Omissions in Tort Law

OXFORD PRIVATE LAW THEORY

Oxford Private Law Theory publishes leading work in private law theory. It commissions and solicits monographs and edited collections in general private law theory as well as specific fields, including the theoretical analysis of tort law, property law, contract law, fiduciary law, trust law, remedies and restitution, and the law of equity. The series is open to diverse theoretical approaches, including those informed by philosophy, economics, history, and political theory. Oxford Private Law Theory sets the standard for rigorous and original work in private law theory.

ALSO PUBLISHED IN THIS SERIES

Relational Justice
A Theory of Private Law Law
Hanoch Dagan and Avihay Dorfman

Methodology in Private Law Theory
Between New Private Law and Rechtsdogmatik
Edited by Thilo Kuntz and Paul B. Miller

Omissions in Tort Law

SANDY STEEL

OXFORD
UNIVERSITY PRESS

OXFORD
UNIVERSITY PRESS

Great Clarendon Street, Oxford, OX2 6DP,
United Kingdom

Oxford University Press is a department of the University of Oxford.
It furthers the University's objective of excellence in research, scholarship,
and education by publishing worldwide. Oxford is a registered trade mark of
Oxford University Press in the UK and in certain other countries

Published in the United States of America by Oxford University Press
198 Madison Avenue, New York, NY 10016, United States of America

British Library Cataloguing in Publication Data
Data available

Library of Congress Control Number: 2024937031

ISBN 9780198866596

DOI: 10.1093/9780191898822.001.0001

The manufacturer's authorised representative in the EU for product safety is
Oxford University Press España S.A. of El Parque Empresarial San Fernando
de Henares, Avenida de Castilla, 2 – 28830 Madrid (www.oup.es/en or
product.safety@oup.com). OUP España S.A. also acts as importer into Spain
of products made by the manufacturer.

Foreword

Several areas of the law draw a distinction between, in broad terms, acts and omissions; or, in the language used in earlier times, between misfeasance and non-feasance. In the law of negligence, the distinction is of fundamental importance when deciding whether one person owes a duty of care to another. For example, there is in general a duty of care not to act so as to cause personal injury to others, but no duty of care to take positive steps to protect others from harm. In the law of nuisance, a distinction is drawn between causing a nuisance and what is confusingly called 'continuing' a nuisance: that is to say, failing to take reasonable steps to avert a nuisance caused by a third party or by the forces of nature. Liability for the former does not depend on negligence, whereas liability for the latter arises only where reasonable steps have not been taken. In human rights law, a distinction is drawn between negative and positive obligations: that is to say, between the state's duty to refrain from acting in a way which infringes an individual's fundamental rights, on the one hand, and the state's duty to take positive steps to protect an individual's fundamental rights, on the other hand. Obligations of the former kind are, in general, more readily imposed than obligations of the latter kind. No doubt further examples could be given from other areas of the law.

Notwithstanding the importance of the distinction between acts and omissions, I am not aware of its ever being given a precise definition. In the context of the law of negligence, scepticism has sometimes been expressed as to whether the distinction is even capable of being drawn: is it not equally possible, it has been asked, to ascribe a road accident to the driver's act in driving too fast as to his omission to brake, and why should it affect the outcome which description is preferred? One response has been to refine the distinction in terms of the difference between an act and a 'pure' omission, but that refinement itself requires an explanation of the concept of 'purity'. Another response, which I suggested some years ago, has been to draw a different and possibly more apt distinction between making things worse and failing to make things better. But that distinction also raises questions of definition. What, for example, are the bases of the comparison between what is worse and what is better? Such conceptual problems are not confined to the law of negligence. In the context of the law of nuisance, the concept of 'continuing' a nuisance is by no means clear, and the circumstances in which liability should be imposed remain unsettled. In the context of human rights law, the distinction between positive and negative duties can be notoriously difficult to draw.

If the point of the distinction between acts and omissions in the law of tort is to rationalise the imposition or non-imposition of an obligation, on the basis that a duty should generally be imposed in respect of acts but not in respect of omissions, it is equally well recognised that there are many exceptions to that general approach. For example, the duty of care owed by a doctor to a patient is not confined to refraining from acts which might harm the patient, but normally extends to taking positive steps to make the patient better. A teacher taking a group of schoolchildren on an outing is under a duty of care to protect them from harm. What is it about situations such as these that makes them exceptions to the general rule? The courts commonly speak of an 'assumption of responsibility', of 'reliance', or of 'control', but what do those terms mean? Is responsibility voluntarily assumed or imposed by law? Is it possible to identify the factors which result in an assumption of responsibility? Is 'reliance' a meaningful concept, where for example a doctor is treating an unconscious patient or a teacher is looking after a young child?

Anyone who tries to make sense of this area of the law soon discovers that the concepts that are used have not been the subject of as much analysis as they require, and are consequently lacking in clarity. Nor has there been much systematic analysis of the case law. Given the nature of a common law system, these two types of analysis—conceptual and casuistic—naturally go hand in hand. What is needed is a careful consideration of the concepts employed in legal reasoning in this area, such as 'pure omission', 'assumption of responsibility', 'special relationship', 'control', and 'reliance', and that analysis has to be grounded in the case law from which such reasoning is derived and in which it has been applied. That is not, of course, to say that all the cases have been correctly reasoned or decided. Nor is it to ignore the fact that they have been decided at different times and in different circumstances, and have to be understood in their historical and social context. Nevertheless, it should be possible to identify rational criteria for determining what is or is not an adequate similarity to the core cases.

The present work is the first, to my knowledge, to carry out an extended analysis of this kind. By carefully elucidating the rationales of the distinctions and analogies to be found in the case law, it succeeds in clarifying the nature and purpose of the distinction drawn in the law of tort between acts and omissions, and of the rationale of treating some situations as exceptions, in which a duty to act is imposed. However, the objectives of the book, and its achievement, are not confined to a descriptive analysis of the existing law and of the conceptual framework within which it is expressed. The analysis also enables an assessment to be made of the aptness of the different ways in which the relevant distinctions have been described, and of the appropriateness of treating certain situations as exceptional. It enables ambiguities and uncertainties in the existing law to be identified, and possible methods of resolving them to be proposed. Analysing the law in this way is not easy, and the book makes demands on its readers. However, it repays the intellectual effort involved.

Keynes famously observed that practical men, who believe themselves to be quite exempt from any intellectual influence, are usually the slaves of some defunct economist.[1] Academic analysis of the kind carried out in this book has an influence on the development of the law whether its practitioners are consciously aware of it or not.[2] Professor Steel's work has already influenced the law in this area,[3] not only in the United Kingdom but also in Australia and Canada. It can be anticipated that the present work will also influence thinking in the courts and elsewhere about the law of tort.

Robert Reed
The Supreme Court
June 2024

[1] J M Keynes, *The General Theory of Employment, Interest, and Money* (Macmillan 1936) 383.

[2] For example, the influence of the work of HLA Hart can be seen in such disparate areas as company law (cf Lord Hoffmann's seminal speech in *Meridian Global Funds Management Asia Ltd v Securities Commission* [1995] 2 AC 500 with Hart's inaugural lecture, 'Definition and Theory in Jurisprudence' (1954) 70 Law Quarterly Review 37), constitutional law (eg the use of the concept of the rule of recognition, developed in *The Concept of Law* (1961) in *R (Miller) v Secretary of State for Exiting the European Union* [2017] UKSC 5), and the law of contract (eg the citation of *Causation in the Law* (OUP 2nd edn, 1985) in *Financial Conduct Authority v Arch Insurance (UK) Ltd* [2021] UKSC 1).

[3] For example, his article 'Negligence Liability for Omissions and the Police' (2016) 75 Cambridge Law Journal 128, co-authored with Dr Stelios Tofaris, has been cited in six decisions of the Supreme Court and the Privy Council.

Acknowledgements

I am indebted to Mark Geistfeld, Nick McBride, and Rob Stevens for enormously valuable comments on several parts of the manuscript.

For excellent comments on chapters of the book at an online seminar series, and/or at an in person workshop, I thank Birke Haecker, Donal Nolan, Helen Scott, Sam Williams (who gave me several good pieces of advice, all the more admirable given his faltering squash record against me, which I note here before the tides turn), Jeff McMahan, Tom Cornford, Irit Samet, David Owens, Emily Gordon and Colm McGrath (who very kindly hosted the workshop on the draft book in the garden of his home in London when it became impossible to hold it at King's).

For other helpful comments, conversations, and observations on drafts or issues related to the book, I am grateful to Crescente Molina, Jane Stapleton, Tim Liau, Adam Perry, James Penner, Jason Neyers, Andrew Simester, Jeffrey Hackney, Roderick Bagshaw, David Enoch, Yip Man, Arthur Ripstein, Greg Keating, John Goldberg, Courtney Cox, Christine Beuermann, Neil Foster, Hanoch Dagan, Ben Zipursky, Aruna Nair, Emily Gordon, Victor Tadros, Leo Boonzaier, Alex Kaiserman, Jonathan Morgan, Irina Sakharova, Irit Samet, Alex Georgiou, Rachel Leow, Steve Schaus, Hugh Collins, Tarun Khaitan, Charlie Webb, Chunsen Bai, Becca Stone, Laura Seymour, Adam Slavny, Shazia Choudhry, Gary Chan, and Erik Encarnacion.

The comments of participants at workshops at Oxford, the London School of Economics, New York University, King's College London, the National University of Singapore, the University of Newcastle, and Singapore Management University (SMU), where I was Lee Kong Chian Visiting Professor of Law in 2023, significantly enhanced the final work. I gratefully record my thanks to SMU for providing a stimulating environment in which to complete the manuscript.

I also record my thanks to Lord Reed for very kindly agreeing to write the Preface to the book.

I started down the path of investigating positive duties in tort as a result of a joint article on the liability of the police with Stelios Tofaris; the work with Stelios has continued to influence my thinking in the book, for which I am grateful.

I have benefitted considerably from research assistance by Justin Tan, Gabriel Tan, Georgios Dougenis, and Cher-Yi Tan. John Yap's research assistance in the final stages was invaluable; it improved the book substantively and otherwise. I also thank Lisa Butts, Akila Mari, and Fiona Tatham, at OUP, for their excellent work in preparing the manuscript and otherwise.

For almost a decade, I have been lucky to be Dr Lee Shau Kee's Sir Man Kam Lo Fellow in Law at Wadham, and a member of the Oxford Law Faculty. Both institutions have been supportive in various ways, not least by employing superb colleagues and admitting talented students.

As ever, I'm indebted to my mum. This one's for CB, with love.

Sandy Steel
London, July 2024

Contents

Table of Cases

Table of Legislation

FRANCE

GERMANY

DENMARK

CZECH REPUBLIC

AUSTRALIA

SINGAPORE

INTERNATIONAL TREATIES

Introduction

1. Why Omissions Liability in Tort

It is difficult to imagine a legal system that attributed no significance to a distinction between doing something and allowing something to occur. Even in legal systems which recognise a tortiously enforceable duty to assist strangers at low cost, the duty is precisely that—a duty to assist *at low cost*. By contrast, the costs a person is required to bear to conform to their duties not to create unreasonable risks of harm may be significant. While it may not be required to take any precaution which costs less than its expected benefit, avoiding the creation of unreasonable risks to strangers can be a costly business.[1] Not only this, in systems which recognise them, duties to assist strangers at low cost are tied to the avoidance of serious harms, such as death or life-threatening injury. By contrast, there is no parallel restriction in duties not to *do* harm: harm includes minor bodily damage or minor property damage. And, a third contrast, duties to assist strangers at low cost are, at least in practice, only enforced in tort law in relation to strangers in physical proximity. This is not true of duties not to do harm to others, which are territorially wide-reaching. If a US manufacturer creates a defective product which damages people in the UK, it is potentially liable.

A tort law system which attributed no significance to the distinction between doing and allowing would, then, involve duties to protect strangers from minor bodily and property damage, trespasses against their person and property, injury to their reputation, at potentially significant cost; and not only strangers in the UK but across the planet. Such a system might be desirable. But it would be a radical re-invention of tort law as we know it. This being so, the distinction between doing and allowing seems likely to be with us in tort law for some time.

Despite the distinction's importance to the kinds of duties and liabilities recognised in tort law, it is underexamined in two respects. First, the content of the distinction is unclear. So far, I have compared 'doing' to 'allowing'. The predominant formulation of the distinction in English law refers to 'acts' and 'pure omissions'. Tort law's concept of an act or a pure omission is rarely given much sustained analytical attention in the cases, however,[2] and the distinction between acts and

[1] See *Bolton v Stone* [1951] AC 850, 867: 'If cricket cannot be played on a ground without creating a substantial risk, then it should not be played there at all', and at 867–68.

[2] For exceptions, see Chapter 1, section 3.

Omissions in Tort Law. Sandy Steel, Oxford University Press. © Sandy Steel 2024.
DOI: 10.1093/9780191898822.001.0001

pure omissions is sometimes elided with other distinctions—such as that between 'making things worse' and 'not making things better'.[3] These distinctions are not equivalent and it is not clear which is descriptively the best or otherwise preferable.

Second, while there is an enormous literature on the normative issues of why omissions should be treated differently from acts and concerning tort duties of easy rescue, there is not much systematic analysis of the existing law on when duties to promote the positions of others arise. The focus of attention, in other words, is on the reasons why liability in respect of omissions is exceptional. By contrast, the situations in which and reasons why such duties arise under the current law, and the relationships between these situations and reasons, are underanalysed. This book is motivated in part as a response to these two gaps in the understanding of this part of the law.

A third reason for this book is the increased prominence of the distinction as a rationale for decisions in the law of negligence.[4] The Supreme Court has invoked the distinction as the primary rationale for the absence of a duty of care on the part of public authorities who carelessly fail to assist persons. Although the distinction has been articulated throughout the twentieth century as an important determinant of the existence of duties of care,[5] it seems true that it has taken on particular importance more recently.

The title of the book is, in two respects, problematic. First, as we shall soon see, the law's true distinction is between acts and *pure* omissions, not *omissions* simpliciter.[6] Second, the law's own characterisation of the distinction is problematic. In so far as the law's concern is with acts and something that contrasts with acts, it is really concerned with acts and not-doings, or 'non-feasance'.[7] Further, part of the argument of Chapter 1 is that the distinction between acts and pure omissions should be replaced, or at least supplemented, with a distinction between making worse and not making better. It is hoped that the book will not be judged on its title, which is a label chosen simply on the basis that, although strictly inaccurate, it

[3] See Chapter 1.

[4] *Michael v Chief Constable of South Wales* [2015] UKSC 2, [2015] AC 1732 [97]–[98]; *Robinson v Chief Constable of West Yorkshire* [2018] UKSC 4, [2018] AC 736 [4], [34], [40]; *N v Poole Borough Council* [2019] UKSC 25, [2020] AC 780 [28], [76]. Contrast the unusual (and, with respect, incorrect) remarks in *The Airport Authority v Western Air Ltd (Bahamas)* [2020] UKPC 29 [48] (Lord Kerr): 'these claims are to be adjudicated upon applying the ordinary rules applicable to the common law of negligence. Those rules apply equally to negligent omissions as they do to actions which are lawfully remiss.'

[5] See, eg, *Deyong v Shenburn* [1946] KB 227, 232–33 (Parcq LJ): 'It is not true to say that wherever a man finds himself in such a position that unless he does a certain act another person may suffer, or that if he does something another person will suffer, then it is his duty in the one case to be careful to do the act and in the other case to be careful not to do the act. Any such proposition is much too wide.'

[6] See Chapter 1.

[7] See Chapter 1. Compare J Salmond, *The Law of Torts* (Stevens & Haynes 1907) [5]: 'He who ventures on dangerous activities is bound, save in special cases, to take care that he does no harm thereby; but in respect of a mere non-feasance every man is entitled in law, save in special cases, to say that he is not his brother's keeper.'

will give potential (including non-specialist) readers a clearer idea of the material that will be discussed.

2. Aims

The book has three main aims. The first is to elucidate, analytically, the content of the law's distinction between acts and pure omissions and its legal significance in the current law. The second is to elucidate the content of the core features of the exceptional situations in which duties to promote other persons' positions arise in tort and to explain the analytical relationships between these exceptional situations. The third is to assess, normatively, whether these exceptions are appropriate. The concluding chapter of the book provides a 'restatement' of the current law. The restatement describes the current position with the benefit of the analytical elucidation provided in the earlier chapters, alongside some normative recommendations as to how the law could be improved.

There are three overarching arguments made across the book, alongside more specific theses defended in each chapter. The first is that the distinction between acts and pure omissions is better replaced, in the law's understanding, with a distinction between making things worse and not making things better. The second is that there is no intrinsic objection to positive duties compared to negative duties—that is, the mere fact that a duty is a positive duty does not itself raise an objection that would not apply were the duty a negative one. What justifies the contrast between positive and negative duties in tort law is rather a set of considerations that *typically* apply to positive duties, but not to negative ones. Two central considerations are (a) a concern not to instrumentalise a person for the benefit of others, and (b) a concern not unduly to reduce a person's freedom. The upshot is that there can be no bright-line exclusion of positive duties in tort. The third is that the existing recognised bases on which a person may be subject to a positive duty in tort are poorly understood and, in some respects, defective. Each chapter identifies major ambiguities in the scope of the current grounds of positive duties and suggests ways of resolving them.

3. Kinds of Claim Made and Method

The book makes descriptive, analytical, and normative claims.[8] A significant part of it is simply aimed at determining the content of the existing positive law on

[8] For a more extensive treatment of different kinds of claim that can be made about law, and how these different claims impact upon methods, see T Khaitan and S Steel, 'Theorizing Areas of Law: A Taxonomy of Special Jurisprudence' (2022) 28 Legal Theory 325

when a person will be subject to a special tort duty to prevent harm to another. This involves a familiar amalgam of description and conceptual analysis. Often a legal concept, such as 'control' or 'assumption of responsibility' or 'reliance', is applied over a series of decisions without its conditions of application being fully or even partially articulated. The book describes these applications and provides an analysis of a set of elucidatory conditions of the concepts, tested by reference to the existing law and hypothetical variations on the existing law, and its relationship to other nearby concepts. If it were trivially obvious what is meant by, for instance, an 'assumption of responsibility' or 'special relationship', this analysis would not be particularly important. However, that is not so: as each substantive chapter shows, there are fundamental ambiguities surrounding the central concepts used to determine the scope of special positive duties and when they arise.

The other main form of analysis is normative. It is directed at what the law ought to be. Part of this is directed at the content of the rules that should apply and the normative reasons that should be considered to support those rules. Part of it is normative taxonomy: it is directed at how the law ought to be conceptually organised.[9]

Given this normative orientation or aspiration, it may be surprising how much the book devotes to analysis of legal decisions. Why not start from first normative principles?

First, straightforwardly, the current legal position is uncertain in several respects; there is value in establishing the current position before offering any normative critique.

Second, sometimes I criticise the existing law for inconsistency; this is necessarily tied, then, to the existing law. This is a normative criticism which, if valid, entails the conclusion that the law ought to resolve the inconsistency—although, standing alone, it does not deliver a verdict on which way. Sometimes, though, if there is one aspect of the law which is inconsistent with many other relatively independent parts of the law, this can be an indication that that inconsistent aspect is unjustified.

Third, on some questions, if certain moral theories are true, the law's position is worthy of attention as a weakly defeasible guide to the moral position; or, even more weakly, the law identifies morally relevant considerations. If act-utilitarianism is true, it seems doubtful that the law provides a defeasible guide to the moral position. Common law tort judgments are replete with deontological distinctions and notions. It is unclear why a judicial decision reached on the basis of such notions will likely track what ought to be done if act-utilitarianism is true. Further, if only the consequences of decisions matter, there are familiar reasons why judicial assessments of the consequences of decisions are unlikely to be reliable: perhaps

[9] On normative taxonomy, see ibid.

most importantly, a lack of specialist knowledge about the complex domains of activity which their decisions will impact upon and a highly limited ability to remedy this lack of knowledge within the context of litigation. This is not to say that judges should never make such assessments. It is simply that these assessments would be an unlikely starting point for a normative analysis.

Suppose, however, that some non-consequentialist morality, which attaches significance to the mode by which an agent is involved in an outcome, is true. Then there seems to be reason to pay attention to judicial views about the morally relevant connections between agents and outcomes, and the morally relevant concepts that apply to determine when a person may be forced to benefit another. These views reflect decisions about the application of a deontologically relevant concept that have been arrived at after argument that need not depend upon fraught empirical assessment of consequences. This argument is often based upon hypothetical thought-experiments that are continuous with the kind found in the work of analytical moral philosophers, but tied to more realistic situations suggested by the facts litigated.

Standing alone, however, I doubt whether the argument in the last paragraph justifies the level of attention I give to the current law in this book for normative purposes. Not all judicial decisions are reached in circumstances in which they will be a reliable reflection of the moral position, even if some non-consequentialist morality is true. Or, even if they have some degree of reliability, they are less likely to be reliable *comparatively* to the considered analysis of a moral philosopher on the same questions. For example, a decision by a first instance judge with a heavy caseload and/or in a case involving a litigant in person seems comparatively less likely to be a reliable guide to the moral position.[10] Furthermore, judicial decisions are sometimes motivated by, not only a view on the interpersonal moral situation of the parties, but also a concern for the negative consequences of their decisions. This would not pose a problem to the argument in the last paragraph if there was a neat separation in judicial decisions between these two issues. But frequently the legal analysis of the interpersonal moral situation is distorted by concern about the negative consequences of the decision. A decision, truly based on a concern for negative consequences, is 'packaged' as a decision about the interpersonal moral situation, perhaps to avoid criticisms about over-stepping the proper judicial role.[11]

Here, then, are two more reasons for my focus on the current law, despite the normative orientation. The first is that the book immodestly aims to have some practical applicability. If the bulk of the examples are sci-fi thought experiments, rather

[10] Their decision may still be morally binding on the litigants. The point is, again, purely methodological: one would not *start* with these decisions in a purely normative analysis.

[11] For instance, decisions about 'duty of care' in negligence often have nothing to do with what the defendant ought to do generally or ought to have done in the particular case at hand. Hence, they are not about 'duty' in any reasonable sense of the term. See N Jansen, *The Structure of Tort Law* (OUP 2021).

than decided cases, then the book will say less about how the current law ought to be understood and improved. The second is that real-world examples are immunised from an often-made criticism of thought-experiments: that they are unrealistic, far-fetched, or wacky.[12] This criticism is often, in my view, unpersuasive. For one thing, sometimes, as in a scientific experiment, the *point* of the experiment is to abstract significantly from features of a real-world situation in order to identify which features of the situation drive a moral judgement, just as the removal of features of the world is needed in a scientific experiment to test a causal hypothesis. Nonetheless, the use of real-world examples will avoid the need, in some cases, repeatedly to obviate concerns about far-fetchedness. There are still many thought-experiments in the book. It seems impossible to assess whether there are *distinct* grounds of positive duties in the law without testing this by hypothetical examples which remove one possible ground of the positive duty in question. Often real-world cases involve multiple morally relevant factors. It is impossible to isolate the relevance of a particular factor without considering cases which isolate that factor from the others.

More substantively, my approach is non-consequentialist. This means that I reject the view that only valuable consequences or valuable states of affairs matter to what may be done. Some beings have a moral status which prohibits their being used or harmed non-consensually even when this maximises value (*constraints*), and some beings are such that they are permitted not to maximise value (*permissions or options*). I further articulate this view and provide some modest support for it in Chapter 2. This non-consequentialist approach does not require us to set aside consequences in determining the normatively desirable content of tort law.[13] In Chapter 2, I explain why the positive and negative consequences of liability are relevant to liability in a way that is consistent with, and potentially required by, the existence of constraints and options. This is pertinent to the topic of liability for pure omissions since some of the arguments given against more extensive tort liability for pure omissions are based upon predictions of negative consequences.

4. Tort Law

My intention is to analyse pure omissions in relation to the rules normally referred to by the words 'tort law'. These are rules which (a) determine what primary legal rights and duties exist between persons independently of contract and trust,[14] (b) determine what secondary and remedial rights a person has against

[12] For discussion of this objection and others, see K Brownlee and Z Stemplowska, 'Thought experiments' in A Blau (ed), *Methods in Analytical Political Theory* (CUP 2017).

[13] It may be belabouring the point, but non-consequentialism only requires a denial of the view that *only* consequences matter. So Jane Stapleton is a non-consequentialist: she accepts a 'sensitivity' to consequences is required, without consequences being the sole normative criterion: J Stapleton, *Three Essays on Torts* (OUP 2021) 31–32.

[14] A primary right is a right that does not arise from the breach of another right.

other persons and courts when (i) such a primary right or secondary right has been or may be violated, or (ii) when one person inflicts harm upon another non-wrongfully.[15] This is obviously an inadequate 'analysis' of tort law in so far as it relies upon an unarticulated distinction between tort, contract, and trust, but it should be enough to isolate the book's subject.

The book is about tort law, not just the tort of negligence.[16] It seeks to examine the role of the act and pure omission distinction in other torts too. However, it is true that the tort of negligence occupies much of the analysis. This is, in part, because discussion of the distinction between acts and pure omissions has largely taken place in relation to the tort of negligence.

5. Terminology: Positive and Negative Duties, Rights, Liabilities

Chapter 1 examines the distinction between 'acts' and 'pure omissions', and the related distinction between 'making worse' and 'not benefitting'. The phenomena to which these terms refer are explained in detail. I refer to duties to act or to benefit another as positive duties—'P-duties'—and duties not to act or not to worsen another's position as negative duties—'N-duties'. As will become clear, the more accurate distinction is the one between 'benefitting' and 'worsening', relative to a baseline as I explain.

Generally, in discussing positive duties, I could equally have spoken of positive *rights*.[17] Most of the legal P-duties discussed in this book correlate with legal rights. In Chapters 9 and 10, when we consider duties of easy rescue and the P-duties of public authorities, there will be occasion to examine in a bit more detail when and why a P-duty correlates with a right, and why this matters. This issue arises in these contexts because it is sometimes thought that positive (moral) duties to assist a stranger in dire need do not correlate with any moral right on the part of the stranger, and this is the justification of why tort law should not legally enforce such duties. This view is rejected. Similarly, certain duties of public authorities are sometimes described to be inherently 'public' duties that do not correlate with any individual's right, and for that reason ought not to be enforced in tort law. Chapter 10 suggests that at least some of the P-duties distinctively owed by public authorities correlate with 'rights' in the sense relevant to generating compensatory duties.

[15] ii(b) reflects the fact that the conventional reference of 'tort law' also includes some rules which merely impose compensatory duties when a condition is met, regardless of whether the condition is a breach of a duty. An arguable example is the rule in *Rylands v Fletcher* (1868) LR 3 HL 330.

[16] For a treatment of the criminal law, see, eg, A Ashworth, *Positive Obligations in Criminal Law* (Hart, 2015) Part 2.

[17] In the Hohfeldian scheme, duties always correlate with (claim-)rights: W Hohfeld, *Fundamental Legal Conceptions as Applied in Judicial Reasoning and Other Legal Essays* (Yale 1923). Even if this is true, it does not follow that all duties correlate with the claim rights of *individuals*. In any event, I doubt it is true.

I use 'general rights' to refer to rights which protect an interest or set of interests against invasion by everyone else. For example, a person's interest in bodily integrity (or ability to control interferences with their body) is protected (in different ways) against everyone through the torts of trespass and negligence. By contrast, 'special rights' are rights that one has against specific others in virtue of a 'special fact'—a fact going beyond a person's existence. A right that arises by virtue of an assumption of responsibility is (sometimes) a special right: one acquires the right by virtue of another conferring it.[18] 'Liability' refers to a person being situated such that another person or institution can exercise a power to impose a duty upon them. Normally, in this book, that duty is a duty to compensate.

6. Jurisdiction

The book focuses on the law of England and Wales, which I abbreviate to 'English law'. Although the book has this focus, the conceptual and normative issues it discusses are not local to English law; the distinctions it draws, for instance, between general and special rights, worsening and not-worsening, and concepts of assuming responsibility are of potential relevance to any system of tort liability. Relatedly, the book draws on judicial decisions in other common law jurisdictions and, much less frequently, civil law jurisdictions. These decisions are sometimes concerned with the same concepts as the concepts applied in English law, and so may shed light upon their conditions of application. These decisions also serve as a repository of normative intuitions and reasoning about enforceable tort duties and so may contribute, in the manner described above, to normative arguments about tort liability. The book is not a comprehensive guide to the positive law in England; it rather aims to elucidate the central foundational conceptual and normative issues raised by the law on pure omissions.

7. Overview

(i) Chapter 1: Isolating the Distinction between Acts and Pure Omissions

This chapter explains the legal significance of the distinction between acts and omissions in tort law. It explains its significance in terms of a boundary between general and special rights: rights that all of us have by existence (general)

[18] See, in more detail, Chapters 1 and 4.

compared to rights that we only have when some special fact holds beyond existence (special). Rights that others not interfere by pure omissions are 'special' rights in English law. The key upshot of the distinction, then, is that a person needs to demonstrate a *special fact* in order to be owed a duty in respect of a pure omission. The chapter then offers an account of the law's distinction between acts and 'pure' omissions, before considering whether the distinction the law seeks to track is in fact this distinction. It proposes a modified distinction based on whether a person's conduct makes another worse off than if that person or their resources had not been present at the time of the impugned conduct.

(ii) Chapter 2: Justifying a Distinction

This chapter turns from conceptual analysis of the distinction between acts and pure omissions to the normative issue of why this or a cognate distinction matters for tort liability. I distinguish between intrinsic and non-intrinsic justifications at a foundational moral level. Intrinsic justifications point to a moral difference that obtains simply in virtue of the mode of a person's involvement in an outcome (act or pure omission). Non-intrinsic justifications point to a moral difference that always or typically tracks the distinction between acts and pure omissions but attribute no significance to the mode of involvement *as such*. I argue that the most powerful non-intrinsic justifications involve (a) a concern not to instrumentalise persons, and (b) a concern to preserve a significant domain of freedom for each person. I cast doubt on intrinsic justifications such as the claim that only acts can be causes while omissions are not true causes, although I accept that certain forms of positive involvement in an outcome are harder to justify than others. I then consider whether there are distinctive moral objections to the legal enforcement of P-duties. I argue that there are none, though there are contingent objections to their enforcement in tort law.

(iii) Chapter 3: Innocent Creation of Risk and Interference

This chapter begins the analysis of exceptional situations in which, according to the current law, P-duties arise in tort. It demonstrates the existence of a principle based on innocent creation of a risk. This grounds duties to take care to prevent the materialisation of risks which one non-wrongfully created. Suppose, while driving carefully, one knocks over and kills an animal and this creates a risk to oncoming road users. One incurs a duty to take reasonable steps to protect others. I explain (i) what it means to create a risk for the purposes of this principle, and (ii) how to think about the demandingness of the duty that arises: it depends upon multiple factors, including the extent to which the innocent risk was voluntarily created for one's own benefit and one's degree of causal involvement in the risk. The second part of the chapter explains the closely connected 'interference' principle, which the law appears to be on the verge of recognising. This principle grounds legal duties to act when a person has interfered with, or risks interfering with, the provision of assistance.

(iv) Chapter 4: Assumptions of Responsibility: Part 1—The Law

It is clear that assuming responsibility can create a P-duty. It is less clear what it means to 'assume responsibility'. This chapter argues that these words refer to a number of distinct phenomena. It identifies a principle based on the risk of detrimental reliance upon a promise, a principle based on assumption of a role (such as parent or doctor), a principle based on special relationships, and a principle based on taking charge of persons or things. These principles have different requirements and rationales and should be disaggregated from the single label of 'assumption of responsibility'.

(v) Chapter 5: Assumptions of Responsibility: Part 2—Normative Issues

This chapter considers four central normative issues relating to the law on assumption of responsibility. First, it examines what justifies a person acquiring a right to another's careful assistance in the absence of a contract. It proposes that some of the law on assumption of responsibility can be understood as responding to the inherent risks of promising and making promise-like commitments. Because these activities generate risks of detrimental reliance, promisors may come under duties to take care to prevent the foreseeable detrimental reliance upon promise, either by performance of the promise or some other step. Other parts of the law, it is suggested, are justified by assumed moral responsibilities that are appropriate, for various reasons, for the law to enforce even in the absence of consideration. Second, the chapter considers what normative considerations bear on when the law should attach P-duties to special relationships or roles—or, indeed, construct such relationships or roles by constitutive P-duties. Third, it argues against the idea that merely taking on the task of assisting another person generates P-duties. Fourth, it considers how the rules on assumption of responsibility apply in cases involving public authorities and whether the case law can be understood to be consistent; it suggests a partial reconciliation.

(vi) Chapter 6: Control

The current law imposes P-duties when a person has 'control' in some sense. The chapter first aims to elucidate what 'control' means in this context. It distinguishes between control as a source of P-duties to the controlled and control as a source of P-duties to third parties. It exposes a tension in the law between acceptance of 'control' as a justification for P-duties and the absence of a general duty of easy rescue, since control often appears largely to identify a person as particularly well-placed to assist another.

(vii) Chapter 7: Statute

This chapter considers the extent to which statutory P-duties are consistent with the common law's normative position. It shows that, by and large, so far as private individuals are concerned, statute operates to concretise abstract P-duties that exist at common law: the statutory duties are justified, fundamentally, by the same grounds as P-duties at common law. The main exceptions are civilly actionable statutory duties on public authorities. Here it is argued that the law is too restrictive: in construing the intention of the legislature, the courts too readily assume an intention not to go beyond the common law position, failing to give due weight to the fact that the common law position is designed by reference to private individuals.

(viii) Chapter 8: Current Protection from a Risk

'Current protection from a risk' is not usually listed as a special fact that triggers a P-duty. While this chapter argues that current provision of protection is indeed insufficient, it draws attention to situations in which a person is under a duty to take care to continue the benefit provided by their resources by not doing a positive act that would disrupt that provision. It considers various explanations of these duties, based on limits of the privilege of self-help and assumption of responsibility, but rejects them. Instead, it is suggested that current protection, when one cannot remove the protection without doing a positive act that removes a person from the safety they currently enjoy, generates a distinctive duty.

(ix) Chapter 9: Easy Rescue

No book on omissions in tort would be complete without an extended discussion of people walking past other people drowning in shallow pools of water. First,

I aim to show that various common law rules come very close to a duty of easy rescue and there is a reasonably strong argument of consistency for such a duty based on the existing law. Then I aim to show that the normative issue of whether there ought to be a legal duty of easy rescue enforceable in tort law by claims for compensation is fundamentally a question of weighing up the positive and negative consequences of such a duty. I criticise Kantian views which seek to exclude such duties from tort law on the basis of facts about the interpersonal moral situation between the person in need of assistance and the person able to provide it (specifically, the claim that, while there is a moral duty to provide assistance, the recipient has no *right* to it). The chapter concludes by considering whether rational limits can be found for duties of easy rescue in tort law (drawing on some examples in other jurisdictions). It suggests that the moral duty of easy rescue is not limited by considerations of physical proximity, but that the enforcement of duties of easy rescue in tort law is justifiably subject to territorial restrictions.

(x) Chapter 10: Public Authorities

This chapter examines the P-duties owed by public authorities in tort. Its starting point is an explanation of the idea, accepted by and large in English law, that public authorities owe all and only the P-duties owed by private individuals, so far as tort is concerned. In other words, the law accepts the *positive equality principle*, that public authorities will owe a P-duty when a special fact which triggers a P-duty for a private individual exists; and the *negative equality principle*, that such P-duties exhaust the P-duties of public authorities in tort. The chapter then considers whether this position can be justified, focussing upon the *negative equality principle*. It shows that the justifications typically adduced for this principle fail. It considers a more plausible justification for the principle—that the kinds of duties owed by public authorities that go beyond those justifiably owed by private individuals are not *owed to* individuals in the relevant sense. It rejects this argument, too. The *negative equality principle* is at best, the chapter concludes, a rough-and-ready rule that delimits judicial competence to develop the law on P-duties.

(xi) Chapter 11: Beyond Duty Issues: Breach, Causation, Remedies

Almost all of the book is concerned with when primary P-duties arise. This chapter considers whether the classification of a person's conduct as a pure omission has other consequences—upon the standard of duty owed by a person, causation, and the remedial orders that may be made. It argues that the standard of duty, in cases in which the P-duty does not arise by virtue of an assumption of responsibility, justifiably varies depending upon the nature of the duty-bearer's involvement in the outcome. Persons with no causal responsibility for a risk are not required to bear significant burdens to protect others from a risk, with the demandingness of the P-duty increasing depending upon the level of a person's causal responsibility, the wrongfulness of the risk imposition, and the level of culpability. As to causation, the book finds little evidence of a distinction in the law's approach to causation depending on whether the breach is a pure omission or not. The chapter largely rejects arguments that special causal rules should apply in cases of pure omission. Finally, the distinction between mandatory and prohibitory injunctions is considered. It is shown that, in relation to remedies for breach of a duty, the distinction between acts and pure omissions should not be of central importance.

(xii) Chapter 12: Conclusion

The book concludes with an overview of the central conclusions and some reflections on their implications for the current law.

1
Isolating the Distinction between Acts and Pure Omissions

> The distinction between acts and omissions is fundamental, although it can be difficult to draw in borderline cases.[1]

Tort law purports to attach significance to a distinction between 'acts' and certain kinds of 'omissions'. Holding everything else fixed—the type of damage or outcome caused, fault with respect to that outcome, and so on—liability is claimed to hinge upon whether the outcome came about by an act or a 'pure' omission. This chapter examines the way the distinction is drawn in the current law and the significance attached to it. It is in nine sections. The first three are concerned with providing a more precise statement of the significance of the distinction, a preview of the situations in which duties to act arise in the current law, and an analysis of how the distinction is ordinarily drawn in the current law. The next three sections examine alternative ways of understanding the distinction that the law is seeking to capture—primarily the distinction between making worse and not benefiting. It is argued that the distinction between acts and pure omissions should be replaced with, or at least supplemented by, a particular version of this distinction. The final two substantive sections respond to objections.

1. The Legal Significance of the Distinction between Acts and Pure Omissions

The first and primary significance of the distinction between acts and pure omissions is that for a person to have a primary right (a right that does not arise from breach of another right) that another not interfere by *pure omission* with their interests, a special fact must be shown. By a 'special fact', I mean 'a fact other than that person's existence'.

Most primary tort rights are rights one has by existence. These include rights not to be falsely imprisoned, defamed, have one's body used without permission, and have one's body damaged by an unreasonable imposition of foreseeable risk. These rights correlate with duties upon everyone else.

[1] *Chief Constable of Essex v Transport Arendonk BvBa* [2020] EWHC 212 (QB), [2020] RTR 22 [66] (Laing J).

Omissions in Tort Law. Sandy Steel, Oxford University Press. © Sandy Steel 2024.
DOI: 10.1093/9780191898822.003.0001

Other tort rights are not like this. They exist only when a fact beyond the right-holder's existence obtains—a special fact.[2] Rights that others not use one's property without permission or damage it by unreasonable risk imposition are acquired when the facts triggering a mode of acquisition hold (existence is not currently such a fact).

Rights that others not interfere with one's interests by *pure omission* are like acquired property rights—they exist when a special fact holds. The main difference is that rights against interference by *pure omission* are, when acquired by a special fact, not enjoyed against *everyone*, but only against another person or a subclass of persons. For instance, neighbouring landowners have reciprocal rights to the support of their land: these are rights arising from the special fact of property ownership but exist only between the neighbours. A child's right against the person who holds the role of parent, that the parent take reasonable care to protect the child from dangers caused by others, is held only against the parent.[3] The right arises in virtue of another person's assuming a role. Hart called these rights 'special rights'.[4]

The point in the last two paragraphs can be put by saying that tort rights against interference by pure omission are 'exceptional'. This may mislead, however. The relevant point is not that rights and duties in relation to pure omissions are statistically unusual or that the facts which generate them are statistically unusual occurrences. The point is simply that these rights and duties only exist when something beyond people's existence is made out. This, and the fact that these rights only correlate with duties in a sub-class of persons, is what makes these rights distinctive within tort law.

The need to show a special fact is the central significance of the distinction between acts and pure omissions. In the tort of negligence, the general right in relation to one's body is typically described as a right that others not cause reasonably foreseeable damage to one's body by an unreasonable *act*. If the claimant successfully shows that the defendant's unreasonable conduct is an *act*, and thus that this right is applicable, then no special fact will need to be shown.

A second significance is that, if a person is under a duty to *act*, this may have implications for the nature of that duty. For instance, a person may be able to point, to a greater extent, to their personal difficulties in conforming to such a duty.[5] Further, the stringency of the duty may be diminished.[6] The stringency of a duty is

[2] Sometimes tort law is defined as concerned with rights one has by existence and property rights are included in this. But it is false that one has property rights by existence.

[3] For analysis of this situation, see Chapters 4 and 5.

[4] H L A Hart, 'Are There Any Natural Rights?' (1955) 64 Philosophical Review 175, 183: 'When rights arise out of special transactions between individuals or out of some special relationship in which they stand to each other, both the persons who have the right and those who have the corresponding obligation are limited to the parties to the special transaction or relationship. I call such rights special rights to distinguish them from those moral rights which are thought of as rights against (i.e., as imposing obligations upon) everyone.'

[5] See Chapter 5 on *Goldman v Hargrave* [1967] 1 AC 645, [1966] 3 WLR 513.

[6] See Chapter 5.

a measure of the cost that a person is expected to bear to conform to the duty. Duties not intentionally to kill innocent others are exceedingly stringent: if the only way of saving your life is to kill an innocent stranger, arguably you must allow yourself to die. When the law imposes duties to act for the benefit of others, however, absent a prior wrong, creation of risk, or choice, the duties are only of minimal stringency. Sometimes only a relatively non-costly measure, such as a warning, is required, even when the consequences for the right-holder are severe.

A third significance of the distinction is its impact, not upon the existence or nature of a primary duty, but upon the nature of the liability to which a person is subject when that duty is breached.[7] The rules or principles which determine the availability of injunctions are affected by whether the injunction is mandatory or prohibitive. This is considered to be an application of the distinction between acts and pure omissions.[8] In certain torts, a person has a defeasible right to a prohibitory order requiring cessation of the wrong.[9] By contrast, with mandatory orders, a person has a much weaker entitlement, something like a right that the court award a mandatory injunction if the balance of reasons supports this.[10]

A fourth significance of the distinction relates, not to the content of the legal rules themselves, but to a normative principle which judges accept as justifying that content. The principle is that if the conduct to which a duty or liability is sought to be attached is a *pure omission*, it calls for exceptional justification why the duty or liability should be imposed. The justification has to be 'exceptional' in the sense that the mere fact that a person's acting will foreseeably prevent a harm, even a severe harm, to another is not a sufficient justification for the duty.[11] In extending the law on actionable pure omissions, then, something more is needed from the law's perspective by way of justification.

There is sometimes said to be a further significance of the distinction between acts and pure omissions. This further significance is said to be that liability in respect of a pure omission requires the existence of *duty to act*.[12] This is particularly

[7] See Chapter 9.

[8] *Shepherd Homes Ltd v Sandham (No 1)* [1971] Ch 340, 348 (Megarry J): 'whereas a prohibitory injunction merely requires abstention from acting, a mandatory injunction requires the taking of positive steps'.

[9] For instance, in the tort of private nuisance: *Coventry v Lawrence* [2014] UKSC 13, [2014] AC 822. The language of 'rights' to an order may be objected to on the basis that injunctions are a discretionary remedy. The objection fails. The difference between a right to an order to pay damages and a right to an injunction requiring cessation of an act is a difference in the defeasibility of the right. In relation to injunctions, there is a wide range of defeating circumstances, not all of which have been enumerated. In relation to damages, there seem to be no defeating circumstances. However, not any countervailing reason against an injunction will do, and some reasons are excluded. Further, this exclusion is partly based upon a concern for the claimant's interests. So, the court has a reason to award an injunction and a reason to exclude certain reasons for doing so, and these reasons are both rationally traceable in part to the claimant's interests. That state of affairs involves the claimant having a defeasible right to an injunction.

[10] See, eg, *Redland Bricks v Morris* [1970] AC 652 (HL), [1969] 2 WLR 1437.

[11] It may not even be, from the law's perspective, a complete reason for a duty.

[12] See, eg, *R v Iqbal (Amar)* [2008] EWCA Crim 2066 (misfeasance in public office).

emphasised in the criminal law on liability for omissions.[13] Call this the 'duty requirement' ('DR').

The claim that there is a DR for pure omissions may be true, but it is puzzling why it is asserted as a distinctive feature of liability for pure omissions. It seems true, in other words, that tort liability generally, inclusive of *acts*, requires the breach of a primary legal duty.

Consider, first, whether the DR is true in the tort law on pure omissions. If a duty not to omit x-ing means 'having a pro tanto weighty legal reason not to omit x-ing', then DR seems true. It is difficult to imagine any examples in which the law holds a person liable in tort for omitting to do something which it considers there to be *no weighty reason* not to omit. There is always a relatively weighty reason to protect a person's body or property from damage. While there is sometimes no reason at all, grounded in a person's own welfare, to protect that person's economic wealth, there is generally a weighty reason not to deprive a person of wealth in the ways which tort law prohibits.[14]

If a duty not to omit x-ing means 'having a legal reason not to omit x-ing which always defeats countervailing reasons, or which defeats countervailing reasons in ordinary contexts', then DR is probably true, for the same reasons.

If a duty not to omit x-ing means 'one legally ought not to omit x-ing, all-things-considered', then matters are more complex. Suppose a parent has a contractual duty to deliver goods at exactly 9am on Monday. Suppose that, unexpectedly, the parent's child will die unless he is taken to hospital around that time. No one else can deliver the goods. Here the parent is likely to be under a duty to compensate for any non-remote loss caused by the failure to deliver. Morally, it is clear that the parent ought, all-things-considered, to save their child and thus fail to deliver the goods. Did the parent have an all-things-considered legal duty to deliver the goods at 9am? It is possible that the law makes contradictory demands here. The law could be saying that one has an all-things-considered duty to deliver and an all-things-considered duty to save. In this way, the law would give no conclusive guidance about what to do here.[15] Alternatively, it is possible that one has a legal permission to fail to deliver here, in the same way as one has a legal permission to damage a person's property to save one's life. If so, then one's duty to compensate is not contingent upon a breach of an all-things-considered legal duty. One's omission to deliver is then a source of compensatory liability absent the breach of an all-things-considered duty. That is an example of a permissible omission giving rise to contractual compensatory liability. It is more difficult to identify situations in which an all-things-considered legally permissible omission gives rise to tortious

[13] See, eg G Yaffe, 'The Duty Requirement' in D Nelkin and S Rickless (eds), *The Ethics and Law of Omissions* (OUP 2017).

[14] Consider stealing $500 from Jeff Bezos.

[15] See S Smith, *Rights, Wrongs, and Injustices: The Structure of Remedial Law* (OUP 2019) 261.

compensatory liability. If there are no such cases, then there may be a reading of DR—one involving all-things-considered duties—which is distinctively true of *pure omissions*, but not true of *acts*. It seems reasonably clear that an *act* can give rise to a tortious compensatory duty in the absence of a breach of an all-things-considered legal duty.[16]

Gideon Yaffe has argued that the DR is distinctively true of omissions in the criminal law.[17] In his view, the 'duty' insisted upon in order to generate criminal liability for an omission is a duty that 'has its source in some part of the law distinct from the criminal prohibition the defendant is accused of violating'.[18] A person guilty of a crime by omission necessarily breaches *two* duties, then: a duty which is external to the criminal law, such as a contractual duty, and the duty constituted by the criminal offence in question. The DR does not, however, apply to crimes committed by action.

Whatever the merits of this view as an account of the criminal law, it is not the position in tort. There is no requirement in tort to identify a duty not to pure omit existing in another area of law.[19] This is not surprising if Yaffe is correct about the rationale for this understanding of the DR in criminal law. Yaffe defends the DR, normatively, on the ground that a criminal prohibition to refrain from x-ing should not be interpreted, as a matter of 'lenity' to defendants, as giving a person a legal reason to do anything other than not x-ing.[20] If a prohibition on x-ing gave rise to criminal liability when x-ing occurred by the defendant omitting to y, then, for this liability to be based on *culpability* for omitting to y, the prohibition would have to be interpreted as giving a legal reason to y. According to Yaffe, this interpretation would be contrary to the principle of lenity in interpreting criminal prohibitions: the prohibition against x-ing should be interpreted as only giving legal reasons not to x, and no more.[21] This principle of lenity simply does not apply in relation to tort liability, or applies with considerably less force.

2. The Special Facts in English Law: A Preview

The book follows the presentation of the special facts that generate duties to act in the current law—creation of risk, assumption of responsibility (including special

[16] *Vincent v Lake Erie Transportation* Co 109 Minn 456, 124 NW 221 (1910). The position is not exclusively Minnesotan. For the similar German law position and that of some other European legal systems, see Nils Jansen, *The Structure of Tort Law* (Sandy Steel tr, OUP 2021) §1, esp 39–40.

[17] Yaffe (n 13). It is not clear whether Yaffe intends to refer to what I mean by *pure* omissions or simply omissions; it is probably the former.

[18] ibid 203.

[19] See Chapters 2–5.

[20] As Yaffe (n 13) acknowledges (at 214), this gives the DR a limited scope: if a criminal prohibition *explicitly* bans *omissions*, then the DR does not apply.

[21] ibid 211, 212.

relationships), and control. It will argue, however, that on analysis the current law recognises the special facts in Table 1.1 as generators of duties in respect of pure omissions in English tort law.

Table 1.1 Special facts generating duties to act

Special facts that generate primary duties to act	Responsibility for conduct that innocently infringes or threatens to infringe a general right (including interference with provision of protection)[22]
	Assumptions of responsibility[23]
	Rights of control over persons, land, and things[24]
	Current provision of protection from harm by a person's resources[25]
	Public authority[26]

Each of these concepts will be explained in detail in later chapters. It will be shown that there is partial overlap between these categories; for instance, some cases of assumption of responsibility are justified by responsibility for a risk of detrimental reliance. However, each special fact has some conceptual and justificatory independence from the others. The final chapter restates the current law's special facts in line with the book's proposed analysis of the distinction between positive and negative duties.

3. The Tort Law Understanding of the Distinction between Acts and Pure Omissions

It bears immediate emphasis that, despite numerous judicial invocations of the distinction between 'acts and omissions', and despite the title of this book, this is not the legally relevant distinction.[27] The legal distinction is between acts and *pure omissions*: 'the common law does not impose liability for what are called pure omissions'.[28] This section elucidates this distinction in three sub-sections concerned with the concept of an omission, the concept of a *pure* omission, and the concept of an *act*.

[22] Chapter 3.
[23] Chapters 4 and 5.
[24] Chapter 6.
[25] See Chapter 8.
[26] Chapters 7 and 10.
[27] For examples of judicial emphasis on the distinction, see, eg, the quotation that opens this chapter and *Stovin v Wise* [1996] AC 923 (HL) 945, 946 (Lord Hoffmann).
[28] *Smith v Littlewoods Organisation Ltd* [1987] AC 241 (HL) 270 (Lord Goff); *Robinson v Chief Constable of West Yorkshire Police* [2018] UKSC 4, [2018] AC 736 [69], [71]–[72] (negligence) (Lord Reed JSC); *Iqbal v Prison Officers Association* [2009] EWCA Civ 1312, [2010] QB 732 [15]–[23] (false imprisonment) (Lord Neuberger MR).

(i) Omissions and Not Doings

An omission is a failure to act. It is not equivalent to not doing something. This is for two reasons. First, an omission involves not doing something which one had certain capacities to do. If I am unconscious, I do not *omit* to have lunch with you. Second, when I (as is my custom) do not set fire to my desk, I am not omitting to set fire to my desk; nor is King Charles omitting to water my avocado tree, though he does not do it. An omission is not doing something that is contrary to some kind of normative standard.[29]

This normative aspect to the concept of an omission poses an apparent problem of circularity. In employing the distinction between *act* and *pure omission* in law, one is trying to ascertain whether the defendant *legally ought* to have done something. However, in order to determine whether the defendant *omitted* to do the thing, one must already know whether the defendant *ought* to have done it.[30] So, it seems that the issue of whether the defendant is under a legal duty is logically anterior to whether their conduct is an *omission*.

There are two ways of avoiding this circularity problem. First, one could say that one is not truly concerned in tort law with *omissions*, but not-doings: the absences of action. 'The absence of an action' is not itself a normative concept. Second, one could say that the relevant normative standard for assessing whether the absence of action is *omissive* is non-legal, or at least not sourced in tort law: if the failure is in breach of a moral or social norm, for instance, one could say it is an omission. Then the question is whether there is a *legal* duty that enforces the moral or social norm. The law does not follow this process of first identifying a moral or social norm breached, however. Therefore, since my aim is to capture the legal distinction, in what follows, though I retain the law's terminology of 'pure omission', strictly what is meant by an 'omission' is 'a not-doing' or 'the absence of an action'.

(ii) Pure and Impure Omissions

In *Robinson v Chief Constable of West Yorkshire Police*, Lord Reed described these as 'commonly given examples' of *pure* omissions: 'someone who watches and does nothing as a blind man approaches the edge of a cliff, or a child drowns in a shallow pool'.[31] The classic example of an *impure* omission, which is treated equivalently to

[29] It need not be a distinctively moral standard; non-compliance with (a potentially immoral) legal rule or social convention might still be an omission.

[30] This problem convinces Jeroen Kortmann to speak of *not doing* rather than *omitting*: see J Kortmann, *Altruism in Private Law* (OUP 2005) 5.

[31] *Robinson* (n 28) [72].

an act for the purpose of general tort duties, is a failure to brake or to indicate while driving.[32]

Beyond description of paradigm examples, however, the concept of a pure omission almost never receives any sustained analysis in the authorities.[33] It is asserted that a case is or is not a case of pure omission without articulation of what makes an omission such.[34] This gives rise to an obvious concern: the concept may be applied inconsistently without an articulation of its conditions of application. Less obviously, it raises a question as to whether the concept *can* be given an intelligible articulation. If it cannot, then the concept must be abandoned as a determinant of liability.

I will consider a number of possible analyses of the concept of a 'pure omission', as it is employed in the law, and show that the idea can be given a more precise rendering.

One possibility is that a failure to act—or not doing something (I will use these equivalently here)—is a pure omission if and only if it cannot be redescribed as doing an act or activity. The failure to brake while driving can be redescribed as performing the act of driving and thus is not a pure omission. Call this *Proposal A*. *Proposal A* raises the question of when a not-doing can indeed be redescribed as an act. The obvious difficulty is that this seems to be possible in virtually all cases of not-doing. One could be eating a sandwich (an act) while not saving a stranger's drowning child: one's failure to save can thus be redescribed as the act of eating.[35]

Consider a second proposal, *Proposal B*: a failure to act is a pure omission if and only if it does not take place during an act. *Proposal B* takes us no further. A failure to rescue a drowning child can be described as taking place during the act of eating a sandwich: the eating of the sandwich and the failure to rescue occur at the same time.

Consider now *Proposal C*: a failure to act counts as a pure omission if and only if it does not constitute improper performance of an *act*. Failing to rescue a child does not constitute improperly eating a sandwich, but failing to brake does constitute improperly driving a car. *Proposal C* fails, however. Consider *Michael v Chief Constable of South Wales Police*.[36] In this case, an emergency call operator carelessly failed effectively to communicate the urgency of a threat to the victim's life to the relevant

[32] *Mitchell v Glasgow City Council* [2009] UKHL 11, [2009] AC 874 [76] (Baroness Hale); J Steele, *Tort Law: Text Cases and Materials* (4th edn, OUP 2017) 170.

[33] The position appears the same in French law, which draws a distinction between *faute d'abstention* (pure omission) and *faute dans l'action* (impure omission) under (now) article 1240 of the French Civil Code: Cass 1re civ, 18 avr 2000.

[34] See, eg, *Iqbal* (n 28); *Aitken v Scottish Ambulance Service and others* [2011] CSOH 49, 2011 SLT 822 [50]–[51] (Lord Mackay); *Al-Najar v Cumberland Hotel Ltd* [2019] EWHC 1593 (QB), [2019] 1 WLR 5953 [181]–[182] (applying the concept without defining it) (Dingemans J).

[35] For an overview of discussion of this problem in the philosophical literature, see M Moore, *Act and Crime: The Philosophy of Action and its Implications for Criminal Law* (OUP 1993) 29–31.

[36] *Michael v Chief Constable of South Wales* [2015] UKSC 2, [2015] AC 1732.

police authority with the result that, the police failing to arrive in time, the victim was murdered. The operator was held not to be under a duty of care because this was a case of pure omission.[37] However, the failure to communicate the threat effectively could be described as improperly communicating the threat, since the operator did speak to the police authority. *Proposal C* therefore misclassifies *Michael* as a case of *impure* omission (on the assumption that all omissions which are not pure are impure). Moreover, *Proposal C* risks the circularity problem addressed earlier: to know whether the conduct is *improper*, it seems one already needs to know whether it ought to have been undertaken. *Proposal C* cannot then serve as a basis for determining whether the conduct ought to have been undertaken.

Consider the following revision, *Proposal D*: a failure to act is a pure omission by a person A in relation to damage if and only if it does not take place during an act of A of which it is true that, had the act not occurred, the damage would not have occurred. Failing to rescue a child may take place while eating a sandwich, but had the sandwich eating not occurred, and holding everything else as close as possible to the actual world, the drowning of the child would still have occurred. Furthermore, had the operator in *Michael* not acted at all, then the damage would (probably) still have occurred. This formulation also arrives at the correct result in the failure to brake example: the failure to brake while driving is a failure to act which occurs during an action (driving) of which it is true that, had the driving not occurred, the damage would not have occurred. Consequently, it is not a pure omission. *Proposal D* delivers the correct results, then, in Lord Reed's examples, *Michael*, and the failure to brake case.

Nonetheless, *Proposal D* raises an awkward question of whether an omission occurs 'during an act'. Suppose that A hits a golf ball without first checking whether the area ahead is clear. On the face of it, the omission to check whether the area is clear occurs *prior* to the act of hitting the golf ball. Therefore, it is a pure omission under *Proposal D*. This result is not necessarily problematic. First, there is clearly an *act* to which liability would in principle attach—the striking of the ball—even if the omission is counted as pure. Second, *Proposal D* could be modified slightly to require that the omission not take place during an act or activity of A (here, golfing) of which it is true that, had the act or activity not occurred, the damage would not have occurred.[38]

Consider a final, apparently simpler, proposal, *Proposal E*: a failure to act is a pure omission if and only if it is not a failure to take steps to control a risk of one's own creation.[39] In the drowning person example, and in *Michael*, there was no

[37] ibid [97], [130].

[38] In removing the 'activity' one needs to suppose a counterfactual in which the actor's body and resources are removed from the scene. Suppose that I move my boat before you reach it to save yourself. This would apparently count as an impure omission on the understanding in the text: if I had not moved the boat, you could have used it to save yourself. But this is likely to be counted as a pure omission. Thanks to Jeff Helmreich here.

[39] cf *AJ Allan (Blairnyle) Ltd v Strathclyde Fire Board* [2016] CSIH 3, 2016 SLT 253 [60] (Lord Drummond Young).

failure to control a risk created by the defendant. By contrast, a failure to brake and a failure to inspect an area prior to striking a golf ball are failures to take steps to control a risk created by the omitter. *Proposal E* delivers, then, the correct results.

Proposal E is opaque, however. It is not clear what must be the case for a person truly to be said to 'create a risk'. A risk is a probability of a negative outcome. If A had not failed to act, *but instead attempted to rescue the drowning person*, then the risk of the negative outcome—drowning—would have been smaller (possibly non-existent). In this way, A may be said to have created a risk of drowning. Thus, for *Proposal E* to deliver the correct results, it must *either* specify an appropriate counterfactual world in which the failure to act does not occur *or* rely upon some as yet unspecified non-counterfactual notion of risk creation.

Here, then, are two workable, if not fully elucidated, understandings of the concept of pure omissions:

> A failure to act is a pure omission by a person A in relation to damage if and only if the failure does not take place during an act or activity of A of which it is true that, had the act or activity not occurred, the damage would not have occurred.
>
> A failure to act is a pure omission if and only if it is not an omission to take steps to control a risk of one's own creation.

(iii) Acts

The legal concept of an *act* in this context has received even less analytical attention in the authorities. In cases affirming that the defendant's conduct is an *act*, it is simply emphasised that the defendant's conduct was 'active'. Thus, in *Robinson*, in deciding that police officers' attempt to arrest a suspect who resisted was an *act*, no analysis is given other than that the conduct played an 'active part in the critical events' which led to damage to the nearby claimant.[40] This is understandable on the facts of *Robinson*: although the case reached the Supreme Court, the police officers' conduct seems *obviously* an act or set of acts. There may, however, be more difficult cases.

One suggestion is that an act is a willed movement of one's body.[41] This works in many cases, so long as 'willed' is not restricted to 'consciously intended', but refers to any movement of one's body that is subject to some kind of voluntary control. Driving, baking, whistling, piano-playing—all *acts*—are at least partly constituted by willed movements of the body, in this sense.

[40] *Robinson* (n 28) [72] (Lord Reed). See, similarly, *Begum v Maran (UK) Ltd* [2020] EWHC 1846 (QB) [38]–[39] (Jay J), aff'd (on this point), [2021] EWCA Civ 326 [64] (Coulson LJ).

[41] Michael Moore holds something like this thesis: Moore (n 35) 79.

There is a class of acts, however, which is identical to willed non-movement of the body (eg sitting still for a portrait or staring at someone) and there are mental acts of making decisions, and so on.

It is clear that keeping one's body perfectly still can give rise to tort liability.[42] This is clear from the discussion of impure omission: a failure to brake in one's car may involve not moving one's body at all. So, one could potentially accept, for the purposes of tort law, that an *act* is a willed movement of the body, and allow the concept of an *impure omission* to cover situations in which a duty should attach (without a special fact existing) when a person does not move their body.

Consider these examples:

> *Crushing Person.* There is an explosion on a busy street. You are rendered unconscious. You wake up to find that you are crushing a business rival, who is gasping for breath. You stay perfectly still.

> *Watch.* As you stand on a bridge, you find that the sunlight has moved onto the face of your watch in such a way that the light is deflected, with a blinding effect, into the eye-line of oncoming drivers. You decide to continue occupying this position, as you are greatly enjoying this particular view from the bridge. An oncoming driver is blinded by the light and their car careens off the bridge.

These examples are difficult because neither do they involve movement of the body nor are they clearly impure omissions. Recall one definition of a pure omission:

> A failure to act is a pure omission if and only if it is not an omission to take steps to control a risk of one's own creation.

There is a hesitancy to describe these examples as ones in which one's failure to move one's body is a failure to control a risk of one's own creation. In *Crushing Person*, it might be said that you did not create the risk to the business rival in the sense that your agency was not significantly involved in causing the initial existence of that risk. In truth, however, in both examples your agency—your action in moving to that position on the bridge and walking down the street near the explosion—was a cause of the present existence of a risk to the driver and the rival. It is suggested that these are examples in which one's agency is innocently a cause of risk to another and, when this risk becomes reasonably knowable, one comes under a duty to act. These are, then, unusual examples of duties to take reasonable care that one's agency does not cause (certain kinds of) harm to others. In effect, then, these are examples of duties (to take care) not to be a cause of harm by impure omission.

[42] See also C McIvor, *Third Party Liability in Tort* (Hart 2006) 9–10.

4. Replacing the Act versus Pure Omission Distinction: Making Worse and Not Making Better (or Failing to Confer a Benefit)

In *N v Poole Borough Council*, Lord Reed preferred:[43]

> a distinction between causing harm (making things worse) and failing to confer a benefit (not making things better), rather than the more traditional distinction between acts and omissions, partly because the former language better conveys the rationale of the distinction drawn in the authorities, and partly because the distinction between acts and omissions seems to be found difficult to apply.[44]

The distinction between *making things worse* and *not making things better* has also been articulated in earlier decisions. For instance, a person who erected a wall on their land which protected neighbouring land from floodwater, but then removed it, leaving things as they would have been had the wall not been erected did not breach a duty in private nuisance: 'If this wall had been erected by the freeholder and taken down by the freeholder the next day, or a week, or a year afterwards, with the result that the floodwater took the course which it would have taken if the wall had never been there, I cannot see, on any principle known to me, that the respondents would have been entitled to complain.'[45]

As Lord Reed says, this formulation has two *prima facie* benefits. First, it tracks an intuitively important moral difference between affecting the world for the worse and failing to improve the world; it thus seems to make the law's attention to the distinction between acts and omissions morally intelligible.[46] Second, it avoids the difficulties of determining whether an omission is pure or impure. One simply asks whether the defendant's *conduct* made the claimant worse off or merely failed to make them better. Strictly, the true advantage is an advantage over the distinction between acts and *pure* omissions—not over the distinction between 'acts' and 'omissions', which has never been the legally relevant distinction.

[43] Chapter 1, section 4 was first published in S Steel, 'Rationalising Omissions Liability in Negligence' (2019) 135 Law Quarterly Review 484. It is reproduced by kind permission of Thomson Reuters.

[44] *N and another v Poole Borough Council* [2019] UKSC 25, [2020] AC 780 [28]. See also *Robinson* (n 28) [69] (Lord Reed); D Nolan, 'The Liability of Public Authorities for Failing to Confer Benefits' (2011) 127 Law Quarterly Review 260, 260, claiming that it is normally more straightforward to ask if 'the defendant has made things worse for the claimant or simply failed to confer a benefit on him or her'. See, similarly, R Stevens, *Torts and Rights* (OUP 2007) 9.

[45] *Thomas & Evans Ltd v Mid-Rhondda Cooperative Society* [1941] 1 KB 381, 389 (Wilfred-Greene MR). The decision is now qualified by *Goldman* (n 5), which imposes a duty to make things better in certain circumstances.

[46] See, articulating the idea that acts are more morally problematic because they involve interventions on the status quo, T Honoré, 'Are Omissions Less Culpable?' in P Cane and J Stapleton (eds), *Essays for Patrick Atiyah* (OUP 1991) 41–42.

Here is a third possible benefit: the distinction correctly identifies 'acts' which should be treated as 'pure omissions'—that is, acts which are only subject to a duty when there is a special fact. Consider this example:

> *Cancellation.* I set up a direct debit which provides funds to an exceptionally talented brain surgeon, who uses those funds to perform operations that are unavailable through the National Health Service. Having carelessly misread a newspaper article as saying that the surgeon had negligently performed certain operations, I instruct my bank to cancel the payment. Suppose that had that payment been made, the surgeon would foreseeably have been able to save one life.[47]

Here I have done a careless *act*—instructing my bank to cancel a payment—which foreseeably led to another's death. It seems highly unlikely that I face any legal liability with respect to the death in *Cancellation*.[48] If we ask—did I make the patient worse off or merely fail to benefit them?—the answer may seem to be that I simply failed to benefit them. If so, here is an *act* which amounts to a failure to benefit. It follows that the distinction between *acts* and *pure omissions* is not equivalent to the distinction between *making worse* and *failing to benefit*. Further, this non-equivalence appears to be beneficial: the latter distinction allows us to reach the correct result in *Cancellation*.

One might be tempted to resist the claim that this example involves an 'act'. It seems to me that this resistance is sourced in the idea that, in order to protect me from a duty of care, the situation needs to be characterised as an omission. If, however, the act versus pure omission distinction is recast as a distinction between making worse and failing to benefit, then there is no such need. The courts have at any rate accepted, in cases involving the withdrawal of life-sustaining treatment such as the removal of a nasogastric tube, that the withdrawal is 'undoubtedly a positive act' albeit one which should not always be treated in law as having the usual incidents of a positive act.[49] This suggests a fourth argument for the *making worse* versus *failure to benefit* formulation: it avoids the potentially confusing artificial recharacterisation of acts as somehow, in reality, omissions.

The central difficulty with the making worse versus not making better formulation, however, is how to specify the baseline relative to which one judges that a person is made worse off or merely not benefitted.[50] Consider *Cancellation*. It might be said that my instruction makes the victim worse off than they would have been had I not given the instruction: had I not given the instruction, they would

[47] This case is modelled on one given in S Kagan, *The Limits of Morality* (OUP 1989) 108. See further J McMahan, 'Killing, Letting Die, and Withdrawal of Aid' (1993) 103 Ethics 250.

[48] At least on the assumption that my giving did not lead to the recipient refusing an alternative source of aid. See Chapters 3 and 4.

[49] *Airedale NHS Trust v Bland* [1993] AC 789 (HL) 881 (Lord Browne-Wilkinson).

[50] This crucial issue is often given little attention in the literature. See, eg, Stevens (n 44) 9.

have lived. Alternatively, it could be said that my act merely causes the victim not to be benefitted because, had I not given to charity at all, they would still have died. As yet, the formulation provides no guidance on which baseline to use.[51]

Here, then, is one way of defining the baseline:

> *W1*: A's conduct makes B worse off if and only if it makes B worse off than had A not existed.

This reaches the intuitively correct answer in *Cancellation*: the cancellation of the payment does not make the victim worse off than had I never existed. But *W1* survives only the least scrutiny. Suppose that I saved your life when no one else would have. Then I carelessly run you over in my car. My carelessly running you over does not, or need not, make you worse off than if I had never existed. But it is clearly conduct which should give rise to liability without any special fact needing to be shown (in virtue of the kind of conduct that it is).

A different suggestion is as follows:[52]

> *W2*: A's conduct makes B worse off if and only if there is a time such that, had A not existed at that time, B would have been better off.

This deals with the careless car collision example in the last paragraph. There is a time (the time of the collision with B) when, had A not existed at that time, B would have been better off. But this formulation reaches the incorrect result in *Cancellation*: there is a time, namely, when A orders the cancellation, at which, had A not existed then, B would have been better off. Thus, *Cancellation* is incorrectly treated as a case of making worse.

A third suggestion:

> *W3*: A's conduct makes B worse off if and only if it makes B worse off than the position B is entitled to be in with respect to A.

This suggestion is uninformative. Consider the drowning stranger. Does walking past the stranger make the stranger worse than the position the stranger is *entitled* to be in with respect to the walker? If the walker has a duty to intervene which correlates with a right on the part of the stranger, then this is so. But whether the walker has a duty to intervene is the very issue that principles such as *W3* are supposed to assist in resolving. One's entitlements with respect to others are generally entitlements not to be made worse off, on the proposal we are considering. But if

[51] Moore makes this criticism: Moore (n 35) 28.

[52] This suggestion and the next are discussed in K Draper, 'Rights and the Doctrine of Doing and Allowing' (2005) 33 Philosophy & Public Affairs 253, 260–62.

determining whether one is worse off depends on a *prior* account of one's legal entitlements, then *W3* is of no assistance whatsoever.

Consider, then:

> *W4*: A's conduct makes B worse off if and only if it makes B worse off than B would be independently of the presence of A's body or resources at the time of the conduct alleged to constitute, or part-constitute, a tort.

This formulation is appealing. It deals with *Cancellation*. In this case, the defendant's act does not make the victim worse off compared to the position they would have been in had the defendant's body or resources (their charity payments) not been present at the time of the cancellation: if the defendant's body and resources had evaporated at that point, then the victim would still have died. This formulation also deals with the careless collision example: A's carelessly colliding with B makes B worse off than B would have been had A's body or resources not been present at that time, even if A's body or resources benefitted B at an earlier time.

Unfortunately, *W4* faces two problems. These are the problems of (i) overinclusiveness and (ii) underinclusiveness.

(i) The Problem of Overinclusiveness

(a) OLL Ltd *v Secretary of State for Transport*

In *OLL*,[53] May J held that no duty of care arose on the part of the defendant coastguard when they misdirected other rescue services in the coordination of a rescue attempt. Thus, although the defendant did something which made the victim worse off than they would have been had the defendant not been present, they were under no duty of care. Rather, a duty only arose not to 'inflict direct physical injury', and misdirecting 'other rescuers' could not be so classified.[54] The objection, then, is that *W4* would entail that a duty should have been owed in *OLL*, since it is a case of making worse with respect to the physical integrity of a person's body.

It may, however, be argued that *OLL* is consistent with the general principle that one is under a duty of care not to render persons foreseeably physically worse off than if one had not intervened. The argument is that the defendant coastguard did not render the victims worse off than if they had not intervened because all public

[53] [1997] 3 All ER 897.

[54] ibid 908; cf *Darnley v Croydon Health Services NHS Trust* [2018] UKSC 50, [2019] AC 831, in which a receptionist was held to be under a duty of care in giving information as to waiting times to the claimant visitor to an Accident and Emergency ward, with the result that the claimant did not wait to see a triage nurse.

rescue services should be treated as one single legal entity.[55] The defendant's act did not render the claimant worse off than if no public rescuer had intervened. This is a somewhat strained interpretation of *OLL*, however, as May J does not distinguish between public and private rescuers and one private rescuer was alleged to have been misdirected in the case.[56] Moreover, there seems to be no normative justification for grouping together all public rescue services in so far as they are distinct legal persons.

The better view is that *OLL* was incorrectly decided. There is a further reason for this conclusion. It is arbitrary to distinguish between cases where a person prevents an object from preventing a risk materialising and cases where a person prevents a person from preventing a risk materialising. It is clear that there can be a duty of care in the former type of case. If the fire brigade turn off a sprinkler system with the result that damage occurs which would not have occurred if they had not intervened at all, then they can be liable in respect of that damage.[57] It is not clear why one should distinguish between turning off a sprinkler and misdirecting a person, at least when the person misdirected could reasonably act upon the basis of the direction.

(b) *Kalma v African Minerals Ltd*

In *Kalma*,[58] the claimant villagers were brutally attacked by police officers in Sierra Leone. The police had been engaged by the defendant mine operator. The defendant had provided funding, accommodation, and vehicles to the police—an arrangement said to be common in Sierra Leone—to provide a presence around the mine.[59] The claimants argued that the defendants were under a duty of care to carry out risk assessments and construct a crisis management plan in relation to engaging the police, and to liaise further with police in their handling of the situation.[60] Despite the defendant's provision of assistance to the police, this was held to be a case of 'pure omission'.[61]

The difficulty for *W4* is that it treats this case as one of *worsening*: had the defendant and its resources not been present at the time of the conduct alleged to part constitute a tort (the failures to carry out risk assessments, etc) then the claimants would not have been attacked by the police: if there had been no mine and no police funding, the events would not have taken place.

Here are three responses to this difficulty. First, the holding that the alleged failure to liaise with the police and carry out risk assessment is a pure omission

55 R Bagshaw, 'The Duties of Care of Emergency Service Providers' [1999] LMCLQ 71, 83.
56 *OLL* (n 53) 908.
57 *Capital & Counties Plc v Hampshire County Council* [1997] QB 1004, [1997] 3 WLR 331.
58 [2020] EWCA Civ 144.
59 ibid [124].
60 ibid [126].
61 ibid [125]–[126].

seems incorrect. The mine operator bore substantial responsibility for the presence at the mine of police by providing accommodation and funding. For this reason, it is plausible to consider them to be causally responsible for the risk posed by the police. Certainly, any duty upon them may have been relatively non-stringent, given that their responsibility for the risk was relatively minimal, but that is an issue of breach not the existence of a duty. Second, even if the last point is incorrect, the fact that *W4* classifies *Kalma* as a case of worsening is not necessarily problematic. The aim of the distinction is to identify cases in which there is *defeasibly* a legal duty without a special fact being shown. Even if the distinction entails that *prima facie* there should be a legal duty in *Kalma*, there may be a competing consideration which defeats that conclusion. The defeating consideration relates to a concern about responsibility for the culpable criminal wrongdoing of others: one might consider it unfair to burden people with legal duties to hinder the culpable criminal activity of others.[62] Third, *W4* can be modified to avoid this problem entirely: the conduct in question must be a *significant* causal factor for why the victim is worse off: although *but for* the presence of the defendant and its resources, the victims would not have suffered damage, the presence of the defendant and its resources would not itself be counted as a significant part of the causal explanation why this occurred.

(ii) The Problem of Underinclusiveness

(a) Damaging, but Benefitting Overall

Let us now consider an example which appears to show that *W4* is underinclusive in what it treats as making worse.[63] Consider:

> *Rescue*. A sees a stranger, B, drowning in a pool of water. No one else is around. A wades in to save B. In pulling B to the shoreline, A forgets to secure her gun in its safety position. The gun goes off and damages B's foot. If A had not intervened at all, B would have drowned. If A had secured her gun, B would have avoided permanent damage to B's foot.

The going-in-the-vicinity-of-another-without-securing-a-gun seems to be conduct which, like driving-without-working-brakes, is in breach of a general duty not to impose an unreasonable risk of physical harm upon another. The difficulty here is that *W4* does not reach this result. If A's body or property had not been present at the time of the conduct that would amount to a breach—the failure to secure the

[62] This is considered later in Chapter 2, where it is argued that the current law gives too much weight to this consideration.

[63] See Chapter 3 for more extended discussion of this problem in the current law.

gun—B would be dead. A's causing B's foot to be damaged does not therefore make B worse off compared to A's body or property being absent.

This suggests the following modification of *W4*:

> *W5*. A's conduct makes B worse off if and only if A's conduct causes B to be in a negative state that B would not have been in but for the presence of A's body or resources at the time of the causative conduct.

This formulation reaches the correct result in *Rescue* because A causes B to be in a negative physical state—having a damaged foot—that B would not have been in but for the presence of A's body or resources at the time. *W5* does not require that the negative state one is in be worse than the state one would have been in had the defendant and their resources not been present.[64]

(b) Overdetermination

Suppose that A and C negligently fire in B's direction and each bullet strikes B's head at the same time (*Shots*). This is a situation in which B's damage is overdetermined: there are multiple sufficient causal conditions for its occurrence.[65] According to *W5*, this appears to be a situation where A and C would not generally be liable to B in negligence. This is because, if A had not been present, B's damage would still have occurred because of C's firing. Similarly, if C had not been present, B's damage would still have occurred because of A's firing. If there is an objection to holding A and C liable here, it should not stem from the distinction between *acts* and *pure omissions* (or a cognate distinction). It therefore seems that *W5* is underinclusive: it fails to find that A and C would be generally in principle liable in overdetermination situations such as *Shots*.

If we understand *W5* as a *heuristic* which generally accurately identifies situations in which a general right is triggered, we can accept this imperfection. It is possible to argue that, in almost all cases, A and C will have inflicted different 'damage' upon B. Even if the bullets simultaneously strike at one particular part of B's body, there will most likely be a sub-part of B's body which is negatively affected only by each bullet considered individually. It will, then, be possible to say under *W5* that A's conduct caused a damage to exist which would not otherwise exist. [66] In

[64] See D Nolan, 'Rights, Damage, and Loss' (2017) 37 Oxford Journal of Legal Studies 255, 270–74. It only follows that A wrongs B here, not that A is liable to pay substantial compensation to B.

[65] This is a somewhat loose definition of overdetermination. See further S Steel, *Proof of Causation in Tort Law* (CUP 2015) 20.

[66] A vaguer version of *W5* which appeals to whether the conduct 'typically' increases the probability of damage that would not otherwise occur without the presence of A's body or resources would also offer a solution. A's conduct typically increases the probability of damage of that description even if it does not in the particular case.

section 5, I consider a view which deals better with overdetermination situations, but is overall more problematic than *W5*.

(c) Removal of One's Own Property

Consider *Ploof v Putnam*.[67] It was alleged that a 'violent tempest' arose while the plaintiff was sailing on a sloop with his wife and their two minor children, and that the plaintiff moored his boat to the defendant's dock to protect them from a substantial risk of death or serious injury. The defendant's employee unfastened the boat, with the result that the plaintiff's wife and children suffered serious injuries and their property was destroyed. The Supreme Court of Vermont held that this allegation disclosed an actionable wrong on the part of the defendant. The plaintiff's interference with the dock was justified by necessity, and it was wrongful for the defendant to interfere with this justified use in such a way as to endanger the plaintiff's life without sufficient reason.

According to *W5*, *Ploof* is not a case of making worse: the defendant's conduct likely did not make the claimant worse off than if the defendant's body and resources had not been present. Yet, the defendant owed a duty without any special fact being shown. More generally, it seems clear that A would owe a duty of reasonable care not to dislodge B from A's property in such a way as to cause them reasonably foreseeably physical damage, even if this does not render B worse off than B would be had A and A's property not been present. *W5* cannot explain this, it seems, since *W5* asserts that a necessary condition of general tort duties is that the defendant make worse off, not merely fail to benefit. But *Ploof* is an example of a general tort duty which does not meet this criterion.

Here is my attempt to salvage *W5*. We might reasonably say that *Ploof* is an example of a duty that arises by virtue of a special fact: another's use of your property in an emergency.[68] So *W5* could still be a good articulation of the conditions of a *general* duty in tort. The duty which arises in *Ploof* is an exceptional duty to take care not to act in such a way that fails to benefit a person. This is clearly not a general duty in tort. It only exists when a special fact obtains. We should add 'emergency use of another's property to protect one's life or similarly weighty interests' to the list of special facts.[69]

[67] 81 Vt 471, 71 A 188 (1908).

[68] I am not aware of any cases which raise the same problem in the context of use of a person's body. Suppose that my only way of saving myself from a substantial risk of death by drowning is to hold on to your ankle for a minute or so until the emergency services arrive. Are you legally permitted to dislodge me from your ankle, thereby likely causing my death? While interference with a person's body might be substantially harder to justify than interference with their property, it seems difficult to draw a firm line. If that is correct, it is likely that there is an analogous *Ploof* duty in cases in which a person is currently receiving assistance from the use of your body. If so, the special fact would be 'another person's use of your body or property in an emergency'.

[69] See further Chapter 8.

In summary, *W5* provides an appealing formulation of the general rule. This formulation leads to the correct results in the simple case where a stranger fails to rescue a drowning child, it avoids the conceptual complexity surrounding 'impure' omissions, and it deals with *acts* which should not give rise to a general duty without a special fact being shown (such as in *Cancellation*). It correctly classifies duties not to dislodge people using one's property in emergency situations as duties arising from the special fact of another using one's property in an emergency.

5. Replacing the Act versus Pure Omission Distinction: Causing and Not Preventing Harm

Lord Reed's *dictum* in *N* also refers to a distinction between *causing* and *not preventing* harm.[70] This suggests a further different idea to the idea of making worse versus not making better. This idea focusses on the actual sequence of events by which a person's conduct is connected to harm. In light of the discussion of *W5*, there is some reason to think an idea like this could be a better account of the distinction. First, what seems significant in cases like *Ploof* is the direct mode of agency by which one is connected to the person's damage, rather than whether one's agency makes the person worse off. Second, it seems immediately clear in overdetermination cases that one is connected to the damage in a way which should fall within a general right, even without it being the case that the claimant is made worse off compared to the position they would be in had the defendant's body or property not been present.

In this section, I will explain the most sophisticated version of this type of view, developed by Fiona Woollard, to account for the moral distinction between *doing* and *allowing harm*.[71] My aim is to consider whether an account like Woollard's can account for the legal distinction in play in tort law. I will show that this account is not successful as an account of the legal distinction. My conclusion is limited: I will reveal problems with Woollard's account *as an account of the legal distinction*, but it may be that there is some possible superior sequence view—I have not so far been able to develop one.

To understand the basic idea behind this sort of view, consider:

No Rescue. A walks past B, an unconscious stranger, who is drowning. B drowns.

[70] See n 44.

[71] F Woollard, *Doing and Allowing Harm* (OUP 2015) chs 1–5. She identifies her account as one based around the notion of a relevant sequence: see, eg, ibid 24.

Contrast this with:

> *Collision*. A negligently thrusts his arms towards B, a stranger, who resultantly falls into a pool of water and drowns.

A is 'relevant to' B's drowning in both cases, in the following sense: A's non-intervention is a necessary condition of B's drowning in *No Rescue* and A's thrusting is a necessary condition of B's drowning in *Collision*. Let's say that 'relevance to an outcome' means 'being a necessary condition or a NESS condition of the outcome'.[72] Although A is relevant to the outcome in both cases, there is nonetheless an intuitive difference in the nature of this relevance. If A is relevant to B's death in *No Rescue*, it will only be through a negative fact: not providing assistance. By contrast, A is relevant to B's death in *Collision* by a positive fact: thrusting his arm towards B. Drawing upon Bennett's work, Woollard offers this analysis of positive and negative facts about a person's conduct:[73]

> A fact about an agent's conduct is a positive fact if, of all the possible movements the agent could have made of his body, most are such that, if he had moved that way, the fact would not hold.
>
> A fact about an agent's conduct is a negative fact if, of all the possible movements the agent could have made of his body, most are such that, if he moved that way, the fact would hold.

On this account 'A thrust his arm towards B' states a positive fact since most of the available movements of A's body do not amount to thrusting his arm towards B. By contrast, 'A's not assisting B' states a negative fact about A's conduct since, of all the possible movements of A's body, most of them are such that they would amount to 'not assisting B'. The intuitive idea is that a positive fact singles out a relatively specific fact about the agent's conduct; it is an informative fact about an agent's conduct. A negative fact is less informative: it leaves open many ways in which the agent might have behaved. Woollard extends this idea, of positive and negative facts about an agent's *conduct*, to positive and negative facts more generally.[74] A fact about an object's whereabouts, for instance, is a positive fact if and only if most of the ways the object could have been placed would not make the proposition about the whereabouts true. So, the fact that the cat is on a tree branch is a positive fact about the cat's whereabouts: most of the ways in which the cat could have been placed are not such that the cat is on a tree branch.

[72] It is controversial whether this is the same as 'causal' relevance; this does not matter here. 'NESS' stands for 'Necessary Element of a Sufficient Set': for the classic presentation of this idea, see R Wright, 'Causation in Tort Law' (1985) 73 California Law Review 1735. For slightly more discussion of this, see Chapter 11.

[73] Woollard (n 71) 41. (I have modified the terminology in minor ways.)

[74] ibid 42–43.

This suggests the following alternative formulation of the distinction traditionally tracked by 'acts' and 'pure omissions':

> *N1*. A is generally not liable to B in tort when A's conduct is only relevant to B's damage by a sequence which involves a negative fact.

In *Cancellation*, Woollard would claim that A's conduct is connected to B's damage by a sequence which involves a negative fact. This is so even although the act of cancellation is a positive fact about A's conduct. A is relevant to the death in *Cancellation* only by making it the case that there is an absence of resources to save the patient. The absence of resources is a negative fact about the world: most of the ways the world could be at that particular time would make it true that that there is an absence of resources at that time. Therefore, A is relevant to the death in *Cancellation* only through a sequence that includes a negative fact.[75]

However, as Woollard realises, *N1* leads to incorrect conclusions in at least two (overlapping) categories of case: (1) cases in which the creation of a negative condition leading to harm appears morally equivalent to directly producing the harm, and (2) some cases involving a removal of a barrier to harm.

An example of (1) is when A uses a device which removes all of the oxygen from a room, with the result that B dies.[76] In tort law, an example would be the encroachment of tree roots which suck moisture from sub-soil, leading to the collapse of another's land.[77] The absence of oxygen or moisture is a negative fact. Most of the ways the world could be are such that there is no oxygen or moisture there. So, this would not be a situation in which A is generally liable under *N1*. Woollard's strategy here is to say that some fact other than a positive fact can be relevant to a sequence leading to harm, so as to count as doing the harm, if the obtaining of the negative fact is contrary to our normal presuppositions.[78] She elaborates that a fact is contrary to what is normally presupposed if it is contrary to 'the assumptions we take for granted unless we are told otherwise'.[79] She says, for example, that we assume that motorways are free of holes and cars have working brakes.[80] And it is normally presupposed that there is oxygen in the air. Thus, we have:

> *N2*: A is generally not liable to B in tort when A's conduct is connected to B's damage by a sequence involving a negative fact, unless A introduces the negative fact, which is contrary to what is normally presupposed.

[75] ibid 31.
[76] ibid 57.
[77] See, eg, *Russell v Barnet LBC* (1984) 271 EG 699.
[78] Woollard (n 71) 57–59.
[79] ibid 82.
[80] ibid 58.

Under *N2*, all cases of the removal of a barrier (category (2) above) are counted as ones in which there is generally no liability, unless the barrier removal is contrary to a normal presupposition. This is because, in these cases, a person will only be relevant to the damage through a negative fact: removing a barrier to harm. This leads to incorrect results in some cases. Suppose B is about to jump from a burning building to a bouncy structure provided by C. A, knowing this and knowing that A's dog is fond of piercing such objects, carelessly permits the dog to run towards the bouncy castle. B jumps and is killed falling into the deflated structure. Call this case *Burning Building*.[81] This is a situation in which A has done harm and ought to be under a legal duty without a special fact being shown. *N1* does not reach this result. By contrast, cases such as *Cancellation* appear to be ones in which the removal of a barrier (the 'barrier' is constituted by the provision of one's own resources) ought not to be treated as morally akin to doing harm. Consider, then, this revision, which partly follows Woollard's strategy of dealing with this problem:

> *N3*. A is generally not liable to B in tort when A's conduct is connected to B's damage by a negative fact, unless (a) A introduces the negative fact that is contrary to what is normally presupposed, or (b) the negative fact consists in A's removing a barrier belonging to B, no one else, or another person, C.[82]

N3 distinguishes between who owns the barrier.[83] If the barrier is owned by the person removing the barrier, it counts as merely allowing harm and a situation in which a special reason is needed for the imposition of liability. Thus, *Cancellation* is preserved as a general no liability case, as is *Ploof* since A would be removing A's own barrier (the dock); but the contrary result is rightly reached in *Burning Building*. It bears emphasis that the upshot is *not* that A is *never* under a tort duty in cases like *Cancellation* and *Ploof*—it is that a duty will only exist, if it does, by virtue of a special fact being shown.

(i) Objections to N3

(a) Removing Barriers

A first objection to *N3* is that it reaches the incorrect conclusion about the apparently simple case in which A fires a gun and the bullet kills B.[84] This is clearly a paradigm case of doing harm in which no special reason is needed for a duty to

[81] This is modelled on the *Burning Building* case in McMahan (n 47) 254.
[82] Woollard adds that C authorised, or would have authorised, the use of the barrier to prevent harm to B: Woollard (n 71), 74–75 (see also 81, 94).
[83] 'Barrier' should be read to include objects, but also persons. If a person removes their own body, they can be said for this purpose to remove something they morally own.
[84] Woollard (n 71) 82–84.

exist. However, by pressing the trigger of a gun, A removes the sear which holds a coil in place. The coil violently unfurls and fires the bullet. Therefore, A's conduct is connected to B's damage only by the interposition of a *negative fact*: the absence of the sear being in position. Further, though it removes a barrier to harm occurring, the barrier belongs to A. This would therefore be a case of merely allowing harm to occur under *N3*.

In response, here is a modification of *N3* which parallels Woollard's:

> *N4.* A is generally not liable to B in tort when A's conduct is only connected to B's damage by a negative fact, unless (a) A introduces the negative fact which is contrary to what is normally presupposed, or (b) the negative fact consists in A removing a barrier belonging to B, another person, C, or to no one else, or (c) A introduces the negative fact which consists in an absence of a barrier to a risk posed by A's own conduct.

This addition of (c) is similar to the law's gloss concept of an impure omission: impure omissions are failures to act to respond to risks of one's own creation, including risks posed by one's resources. *N4* allows this account correctly to classify cases in which there is a negative fact interposed by a person in the causal mechanism when the negative fact allows the agent's resources to inflict damage. Thus, the removal of the sear is the introduction of a negative fact which removes a barrier to the risk posed by A.

It seems to me that Woollard's account is still vulnerable to counterexamples concerning barriers. Suppose that I put up a massive clear sign next to my drawbridge which states that I may sometimes, without warning, open a large door on the road surface of the bridge, even when people are crossing the bridge. You come onto the bridge and I open up the door in preparation for the high-altitude diving from that spot which I will do later. You fall to your death. It seems obvious that I have *done* harm here, but I have removed my own barrier and there is no normal presupposition, given the warning, that the barrier will not be removed. It may be that you are partly responsible for your own fate, but this does not alter the fact my conduct falls on the *doing* side of the *doing v allowing* distinction.[85]

[85] Woollard offers a response to similar examples: see ibid 88–89. She says that her account treats an agent as merely allowing harm 'if he removes a barrier that requires the continued use of resources belonging to the agent'. For this purpose, an object counts as a 'resource' if and only if '(1) it is either generally valuable or useful to the agent or valuable or useful to the agent in this particular case and (2) being forbidden from removing the barrier in the way the agent plans will undermine the agent's possession of the object, by damaging or destroying it, preventing him from using it now or at a later stage or in some other way decreasing the value of the resource for the agent'. This qualification does not seem to me to avoid the counterexample in the text. We can suppose that my opening the door to dive at that particular time was valuable, and being required not to do so would impair the value of the resource by preventing its being used for high altitude diving at a suitable time.

(b) Conventional Presuppositions

A second objection to Woollard's proposal relates to its incorporation of the idea of what is 'normally presupposed'.[86]

First, suppose that we move to another planet where no oxygen is present in the general atmosphere, except in certain isolated locations. If A removed the oxygen from one of those locations with the result that B died, this would surely still count as doing harm to B, even though no assumptions may yet have been formed about the presence of oxygen in particular locations on the planet. Second, it seems problematic that the moral quality of one's conduct could turn *solely* upon everyone else's assumptions. If everyone assumed that the charity payment would continue to be made in *Cancellation*, that alone should not be determinative of whether the act constitutes doing or allowing harm. Third, it also seems underinclusive. Even if we lived in a world in which few people kept their promises, if you know that *I* keep my promises, and I induce you to take some detrimental action by making you a promise, it seems that I *do* harm rather than merely allow harm to occur.

(ii) Summary

This section has considered a possible causal sequence view of the distinction embedded in the law's distinction between 'acts' and 'pure omissions'. It has suggested that the best version of this view is *N4*:

> *N4*. A is generally not liable to B in tort when A's conduct is only connected to B's damage by a negative fact, unless (a) A introduces the negative fact, which is contrary to what is normally presupposed, (b) unless the negative fact consists in A removing a barrier belonging to B, another person, C, or to no one else, or (c) unless A introduces the negative fact which consists in an absence of a barrier to a risk posed by A's own conduct.

N4 seems inferior, however, to *W5* since it is subject to counterexamples in cases involving the removal of barriers and the notion of a 'normal presupposition' seems to lead to problematic results. The better account of the law's distinction is *W5*.

6. A Kantian Alternative

Ripstein and Benson have also rejected an account of the relevant distinction in terms of *acts* and *omissions*.[87] Benson holds that (in my terms) our general rights

[86] For other criticisms of this, see S Rickless, 'Review: *Doing and Allowing Harm*' (2016) 126 Ethics 862, 864.

[87] A Ripstein, *Private Wrongs* (Harvard UP 2016), ch 3; P Benson, 'Misfeasance as an Organizing Normative Idea in Private Law' (2010) 60 University of Toronto Law Journal 731.

are 'exclusionary rights', whereas rights that are triggered by a special fact are not of this kind. An 'exclusionary right' seems to be a right of control, in some sense, over one's body or an external resource. In explaining the absence of a general duty to rescue a stranger, Benson writes:

> Since it is the plaintiff's life or property that is in danger, the only legally recognized interests which the plaintiff can possibly assert vis-à-vis the defendant are her rights of bodily integrity and property. But these interests are protected through rights to exclude the defendant . . . Now, supposing that the defendant has not in any way contributed to the danger, what the plaintiff can assert to the exclusion of the defendant is just her bodily existence or property in this condition of danger.[88]

And it is true that, on any intuitive understanding of 'control', the person who fails to rescue does not exercise control over the endangered stranger. This idea is also used to explain the absence of a general right in relation to pure economic loss: if you damage T's property with the effect that it causes me economic loss, you do not exercise illegitimate control over my resource—you simply negatively change my circumstances.

This view is subject to a dilemma. If it adheres to the notion of rights against 'control' over one's body or property, then it reaches untenable (and legally incorrect) conclusions. If it extends the notion of 'control' to rights against 'interference', it becomes analytically unilluminating.

The first part of the dilemma emerges when one thinks about situations in which one person carelessly removes a barrier to protection from harm. Suppose that you carelessly weaken the foundations of a public bridge on which I am standing. The bridge collapses and I drown. Do you exercise 'control' over my body or resources? If 'control' is understood as involving a trespass, then the answer is 'no'. Or suppose that you set fire to an unowned life-raft that is heading my way and will otherwise save my life. It's not clear that you have done something amounting to 'control' over my body, and yet no special fact would need to be shown here for there to be a duty not to do this.

To deal with this kind of case, the view might expand the general rights to cover, not only rights to 'control' over one's body or resources, but rights against *interference*. If one has exclusionary rights, one has a right against *interference* with one's body or resources. Then the second part of the dilemma emerges: now we need an account of why *Cancellation* does not involve 'interference', whereas the examples in the above paragraph do involve interference. *W5* and *N4* provide such an account, whereas this view does not.

[88] P Benson, 'Misfeasance as an Organizing Normative Idea in Private Law' (2010) 60 University of Toronto Law Journal 731, 737.

At points, there are hints of other ideas in these authors. One is that the relevant distinction is irreducibly normative and is perhaps to be answered by considering whether the duty involves one person potentially being 'in charge of' another. The relevant issue, however, is *in relation to what kinds of duty* does this risk arise, such that a special fact needs to be shown. A concern about one person being in charge of another might underpin the distinction, but it is not an account of what the distinction *is*.

Another is the idea that our general rights protect our capacity to set ends by protecting our means to set ends, but do not require others to serve our ends or any particular end that another has. This fails to explain the absence of a duty of easy rescue, which can be understood as a duty to protect a person's capacity to set ends through preserving the continued existence of their capacities, and not a requirement to serve a particular end of a person.

There is, however, one point on which Kantian accounts have an advantage over *W5*. The kind of control that is involved in trespass is only awkwardly describable as a 'negative state'. If someone encounters an unconscious injured person, and briefly stands on the latter's body purely in order to reach an attractive fruit on a nearby branch, this would be a trespass, even if the pressure momentarily benefitted the person. Intentionally altering the position of a person's body without permission calls for justification. Even here, however, 'intentional alteration of a person's body' is not enough to characterise the general right in trespass: in *Cancellation*, the cancellation may alter the position of a person's body, but is no trespass. The person's conduct must lead to an alteration in the other's body which would not have occurred relative to the baseline in *W5*.

7. Rule and Exceptions

It is usually said that a person is not *generally* liable in tort for a pure omission, but that there exist *exceptions* to this general rule. For example, Stelios Tofaris and I formulated the rule (in the context of the tort of negligence) and the exceptions in this way:

> ... a person A is not under a duty to take care to prevent harm occurring to person B through a source of danger not created by A unless (i) A has assumed a responsibility to protect B from that danger, (ii) A has done something which prevents another from protecting B from that danger, (iii) A has a special level of control over that source of danger, or (iv) A's status creates an obligation to protect B from that danger.

The intention behind this formulation was to provide a rule which identifies conduct that does not attract a duty of care unless certain special facts are satisfied.

The exceptions are thus situations in which the category of conduct identified does generate a duty.

Sometimes, however, the exceptions to the rule are formulated in a way which makes them only apparent exceptions. The exceptions really identify conduct which, on proper analysis, is *not* a pure omission after all. If all of the exceptions to the rule are only apparent, there is no value in structuring the law as based upon a rule subject to exceptions. It is akin to saying that there is no liability for pure omissions unless the conduct is not a pure omission. Here are three examples of this phenomenon. First, it is sometimes said that a person is not liable for a pure omission unless they have made matters worse.[89] This makes no sense if we follow Lord Reed's formulation in *N*: the 'pure omission' category is just the category of situations in which one has *not* made matters worse. Second, it is sometimes claimed that when an exception is satisfied, the conduct is no longer a pure omission. Thus, when a person assumes a responsibility towards another person to benefit them, a failure to discharge the responsibility with care is then described as no longer a pure omission.[90] Third, perhaps most frequently, it is said that a person is exceptionally liable for a pure omission when they create a danger. If the omission is a failure to protect against the materialisation of a risk one chose to create, however, then it is almost certainly an *impure* omission and so not within the general no-liability rule at all.

Kenneth Abraham and Leslie Kendrick have argued that, properly analysed, all of the 'exceptional' cases in which the law (in the United States) imposes 'affirmative' duties are simply situations which fall within the 'general duty' attached to 'active conduct'.[91] Thus, when a parent is held to be under an affirmative duty to their child to protect them from drowning at a swimming pool, this is because the parent has created danger to the child by bringing them within proximity of the pool. If all of the 'exceptions' can be re-analysed in this way then the idea that there are, exceptionally, duties in relation to pure omissions should be abandoned.

Their thesis is, however, false. We have already seen one reason why. The duty in *Ploof* situations is a duty to take care not to do something which will fail to benefit another person. There is no such general duty. It will be shown in later chapters that their thesis is false in other ways in English law. First, some duties arising from 'assumptions of responsibility' and 'control', cannot be understood simply as instantiations of any general duty.[92] These are special tort duties to (take care to) improve a person's position. Second, there is no such thing as the 'general tort duty' attached to active conduct—there are different general tort duties, and these are not usefully considered as a single duty as they have separate requirements and

[89] *AJ Allan* (n 39) [71] (Lord Drummond Young): 'there is no liability for pure omissions unless matters are made worse'.

[90] *Aitken* (n 34).

[91] K Abraham and L Kendrick, 'There's No Such Thing as Affirmative Duty' (2019) 104 Iowa Law Review 1649.

[92] Chapters 4–6.

stringencies.[93] However, the truth in their view is the one expressed above: what is classified as an exception to the rule ought not merely to be an instantiation of conduct that generally attracts a duty. And we will see that some of what is classified as a duty arising by virtue of a special fact is not properly so classified.

8. An Impossible Distinction?

The distinction between acts and pure omissions or related distinctions has often been criticised. The next chapter considers normative objections to it. But the distinction has also been criticised, on conceptual grounds, on the basis that the distinction it draws simply cannot be drawn in many cases:

> . . . there is no firm line capable of determination between a case of omission and of commission. Some cases may fall clearly on one side of the line . . . But the great majority of cases can be analysed in terms of either.[94]

> . . . there are many situations in which it is impossible to draw any logical line between misfeasance and nonfeasance. A solicitor instructed to make a will allows it to be wrongly witnessed so that it is invalid: this may be seen as misfeasance in making the will or as a failure to ensure that it was properly witnessed. A person digs a hole on their land and a visitor falls into it: this may be seen as affirmative conduct in digging the hole or as nonfeasance in failing to fence the hole or give a warning. A person turns right across a line of traffic without signalling: this is either positive bad driving or a negative failing to signal. More generally, whether failure to act is viewed as nonfeasance or misfeasance depends largely on whether we view the failure in isolation or as part of a larger activity.[95]

An initial difficulty with the first of these passages is that the distinction invoked is between *acts* and *omissions*. The legal distinction is, however, between *acts* and *pure omissions*. Suppose the passages are read as invoking the latter distinction. There is then a weak and a strong version of the objection in these passages. The weak version is that there are occasional borderline cases in which it is conceptually unclear whether conduct constitutes an act or a pure omission. If this is the objection, it does not justify a *wholesale* rejection of the distinction between acts and pure omissions. Virtually all concepts have borderline cases. The strong version is that *in many* or *most* cases conduct can logically be analysed as an *act* or *pure omission*. This would be problematic if true. The examples given in the second passage do not vindicate

[93] See especially Chapter 2.

[94] *Robinson* (n 28) [117] (Lord Hughes).

[95] P Cane, *Atiyah's Accidents Compensation and the Law* (6th edn, CUP 2010) 60. The passage is cited with approval in *Bellefield Computer Services Ltd v E Turner & Sons Ltd* [2000] 2 TCLR 759, 764–765 (Schiemann LJ).

this objection, however. The examples identify cases in which one can identify an action or *an omission*. However, the tests for determining whether an omission is *pure* omission developed earlier are not satisfied in these cases. Failure to take steps to prevent a danger one created is not a pure omission. Thus, failing to signal when driving and failing to warn in relation to a hole one created on one's land are *impure* omissions, which do not require a special fact for the imposition of a duty.

9. Conclusions

The current tort law conceptualises the distinction between general rights and rights arising when a special fact exists as a distinction between rights against *acts* (inclusive of *impure omissions*) and rights against *pure omissions.*

The aim of this chapter has been to clarify this distinction and consider whether it should be replaced with another that better characterises the division which the law is seeking to track.

As to clarification, it was suggested that a *pure omission* is:

> a failure to act by a person A in relation to damage if and only if the failure does not take place during an act or activity of A of which it is true that, had the act or activity not occurred, the damage would not have occurred;
>
> or
>
> a failure to act if and only if it is not an omission to take steps to control a risk of one's own creation.

An *impure omission* is thus a failure to act to take steps to control a risk of one's own creation, or a failure to act during an act or activity which is a but-for cause of the damage.

An *act* is a willed bodily movement. So long as it is realised that tort general rights are rights against acts *and* impure omissions, this definition of *act*, while philosophically flawed, is not underinclusive.

As to replacement, it was shown that the alternative distinction between making things worse and not making things better can be understood in several different ways, depending upon the specification of the relevant baseline. It was argued that the best version of this alternative is:

> *W5.* A's conduct makes B worse off if and only if A's conduct causes B to be in a negative state that B would not have been in, but for the presence of A's body or resources at the time of the causative conduct.

W5 has two primary advantages over the current law's conceptualisation. First, it avoids the complexity surrounding whether an omission is pure or impure. Second, it is extensionally more adequate: it excludes cases such as *Cancellation* from the scope of general rights.

2
Justifying a Distinction

This chapter turns to the normative question of whether the significance attached in tort law to the distinction between *acts* and *pure omissions* can be justified. The issue addressed is not whether the details of the current law can be justified, but whether the law is right to recognise that legal positive duties (P-duties) should arise only in limited situations when a special fact obtains, such as an assumption of responsibility.[1]

In Chapter 1, I argued for this account of the 'act' part of the distinction that the law is seeking to track in using the distinction between 'acts' and 'pure omissions':

> *W5*. A's conduct makes B worse off if and only if A's conduct causes B to be in a negative state that B would not have been in, but for the presence of A's body or resources at the time of the causative conduct.

We can, then, draw a distinction between duties not to *worsen* a person's position where worsening is understood according to the baseline in *W5*, and duties to *improve* a person's position where improvement is understood as improvement relative to the same baseline. I will refer to the first duties as negative duties ('N-duties') and the second as positive duties ('P-duties').

The central concern of this chapter is whether there is a normative distinction between N-duties and P-duties such that the legal recognition and enforceability of P-duties in tort is justifiably subject to more demanding requirements than N-duties.

It is useful to distinguish at the outset between different kinds of distinction and different stages at which a distinction may arise. The distinction between N-duties and P-duties could either be one that holds, *intrinsically*, in virtue of the nature of a P-duty, or it could be one that holds contingently but *typically*. In the former case, there is always some moral difference between N-duties and P-duties such that P-duties are intrinsically more difficult to justify. In the latter case, there is a consideration or set of considerations that often or normally apply to P-duties, but not in every case.

A distinction between N-duties and P-duties, whether intrinsic or contingent, could arise at two different stages. First, there could be a difference between the

[1] See Chapters 4 and 5 on 'Assumption of Responsibility'. For the notion of a 'special fact', see Chapter 1.

Omissions in Tort Law. Sandy Steel, Oxford University Press. © Sandy Steel 2024.
DOI: 10.1093/9780191898822.003.0002

two which exists at a fundamental moral level, independently of the institutionalisation of these duties. Second, there could be a difference which emerges when it comes to the legal institutionalisation of the duties.

In the first section of the chapter, I argue against the idea that there is an *intrinsic* objectionability at the fundamental moral level to P-duties, though I endorse the view that P-duties are more difficult to justify in virtue of a special kind of involvement of one person in the life of another, which by contrast obtains in relation to N-duties. I defend the view that there are important contingent considerations that sometimes make P-duties more difficult to justify. I then consider whether there are moral objections to the institutionalisation of interpersonal moral duties and liabilities in respect of pure omissions as such. I reject the idea that there is an intrinsic objection to the enforcement of moral duties in respect of pure omissions, and largely reject the claim that there are negative consequences distinctively associated with their legal enforcement.

It bears emphasis at the outset that the limited concern of this chapter is to assess the justifiability of a different pattern of legal regulation of acts and pure omissions in tort. Specifically, what calls for justification is (a) that duties and liabilities in respect of *acts* are established by different broader requirements, while additional requirements must be satisfied in relation to *pure omissions*, and (b) that the kinds of duty that arise in relation to *pure omissions* may be of a less stringent character than those arising in respect of *acts*. If this differential treatment is justified, it does not follow that the current law is justified. The current law embodies one particular vision about the normative difference between *acts* and *pure omissions*. It may be, as I later argue,[2] that it attributes too much weight to the difference and adopts an overly narrow position on when liability for *pure omissions* is justified or not.

1. Justifications for a Moral Difference between N-Duties and P-Duties

(i) Intrinsic Differences

(a) Being Treated Merely as a Resource

Kimberly Ferzan argues that the distinction between P-duties and N-duties is explained by a person's entitlement 'not to be forced into servitude of the greater good':[3] unlike N-duties, P-duties involve a person 'being treated as a resource for others'.[4]

[2] Chapter 9 on 'easy rescue'.

[3] K Ferzan, 'Omissions, Acts, and the Duty to Rescue' in D Nelkin and S Rickless (eds), *The Ethics and Law of Omissions* (OUP 2017) 221.

[4] ibid 222.

This kind of view is attractive.[5] It is supported by an idea that underpins the rejection of consequentialism. Part of what is objectionable about consequentialism is its failure to recognise persons as having a distinctive moral status, rather than as mere sites of impersonal value. If there were no distinction between N-duties and P-duties, with P-duties being assimilated to N-duties such that each of us had to promote others' interests whenever the costs to our own are less than the benefit to be conferred, then there would be a sense in which each of us would be mere a site of value with no independent significance.

Furthermore, a person's distinctive moral status as a setter of their own ends seems to give a person a strong objection to being used non-consensually for the benefit of others. This objection is the same one which prohibits other intuitively impermissible uses of a person's body to protect others, such as non-consensually using a large innocent person's body to stop a runaway train (or 'trolley') which will otherwise kill five other innocent people. Given the large person's moral status, the extent to which they can be required to use their body as means to benefit others is limited. A requirement to use one's body to benefit others whenever there is a greater benefit to others would not acknowledge an individual's distinctive moral status as an end-setter.

Some authors, such as Arthur Ripstein, take this, or a highly similar, thought to entail the absence of any general relational moral P-duties, even P-duties that are highly constrained in character such as a P-duty to provide non-costly assistance to a stranger in urgent need.[6] On Ripstein's view, one never has a P-duty owed to another to provide them with assistance: this would involve the other's need determining the use of one's means. If this view is true, there is a very sharp moral distinction between N-duties and P-duties.

One can accept that P-duties need to be more limited than N-duties, on the ground that individuals have a moral claim not to be treated merely as instruments for others' welfare, without being committed to the absence of any general relational P-duty, however. There are at least two reasons. First, the non-consequentialist objection to an equivalence between P-duties and N-duties is based on the concern that this equivalence would treat persons *merely* as means for the improvement of others' welfare. This concern does not support the absence of a general duty of easy rescue. If I have a duty to try to save your life when there is a tiny cost to me, it is not the case that I am required to bear a setback to my interests *whenever* there is a greater promotion of your interests. Rather, this duty only

[5] It might be considered incoherent to speak of 'morality' treating a person as a resource. On the one hand, morality is not an agent and so cannot literally 'treat' anyone in a particular way. On the other hand, if there is a moral objection to being treated as a resource, then one cannot *have* a moral duty that partakes of that objectionability; the moral duty simply would not exist. I intend the following: in investigating whether there *could be* a moral duty, one considers what moral objections there would be to such a duty. If one finds that the putative moral duty would sit uneasily with some moral conviction, then this is a reason for believing that the duty does not exist at all.

[6] A Ripstein, *Private Wrongs* (Harvard UP 2016) 56.

requires me to bear a cost, perhaps up to a certain threshold, when the costs to you of my not doing so are *much* greater. This hardly treats me *merely* as a means for the promotion of your interests. Second, my separateness as a person seems to bear mainly on requirements to use my *body* for the benefit of others. Without a wide-ranging moral veto on when my body can be used, my special status as a person is not respected. Such a consideration has less force in relation to the use of my external resources. If I were required to use my property in an impartially good-maximising way, then I would not have a moral veto on the use of my external resources. But the strength of my claim not to make my resources available for use by others seems less powerful: the intimate connection I enjoy with my body does not exist as significantly in relation to my property.

If this is correct, then the moral fact that a person is not a mere resource is not itself inconsistent with the existence of general P-duties. Whether one is treated as a mere resource rather depends upon *the specific kind* of P-duties to which one is subject. More specifically, those that require excessive self-sacrifice for the benefit of others, or which give no recognition to the separateness of people's lives, are those which would offend against this value.

(b) Causation

Michael Moore contends that the moral difference between acts and omissions stems from a metaphysical difference: in his view, acts can, while omissions cannot, be causes.[7] This is because, according to Moore, an omission is simply a nothing and nothing causes nothing.[8] Moore accepts, however, that a person can be *responsible* for an outcome which counterfactually depended upon that person's omission. Counterfactual dependence is not causality, however, on his view—instead, responsibility for outcomes that are counterfactually dependent upon one's omission to do something is a form of *non-causal* responsibility. Here are two claims, then, which are central to Moore's view:

(1) Omissions cannot be causes, while acts can be causes.
(2) The difference in the causal properties of acts and omissions explains the moral difference between acts and omissions.

Moore's argument for (1) runs into serious problems. The basis of the argument is that an omission is a nothing. Moore's physicalist intuitions about causation convince him that therefore omissions cannot be causes. The problem is that paradigm cases of causation often involve the interposition of a nothing with apparent

[7] M Moore, *Causation and Responsibility: An Essay in Law, Morals and Metaphysics* (OUP 2009) esp ch 3, s B.

[8] See, eg, ibid 55–56: 'omissions cause nothing. "Nothing comes from nothing, and nothing ever can"'; see also 129; see further M Moore, *Act and Crime: The Philosophy of Action and its Implications for Criminal Law* (OUP 2010) 28–29.

causal effect. If you are leaning on me, and I move away, it seems that my not-being-there—my absence—causes you to fall. If a person is decapitated, it is the absence of oxygen to their brain which causes their death.[9]

It is true that these examples involve the interposition of a 'nothing' between a positive occurrence (the movement of my body) and the outcome. Moore could reply that omissions cannot *start* causal chains, but that causation can transmit *through* an omission. This response also runs into difficulty, however. Every omission is part of some causal chain going back to the Big Bang and that causal chain will include suitably 'positive' occurrences. If so, then every omission could then count as causative, since in reality it is part of a larger causal chain that includes positives.[10]

Another common argument against absences (and therefore, also, omissions) as causes is the following dilemma: if one accepts causation by absence, then *either* there is a problematic proliferation of causation *or* causation is made to depend upon normative facts. Since both horns are unappealing, we ought to reject causation by absences. Take the first horn of the dilemma: the idea is that if absences are causes, then King Charles is a cause of the death of my lemon tree since he did not water it, and so too everyone else on the planet who did not do so. This proliferation can be avoided if we accept that only absences which amount to normative failures of some kind can be causally relevant. So, King Charles is ruled out because he has no duty or responsibility to water my lemon tree. This, however, takes us to the second horn: it is supposed to be implausible for causation to rest upon normative facts like this.[11]

This argument is unpersuasive. First, one could run the same argument for *acts*: if one accepts causation by *acts*, then either there is a problematic proliferation of causation *or* causation is made to depend upon normative facts. If one's working notion of causation is counterfactual dependence, then there is an enormous number of acts on which any outcome is counterfactually dependent. My writing this now is counterfactually dependent upon my great-great-great-grandfather's doing some particular act. But no one denies causation by acts. Second, unless one already has something like Moore's physicalist intuitions about causation, the argument provides no reason to depart from the ordinary understanding of causation according to which normative considerations *do* bear upon causal conclusions.[12]

Suppose, however, we grant that omissions cannot be causes while acts can. It does not follow that omissions cannot generate responsibility for an outcome, as Moore's own view shows: this would require one to deny the possibility of non-causal responsibility for outcomes. If one accepts (1), this denial would come at

[9] See J Schaffer, 'Disconnection and Responsibility' (2012) 18 Legal Theory 399, 405–06, 426.
[10] For this response to Michael Moore, see A Walen, 'More Contra Moore on Omissions as Causes' (2022) 58 Criminal Law Bulletin 375.
[11] For consideration of this problem (and a different response), see ibid s IV.C.
[12] See, eg, H L A Hart and T Honoré, *Causation in the Law* (OUP 1985); A Kaiserman, 'Necessary Connections in Context' (2017) 82 Erkenntnis 45, especially s 6.

an untenable cost: for example, a parent who starves their child would not be responsible for the child's death. If we accept, however, that there can be non-causal responsibility for outcomes, we need a further argument why non-causal responsibility is less extensive than causal responsibility. Pointing to the metaphysical difference between the two does not yet proffer a moral explanation of the difference.[13] The mere fact that two things are metaphysically different does not *explain* why they have different moral properties.

(c) Involvement

Consider these two examples:[14]

> *Duck*. A bullet is heading in my direction and will paralyse me. If I duck, I know that the bullet will kill you, a stranger to me.

> *Swivel*. A bullet is heading in my direction and will paralyse me. You and I, strangers, are opposite each other on a turntable. I know that if I move in one direction, the turntable will locate you in front of the bullet, with the result that you will be killed and I will be protected. If I stay still, I know that the bullet will paralyse me and this occurrence will protect you.

The impact on you—death—is the same in both cases. Further, in both cases, if I act, I prevent my body being useful to you. If I had a duty not to act in both cases, I would be required to allow my body to be useful to you. In both cases, then, there is a sense in which I will be required to treat myself as an instrument of your safety if I am required to save you. Despite the fact that I must either allow myself to be useful to you or act with the result that you will die in both cases, my conduct in *Swivel* seems harder to justify. In *Swivel*, I put you in harm's way. This suggests that there is something more than a concern for self-partiality and a concern to avoid a person being treated as an instrument, which explains the difference between these examples. Partiality cannot be the full explanation of the difference since the costs to me are the same in both cases. Similarly, in both cases, if I were required to save you, I would be required to use my body as a means of your preservation.

Victor Tadros writes that the 'relational' idea that underpins the intuitive difference between cases like these is 'the idea that it is distinctively objectionable for one person to involve herself in the life of another if that makes the person worse off, or the idea that it is distinctively objectionable to involve another person in one's own life if that makes the person worse off'.[15] In *Duck*, the thought

[13] We might agree with Moore that all moral differences supervene upon metaphysical differences. Clearly, however, this is not to say that metaphysical differences entail moral differences.

[14] These are based on examples in V Tadros, *To Do, To Die, To Reason Why: Individual Ethics in War* (OUP 2020) 97. The 'ducking' type of example seems to originate in C Boorse and R Sorenson, 'Ducking Harm' (1988) 85 Journal of Philosophy 115.

[15] Tadros (n 14) 97.

is that you are less involved in my life than in *Swivel*; when a person walks past a drowning stranger the person nonetheless does not involve that person in their life.[16]

This comes very close to a restatement, however, of the distinction we are trying to explain. Why are acts or makings-worse harder to justify than omissions or not-benefitting? On this answer, it is because the former involve greater personal involvement. The idea does very loosely sit well with the idea that persons are morally separate, and so a harmful involvement of another in one's own life is particularly difficult to justify. But why do we rationally regard a person's connection to an outcome in N-duty cases as more of an involvement in the life of another than in P-duty cases? An argument is needed to explain the intuition that the kind of involvement in *Swivel* is more of an expression of a deeper personal involvement in an outcome than that in *Duck*.

In some cases, it will literally be true that *you* are constitutive of a risk of a person's being worse off. In these cases, it may make particular sense to say that you are more personally involved. Suppose, as in the last chapter's example, that you awake to find yourself crushing another person. Suppose that if you roll off the person, saving them from the weight of your body, you will put yourself out of reach of a button, which you could press to save an identical person from being crushed by a weight. Intuitively, it seems that you ought to roll off, rather than remain and press the button. The fact that your body will crush the person gives you decisive reason to avoid this, rather than save another person from being crushed. The connection you would bear to the former person's death is importantly different to the connection you would bear to the latter's.

The sense in which you are *more* personally involved here and in similar cases is that, in one respect, the metaphysical connection which you bear to an outcome in cases of pure omission is the same connection that many people bear. The events that each of us is currently not preventing are many. The events that each of us is 'involved' in are not as many.

Accepting that there is something to the idea that certain forms of metaphysical connection to an outcome involve a deeper involvement of one person in the life of another, what this would show is that it is more difficult to justify bearing this connection to an outcome than the connection that exists in cases of P-duties. It does not show, however, that there is something inherent in the very nature of a P-duty that makes it *prima facie* morally objectionable. It is just that the moral case for a P-duty cannot rely upon the distinctive involvement that obtains with (the breach of) N-duties.

[16] See also T Honoré, 'Are Omissions Less Culpable?' in P Cane and J Stapleton (eds), *Essays for Patrick Atiyah* (OUP 1991) 41–42.

(ii) Contingent Considerations

(a) Being Treated Merely as a Resource

Although the moral fact that a person is not a mere resource does not speak against P-duties *as such*, it does speak against P-duties being exactly equivalent in moral character to N-duties. Specifically, if P-duties were such, then individuals would not be able to pursue their own projects or enjoy personal relationships with others.

If the moral P-duty to prevent harm to others were 'akin to' the moral N-duty not to harm, this would involve four things. First, the P-duty would be demanding: conformity to it would at least have to be such that one would be required to bear very significant harms for the sake of preventing even greater harms to others. If the P-duty to protect others from harm were equally as stringent as the N-duty, it may even involve bearing harms of *greater* magnitude than the harms that breach of the duty would cause another. Second, as with the N-duty not to harm, we would always be subject to the P-duty. It would govern all aspects of our lives. Third, as with the moral N-duty against harm, the P-duty would be in principle *enforceable*—when a person is about to violate the duty, it would be permissible to take certain forcible measures to prevent this. Fourth, as with the moral N-duty against harming, the P-duty would generate derivative duties such as duties to take care to avoid harming.

Suppose, then, that the P-duty to protect from harm were in these ways akin to the moral N-duty not to harm: it would then be (1) equally stringent, (2) equally applicable, (3) equally enforceable, and (4) equally generative of derivative duties to take care to conform.

If this were the case, then our lives would involve frequent substantial sacrifice for the benefit of others. We would frequently be liable to suffer forcible measures to see to it that those benefits were conferred. And, given the derivative duties of care, we would need to be on the lookout for the possibility of failing to protect people from harm whenever this could be avoided by our bearing a smaller harm.

There would, then, be enormous personal cost to a person's ability to set and pursue their own goals if the P-duty to protect from harm had these features in our world. If one were living with the constant possibility of one's bodily resources being harmfully taken to protect others from slightly greater harm, then one's ability to plan one's life, and adopt and pursue goals, would be severely negatively affected.[17] One's body would be available for use whenever it would confer greater benefit upon another.

[17] See, eg, R Kumar, 'Defending the Moral Moderate: Contractualism and Common Sense' (2005) Philosophy & Public Affairs 275, 298. For autonomy-based objections to duties to rescue, see T Pummer, *The Rules of Rescue* (OUP 2022) ch 1.

If the P-duty to protect from harm generated a derivative duty to take care to conform to it, this would likely require significant mental attention. Our mental life would be taken up substantially more with the needs of others. One's ability to enjoy intimate relationships, in which one privileges another person's interests over the equally valuable interests of other people, would be narrowed enormously. One would not be able to devote one's resources to that relationship whenever those resources could be employed more beneficially to protect from harm elsewhere. The ability to devote attention and resources to specific persons to the exclusion of others seems a precondition of having intimate relationships.

These arguments depend upon contingent features of the world. In our world, the prospect of having to make a significant personal sacrifice to conform to an N-duty is not something that bothers most of us: the probability of this occurring absent our choices is minimal. If we supposed that the prospect of having to make a significant sacrifice to conform to a P-duty to protect from harm were similarly low, then the negative effects on personal projects and relationships described in the last paragraph would not occur. Nonetheless, these are relatively stable contingencies: there seems to be a significantly greater probability of being required to make enormous personal sacrifice if there were a P-duty akin to the N-duty in the ways described above. This is not merely a contingent fact about our own unjust world in which much suffering is due to the failure to conform to moral P-duties.

However, the fact that a general P-duty equivalent to the general N-duty would be exceptionally demanding is not itself a reason for rejecting its existence. The considerations mentioned above simply point out that life would be very tough if there were no distinction between N-duties and P-duties. Part of the response to this objection is that our moral status as separate beings with our own lives itself gives reason to permit the pursuit of our own projects, including valuable relationships. If one were asked to accept a P-duty equivalent to the N-duty, one would be giving up on the possibility of an ability to pursue one's own goals and personal relationships. Each of us would have a decisive reason to reject such a moral duty: we would be subscribing to a morality which denied us the prospect of a meaningful life.[18]

(b) Freedom and Options

P-duties are often said to be more difficult to justify because they are more invasive of a person's freedom than N-duties.[19] The general idea is that conformity to a P-duty to do an act closes off more options for the duty-bearer than conformity

[18] Kumar (n 17) 299 (rejecting the idea that increasing one's life expectancy can sufficiently compensate 'for the erosion of effective control over [another's] life'); see also 278 (recognising that one's 'cares, commitments, relationships, goals and so forth' may all be relevant in one's assessment of whether to follow or reject a proposed moral principle).

[19] For a well-known judicial statement of this point, see *Stovin v Wise* [1996] AC 923 (HL) 943, [1996] 3 WLR 388, 406 (Lord Hoffmann).

to an N-duty not to do an act. Duties not to act in a certain way leave open the duty-bearer's options to do everything except that act. By contrast, duties to act in a certain way preclude all other options except the doing of that act.[20] For example, if I am required to help you when you have fallen off your bike, conforming to the duty uses up my time and resources in such a way that I cannot do various other things at that time. By contrast, if I am required not intentionally to knock you off your bike, this is consistent with me pursuing virtually any of my projects while conforming to the duty.

Now consider more precise versions of the argument. One version is that conformity to *all* P-duties *always* removes more options than conformity to *all* N-duties. This is false. Suppose that my only way of avoiding being paralysed for a year is by running over and killing an innocent stranger. If I conform to my N-duty not to kill an innocent stranger here, then I will be paralysed for one year and thus many options will be closed off to me. By contrast, conformity to a P-duty to save a person's life by pressing a button will only have a temporary negligible impact upon my options. Or consider a duty to maintain the support one's land provides for one's neighbour's land. This is a P-duty since, even though it requires one not to do certain acts, doing those acts will not make one's neighbour's land worse than if one's land had not been present at all.[21] Conformity with this P-duty is, however, generally compatible with doing many other things. Compare this with conformity to one's N-duty not to damage another's body through carelessness when walking down an extremely busy street. To conform, one will typically need to have a level of attention to the interests of others that may shut off a variety of other options, such as listening to loud music, daydreaming, stretching, closing one's eyes for an extended period, and so on. It is true that, to avoid this restriction upon one's options, one could choose not to go amongst others. But that is an intolerable alternative and surely therefore does not do any, or much, justificatory work in explaining why one can legitimately be required to attend to others' interests in this situation, despite that attention closing off a number of alternative options.

A different, weaker, version of the argument is that conformity to a P-duty to do an act always removes more options than, in some sense, a *corresponding* N-duty. Consider an N-duty not intentionally to imprison a person without justification. Contrast this with a P-duty not intentionally to fail to protect a person from imprisonment without justification. It is possible to conform to the N-duty while doing any number of things. By contrast, it is not possible to conform to the P-duty to protect a person from imprisonment without interventions that preclude other activities. This weaker view still seems false. If you are a judge with the power to imprison a person, it may be rather difficult to conform to the N-duty: it may require significant investigation, assessment of evidence, and so on. Conversely, if

[20] See, eg, P J Fitzgerald, 'Acting and Refraining' (1967) 27 Analysis 133, 139.

[21] For a defence of this understanding of a P-duty, see Chapter 1 on '*W5*'.

I can rescue a person from unjust imprisonment by pressing a button, then the effect of conformity on my options is minimal.

A third, even weaker, claim seems more apt: conformity to a P-duty to do an act *typically* removes more options than conformity to a corresponding N-duty. For most people, most of the time, the freedom-related contrast between the P-duty in relation to imprisonment and the N-duty in relation to imprisonment holds. If only this weaker claim is correct, then the freedom argument does not identify an intrinsic moral difference between P-duties and N-duties such that there is always a further justificatory burden to be met simply by virtue of a duty being a P-duty. It merely identifies a consideration that often arises in the context of P-duties, which might typically make them harder to justify.

To see especially clearly the contingency of the connection between freedom and P-duties, consider this example:

> *Button.* You are walking past a drowning stranger. If you continue on your planned route, you will step on a button which, as you know, will trigger a device that rescues the stranger from certain death. No one else is around to help.

If you were subject to a P-duty to rescue this stranger, you could continue with your planned activity. Conformity to the duty would be perfectly consistent with pursuing your projects.

2. Legal Enforcement: Intrinsic Objections to Enforcement of P-Duties

If one person owes a moral duty to another, it is obviously a further question how, if at all, the law ought to respond to this fact. This section considers whether there is an intrinsic objection to legal enforcement of P-duties which does not apply to N-duties. Let's distinguish private legal enforcement from public legal enforcement. Private enforcement involves (a) legal subjects being empowered to trigger a court's jurisdiction to determine authoritatively whether the duty has been breached, (b) the court being empowered to issue orders to conform to the duty, or to the secondary duties (such as duties to compensate) which arise from its breach, and (c) the court being empowered in such proceedings to impose sanctions for the non-conformity to its orders to conform. Public enforcement involves an official or set of officials being empowered to (a) trigger the jurisdiction of a court in relation to a breach of a duty, (b) the court being empowered to issue orders for conformity with the duty or secondary duties arising from its breach, and (c) the court being empowered to sanction non-conformity to its orders to conform.

It might be argued that P-duties raise special normative considerations at the level of one or both of these legal responses. Section 3 of this chapter considers whether there are any negative consequences particularly associated with the legal enforcement of P-duties. This section is concerned with whether there is an intrinsic objection to the legal recognition of P-duties.

(i) Virtue, Not Right

One claim sometimes made is that P-duties are duties of *virtue* not duties of *right* and, because of this, they should not be legally enforced.[22] Without more, however, this distinction is at most a placeholder for an explanation of which duties are properly legally recognised and which are not. In other words, if the distinction between 'virtue' and 'right' is simply the distinction between 'duties which should not be legally enforced' and 'duties which may be legally enforced' then clearly it can do no work in determining which duties belong to which category.

One possible deeper explanation of the distinction between 'duties of right' and 'duties of virtue' is that the value which justifies certain duties is only respected or promoted if the duty-bearer decides for themself what specifically the duty requires, or conforms with the duty without compulsion. Suppose that generosity requires me to allow my neighbour to use my car to travel to work for a week when theirs is being repaired if the costs to me are negligible. If I were subject to a legal duty to compensate for not being generous, then my granting the car would, it might be argued, no longer be an act of *generosity*; or, if it is an act of generosity, one that fails to instantiate the value of generosity. This would be so if I granted you the car, at least in part, in order to avoid being forced by the law to do the act or some substitute. In this case, what my act communicates to you would be changed if you know my motivation for acting. If there were legal recognition and enforcement of the acts required by duties of generosity (or gratitude), then those acts would lose their communicative value in many cases.

Ultimately, the argument in the last paragraph reduces to a concern about negative consequences: the negative consequence that legal recognition will alter the communicative value of certain acts. And it points to a valid concern: such consequences are one reason against the enforcement of such acts. But this kind of concern is only highly contingently connected to something being a P-duty. Duties to pay tax are, sometimes, P-duties, but their justification does not require that anyone act for a particular motivation or in the absence of compulsion. Similarly, the most plausible bases for duties of easy rescue point to the interests of the beneficiary of the duty.[23]

[22] See R Stevens, 'Private Rights and Public Wrongs' in M Dyson (ed), *Unravelling Tort and Crime* (CUP 2014).

[23] See Chapter 9.

(ii) Rights and P-Duties

Here is a different argument, call it *Rights*:

(1) P-duties do not correlate with rights.
(2) Only duties correlated with rights may be legally enforced.
(3) Therefore, P-duties may not be legally enforced.

(1) is implausible: promissory duties correlate with rights in the promisee, but a promissory duty may be a P-duty.

A weaker version of (1) is more plausible: (1*) P-duties typically do not correlate with rights, particularly P-duties not arising from a special transaction such as a promise.[24] A moral duty to pay tax, for instance, is not obviously correlated with a right. If a duty correlates with a right only if another person's interest is itself sufficient to justify the duty, then arguably the duty to pay tax does not so correlate. Arguably, no particular individual's interest is sufficient to justify the duty. One argument for this is that no individual's contribution to tax will prevent harm on its own, and so no individual's interest could alone justify that contribution, since their interest will not be promoted by that payment of tax. If that is true, though, it becomes very difficult to defend (2), on pain of being unable to justify any form of taxation (other than taxation that amounts to a justifiable response to breach of an N-duty). More generally, it is difficult to see why the rights-relationality of a duty should matter to *whether* the duty is enforced, even if it should have a bearing upon whether the enforcement is private or public. If a person is subject to a duty, and enforcing that duty would not undermine the value (or values) which ground the duty or lead to other negative consequences, there seems to be no reason why the duty must be related to a right to be enforceable, even if correlativity with a right may be a justifiable requirement for certain *kinds* of legal enforcement.

This last point suggests a revised version of *Rights*:

(1) P-duties do not correlate with rights, absent a special transaction.
(2) Only P-duties correlated with rights may be legally enforced by private enforcement.
(3) Therefore, P-duties, absent a special transaction, may not be legally enforced by private enforcement.

The success of the revised argument clearly hinges on what it is to have a 'right'. Here are different things to which the word 'right' can be used to refer:

[24] cf F M Kamm, *Intricate Ethics: Rights, Responsibilities and Permissible Harm* (OUP 2007) 286.

(a) A duty correlates with a right held by P if and only if the duty's main justification is P's interest[25] or moral status.[26]
(b) A duty correlates with a right held by P if and only if the duty is waivable by P.[27]
(c) A duty correlates with a right held by P if and only if P may (normally) demand performance of the duty in the event that the duty is at risk of being breached.[28]
(d) A duty correlates with a right held by P if and only if P or a person acting on P's behalf may use force to ensure conformity to the duty.[29]

Later I will argue that there are P-duties, absent a special transaction—P-duties of easy rescue—which correlate with 'rights' in senses (a), (c), and (d).[30] If sense (b) is insisted upon for the purposes of the revised *Rights* argument, this substantially diminishes the plausibility of premiss (2)—that only duties that correlate with rights in the sense of waivable duties are apt for private legal enforcement. It would entail that non-waivable duties not to harm young children are not the appropriate subject of private law relations. I conclude that the revised *Rights* argument is unpromising. The first premiss is false on three prominent conceptions of rights; and on a fourth conception, the second premiss is implausible.

A further simple point about the revised *Rights* argument is that, even if the argument succeeds, it does not demonstrate an intrinsic objection to the private enforcement of moral P-duties. It supports, instead, a more limited claim: that there is an intrinsic objection to the private enforcement of *some* moral P-duties, namely, those which do not arise from a special transaction. Nonetheless, if true, this would be an important limit on the legal enforceability of P-duties. It is far from clear, however, that this would be a *distinctive* limit on the legal enforceability of P-duties, as compared to N-duties. If there are reasons to limit the private enforcement of duties to those which correlate with rights, it seems likely that those reasons apply to N-duties too. It is at least arguable that there are moral N-duties which do not correlate with rights, such as N-duties not to pollute the environment: this will be true on some of the definitions of 'right' in the paragraph above. The fact that there is no particular individual who may waive your duty not to pollute the environment may, for instance, be expressed

[25] See, eg, J Raz, *The Morality of Freedom* (OUP 1988) 166, 183.
[26] See, eg, Kamm (n 24) especially ch 8.
[27] See, eg, R Stevens, 'Defences in Contract' in A Dyson, J Goudkamp, and F Wilmot-Smith (eds), *Defences in Contract* (Hart 2017) 125ff: 'waiver is central to what it is to have a right'.
[28] See generally M Gilbert, *Rights and Demands: A Foundational Inquiry* (OUP 2018), ch 4ff (describing a 'Demand-Right'; although she does not claim that all duty-imposing rights are Demand-Rights, they are simply a 'kind of right's: see 1).
[29] For Kant, the connection between rights and permissions to coerce is 'analytic', see I Kant, *The Metaphysics of Morals* (ed M Gregor, CUP 1996) 6:396.
[30] See Chapter 9.

by saying that the duty does not correlate with a right. At best, it seems likely that there is a wider category of P-duties, compared to N-duties, which do not correlate with rights.[31]

3. Contingent Negative Consequences of Legal Enforcement of P-Duties

(i) Unfairness

A well-worn argument against the legal enforcement of P-duties is that doing so involves unfairly singling out particular persons for the provision of a benefit to others. 'Why pick on me?' is the anticipated objection of those subject to such enforcement.[32]

This objection might be understood either as intrinsic to the nature of P-duties or a contingent objection. It is intrinsic in the sense that, for every P-duty to protect against a certain risk of harm, there must be a reason for the duty-bearer, rather than others, to be the person under such a duty. Given the personal involvement involved in risk creation, this question does not arise with N-duties. The fact that your action led to the risk already identifies a reason for your being duty-bound to respond to the risk. There are many such reasons that can be identified, as we shall see later in the book: for instance, the fact that a person agreed to be subject to the P-duty, the fact that an earlier action of that person was a causal source of the risk, and the fact that a person has authority over others in relation to the space in which the risk originates.

The objection can also be understood as 'contingent' in the sense that recognising P-duties in tort based on certain persons being *well-placed* to deal with a risk may result in the legal system arbitrarily enforcing some P-duties and not others. For instance, in affluent countries, we are generally well-placed to assist others in dire need in non-affluent countries. If the legal system enforces a duty of easy rescue in its territory, it might be singling out some people for legal enforcement when it fails to do so in relation to many others who, despite being well-placed to do so, fail to assist others in other countries. This kind of differential treatment of similarly situated persons is not unique to P-duties—sometimes the legal system will unfairly enforce some people's N-duties and not others'. Still, it does identify an objection that persons subject to the legal system could have against the legal system in these situations. Note, however, that it does nothing to undermine the interpersonal case for liability between the duty-bearer and the potential right-holder. As between those persons, the duty and its enforcement may be entirely

[31] In Chapter 7, I also cast doubt on (2).

[32] See *Stovin v Wise* [1996] 3 All ER 801, 819, and further, Chapter 7.

justified; the complaint is against the legal system, rather than the right-holder, and this complaint need not undermine the permissibility of enforcing the duty through the mechanism of the legal system.[33]

(ii) More Harm than Good

Even if there is no objection to the private legal enforcement of P-duties *as such*, it may be that the legal recognition of moral P-duties typically leads to more harm than good. Before considering whether this is so, a preliminary issue needs to be addressed: what justificatory significance should be attached to the fact that legal enforcement leads to more harm than good?

It might seem obvious: such enforcement ought not to exist. The obvious answer becomes less obvious, however, when one considers that the fact a rule produces greater good than harm is not always sufficient to justify it. Few would accept a rule which permitted the punishment of the innocent even were it clear that the rule's good consequences outweighed the bad. If it is permissible to maintain rules that do less overall good than alternative rules, then it is less clear why it is always impermissible to bring into existence a rule that produces more bad than good.

One view about this is as follows: the law ought to adopt rules that produce more good than bad, unless the rule authorises the use of a person as a means to achieve the good. Consequently, the law ought not to adopt the punishment-of-the-innocent rule, which uses the innocent as a means, but, apart from the prohibition on the use of people as means, the law ought to adopt the rule which does more good than bad.

Suppose that the law established a legal P-duty to contribute to the rescue of strangers in physical proximity when the costs of contributing to the rescue involve minimal risk to one's physical integrity and minimal effort. Grant that this legal P-duty corresponds to a moral duty. Suppose that Tolu breaches this legal and moral duty, and Ulrike's body is severely damaged as a result. Ulrike now seeks compensation from Tolu. Suppose that, if the legal system provided for the enforcement of Tolu's secondary moral duty of compensation, rescue teams who voluntarily operate in mountain regions will cease their operations. Perhaps they will do so because their activities will no longer be considered heroic or because of the difficulty of obtaining insurance for the breach of the duty.[34] As a result, more deaths

[33] See, for this point, H Dagan and A Dorfman, *Relational Justice: A Theory of Private Law* (OUP 2024, forthcoming), chapter on non-feasance. Matters may be more complex when the state's own wrongdoing is implicated in the wrong committed by the duty-bearer; in such cases, it might be argued the state has no 'standing' to hold the wrongdoer to its secondary duties. Even here, however, it is not clear that this is so: the state acts on behalf of the right-holder, rather than on its own account, and so its own wrong is arguably irrelevant in this respect.

[34] On legal enforcement of duties of rescue as sapping rescuers' motivations to rescue, see W M Landes and R A Posner, 'Salvors, Finders, Good Samaritans, and Other Rescuers: An Economic Study of Law and Altruism' (1978) 7 Journal of Legal Studies 83, 91–92.

overall will consequently occur than if there were no legal enforcement of the P-duty. Should the legal system nonetheless enforce the P-duty owed by Tolu, despite this leading to more harm than good?

If we think that the legal system ought to do whatever produces more good than harm unless it authorises the use of a person as a means, then it ought *not* to establish a rule enforcing the P-duty. Not ordering Tolu to compensate Ulrike does not use Ulrike as a means. This is not because the legal system merely fails to help Ulrike. Failing to help a person can constitute using them as a means.[35] If you fail to rescue me in order to harvest my organs when I die to save five other people, you use me as a means. Rather, Ulrike is not used as a means because the harm to Ulrike is not necessary in order to achieve the good consequences—that is, the continued existence of the rescue services in the area. We can see this by noting that Ulrike's being compensated by a third party would not prevent the occurrence of this good. Ulrike's not being compensated, and suffering harm, is not necessary, then, for the production of the good.

It might be thought that, if Ulrike has a moral right to compensation against Tolu, and Ulrike has a moral right against the legal system that it enforces her moral rights, the legal system cannot justify infringing this right by appeal to the bad consequences that will occur if the right is enforced. This is false. Simply because you have a moral right against another person does not justify that person violating other people's rights in order to conform to your moral right. For example, consider:

> *Room.* The only way in which I can save my child from a fire-engulfed building is by opening the door to a room in the building. I realise that this will cause another part of the building to collapse, killing five other children who would otherwise be saved.

It may be excusable for me to save my child, but it seems impermissible. This is so despite the fact that my child plausibly has a special claim upon me to be rescued. Similarly, even if I have a special right against the legal system that it enforce my moral rights, this is, so to speak, morally between us. It does not entail that the legal system may damage other people's rights in conforming to its duty to me. This is important, as some believe that the legal system does have a moral duty to each person to provide that person with private legal enforcement of their moral rights, in virtue of having prohibited private non-legal enforcement of rights.[36] On these views, the legal system owes each of us a special duty to compensate us for

[35] See N Kolodny, *The Pecking Order: Social Hierarchy as a Philosophical Problem* (Harvard UP 2023).

[36] For a critical discussion of such arguments, see S Steel, 'On the Moral Necessity of Tort Law: The Fairness Argument' (2021) 41 Oxford Journal of Legal Studies 192.

the deprivation of private enforcement of our moral rights and the compensation should take the form of private law enforcement of moral rights. Even if that is true, however, the legal system could still be justified in breaching that duty, if this is necessary to avoid breaching some other more important moral duty.

Is *Room* analogous to the situation between Tolu, Ulrike, and the legal system? Hopefully the respects in which it is analogous are now relatively clear: if the legal system assists Ulrike, it will be a cause of many other people dying because those others will not be saved by the rescue services; similarly, in *Room*, if I save my child, I will be a cause of several others dying because those others will not be saved by others.

The disanalogy between the two is that in Tolu's case the causal chain by which the legal system will be a cause of others' deaths is indirect: the legal system's establishing a rule permitting enforcement of Ulrike's compensatory right against Tolu will be a cause of harm by dissuading other agents from engaging in rescue operations. By contrast, in *Room*, my opening the door will directly cause the deaths of five others. In particular, the door opening will cause their deaths without the interposition of a human decision. It might be argued that the voluntary decision of the rescue agencies not to continue their operation is a free decision which 'breaks the chain of causation' between the legal system's decision and the death of those who would otherwise be saved. If so, it might be said, the legal system does not bear responsibility for those deaths. In deciding what one ought to do, one might think, one is permitted to discount those outcomes for which one will have no responsibility, even if one knows that these outcomes will be, in some sense, the upshot of one's conduct.

If it is known that the intervening agent will act in a way which leads to harm, however, it seems difficult to accept that one can entirely ignore their conduct in deciding what to do. Suppose I see that someone has evaded a psychopath, who is trying to kill them, by entering and locking the door to my garage. I can press a button which will allow the psychopath to enter the garage. It seems absurd to think that I have no duty not to press the button, because the psychopath's conduct will be an intentional culpable wrong. If the break in the chain of causation view were true, then I could simply *ignore* the fact I will be assisting a killer because the killer's decision is a voluntary act for which I am not responsible.[37]

An objection to causally linking the legal system's decision to enforce compensatory rights and the negative consequences that ensue might be that the conduct of intervening agents may well be unreasonable, thus breaking the chain of causation. In the rescue operations case, if rescue teams decide no longer to operate, their decision might be criticised as irrational or in some way unreasonable: supposing that those rescuers are only subject to legal duties of *easy* rescue, then they

[37] cf V Tadros, 'Permissibility in a World of Wrongdoing' (2016) 44 Philosophy & Public Affairs 101.

are highly unlikely to face any legal liability for failure to rescue since they will reliably be able to conform. However, a psychopath's decision to kill a person when a garage door is opened is also rather unreasonable, yet it seems that I would be causally responsible by pressing the button. There is no difference between the two causal chains.

The upshot of the foregoing is that the negative consequences of enforcement of a moral duty are morally relevant to the decision whether to enforce that duty. Those negative consequences are relevant since taking them into account does not violate the principle against using a person as a means, and is required of the legal system by an N-duty not knowingly to contribute by positive conduct to foreseeable physical harm to others.

(iii) Negative Consequences Particularly Associated with Legal Enforcement of P-Duties

The empirical literature on tort law enforcement of P-duties tends to focus on the special case of legal duties of easy rescue.[38] Here, there are essentially three causal mechanisms identified by which negative consequences are likely to ensue through tort enforcement of P-duties.

A first concern is with the sapping of altruistic incentives or incentives for benefitting others that arise from a perception that one will acquire social esteem.[39] This may be bad either because it leads to more harm, or simply because it erodes certain valuable motivations which affect the quality of people's interactions with each other.[40] A person's willingness to perform a rescue may be dependent upon the social esteem they will acquire from doing so. This esteem, or the belief that one will acquire such esteem, will be diminished if others consider the rescue to have been undertaken for fear of paying compensation. Probably there are some people like this. If those people would otherwise have undertaken rescues in the expectation of hero status, and the legal enforcement of the duty of easy rescue does not enhance conformity amongst people who are morally motivated to rescue in any event, then the legal enforcement of the duty simply causes more harm than it prevents.

38 See Landes and Posner (n 34); S Levmore, 'Waiting for Rescue: An Essay on the Evolution and Incentive Structure of the Law of Affirmative Obligations' (1986) 72 Virginia Law Review 879; M G Faure, 'Liability for Omissions in Tort Law: Economic Analysis' (2011) 2 Journal of European Tort Law 184 (which despite its title focusses on rescue); D A Hyman, 'Rescue Without Law: An Empirical Perspective on the Duty to Rescue' (2006) 84 Texas Law Review 653.

39 Landes and Posner (n 34) 94. For legal recognition of this concern, see Social Action, Responsibility and Heroism Act 2015, especially ss 2 and 4.

40 On the latter, see E H Atiq, 'Why Motives Matter: Reframing the Crowding Out Effect of Legal Incentives' (2014) 123 Yale Law Journal 1070.

It may, however, be that there is another larger class of persons who do not effect easy rescues out of a misplaced concern for unduly intervening in another's affairs, or who are simply too wrapped up in their own life. This category may be an apt target for legal sanctions. Further, if there is a social stigma associated with legal liability for failure to conduct easy rescues, then those who would otherwise have been motivated by a gain in social esteem will likely be motivated by a concern to avoid social stigma.

A second concern is with an activity-level effect, as in the Tolu–Ulrike example given earlier.[41] The concern here is that enforcement of duties of rescue produces an alteration in behaviour such that more harm is caused than is prevented. The causal mechanism for this alteration is said to be that potential harm-preventers are deterred from being in locations in which rescues are likely to be needed because of the threat of liability for failure to prevent harm. Suppose we treat victims and rescuers as separate non-overlapping categories of persons. If so, then rescuers may well take steps to avoid victims, so far as this is possible. In many cases, it will not be: it depends upon an ability to identify who are the potential victims, and the benefits of association with them being less than the cost posed by the threat of liability. A typical example given is swimmers and beaches. If legal liability were imposed for failure to rescue, strong swimmers (rescuers) will group together, it is said, on their own beaches and avoid weak swimmers (victims). Weak swimmers will thus have fewer potential rescuers available to them. One might speculate as to whether such grouping is likely to occur. Weak swimmers could presumably follow the strong swimmers, unless access to beaches were privately controlled based on swimming skill. If *that* occurred, then weak swimmers would be alerted to their vulnerable position and would likely take steps to restore the supply of rescue by going to beaches with lifeguards.

Suppose we make the more realistic assumption that victims and rescuers are overlapping categories.[42] If so, a person in both categories will stand to benefit from rescue by others and be subject to a cost by virtue of the threat of liability for non-rescue. Under this assumption, it seems there is still a risk of strong rescuers grouping together to the detriment of weaker rescuers. Suppose we imagine a strong swimmer, Yotam, who would normally go to beaches with relatively weak swimmers. He is then alerted to the new tort duty of easy rescue. Suppose he estimates his probability of needing rescue from death on each visit to the beach at 1%, and his probability of having to undertake a low-cost rescue on each visit—say, one costing £500—at 10%. Finally, suppose he values his life at £1,000,000. Will Yotam change his behaviour and head off to the strong swimmers' beach? Presumably

[41] See again Landes and Posner (n 34) 120. The activity-level effect could also occur because of the first causal mechanism in the last paragraph.

[42] See R L Hasen, 'The Efficient Duty to Rescue' (1995) 15 International Review of Law and Economics 141.

the answer is still 'potentially yes'. While a visit to the weak swimmers' beach is still beneficial, Yotam could reduce the probability of having to undertake a low-cost rescue by moving to the strong swimmers' beach; he will maximise benefit by moving to that beach. Again, however, this obviously depends upon the ability to identify such beaches and such beaches not being significantly less valuable to Yotam in some other respect.

The activity-level effect described is inherently tied up with normatively appropriate regulation of P-duties. Some P-duties should only be owed when people *choose* them. Given our free and independent moral status, there are certain tasks we cannot be conscripted into without our agreement. So, a justified legal system will make the acquisition of certain P-duties contingent upon choice. This means that there will be a point at which a person can either choose to become subject to the duty or not. Consequently, the law needs to be careful not to disincentivise appropriate duty-bearers from choosing to incur the duty.

A third way in which negative consequences may ensue by the imposition of P-duties is the unclarity of any legal standard requiring easy rescue.[43] Unclarity around what conformity requires may cause persons to be anxious about legal liability. Further, the unclarity of legal standards may also be considered inherently unfair in so far as persons are ambushed by legal liability when they had no reasonable opportunity to comply. It seems doubtful, however, that these arguments point to particular difficulties with P-duties. The N-duty not to injure a person through failure to take *reasonable* care is hardly a model of legal certainty, and yet it is considered morally tolerable since only tort liability, rather than stigmatic criminal liability, is at stake. More generally, some P-duties involve clear demands, some do not. There is no special clarity problem for legal P-duties as such.

A fourth concern relates to coordination: P-duties tend to implicate coordination problems more than N-duties. For instance, suppose that everyone had a legal P-duty of easy rescue. If ten people are near a person in urgent need of assistance, the fact that all are duty-bound to assist may lead to a worse outcome than if only a sub-set, or none, were legally duty-bound: each may get in the way of each other or unwittingly frustrate the others' efforts. This problem arises in particular with P-duties because it is typically the case that more people can be connected with an outcome in an omissive way than by their action. The proliferation of P-duties can thus pose a risk of spoiled efforts by virtue of duty-bearers failing to coordinate their efforts appropriately. This problem is plausibly a real one. It can be managed, however, in at least two ways. First, P-duties can be specified in ways which identify those uniquely or best placed to deal with a problem. Second,

[43] For a discussion of the importance (or unimportance) of legal certainty in tort law, see generally K Oliphant, 'Against Certainty in Tort Law' in K Oliphant and others (eds), *Tort Law: Challenging Orthodoxy* (Hart 2013).

P-duties can be coupled with N-duties to take reasonable care not to interfere with the performance of P-duties. A related point is that some P-duties are likely only to be effective at achieving the good which justifies them if there is a system of coordination in place. A duty to pay tax would be unjustifiable if the lack of coordination in the use of tax means the tax could not reasonably be expected to achieve any of the goods that justify the duty.

A fifth concern is that determining the content of justified P-duties sometimes depends upon 'systematic' considerations, such as the other benefits conferred upon the duty-bearer by the legal system and the other demands made by the legal system.[44] This gives a reason for caution in *judicial* development of the law on P-duties. For instance, the design of an appropriate system of P-duties to pay tax is clearly unsuited to judicial determination alone.

(iv) Conclusions on Consequences

The positive and negative consequences of enforcement of P-duties are morally relevant to the decision whether to create tort P-duties. There is no simple moral calculus that will determine when such duties are permissibly created. The risk of positively contributing to causing harm has greater moral weight than the chance of contributing to the alleviation of harm. This supports some caution in extending the scope of legal P-duties *and* N-duties. Nothing in the discussion of consequences reveals a generally applicable consideration which should always point against the recognition of a tort P-duty, however. Ultimately, each situation needs to be considered on its merits.[45] The specific case of the duty of easy rescue will be considered in more detail later.[46]

4. Tort Law as an Inept Regulator of Moral P-Duties

Suppose it is accepted that there is a valid moral P-duty, that enforcing it *in some way* would not frustrate the value that grounds the duty, and that the duty would likely do more good than harm. It does not follow that the duty should be enforced by tort law.

[44] See especially R Stone, 'Private Liability without Wrongdoing' (2023) 73 University of Toronto Law Journal 53, 78–79. Stone recognises, however, that this concern does not preclude development of duties of 'very' easy rescue: 79.

[45] This does not entail that there can be no general guidance rules. For instance, the rule that promises made in purely social contexts are not intended to be contractually binding constitutes a legal presumption that reflects presumed intention, but also avoids the law casting too great a shadow in such settings, potentially undermining the communicative value of promises undertaken in those contexts.

[46] For a defence of the existence of such secondary duties, see Chapter 9.

(i) Inherent Ineptness

Tort law enforcement might be inherently inept in the sense that it will fail to enforce the duty when it ought to be enforced, or enforce it in morally unappealing ways. Suppose that we all have an enforceable moral duty to pay tax. It will almost always be impossible for an individual to prove that they have suffered loss as a result of the breach of this duty. At the very least, this is a reason for establishing an additional enforcement mechanism beyond tort law. Further, even if we could envisage a class action suit which, given the numbers involved, could prove that at least some people in society had suffered loss as a result of a breach of a duty to pay tax, the compensatory payment by the tax duty-bearer may, in current circumstances, be morally required elsewhere; this is not a decision which can legitimately be taken by a court.[47] Given the live possibility in each case that the tax payment is morally required to meet some other social need, this is a reason for thinking that no individual has the moral power to enforce the duty.

(ii) Doctrinal Objections

It has been argued that tort law is characterised by primary rights which are held by all against all.[48] By contrast, it is plausible to think, the argument runs, that P-duties are only owed by *some* against *some*, and so are not naturally regulated in tort law. In this way, P-duties are analogous to contractual duties. These correlate with rights but are nonetheless not properly regulated in tort law.

This argument, if understood as a general objection to enforcing P-duties in tort law, is unpersuasive. First, it is not the case that all rights regulated by tort law are held by all against all. The obvious counterexample are rights generated by assumptions of responsibility, which impose a special duty upon a particular individual for the benefit of another particular individual or set of individuals. These duties are requirements *not* owed by *everyone* to *everyone*. Second, even if one accepts both that tort law is so characterised and that it follows from that character that it ought not to enforce special duties, not all P-duties are special. It may be that the law ought to recognise a legal duty of easy rescue which gives rise to a compensatory claim for its non-fulfilment. If so, this duty may be owed by all against all, and so, accepting the premise of the objection, should be naturally housed within tort law. A more plausible version of this kind of objection is that there are some

[47] There is no guarantee, even if we have large numbers of persons in the class action—even the whole of society—that any individual will have suffered 'loss' in the traditional sense. It may be that the failure to pay tax causes tiny detriments to everyone, and only harms in combination with other failures to pay tax.

[48] See, eg, D Nolan, 'Negligence and Human Rights Law: The Case for Separate Development' (2013) 76 Modern Law Review 286, 294.

P-duties which are properly only owed in law by public authorities, and whose regulation attracts special considerations not applicable to private persons. I consider this view in a later chapter, but whether it is true or not does not rule out the justifiable existence of P-duties in tort law.[49]

5. Conclusions

The three central fundamental considerations which justify a differential treatment between P-duties and N-duties are: the moral need to allow individuals to pursue their own valuable projects and special relationships, the fact that we are beings with a special moral status that entitles us not to be treated merely as instruments for the promotion of others' well-being, and the greater involvement of ourselves in outcomes caused by action as opposed to omission. The law's general differential treatment of N-duties and P-duties is justified, then, simply in virtue of the moral position. We can already see the outlines of when legal P-duties are likely to be consistent with these considerations: when the P-duties are part of arrangements that allow people to pursue valuable projects, in the context of special relationships, and when a person's consent defeats the objection that they are being treated as a mere instrument.[50] If a P-duty is consistent with these considerations, it does not follow that it ought to be legally enforced in tort. It has been shown that the decision whether to enforce a P-duty in tort law depends in principle upon the answer to a series of questions: (1) Would the enforcement of the P-duty frustrate the value that grounds the P-duty? (2) Would legal enforcement do more harm than good? and (3) Is tort law an inept regulator of the duty in question?

[49] Chapter 10.

[50] In Chapter 9, I will argue that these considerations do not exclude the justifiability of a general duty of easy rescue.

3

Innocent Creation of Risk and Interference

This chapter begins the analysis of the special facts which, from the perspective of the current law, trigger P-duties in tort. It considers two special facts: 'innocent creation of risk' and 'interference'.[1] The first section focusses on innocent creation of a risk. It shows that the law accepts this principle: if A substantially causally contributes to an interference with B's general right-protected interest, or to a non-minimal risk to B's general right-protected interest, and A ought to know that this poses a foreseeable risk of injury to that interest, then A is under a duty to take reasonable steps to protect B from that risk. For example: A non-negligently collides with a large cow while driving, knocking it dead. A acquires a P-duty to take reasonable steps to protect other drivers from the risk due to the cow being on the road. This principle gives rise to particular difficulties in relation to risks created through human agency. It is shown that the law adopts too restrictive an approach to when A can be said to create a risk through another person, C.

The second part focusses on interference. There is evidence that the law is about to accept this kind of principle: If (i) A non-wrongfully does something at *t* and (ii) A knows or ought to know at *t* or $t + n$ that A's act did or will non-minimally increase the probability that B will be worse off with respect to B's general right-protected interests than if A or A's resources had not been present at *t*, by interfering with those interests being saved from harm by B, C, or a natural event, then A is under a P-duty to take reasonable steps to prevent B being in a worse position than if A and A's resources had not been present at *t*. For example: A innocently damages B's lifejacket before B is about to set sail. A acquires a P-duty to protect B from the risk which the lifejacket protected him from. It is argued that acceptance of this principle would be a desirable development.

The justification for treating these two special facts together is that they are closely connected in two respects. First, it is arguable that these two facts are really instances of the same fact: innocent creation of a risk. It is possible to describe interfering with harm-preventive events as a mode of risk creation.[2]

Second, although the law presents the duties arising in these situations as exceptional P-duties, this may be mistaken. In both cases, A does something

[1] I use 'danger' and 'risk' interchangeably.
[2] See section 2(ii).

Omissions in Tort Law. Sandy Steel, Oxford University Press. © Sandy Steel 2024.
DOI: 10.1093/9780191898822.003.0003

which then, later, requires A to take some preventative step. What triggers the preventative step, however, is the foreseeable prospect that A will be causally responsible for B being worse off compared to B's position had A not done the initial act. So A comes under a duty here to do an act for B's benefit, but only when this will foreseeably prevent B being worse off than if A had not earlier done an act in relation to B. In this sense, these duties could be considered not truly P-duties. These duties are similar, in this respect, to duties not unreasonably to be a cause of damage by *impure* omission. Further, it is not clear that these duties arise from a 'special fact'. If one treats duties arising from a creation of a risk as exceptional duties, which arise when the special fact of 'creation of a risk' obtains, then much of the tort of negligence involves such a special duty. Duties to take positive risk-reducing measures while driving, for instance, would count as special duties. Not all tort duties would then be classified as 'special': duties not to interfere intentionally with a person's body or property without permission would still, for instance, count as general duties existing absent a special fact as these duties are triggered only by existence. And *some* duties even in negligence would count as general duties. For instance, I have a duty not to drive a car which I know does not have a working brake system: this follows from my general duty not to impose unreasonable risks of actionable injury. It is not possible to construe this duty as *arising from* the creation of a danger: the duty exists as a constraint on conduct *prior to* the creation of any danger.

If we accept the view defended in Chapter 1 that a P-duty is the duty of A to improve B's position compared to the position B would be in had A's body or resources not been present at the time of conduct required by the duty, including the causal effects of A's body or resources, then we reach the conclusion that the duties in this chapter are not true P-duties.[3] Consider the cow example: A non-negligently knocks over a cow and this poses a risk to other road-users. If we consider a putative duty to give a warning about the cow's being on the road, this duty is not a duty to improve others' positions compared to what those positions would have been had A's body or resources *and their causal effects* not been present at the time. If these causal effects had not been present, then there would be no cow in the road, and so no danger in the first place. Nonetheless, partly because of the traditional classification of these duties as P-duties, and partly because elaborating the basis of these duties will allow me to explain other supposed (but not true) P-duties as implications of the ones discussed in this chapter,[4] I consider them here.

[3] The 'causal effects' point is necessitated if we are to arrive at the correct result in cases like *Cancellation* (see Chapter 1, section 4).

[4] In Chapters 4 and 5.

1. Innocent Creation of Risk

(i) Innocent Creation of Risk: The Law

Here is an initial characterisation of the kind of situation under discussion: A contributes non-wrongfully to a substantial risk to B's right-protected interests, either by damaging those interests or simply by altering the world such that B's right-protected interests are now subject to this risk. Suppose A collides with B while driving carefully, rendering B unconscious. This involves damaging B's right-protected interest in his body and thereby creating a risk of further damage to that interest. Suppose that A knocks over and kills a cow, which has strayed onto the road.[5] This involves creation of a risk to B's (and others') right-protected interests in their body and property, without itself damaging them.

(a) Innocent versus Wrongful Creation of Risk

In each of the examples, A *innocently* creates a risk in the sense that risk is created without a wrong, or at least without a wrong to the person subject to the risk.[6] If, in the first example, A had carelessly injured B as a result of being distracted while talking on the phone, the risk that B's damage will worsen would then have been caused by a wrong. It seems true that, in this case, A would have a legal duty to take reasonable steps to protect B from this worsening.[7] A's breach of their N-duty not carelessly to damage B gives rise to a P-duty to give reasonable assistance to B.

It is difficult to envisage a situation in which B would need to rely upon this duty in the tort of negligence, when the initial damage is wrongful: if B is seeking compensation from A for loss caused by the breach of the N-duty, the fact that there is a breach of this P-duty seems unnecessary to explain B's right to compensation for loss caused by the breach of the N-duty. B can simply argue that B's total loss is causally attributable to A's breach of their initial N-duty.

Nonetheless, it seems important to insist that A *is* under a P-duty in this situation, for four reasons. First, the law is surely not indifferent to whether a person provides assistance in these circumstances: the law *mandates* that one take steps to provide assistance and does not merely require one to compensate if one fails to do so.[8]

Second, if A deliberately, without justification, failed to take steps to protect B with the result that B is worse off than if this had not occurred, this failure could

[5] See *Hardy v Brooks* (1961) 130 Ga App 124.

[6] So, the risk created to unforeseeable third parties, such as Mrs Palsgraf, would be 'innocent': see *Palsgraf v Long Island Railroad* 248 NY 339, 162 NE 99 (1928).

[7] See, eg, *Capital & Counties Plc v Hampshire County Council* [1997] QB 1004 (CA) 1034.

[8] For the general claim that the law imposes duties of care, see N McBride, 'Duties of Care—Do They Really Exist?' (2004) 24 Oxford Journal of Legal Studies 417.

plausibly attract an award of exemplary damages in jurisdictions which permit punitive damages in negligence.[9] Such an award could not be tied to A's breach of their initial N-duty if that breach were insufficiently culpable.

Third, the existence of a P-duty to take preventive or mitigatory steps after the breach of an N-duty could also be significant for the purposes of limitation. This issue arose, for instance, in *Jalla v Shell Petroleum*.[10] The defendant was alleged wrongfully to have allowed oil to leak from its pipe off the shore of Nigeria, with oil reaching the shore and damaging the claimants' properties. If the cause of action in nuisance accrued when the oil reached the shore, shortly after the initial leak, the claim was time-barred. The claimants argued that the defendant had a duty to remediate the damage caused by their initial spill and so the cause of action continued to arise until that remediation had occurred. The Court of Appeal rejected this argument. It held that while the defendant had a duty to abate the nuisance, this duty did not entail taking steps to remediate damage already caused: 'abatement of the nuisance means dealing with the state of affairs that created the nuisance; it does not involve any obligation to remediate the damage caused by the nuisance'.[11] Coulson LJ considered that it would be contrary to principle if the defendant were subject to a duty when 'the defendant itself may not have the ability or the necessary control to effect any remedial works'.[12]

The Supreme Court upheld this decision.[13] It held that there was no continuing nuisance on because there was no repeated activity by the defendant nor an ongoing state of affairs causing substantial interference with use and enjoyment on the claimant's land for which the defendant was responsible.[14] This decision does not, however, preclude a defendant being under a P-duty to prevent *further* damage, as a result of an initial wrongful or non-wrongful, act, when the defendant has the ability to do so. Suppose that the oil had reached the shore, and the defendants knew the claimants were not present, with the likely result that much greater damage would ensue unless preventive measures were taken. The defendants would have a legal P-duty to take reasonable steps in these circumstances, for instance, by contacting the claimants to warn of the risk of further damage. Such a duty should not depend on whether the defendant still had control over the source of risk. As we shall see, a product manufacturer has a duty to warn of risk innocently created by its products even after the product has been distributed. There is no reason for a difference between duties to warn about risks in relation

[9] For example, in Singapore (see, eg, *ACB v Thomson Medical* [2017] SGCA 20) and New Zealand (see, eg, *McGougan and Dingle v Depuy International Ltd* [2016] NZHC 2511 (in the context of personal injury)).

[10] [2021] EWCA Civ 63, [2021] BLR 276.

[11] ibid [71] (Coulson LJ).

[12] ibid [73] (Coulson LJ).

[13] [2023] UKSC 16.

[14] ibid [34]–[40].

to products not in one's control and duties to warn about risks of oil not in one's control.[15]

Fourth, if a person *wrongfully* creates a risk, the preventive steps that may be required of them are plausibly more demanding than what would be required of a non-wrongful risk creator. This is already illustrated by the fact that a person can come under a costly compensatory duty in relation to wrongfully inflicted harm, compared to the kind of P-duty they will come under in relation to innocent risks. For instance, if A wrongfully breaks B's leg, then A is under a P-duty to pay damages to A such that B will not be worse off than if A had not wronged B. Absent insurance, this could be a very costly duty to fulfil. By contrast, if A innocently breaks B's leg, the most that is likely to be required of A is that A provide B with some relatively minimal assistance to protect B from further worsening of B's condition. The level of cost a person is expected to bear to avert a risk is plausibly a function of three variables: (i) responsibility for the risk, (ii) wrongfulness in relation to the risk, (iii) culpability for the risk. Cases of innocent risk involve only (i). In cases in which a person is under a P-duty with respect to risks absent (i), (ii), and (iii), the level of cost they may be required to bear is very low indeed.[16]

(b) Innocent Creation of Risk: Existence of the Principle

In English law, direct authority on the question of duties in relation to innocently created risk is slender. The law appears to be that if A substantially causally contributes to an interference with B's right-protected interest, or a risk to B's right-protected interest, and A ought to know that this interference or risk poses a foreseeable risk of injury to that interest, then A is under a duty to take reasonable steps to protect B from that risk. Let us call this the *Innocent Risk Principle.*

Hobbs v Baxenden supports the existence of the *Innocent Risk Principle.*[17] The defendant's marketing materials described an insulating foam as 'self-extinguishing'. The claimant insulated his barn using the foam. A fire began in the barn due to the careless actions of one of the claimant's employees. The foam did not 'self-extinguish' but rather greatly exacerbated the spread of the fire. The judge held that the defendant ought not to have used the misleading term 'self-extinguish' which, to an ordinary person, comports the general safety of the material in the event of a fire when, in reality, it refers to the behaviour of a material in laboratory conditions. He said that 'a manufacturer's duty of care does not end when the goods are sold. A manufacturer who realises that omitting to warn past customers about something which might result in injury to them must take reasonable steps to attempt to warn them, however lacking in negligence he may been

[15] The Supreme Court accepted that 'control' is not a necessary condition of a continuing nuisance: ibid [43]–[46].

[16] See Chapter 6, p. 146; Chapter 9.

[17] [1992] 1 Lloyd's Rep 54.

at the time the goods were sold'.[18] This explicitly envisages a duty arising in relation to a risk innocently created. Strictly, however, this was unnecessary to decide *Hobbs*: it seems clear that the defendant's use of the term 'self-extinguishing' was itself in breach of a duty of care, and so was not innocent.[19]

The existence of the principle is also supported by *Cambridge Water v Eastern Counties*.[20] A solvent had unforeseeably escaped from the defendant's land and impaired the claimant's water supply. The House of Lords rejected strict liability for damage caused by this solvent, but Lord Goff assumed that the defendant would be under a duty to respond in negligence and nuisance to the damage caused, albeit that the initial escape was unforeseeable.[21]

The duty to correct an innocent misrepresentation can also be seen to support the principle. The wrong which generates an entitlement to damages here is a failure to take reasonable care to disabuse a person of a false representation that was initially made without a failure to take reasonable care.[22] The making of the false statement is an innocent creation of risk, which triggers a duty to take reasonable care to disabuse the recipient.

The other relevant English authorities are complicated by the fact the defendant was alleged to have created a risk through another person's agency, but these also support the existence of the principle. In *Mitchell v Glasgow City Council*, the defender council held a meeting with one of their tenants to discuss a notice of possession proceedings against him.[23] The notice was in effect because of the tenant's violent and anti-social behaviour against his neighbour, also a tenant of the defender. The meeting involved discussion of the latest in a series of altercations with the deceased and notice that any further such behaviour would lead to another notice being served. After the meeting, the tenant inflicted injuries on the same neighbour, resulting in his death. The deceased's estate argued that the defender had a duty to warn the deceased of the risk of retaliation after the meeting. The House of Lords rejected this. It was accepted that *if* the council's conduct could be said to have created the risk of danger to the deceased, then the council would have been under a duty to take reasonable steps to protect him.[24] Lord Scott said: 'If a defendant has played some causative part in the train of events that have led to the risk of injury, a duty to take reasonable steps to avert or lessen the risk may arise'.[25] It was concluded, however, that the council could not be said to have caused the

[18] ibid 65 (Michael Odgen QC).
[19] ibid: the term was 'undoubtedly misleading and should not have been used by Baxenden after the end of 1974'.
[20] [1994] 2 AC 264 (HL), [1994] 2 WLR 53.
[21] ibid 307.
[22] See, eg, *With v O'Flanagan* [1936] Ch 575 (CA), [1936] 1 All ER 727, 583–84 and authorities cited therein (using the language of 'duty') (Lord Wright MR), although Romer LJ merely states that the contractual rights acquired are voidable (at 586)).
[23] [2009] UKHL 11, [2009] 1 AC 874.
[24] ibid [20], [42] (Lord Hope), [55] (Lord Rodger), [83] (Lord Brown).
[25] ibid [40] (Lord Scott).

risk to the deceased: the tenant's decision to engage in criminal violence was not properly causally attributable to the council's conduct.[26]

Admittedly, Lord Rodger appears to take the view that, absent an assumption of responsibility or control over the wrongdoer, only a 'wrongful' act by the council could have generated a positive duty; since the decision to hold the meeting, and the meeting itself, were 'legitimate steps', no duty arose.[27] There are at least three possible readings of this. First, Lord Rodger could be understood as rejecting the *Innocent Risk Principle* entirely by insisting upon a *wrongful* act. Second, Lord Rodger's analysis could be understood as directed specifically to innocent contributions to *wrongful* acts of third parties. Third, Lord Rodger could be employing 'wrongful' in a non-standard sense, where an act is 'wrongful' if there is no objective justification for the act: thus, if A drives carefully and injures B, A act is 'wrongful' because there is no objective justification for injuring B. In the context, the second interpretation seems the most plausible; his Lordship's analysis of the 'wrongful' requirement refers specifically to cases in which third parties are involved. Hence, even taking into account Lord Rodger's analysis, *Mitchell* overall provides support for the *Innocent Risk Principle*.

There are decisions in the tort of false imprisonment which are inconsistent with the *Innocent Risk Principle*, however. In *Herd v Weardale Steel, Coal and Coke Co Ltd*,[28] the defendant coal-mining employer refused their employee's request to be taken to the surface from the mine until two hours after the request was made, and despite the lift being available prior to that point. It was held by the Court of Appeal and House of Lords that this was not false imprisonment. Buckley LJ rested his decision in part on the ground that there was no *act* on the defendant's part and no contractual right in the employee that he be released: 'What kept [the plaintiff] from getting to the surface was not any act which the defendants did, but the fact that he was at the bottom of a deep shaft, and that there were no means of getting out other than the particular means which belonged to his employers and over which the plaintiff had contractual rights which at that moment were not in operation'.[29] In *Iqbal v POA*, the Court of Appeal interpreted *Herd* to have provided support for the view that there could generally be no liability in false imprisonment for a failure to act. In that case, prison officers went on strike with the result that the prison governor took a decision to reduce prisoners' time outside of their cells. The claimant said this was false imprisonment. The claim was rejected, partly on the ground that failure to open the cells was a failure to act.[30] Lord Neuberger

[26] ibid [83] (Lord Brown).
[27] ibid [58].
[28] [1913] 3 KB 771 (CA).
[29] ibid 785–86. Even if there had been a contractual right, he considered that irrelevant to false imprisonment: 789.
[30] *Iqbal v Prison Officers' Association* [2009] EWCA Civ 1312, [2010] QB 732 [34] (Lord Neuberger MR).

endorsed the possibility that a failure to act could give rise to false imprisonment but 'at least, normally' only when there is a breach of an 'independent' duty to the claimant, such as a breach of contract or another tort.[31] No such duty existed in *Iqbal*. The view expressed in *Iqbal* is inconsistent with the approach to innocent risk elsewhere and, with respect, seems doubtful. If a person is lawfully imprisoned but the lawful justification falls away, then a duty to release or a duty to take reasonable steps to release should arise according to the *Innocent Risk Principle*. It also seems normatively implausible that an independent duty, in Lord Neuberger's sense, is always needed to generate a duty to take steps to release a person. If a person is lawfully imprisoned by a police officer, but then the officer becomes aware that the justification for the imprisonment no longer obtains, it is difficult to believe that the officer is legally permitted to leave the person imprisoned.

The *Innocent Risk Principle* enjoys support in other common law jurisdictions.[32] A well-known US example is *Hardy v Brooks*.[33] The defendant, despite driving with reasonable care, knocked over and killed a cow which had strayed onto the road. He did nothing to move the cow or warn others of its presence. The claimant was injured in a collision with the cow. The court stated that 'if one by his own act, although without negligence on his part, creates a dangerous situation in or along a public highway and it reasonably appears that other users of the highway in the exercise of ordinary care for their own safety may be injured by the dangerous situation so created, the one creating the same is under a duty to eliminate the danger or give warning to others of its presence'.[34]

(c) The Meaning and Scope of 'Creation of Risk'

The concept of the creation of risk is rarely stated with any precision.[35] The following definition ordinarily works reasonably well:

> A creates a risk if and only if A does an act which increases the probability of B suffering a damage.

On analysis, though, this definition is too broad and too narrow for the purposes of the *Innocent Risk Principle*.

It is too broad for three reasons. First, the law attributes special significance to the highly responsible interventions of others. If A does an act which increases the probability of B's suffering a damage, by making it more likely that a third party

[31] ibid [35] (Lord Neuberger MR).

[32] See also its acceptance in English criminal law: *R v Miller* [1983] 2 AC 161 (HL), [1983] 2 WLR 539.

[33] *Hardy* (n 5). See also *Montgomery v National Convoy & Trucking Co* 186 SC 167, 195 SE 247 (1938).

[34] *Hardy* (n 5) 127.

[35] See, eg, J Stapleton, 'The Risk Architecture of the Restatement (Third) of Torts (2009) 44 Wake Forest Law Review 1309.

will commit a crime against B, this will not be sufficient to trigger the *Innocent Risk Principle*. Second, it improperly counts certain withdrawals of aid as creations of risk. The withdrawal of the charity payment in *Cancellation* will count as creating a risk, triggering a duty of care.[36] Third, arguably, one's contribution to a risk must, in some sense, be more than minimal. In *Buchanan v Rose*, the defendant drove across a defective bridge.[37] The bridge collapsed. The court accepted that a person who innocently creates a risk comes under a duty to take reasonable steps to protect others from the risk, but held that this principle did not generate a duty to warn others of the collapsed bridge on the facts. The reason for this was framed in causal terms: the bridge 'merely gave way as the result of the usual and legitimate use of the road. It fell as a result of its own inherent defects'.[38]

It is too narrow for two reasons. First, it does not capture cases in which a person acts but the probability, on the evidence, of their act leading to a risk is non-existent, or far-fetched, and yet the person seems to come under a P-duty by their contribution to the risk faced by another. The example was given in Chapter 1 of the person who is rendered unconscious by an explosion and awakes to find their body on top of another person, risking that person physical harm. Here the person is likely to be under a P-duty to move because of the danger their body poses to the other, even if the person cannot be described as having done an act which increased the probability of his suffering a damage.[39] Second, there is the problem of pre-emption and overdetermination. Suppose that A's act releases toxic sludge from a pipe on A's land into B's river. The opening of A's pipe, unbeknownst to A, closes C's pipe, which would otherwise have released the same amount of toxic sludge from C's land into B's river. Here A's act has not increased the probability of damage to B, relative to a baseline in which A does not act.

These difficulties can largely be avoided by the analysis of 'making worse' in Chapter 1. Recall:

> *W5*. A's conduct makes B worse off if and only if A's conduct causes B to be in a negative state that B would not have been in but for the presence of A's body or resources at the time of the causative conduct.

Reframing this in terms of risk, we can say:

> A creates a danger to B if and only if A's conduct causes B to be at an increased risk of suffering a negative state, compared to the risk B would face absent A's body or resources at the time of conduct.

[36] See Chapter 1.

[37] 138 Tex 390, 159 SW2d 109 (1942).

[38] ibid 393. See similarly *Vasquez v Legend Natural Gas III, LP* (2016) 492 SW3d 448 (Court of Appeals of Texas); *Kalma v African Minerals* [2020] EWCA Civ 144.

[39] See the *Crushing Person* example, Chapter 1, section 3(iii).

First, this deals with the withdrawal of aid problem, for the reasons given in Chapter 1. Second, to *cause* B to be at an increased risk involves more than a but-for connection: on the ordinary legal analysis, it requires the absence of highly responsible interventions.[40] This deals with the problems of intervening agency and minimal causal contribution.

Admittedly, the two problems of narrowness are not immediately solved by this reformulation. It seems to suffice if A's *body* or *property* is currently causing B to be at an increased risk, and A is currently in control of A's body or property, for A to be said to be creating a risk to B. Hence the person who awakes to find himself on top of another person is creating a risk of harm to that person. Further, it suffices if A's conduct would *ordinarily* cause B to be at an increased risk, compared to the risk B would face absent A's body or resources at the time of the conduct. Ordinarily, releasing toxic sludge into a river has this effect. This resolves the pre-emption and overdetermination issue above.

Creation of Risk through Other People. It is clearly possible to come under a duty in virtue of the *Innocent Risk Principle* by creating a risk through another person's agency. Suppose A non-negligently collides with C, a pedestrian, while driving. C, seriously hurt, is in a dazed condition and is wandering across the road. A would owe a duty to take steps to protect B and other road users from C's conduct, as well as to C to protect them from further injury. More generally, if A innocently but substantially undermines C's capacity to make rational decisions and this imposes a significant foreseeable risk on B, then A has a duty to take reasonable care to protect B from this risk immediately due to C. In these cases, it is as if A's conduct set off a dangerous machine. The same would be true if A's non-negligently caused collision forced C into the direction of B, injuring B. A would owe a duty to both B and C to take reasonable steps to protect them from deterioration of their injuries. If C reasonably regards A as an epistemic authority on some matter, such that C reasonably defers to A's judgement on some matter, then decisions which C makes in relation to that subject matter may be considered risks created by A towards B and others. If a doctor gives a patient a drug which makes the patient dizzy while driving and fails to warn of its effect, then the doctor creates a risk through the patient's agency to other drivers. If A provides C, a psychologically unstable person, with a firearm, then A can be said to create a risk through C towards B and others.[41] The thread that unites these cases is A's increasing a probability of harm towards B through initiating a process which is responded to by C's innocent, impaired, or reasonable deferential agency.

The more difficult cases are those in which there are wrongful and significantly responsible interventions by a third party. If A breaches a duty of care to B, the

[40] Since certain highly responsible interventions 'break the chain of causation'; see generally HLA Hart and T Honoré, *Causation in the Law* (Clarendon 1985) 41–44.

[41] *Attorney General of the British Virgin Islands v Hartwell* [2004] UKPC 12, [2004] 1 WLR 1273 [31].

chain of causation will not generally be broken by intervening negligence on the part of B or C. Thus one cannot shut one's eyes to the negligence of others when driving.[42] And hence the possibility of A's being liable to B when B is contributorily negligent: B's own carelessness does not generally break the chain, but only reduces the extent of liability under the defence of contributory negligence. In many cases, the fact that B behaves unreasonably, however, when A is *innocent*, will entail that A does not create the risk posed by or to B. For instance, suppose that A is talking to a person at the side of a pavement, and B collides with A from behind because B is answering an email while walking down the street on his phone. B falls, damages his skull, and needs urgent medical assistance. As a general rule, when there are multiple necessary conditions of an event, the ordinary concept of cause isolates the most abnormal conditions—either statistically or normatively abnormal—as causes of it. When A's conduct is a breach of a duty of care, and B's conduct is also a breach of a duty of care, each is therefore classified as a cause of a harm for which their breaches are necessary conditions, if there are no other, more abnormal, conditions. However, when A's conduct is innocent, and B's conduct is a breach of a duty of care, B's conduct is more abnormal than A's conduct, and so generally precludes A's causal status.[43]

This reasoning would initially seem to imply that A should not be said to 'create' a risk whenever A's conduct is innocent, and B's conduct is a breach. If this were true, one would never be held to have a duty to protect against a risk which only arose because of one's innocent conduct and the wrongful conduct of another. The law is indeed resistant to attribute the risk of a highly culpable wrong to an innocent agent, as *Mitchell* shows.[44] The fact that it is reasonably foreseeable that another will commit an intentional wrong and one's act has increased the probability of this is insufficient to generate a duty in negligence in relation to it.[45] The cases in which a duty has arisen in relation to such wrongs involve a further feature. In *Home Office v Dorset Yacht*, the defendant had factual and legal control over the wrongdoer.[46] In *Bullock v Tamiami Trail Tours Inc*, a US case discussed in *Mitchell*,[47] a black Jamaican minister and his wife were assaulted by a person who boarded their bus in Florida in the 1950s when racial segregation was rife.[48] The person learned that the couple were sitting in the zone of the bus segregated

[42] *Grant v Sun Shipping Co* [1948] AC 549, 567: 'A prudent man will guard against the possible negligence of others, when experience shows negligence to be common' (Lord du Parcq).

[43] For this analysis of legal causation, see J Knobe and S Shapiro, 'Proximate Cause Explained: An Essayy in Experimental Jurisprudence' (2021) 88 University of Chicago Law Review 165; cf *Childs v Desormeaux* [2006] SCC 18 (CanLII), [2006] 1 SCR 643 [44]: 'hosting a party where alcohol is served, without more, does not suggest the creation or exacerbation of risk of the level required to impose a duty of care on the host to members of the public who may be affected by a guest's conduct'.

[44] See section 1(i)(b).

[45] *Smith v Littlewoods* [1987] AC 241 (HL) 272 (Lord Goff).

[46] [1970] AC 1004 (HL), [1970] 2 WLR 1140. See further Chapter 6.

[47] *Mitchell* (n 23).

[48] 266 F2d 326 (5th Cir 1959).

for white people as a result of an overheard conversation between the bus driver and police officers during a stop. The Fifth Circuit Court of Appeals held the bus company to be under a duty to protect, by warning or otherwise, a passenger from a reasonably foreseeable assault by another passenger. In *Mitchell*, Lord Rodger analysed the duty in *Bullock* as arising in part because the passengers were shut up together in an environment controlled by the defendant, and so less able to protect themselves. The duty did not arise simply in virtue of the driver's conversation.[49] On this view, if a third party's conversation about the couple had been unwittingly overheard by the attacker, the third party would not have had the duty since, despite their contribution to the sequence leading to the harm, there was no further fact present such as control over the environment.

One possible qualification to this are cases in which a person substantially increases the probability of another's culpable wrong, relative to the *W5* baseline, by failing to take an extremely low-cost precaution. In *Rushbond v JS Design*, an architect was given keys to an empty cinema in Leeds city centre by a company that was entrusted with them by the owner for the purpose of obtaining a tenant.[50] The architect was alleged to have left the door open for around an hour, during which time an intruder entered and caused substantial damage to the premises. The Court of Appeal held that it was arguable that the defendant was in breach of a duty not unreasonably to create risks of harm to others.[51] This case might be considered as justifiable on the basis of an assumption of responsibility—either because the architect's entering the property was justified only on condition that he take reasonable care, or because the architect agreed to discharge the company's assumed responsibility.[52] However, the same result would seem to be appropriate, absent such an assumption, if one innocently drove one's car through the cinema's doors: one would then have a duty to take the low-cost precaution of calling for assistance. This reasoning seems precluded, however, on the current law, by virtue of *Mitchell*: there, too, an innocent act substantially increased the probability of an intentional wrong, and a low-cost precaution would have reduced that probability, yet the *Innocent Risk* principle was not triggered.

If the law accepts that there is no general N-duty *to take care* not to contribute to another's intentional wrong—no such duty generally arises absent some further special fact (such as an assumption of responsibility, control over the intervening agent, or control over the ultimate victim)—then it would be inconsistent to apply the *Innocent Risk Principle* to such cases. Consider:

> *Neighbour Affair.* A person comes to your door and asks where your neighbour lives. You tell him. Moments later, you receive a text message from your

[49] *Mitchell* (n 23) [59]–[61].
[50] [2021] EWCA Civ 1889. See also *Stansbie v Troman* [1948] 2 KB 48.
[51] [2021] EWCA Civ 1889 [70]–[72].
[52] See also [2021] EWCA Civ 1889 [73].

neighbour, telling you not to tell anyone her location as she has been having an affair with the wife of a violent gang member. You now realise you have disclosed the location of your neighbour to the violent gang member.

If there is no general duty to take reasonable care not to do an act which poses a reasonably foreseeable risk of a third party committing a highly culpable wrong, then there ought not to be a duty to take reasonable care to warn in this case. If there is no duty when the risk is reasonably foreseeable *ex ante*, prior to the act, then there can be no duty simply when the risk becomes reasonably foreseeable *ex post*, after the text message.

However, it should not follow that there is never a duty to warn in cases like *Neighbour Affair*. Suppose that you *do* know the person on your doorstop's intentions. Surely, there is at least a duty not knowingly to assist the person in their plan, without justification. A knowledge standard reflects one's lesser responsibility in relation to the culpable wrongs of others. Two arguments may be given against general duties not knowingly and unreasonably to contribute to damage by highly responsible wrongdoers. First, there is the idea that the person who is fully responsible for the harm is the intentional wrongdoer. As Alec Walen points out, though, responsibility is 'not in short supply': it is possible that more than one person is fully responsible in respect of a harm, or one person fully responsible and another partially responsible.[53]

Second, it might be thought unfair that other people's highly culpable and responsible wrongdoing affects one's duties, and thus one's freedom. Consider:

Diabolical Dictator. You live under a diabolical dictator. If the dictator suspects dissent, he kills an innocent member of the population. You know that the dictator considers reading books to be signs of dissent.

It might be thought *unfair* that your freedom could be diminished by the prospect of the dictator's intentional wrongdoing. You lose a valuable option—the option to read books—because of another person's choice to commit a wrong. Being deprived of something of value by another's deliberate wrong is unfair. It might be justifiable to give diminished weight to risks which are the consequence of the deliberate wrongs of others, in virtue of this unfairness. However, the idea that one can discount entirely such risks seems untenable.[54]

Strictly, the prior question of whether there should be a general duty to take care not to contribute to deliberate wrongs is not itself an issue of the normative scope

[53] A Walen, *The Mechanics of Claims* (OUP 2019) 163.

[54] Perhaps the requirement of a particularly *high* degree of foreseeability in earlier cases— such as *Topp v London Country Bus (South West) Ltd* [1993] 1 WLR 976—supports this idea that one can give some kind of discount in weight to the risks created by the deliberate wrongs of others; one must only act when the probability reaches a higher threshold than usual. It should also be noted that when a special fact such as assumption of responsibility exists, this may transform a duty not *knowingly* to

of liability for pure omissions: contribution is not purely omissive.[55] But if this prior question is resolved in favour of a limited duty not knowingly to contribute without justification, then an innocent contribution to deliberate wrongs should trigger a P-duty to take reasonable steps to prevent the wrong under the *Innocent Risk Principle*, when the contributor has knowledge. The fact that the person who contributes to the intentional wrong is far less responsible than the person who commits the wrong could justify the law only demanding relatively minimal measures to be taken. If the N-duty not to contribute to the wrong were relatively non-demanding, then this would also be true of the P-duty to prevent the wrong.

Creation of Risk, and Providing and Withdrawing Aid. A particularly difficult issue arises as to whether a person can be said to have created a risk in the course of, or soon after, alleviating risk to a person. *W5* provides some guidance here—that is, such cases can mainly be resolved by considering whether the person providing aid increased the risk of a negative state relative to the baseline of their and their resources not being present. However, it will be seen that matters are more complex. It will be useful to deal with this issue through a series of hypothetical examples which bring out the possible kinds of case.

No Removal from a Risk

Passing Speedboat. A sees B drowning. A could easily help but drives past in A's speedboat. B drowns.

This is the simple case: A is not under a P-duty absent a special fact; A has not created a risk.

Ineffective Removal from a Risk

No addition of risk:

> *Slow Speedboat.* A sees B drowning in the distance. A mistakenly puts his speedboat's speed to level 2, instead of the highest speed of level 4, which would have been perfectly safe in the circumstances. Consequently, A takes two minutes

contribute to a duty to take care. Suppose that a computer operator in an intelligence organisation has a button on their computer which will send the locations of spies operating in other countries to those countries' intelligence agencies, with the result that the spies will be tortured. It is difficult to believe that the operator does not *create a risk of* harm to the spies if he unwittingly presses the button, simply because the harm will be produced by the intentional wrongs of third parties. The special relation justifies a duty to take care not to create this risk.

[55] Sometimes the issues are conflated. In *Royal Bank of Scotland International Ltd v JP SPC 4* [2022] UKPC 18, [2023] AC 461, a bank's executing an order, which was alleged to have been a fraud on the beneficial owner of money in the account, was held to raise an issue of omissions liability. The execution of the order was clearly not a pure omission, however. This is shown by the fact that, if the bank had *known* of the fraud, it would have been held to have *assisted* in breach of fiduciary duty. The addition of knowledge cannot change the bank's conduct from a *pure omission* to an *act*. The better view is therefore that the conduct was an *act*, whether done with knowledge or not.

> longer than A would have taken if the speed level had been level 4. B suffers brain damage which would have been avoided if A had driven at level 4 speed.

A is, again, not under a P-duty absent a special fact; A has not created a risk. A simply failed to respond effectively to an existing risk not of A's creation.
Addition of a new risk:

> *Speedboat and Dog.* A is out fishing in his boat with A's aggressive dog, Chi. A sees B drowning and drags him into the boat, saving his life. When driving back to shore, Chi viciously bites B's leg while A is on the phone.

A's conduct has not worsened B's position overall relative to the position B would be in had A and A's resources not been present. Death is normally worse than a dog bite. Nonetheless, it is suggested that A is under a general N-duty to protect B from the risk posed by Chi. One sufficient reason for that duty is simply A's involvement in creating the risk of a negative state to B's body.

Removal from a Risk and Re-introduction to the Same Risk
Contrast these examples:

> *Speedboat and Chair.* A rescues B from drowning using A's speedboat. A places B, unconscious, on a chair on A's dock, having returned to shore. In anchoring the boat, A accidentally knocks B off the chair back into the sea. B drowns.

> *Drunken Father.* A lives next to a family whose father, F, is an alcoholic who drinks heavily during the day. A has seen F beat his 12-year-old son, B, when F is drunk. A has called social services who are monitoring the situation. In order to protect B as much as possible, A invites B to stay with A during the day in the summer holidays when B is off school. A sends B home each evening, despite knowing that B's father is often still drunk at this time. On one such occasion, B is violently assaulted by F.

In both cases, A removes B from a source of risk and returns B to that source of risk. In both cases, A's conduct does not make B worse off than if A and A's resources had not been present.

In *Speedboat and Chair*, it seems likely, however, that A is under a duty to take care not to dislodge A from the chair, increasing the risk that A drown. The past fact that A rescued B does not release A from A's duty of care not to impose risks of damage upon B.

Drunken Father is more complicated for two reasons: (1) A is restoring B to a risk that is posed by deliberate human agency, and (2) the cost to A of non-restoration is continued accommodation of B, a significantly greater cost to A than in *Speedboat and Chair*. It seems likely that there would be a duty to take reasonable steps to protect B even in *Drunken Father*, however. This duty arises in virtue of A's becoming involved in the imposition of a risk to B. For instance, if A saw F brandishing a knife on the doorstep, A's duty would be to accommodate B for longer or contact the police or another authority.[56] In these circumstances, A could not justify contributing to B's risk of harm on the basis that F has parental responsibility for B, and so it is reasonable to return a child to their parent. Although A has no duty to become involved to protect B at all, A's involvement results in A's contributing to the risk to B if A returns B to that risk, as in *Speedboat and Chair*. In this way *Drunken Father* is partly analogous to *Ploof v Putnam*, where the court held that sending a visiting elderly person out from one's house into the freezing cold where he almost died could amount to a breach of a duty of care.[57]

Removal From a Risk and Introduction to a Further Risk
One last speedboat variation:

> *Speedboat and Road*. A rescues B from drowning using A's speedboat. A places B, unconscious, near the side of a busy road and leaves B. B awakes, stumbles, and is seriously injured by a passing car.

Again, A's conduct does not make B worse off overall than if A's body or resources had not been present. Nonetheless, A is likely to be under a duty not to expose B to the risk of being injured by a car. A's conduct exposes B to a new risk of B's body being in a negative state.[58]

This series of results can be summarised by saying that A creates a risk if and only if A causes B to be subject to a *new* risk of harm. A risk is *new* if (a) the facts which constitute that risk would not have obtained but for the presence of A's body or resources (*Speedboat and Dog, Speedboat and Road*), or (b) B currently enjoyed protection from a source of risk, but A's act removed this protection (*Speedboat and Chair, Drunken Father*).

Isolating Duty-Bearers Amongst Multiple Innocent Risk Creators. Consider a variant of *Hardy v Brooks*, the cow-on-the-road case, in which the car is a taxi taking a passenger to her destination. Does the passenger also have a P-duty to warn oncoming traffic of the risk posed by the cow, or only the driver? The passenger's booking the taxi is a but-for cause of the risk posed. We could easily imagine other but-for causes of the danger too: suppose that the vet who recently

[56] This is based on an example given by Master Dagnall in *YXA v Wolverhampton City Council* [2021] EWHC 1444 (QB) [80].
[57] See Chapters 8 and 9.
[58] This is the conclusion reached by the *Restatement of Torts (Third): Liability for Physical and Emotional Harm*, vol 2 (American Law Institute 2010) §44 cmt h: 'one who rescues a drowning swimmer and brings the swimmer to shore may not leave the swimmer in the middle of a busy highway.'

prevented a fatal outbreak of disease on the farm from which the cow has escaped is passing in her car. Does she owe a P-duty to warn, given that the cow would not have been there had she not saved its life earlier in the week? Determining which innocent but-for conditions of the existence of risk should have P-duties has been described as a 'major theoretical challenge'.[59]

The source of the challenge is that, in these cases, the law cannot rely upon culpability or wrongfulness to discriminate between the endless but-for conditions of an event: *ex hypothesi*, the conditions are *innocent*. Consequently, the law must instead rely upon a concept of 'causing' or 'contributing to' a risk which goes beyond mere but for, appeal to additional normative considerations to discriminate between but-for conditions, or else allow that *all* of the antecedent but-for conditions of an innocent risk are under P-duties.

The Third Restatement of Torts, §39 attempts to deal with this issue by introducing the concept of a 'characteristic' risk:

> When an actor's prior conduct, even though not tortious, creates a continuing risk of physical harm of a type characteristic of the conduct, the actor has a duty to exercise reasonable care to prevent or minimize the harm.

The concept of a 'characteristic' type of risk is introduced to deal with examples such as the following. A invites B to go to a baseball game. B trips up on the stairs in the stadium and suffers a serious head injury. A is a but-for cause of the risk posed to B by the head injury. The Restatement concludes, however, that A does not owe B a duty *in virtue of innocently creating a risk to B*. Similarly, in the vet variant on *Hardy*, we could intuitively rule out the vet as a duty-bearer on the basis that the risk of a road accident is not a characteristic risk of treating cows.

The concept of a 'characteristic' risk is vague, however. Consider the position of the passenger in the variant: are collisions a *characteristic risk* of hiring a taxi? Or suppose a mobile phone manufacturer discovers that a small number of its phones will explode when used. Is the risk of an explosion a 'characteristic' risk of manufacture or distribution of mobile phones? Suppose a person finds out that their coronavirus test was in fact positive, but having relied upon an erroneous communication that it was negative, they visited a nursing home—is the risk of transmitting a virus a characteristic risk of visiting people? More generally, can a risk be of a type characteristic of an activity if it is unforeseeable? Without further specification of the concept, it is impossible to say.

[59] L Alexander and K Ferzan, *Reflections on Crime and Culpability: Problems and Puzzles* (CUP 2018) 71.

A better view seems to be that (a) one must intend to create the harm or risk, albeit innocently (as in justified defence, or justified necessity), or (b) one must substantially contribute to the existence of the risk of harm, or (c) one's body or resources must be constitutive of the risk.

In (a), one's agency is deeply connected—by one's intending the harm or risk—with the creation of the risk and so this justifies a duty to respond to the risk; this intention identifies one as an appropriate duty-bearer amongst many innocent conditions of a risk. Moreover, when one intends to cause harm to a right-protected interest of another, it is justifiable to require that one take reasonable steps to mitigate the harm after it has been caused. One is only permitted to harm an unjustified attacker to the extent *necessary* to prevent or diminish the effect of the attack. If one harms an attacker and leaves them to die, one will at least sometimes fail the necessity condition: one could instead have harmed-and-taken-reasonable-measures.[60]

(b) is reflective of the general distinction the law draws between being a background condition of an outcome and being a cause of the outcome. Although the vet and the driver's mother are but-for conditions of the cow being struck in the *Hardy* variant, neither would be said substantially to contribute to the existence of the risk posed to other drivers. Driving a car increases the probability of a collision significantly more than giving birth to another person. One will substantially contribute to the existence of a risk if the risk was of a kind which one was reasonably expected to take into account *ex ante*, but which was reasonable to impose given its small size or the justification for imposing it. In these circumstances, it seems reasonable to ask one to take steps in relation to that category of risk *ex post*, when the risk is of a greater size. Hence the phone manufacturer has a duty to warn of exploding phones: the risk of a product malfunctioning is a known risk of manufacture.[61] Similarly, the car operator has a duty to respond to risks of collisions involving their vehicle. As we have all been reminded, the risk of transmitting a virus is a risk which is increased by physical proximity with others; if the risk is sufficiently low, the virus not serious, and perhaps there is a reciprocal general imposition of such risks, then there is normally no duty to warn others about the risk of transmission. However, this is probably different when a person knows that the risk is substantial and the consequences are likely to be severe, as in the nursing home case. The absence of a duty in the baseball example can be explained on the basis that inviting a person to a baseball match does not increase the risk of tripping beyond what virtually any other action would do.

This leaves the difficult case of the passengers in a vehicle or, more generally, passengers on transport. In some cases, the passenger's presence cannot be

[60] The defence of illegality could potentially bar a claim by the attacker here, however.

[61] The same would apply if the phone manufacturer's phones had become explosive due to the malicious actions of a rival. This kind of risk is one in respect of which the manufacturer is expected to take precautions *ex ante*.

described as making a significant causal contribution to the existence of the risk. For example, if I take the 9.59am train from Oxford to London, I do not play a role in the existence of the risk posed by the train: all would be identical except for my presence. In these circumstances, there should be no P-duty upon me on the basis of creation of risk, if there is a train accident that poses risk to others. However, in other cases, one can be reasonably confident that one's presence made a difference to the existence of a risk, as in the taxi version of *Hardy*. If the taxi driver were your chauffeur and employed by you to drive where you please, then it seems plausible that you ought to have P-duty based on creation of risk. In cases where each person is acting merely for their own purposes and one does not act for the other, the case is more finely balanced. Arguably, a P-duty should exist upon people who *make use of* risk-creating devices for their own purposes. By choosing to make use of such a device—by agreeing with another to be transported by that device—one associates oneself with the risk in a distinctive way.

An example of (c) would be when a person's arm uncontrollably and unforeseeably spasms near another person, or when one awakens to find oneself on top of another person crushing them after an explosion. Intuitively one has a greater responsibility to deal with this problem than a bystander. This could be justified on the basis that a person is usually better placed to deal with risks posed directly by their own body or property than others, and that person's own interest in not being interfered with by others. A different justification is the special connection one has with one's own body. One cannot treat one's spasming arm simply as a problem in the world; it is part of you.

It might be tempting to argue, instead, that the law could adopt a simple rule: if A is a but-for condition of B's being subject to a risk, and A is well-positioned to take steps to protect B from that risk, then A has a P-duty to take reasonable steps to provide protection. This would entail, however, that there are P-duties on the part of the passing vet (and the passing vet's mother), the passenger, and the baseball match invitor. Such an expansive rule would prompt similar cost-related objections as a general duty to take care to protect others from harm: it is very often the case that a person is a but-for condition of some risk and able to help.

Steps Required When One Innocently Creates a Risk. An innocent risk creator is required to take reasonable steps to prevent the materialisation of the risk or mitigate the effects of innocently caused harm, when they reasonably ought to be aware of the innocent risk creation. In thinking about the steps required, it is helpful to imagine what measures would be required prior to the conduct which created the risk, if it were reasonably foreseeable that the risk would exist. If one would have been required to take a precaution of cost *n ex ante* to reduce the risk to a reasonable level, one should also be required to take a precaution of at least that cost *ex post*. So, if one would have been required to warn of a risk *ex ante* at cost *n*, one should also be required to do that *ex post* up to that cost. The costs of precautions *ex post* may typically be greater in so far as a risk is no longer within the control of the creator, with the result that a precaution that was required *ex ante* is not required *ex post*.[62]

(ii) Justification of the *Innocent Risk Principle*

The *Innocent Risk Principle* clearly bears a close connection to the general negligence duty to take reasonable care in relation to foreseeable risk of one's creation. Despite the factual differences in the situations to which the *Innocent Risk Principle* applies, it is argued that these differences are not normatively important, so far as the existence of a duty is concerned. It follows that duties to act arising under the *Innocent Risk Principle* are best considered as justified by whatever justifies the general duty. The discussion will initially focus on negligence, before considering the problem in other torts.

The general duty in negligence in relation to body and property is a duty:

(i) Not to impose, by one's voluntary movement, an unreasonable, reasonably foreseeable risk of damage to B's body or property.[63]

The cases under discussion in this part have the following structure:

(i) A's voluntary bodily movement at *t* causes B's body or property to be subject to a non-minimal risk.
(ii) Either (a) it was not reasonably foreseeable at *t* that A's bodily movement will cause B's body or property to be subject to a substantial risk (*unforeseeable risk cases*), or (b) it was reasonably foreseeable at *t* that A's bodily movement will cause B's body or property to be subject to a risk, but it was not wrongful to impose this risk (*justified foreseeable risks*).
(iii) At $t + n$, A ought reasonably to foresee that A's bodily movement has imposed a substantial risk of worsening of B's body or property.

The key question is whether the differences in (ii) and (iii) are normatively significant. That is, the question is whether a duty to take reasonable measures in response to a risk which one, at an earlier time, unforeseeably or justifiably created requires significant further justification.

Let us consider *unforeseeable risk cases* first. Suppose that a drug manufacturer creates a drug which, despite its considerable benefits, is known at the time of

[62] See also section 1(1)(a).
[63] If the reader subscribes to the view that the duty is always a duty not to damage by unreasonable risk imposition, and there is no freestanding duty not to impose unreasonable risk, then please make the appropriate substitutions.

manufacture to carry a significant risk of causing liver damage in certain people—call this risk X. Suppose further that, after distribution, the drug is discovered to carry a risk of severe bodily damage to people who ingest the drug when taking another drug prescribed for pneumonia. A reasonable manufacturer would have been unaware of the latter risk at the time of distribution. Call this risk Y. According to *Hobbs*, the manufacturer has a duty to take reasonable steps in response to the subsequently discovered risk Y.

One apparently normatively salient difference between risk X and risk Y is that the manufacturer can be said to have *chosen* to create risk X. By distributing the product knowing of risk X, the manufacturer can be said to have chosen to impose this risk. Not so risk Y, which is unknown and reasonably unknowable at the time. This difference does not seem normatively significant *in so far as the existence of a duty to respond to the risk* is concerned, however. If we accept that a person has a duty to respond to risks that they *ought to have known* about, even if they did not know about them, then we already accept a duty to take measures in relation to *un-chosen* risk.

A second argument for a normative difference between risk X and risk Y is that risk X is epistemically available to a reasonable agent and this entails that the agent has a reasonable opportunity to avoid imposing risk X; not so risk Y. It is false, however, that the epistemic availability of the risk entails that there is a reasonable opportunity to avoid it. A person may have no reasonable alternative but to drive their car, given their circumstances—yet they reasonably ought to know of the inevitable risk it imposes on others. Nonetheless, it is reasonable that a person has a duty to take steps to reduce the risks of their driving, even if they have no reasonable alternative but to drive.

If one can have a duty to respond to risks one created, even if one did not choose to impose the risk and had no reasonable opportunity but to impose the risk, it becomes difficult to identify a normative distinction between risk X and risk Y. It seems more plausible that the fundamental reason the company has to respond to risk X is simply because they *created it.* The reasonable awareness of the risk is a matter of what one can reasonably expect the company to do. One cannot reasonably expect a person to take steps in relation to reasonably unknowable risks. If so, *when* the company reasonably ought to be aware of risk Y, albeit after its creation, they should also have a duty in relation to that risk. It is possible, of course, that the 'reasonable steps' required differ between time t and $t + n$. Often, the state of affairs constituting a risk will be beyond the physical proximity and control of a person at $t + n$. This (contingently) affects what can reasonably expected of a person in relation to the risk. There may also be important differences in this regard between cases in which the risk *can* be said to be chosen and situations in which it cannot: this may impact upon what can reasonably be required by way of preventative steps.

The moral duty to protect others from risks one created even seems to extend to risks which are not initially a product of one's *agency*. Suppose that my arm unforeseeably spasms uncontrollably around others. I am required to take steps to protect others from my arm. Indeed, it seems that the steps required may be relatively onerous. Suppose my arm is posing a substantial risk of damage to another person's arm. Intuitively I would be required to bear fairly significant costs—breaking my other arm, perhaps, if that were necessary—to protect that person's arm. This is further evidence that, once there is reasonable awareness of risk Y, there is no normative difference between risk X and risk Y so far as the existence of a duty to take reasonable preventative measures is concerned.

Consider now *justified risks*—risks which it is not wrongful to impose. One reason why a risk may be justifiable is that, while reasonably foreseeable as beyond a remote possibility, the risk is insubstantial and there is some benefit to the risk-imposer or others in imposing the risk. If the risk materialises, however, it may now be that the risk is *substantial*. Given the above argument, there now appears to be no reason why a duty would not arise to take significant protective measures in relation to that substantial risk. There is a small risk of my new car's engine failing while driving, with the result that others are exposed to a small risk of serious bodily injury. The small risk is nonetheless justifiable to impose. If the risk materialises, however, and a person is injured, I now owe them a duty to take potentially costly steps to protect them from further harm risked by the materialisation of the justifiable risk.

Consider now risks which are justified by a permission, such as self-defence:

> *Defence.* B poses a culpable threat to A, such that A is at serious risk of suffering a very serious bodily injury, without justification. A's only way of preventing B's threat is to push B away into a swimming pool. A knows that there is a significant risk that B's head will strike the edge of the swimming pool. Suppose it is necessary and proportionate to impose this risk. B's head strikes the edge and B will die without medical attention. A does nothing to assist B. B dies.

It is submitted that A owes B a duty to take reasonable steps to protect B from the harmful consequences of the risk imposed by A. To see this, consider A's duty towards B during the attack. Suppose that A has two possible defensive options: (1) A impales B with a stake, causing B's certain death, (2) A imposes a significant risk of B drowning, but A will endure a scuffle with B causing bruising to A. Killing B ((1)) is unnecessary since there is a much less harmful means of defence, albeit one which imposes a small cost on A ((2)). The necessity limitation on permissible defence—that one must use a less harmful means of defence so long as this is not overly burdensome to the defender—itself implies, then, that one has a duty to protect an attacker from excessive harm. It is possible to be liable in tort when one inflicts harm that goes beyond the necessity condition, without reasonable care.[64] Once A has harmed B, albeit innocently, it is, then, plausible to think that A has a duty to take reasonable care to protect B from harm. This duty, however, may not be as stringent as the other duties which arise from the creation of innocent risks. That is, it may only require A to take very low-cost measures to protect B from harm, such that A would not be required to take a step which posed a non-minimal risk of harm to A. This reflects the fact that A's causal responsibility for the risk (while present) is diminished, given B's much greater causal responsibility and culpability for the occurrence of the risk. In cases in which A and B are both entirely innocent, but A is exceptionally permitted to harm B to protect A's own interests, A may be required to take on more significant burdens to protect B from further harm. Notably, in such cases A is generally required to compensate even for the initial justified harm.[65]

It is true that the existence of a legal duty to take reasonable steps to prevent a worsening of an innocent invasion of, or risk to, another's interests may disincentivise justified, desirable, conduct, such as the eviction of a violent tenant, as in *Mitchell.* So long as it is borne in mind that the stringency of such a duty should be relatively minimal, however, this risk can reasonably be countenanced.

So far the argument has been that if one accepts the justifiability of the general N-duty in relation to risks of one's own creation, one ought also to accept the *Innocent Risk Principle.* It might still reasonably be asked what justifies the general N-duty. Why are we duty-bound, without more, to respond to risks of our own creation? First, in part, the value of other people's lives mandates certain protective measures. Second, the distinctive disvalue of being harmfully involved—in the sense generally picked out by *W5*—in another's life. Third, in relation to risks posed by our bodies and resources, we are typically better placed than others to protect people from those risks, and have reason to object to others having wide-ranging general permissions to intervene to mitigate those risks. Fourth, we can typically plan around risks of our own creation, and thus incorporate them into our plans in ways which are not possible with risks not of our creation. The risks posed by a vehicle are risks one chooses to impose in a particular activity.

(a) Other Torts

The discussion so far has focussed mainly on negligence. It is suggested a general principle can be formulated for other torts:

> If A has caused a state of affairs which is wrongful to B at *t* unless a fact F obtains,
>
> F obtains at *t*, *but*
>
> At $t + n$, F no longer obtains, *and*

[64] See, eg, *Gilchrist v Chief Constable of Greater Manchester Police* [2019] EWHC 1233 (QB) [118] and *Flint v Motor Insurers Bureau* [2015] EWHC 466 (QB), [2015] 1 WLR 4370 [39].

[65] *Vincent v Lake Erie Transportation Co* (1910) 124 NW 221.

A is still causally responsible for the state of affairs at t +n, *then*
A commits the wrong at $t+n$.

Suppose, for example, that A imprisons B at t and this is lawful imprisonment (because justified by F). Suppose further that this lawful justification falls away at $t + n$, but A is still causally responsible for the imprisonment. A then falsely imprisons B. So, if the cell door is stuck when a prisoner is due to be released, the prison should be liable in false imprisonment. Unlike in negligence, the prison does not merely have a duty to take reasonable care to release the prisoner upon their release. The imprisonment is simply wrongful if there is no justification for it. This reflects the different duties in torts: the duty in false imprisonment is a duty not to imprison without justification. When the justification falls away at $t + n$, the duty is being breached. The result may seem harsh, but it is no more harsh than the initial strict nature of the duty at t.

2. Interference

The category of case under discussion in this section can be broadly characterised thus:[66]

(i) A non-wrongfully does something at t
(ii) A knows or ought to know at t or $t + n$ that A's act has significantly increased or will significantly increase the probability that B will be worse off with respect to B's right-protected interests, than if A or A's resources had not been present at t, by preventing those interests being protected from harm by B, C, an object not belonging to A, or an event.

Suppose, for example, that the zip of A's jacket non-negligently rips a life jacket while A is taking a trip on C's boat. A decides not to tell C or anyone else. Later that day, B drowns in an accident due to the defect in the life jacket. The basic idea is that there is a duty to take reasonable measures when one's act raises or has raised the probability of preventing a harm-preventative causal chain.

It might seem to follow immediately from the discussion of creation of risk that B owes a duty in the life jacket example: B faces a greater risk of death than B would have faced but for the presence of A's body or resources. It is true that but for A's act, B would have been subject to a lesser probability of death. This is how the

[66] The 'interference' name is stolen from N McBride and R Bagshaw, *Tort Law* (6th edn, Pearson 2018) ch 6.4. The content of the principle articulated in the text differs, however, from theirs.

US Restatement now (unlike in the Second Restatement) deals with the issue: it is treated as a sub-species of duty based on creation of risk.[67]

In the final section, I will show that, in general, there are no normatively important differences between being implicated in harm through creation of risk and through preventing the prevention of harm. This being so, even if there are conceptual differences between the two kinds of involvement in harm, one need not be concerned about them. Nonetheless, interference with harm-preventive causal chains raises non-obvious issues about what constitutes interference such as to generate a P-duty. For this reason, and because such cases have sometimes been treated as a distinctive category, I will treat them separately. It bears emphasis, though, that there is no pressing need to identify whether a case is properly classified as 'creation of risk' or 'interference'.

(i) Interference: The Law

English law is broadly consistent with the proposition that if A does something non-wrongfully, and later reasonably ought to know that this will raise or has raised the probability of B's right-protected interests being worse than they would be but for the presence of A and A's resources, through preventing B from obtaining assistance, then A has a duty to take reasonable steps to prevent the harm to B.

However, this result has typically been reached on the basis either that (1) A created a *new* risk to B, or (2) A assumed responsibility to B. Less typically, the result has been reached on the basis of (3) interference as an apparently distinctive duty principle.

Consider (1). *Capital and Counties* v *Hampshire* illustrates the point.[68] In this case, the defendant fire brigade attended the claimant's property to fight a fire. In doing so, they turned off the sprinklers. This was itself held to be in breach of a duty of care: the defendant had 'by their action in turning off the sprinklers, created or increased the danger'.[69] The duty breached was conceived as the general duty not to create unreasonable risk of damage. It was not conceived as a distinct duty to take care not to prevent or interfere with a source of aid—the sprinkler system. Suppose that the initial act of turning off the sprinklers had been justifiable for some reason, but nonetheless imposed a substantial risk of worsening the claimant's position. Given that the act was conceived as introducing a new risk, it is likely that the *Innocent Risk Principle* would then entail a duty to take reasonable steps to protect against this risk.

[67] *Restatement of Torts* (n 58).
[68] *Capital & Counties* (n 7).
[69] ibid 1042.

Consider (2). *Kent v Griffiths* is an example.[70] The claimant had an asthma attack. Her attending GP called for an ambulance, requesting it come immediately to transfer the claimant to hospital. The operator affirmed that this request had been accepted. After the claimant's husband called again, the operator repeated that the request had been accepted and said 'give them another 7 or 8 minutes'.[71] Further delay ensued. But for the careless delay in the ambulance arriving, the claimant would have avoided a damaging respiratory arrest. If no undertaking had been given that an ambulance would come, the claimant's husband would have driven the claimant to hospital, where she would have arrived earlier than she did. Lord Woolf MR held that '[t]he acceptance of the call in this case established the duty of care. On the findings of the judge it was delay which caused the further injuries. If wrong information had not been given about the arrival of the ambulance, other means of transport could have been used.'[72]

This passage is ambiguous. The first part suggests that the duty to take reasonable care in the provision of an ambulance is created by a promise that the ambulance would come. The second part focusses not on the promise, but upon the fact that wrong information was given. The promise itself is not wrong information. This makes it unclear whether the duty arose in *Kent* because: (1) a promise was made (*per se*), (2) the fact that the promise was made increased the probability that another person (the claimant's husband) would not provide assistance to the claimant, or (3) the fact that wrong information was given increased the probability that another person would not provide assistance to the claimant. Given that Lord Woolf drew an analogy with the duty of a hospital doctor, which clearly does not depend upon (2) or (3), it seems more likely to have been (1), or each was regarded as independently sufficient for a duty.[73] On the facts of *Kent*, it was possible to avoid reliance upon a distinct duty principle of interference (if one exists), since an assumption of responsibility was found.

Consider now (3), evidence for a distinct duty principle based upon prevention of or interference with aid. Some support is provided by *Transport Arendonk v Chief Constable of Essex Police*.[74] A lorry driver was arrested and taken into custody, having been tested as over the alcohol limit when driving. The driver told the police that he was not permitted to leave the lorry and had to telephone his employer. The arresting officers did not allow this. Despite noticing a rip in the side of the lorry's curtain, the officers recorded that the lorry was left in the layby in a secure condition. The key to the lorry was confiscated at the time of the arrest or at the police station. Thieves stole goods from the lorry and the lorry owners were liable to the owners of these goods. Laing J considered that it was arguable—the

[70] [2001] QB 36 (CA), [2000] 2 WLR 1158.
[71] ibid [4].
[72] ibid [49] (Lord Woolf MR).
[73] ibid [52]–[53] (Lord Woolf MR). See further Chapters 4 and 5 on choice-based duties.
[74] [2020] EWHC 212 (QB), [2020] RTR 22.

issue being whether the claim should be struck out as disclosing no reasonable prospect of success as a matter of law—that the police had a duty of care to secure the lorry on the basis that they 'took steps which prevented others from keeping the lorry safe'.[75]

In *HXA v Surrey County Council*, Deputy Master Bagot QC considered whether a local authority was under a duty of care when it investigated allegations of child abuse against the claimants because it had 'prevent[ed] others from protecting the claimant', and treated this as a distinctive exception to the position that one is not under a duty in relation to a pure omission.[76] On the facts, the judge found that there was no reasonable prospect of establishing that another protective agency would have intervened had the defendant not commenced investigation.[77]

The Court of Appeal decision in *Tindall v Chief Constable of Thames Valley Police* might be considered to have rejected a principle based on interference with aid.[78] A vehicle came off the road due to black ice on the road surface. The driver, injured, exited the car and warned other drivers to slow down their approach. He called the police, emphasising the dangerous condition of the road. The police attended and called an ambulance which took the driver to hospital. They put up a warning sign, cleared up the accident, removed the warning sign, and did nothing further. About one hour later, Mr Tindall was killed in a head-on collision with another vehicle which went out of control on contact with the ice. At first instance, the judge refused to strike out the claim in respect of Mr Tindall's death against the police because it was arguable that an emergency service which 'attends, takes control, and changes the situation such as by removing someone who is warning traffic, or where it renders the situation safer by their signage but then positively decides to remove that signage, . . . may have crossed the line and assumed a duty of care under the current state of the law'.[79]

The Court of Appeal allowed the defendant's appeal. It was accepted that, but for the arrival of the police, the driver would have continued to warn other drivers of the presence of ice and the need to slow down:[80]

> For the purposes of this appeal the Chief Constable accepts that, but for the arrival of the police, Mr Kendall [the first driver] would have continued his attempts to alert other road users. For her part, the Claimant accepts that it was simply the arrival of the police on the scene that influenced Mr Kendall to go in the ambulance. The police did not say or do anything (either directly to Mr Kendall or

[75] ibid [90].
[76] [2021] EWHC 250 (QB) [35]. For this principle in Canada, see *Goodwin v Mainroad North Island Contracting Ltd.* (2007), 237 BCAC 129 (CA), 2007 BCCA 81.
[77] [2021] EWHC 250 (QB) [35].
[78] [2022] EWCA Civ 25.
[79] [2020] EWHC 837 [16]–[17].
[80] [2022] EWCA Civ 25 [8].

> generally) to encourage him to stop his attempts or to go in the ambulance; still less did they direct or in any way coerce him to stop what he was doing or to leave.

The essence of the reasoning against a duty of care was that the police's conduct did not amount to making matters worse.[81] On the face of it, this is difficult to reconcile with the supposition that, but for the arrival of the police, Mr Kendall would have continued to warn, and the absence of evidence that this continued warning would have been ineffective. The idea, however, seems to be that, although the police's conduct was, or may have been, a but-for condition of the worsening of the situation—on the assumption that Mr Kendall would have successfully warned the deceased of the ice—their presence did not *legally cause* the worsening of the situation.[82] The police did not *make* the situation worse, but merely constituted a background condition of its worsening. Hence Stuart-Smith LJ's point that the police did not 'in any way coerce' Mr Kendall to stop his efforts: had they done so, his decision to leave would have been attributable to them. Essentially, the issue is when one person's decision to discontinue aid is reasonably attributable to another; *Tindall* merely affirms that a but-for connection is insufficient. It does not, therefore, rule out the existence of a duty based on interference with aid. Arguably, however, *Tindall* is too restrictive in what it counts as reasonably attributable to the putative interferer. As the next sub-section explains, it should not be a requirement that A does something which generates a right in C that A assist B, for instance, an assumption of responsibility. The fact that the police did not assume a responsibility to Mr Kendall to protect road-users should not be decisive since the gist of the claim is that the police made matters worse with respect to other road-users' bodily integrity.

(a) Scope of Duties in Respect of Interference

Preventing Use of One's Own Resources

There is no general duty on A not to prevent C from assisting B by refusing to allow C to use A's resources. In *Soldano v O'Daniels*, a man was shot in a bar. An employee of the bar crossed the street to a restaurant and requested to use the restaurant's public phone to call the police, explaining that a man had been shot; the request was refused.[83] A wrongful death suit was brought against the restaurant owner. The California Court of Appeal held that there was a tortious duty to allow the use of the phone. It accepted, however, that the facts did *not* fall within §327 of the Second Restatement of Torts ('Prevention of Assistance by Third Persons').[84]

[81] See ibid [66]: 'I therefore reject the submission that the police made matters worse by reference to the departure of Mr Kendall.'

[82] See again ibid [66]. An alternative reading that there was no factual basis for the conclusion that the police made things worse is not tenable.

[83] 141 Cal App 3d 443, 190 Cal Rptr 310 (1983).

[84] It noted that the facts 'very nearly' fell within this: ibid 452–53.

A duty to permit the use of one's resources by a third party comes very close to a duty of easy rescue: one is being required to make a person better off than if one's body or resources had not been present.

Preventing Other People from Helping

It is not obvious exactly what kind of interference ought to trigger a duty to take reasonable steps. It cannot be enough that one's presence is or risks being a but-for cause of another person not helping a person. Consider:

> *Two People.* B suffers a heart attack late at night on a quiet street. C is across the street from B, but does not intervene because he sees A, on the same side of the street to B, and assumes, simply on the basis of A's proximity, that A will intervene. C shouts to A 'this is your problem - you've got to help, you're closest'.

Here A's being proximate to B was a but-for cause of C's not intervening to assist, and A came to know this. In a system which does not accept the existence of a duty of easy rescue simply on grounds of physical proximity, it would be difficult to accept that another person's not intervening on the basis of a belief that physical proximity generates a duty to assist in fact creates such a duty. In general terms, the fact that others did not intervene simply because they believed in facts about a person that would only generate a duty of easy rescue in that person cannot foist a duty upon that person. Likewise, the *mere fact* that others believe one will intervene should not be sufficient, absent some non-minimal responsibility for these beliefs.

If, however, A *promises* C that A will protect B from physical harm, and this foreseeably raises the probability that B will not be protected from physical harm, this seems to be sufficient to generate a P-duty in A. In *Sherratt v Chief Constable of Great Manchester Police*, the police (A) promised a mother (C) that the police would check on her daughter (B) who had severe mental health problems. Relying upon this promise, the mother did not herself attend her daughter's home.[85] The daughter had overdosed and died. The police were held to owe a duty of care on the basis that there was an assumption of responsibility and reliance by the mother on that assumption. Unlike in *Two People*, the mother's non-intervention was not based simply on a belief that the police were well-placed to help: it was based on the assurance given.

An assurance cannot be a necessary condition of a duty arising in cases involving prevention of a third person from helping, however. Suppose the police arrest a mother whose young child is home alone. When the police know or ought to know this fact, they surely have a duty to take reasonable steps to protect

[85] [2018] EWHC 1746 (QB), [2019] PIQR P1.

the child from physical harm. A narrow basis for this duty is the interference with the performance of the mother's duty to the child. This might be taken to suggest that the distinguishing feature between *Two People* and *Sherratt* and the case in this paragraph is the interference with the performance of a *duty*. If A prevents C from performing C's duty to B, then A is plausibly under a duty to take reasonable steps to prevent B's position from being worsened. Conversely, if A deprives B of something to which B had no right from C, it might seem obscure how A could violate B's rights in doing so: how could depriving B of something to which B had no entitlement wrong B? The answer is that the reasons why B does not have an entitlement against C do not necessarily entail that B has no entitlement against A. Quite simply, this is because B's only right against C will be a positive right, and B generally has no positive rights of assistance against C. By contrast, B *does* have a general right that others take care not to worsen B's position with respect to B's general right-protected interests. So if A locks a police officer, C, in a cupboard to prevent the police officer from helping B, this should trigger a P-duty in A, even if C had no private law duty to assist B. Likewise, if A's dog prevents a life-saving tree branch from making its way into B's grasp, A should be under a duty to take reasonable steps in response.

Prevention and Inaction

Consider a variant on *Soldano v Daniels*. Suppose that the restaurant proprietor had been willing to allow use of the phone, but a large person, despite the emergency situation being explained to him, refused to move out of the way of the entrance to the restaurant, blocking access to the telephone. In this variant, the continued presence of the large person's body in its location makes it more probable that the harmed person will be worse off than if the large person had not been present. This distinguishes the example from a standard failure to assist a stranger. The large person's initially moving to the location innocently raised the probability of a person being made physically worse off. For this reason, the refusal to move absent a reasonable ground ought to constitute the breach of a duty to the person needing assistance.

If literally standing in the way of a rescue triggers a duty to remove one's obstruction or more, if one's obstruction has made the situation worse, it might be objected that this leads to the counterintuitive proliferation of duties and liabilities. Whenever a person occupies a role, it is possible that taking up the role prevented another person from occupying the role, and that person might have performed the role non-carelessly. For instance, in *Kent*, the ambulance operator ought to have known that, if he or she did not perform the role carefully, there is a risk that their taking up the role will make others worse off than if they had not done so. Can we think of occupying the role as akin to standing in front of the restaurant, blocking assistance? Clearly, not always: it depends upon whether there is a reasonably foreseeable prospect that one's failure to perform the role carefully enhances the probability of harm relative to had another person been in the role. Depending on the time between the occupation of the role and the specific conduct alleged to be careless, the evidential difficulties in pursuing this argument (particularly in relation to causation) may be insuperable. In principle, however, the argument is cogent.[86]

Liability Limited to Worsening

A difficult issue is the significance of whether the defendant's interference actually worsened the victim's position. Suppose that, in *Sherratt*, the mother had not believed the assurance given by the police, travelled to her daughter's home anyway, but had been killed in a car accident before arriving at her daughter's house. In this instance, the police reasonably ought to have believed that their assurance raised the probability that the daughter would suffer harm. If so, it would seem that they ought to have taken reasonable steps, and those reasonable steps would have prevented the daughter's death. It transpired, in this variant, however, that the assurance in fact made things no worse. It is suggested that liability in damages should reflect this fact. The explanation of why one has reason not to interfere with assistance is the prospect of depriving someone of the avoidance of harm. If that prospect has not materialised, the reasons which justify the duty do not support substantial liability. It is a separate question whether the assurance to do X, as was given in *Sherratt*, should give rise to a free-standing P-duty in tort to take care to do X.[87]

(ii) Interference: Justification

This section considers the issue of whether the law needs a distinctive principle of 'interference'. The answer given is that interference could be subsumed within 'creation of risk' if the latter concept is understood as raising the probability of harm relative to the absence of a person's body and resources. It is shown that this subsumption would not occlude normatively important distinctions. Nonetheless, it is useful to consider 'interference' as grouping together specific instances of creation of risk.

Consider first whether interference could be assimilated to duties arising from an assumption of responsibility. One might argue that, in all of the cases discussed, the defendant 'assumed a responsibility' to assist the claimant. This, however, does violence to accepted principles governing assumptions of responsibility. For

[86] The mere fact of passage of time between the initial act of interference and the subsequent injury is not normatively important: in the zip-rip example, it surely makes no difference if the zip rip happened years before the accident, if the rip was not obvious to a reasonable observer.

[87] As to which, see Chapters 4 and 5.

instance, in *Arendonk* and *Tindall*, a reasonable person would not understand the defendant to be undertaking a task *for the claimant*. There was no antecedent connection at all between the defendant and the driver killed in *Tindall*. Even more obviously, in the zip rip example given at the beginning of this section, there is nothing describable as an assumption of responsibility.[88]

Consider the claim that interference could be subsumed within the creation of danger category. If A is said to create a risk of danger when A's conduct at *t* causes B to be at greater risk of damage than B would have been had A's body and property not been present at *t*, then the categories perfectly overlap. In *Tindall*, for example, the police's taking the driver to the hospital was a but-for condition of the deceased being at greater risk of damage than he would have faced had the police not so acted: the driver would have remained to warn other drivers. So, unlike with assumption of responsibility, it is at least *possible* to group these instances of liability in the same category.

The thornier question is whether this would be desirable. It would be undesirable if there are important normative differences between the two situations and these differences impact upon the existence or nature of the duties. It would also be undesirable if the unified description were linguistically awkward. Conversely, it would be desirable if there were no such differences or, perhaps, if the difficulty of distinguishing between creation of risk cases and interference cases is likely to lead to unpredictable results.

Here is an argument why the division is desirable. Consider:

> *Ambulance*. D is stationary at red traffic lights. An ambulance approaches carrying C, who is in critical condition, with every minute substantially decreasing C's chance of survival from a brain tumour. D does not move from the lights to allow the ambulance through until the lights are green.

Here it is true that, had D or D's resources not been present, C would have had a better chance of survival. If creation of risk is defined in terms of counterfactual risk increase, relative to this baseline, then D creates a risk to C. But it seems awkward to describe D as creating a risk to C here. It is more natural to say that D's failure to move causes C's pre-existing risk—the risk constituted by the brain tumour—to be prevented from being alleviated. So, there is linguistic awkwardness in grouping all cases within creation of risk.

In many cases, there seems, however, to be no normatively important difference between being involved in a harm through 'direct' creation of risk and 'indirect' creation of risk—the latter being preventing the prevention of harm. Suppose one can impose a probability of 10% physical harm to a person's body either through

[88] See further ibid.

damaging a person's brake cables (risking preventing the prevention of harm) *or* through colliding with the person in one's car. It seems odd to think that one ought to take greater precautions against, or otherwise be more morally attentive to, one probability of harm rather than the other.

There is one puzzling category of case in which it may seem that interference is morally distinctive. Suppose that, after a shipwreck, there is one plank of wood which is available to serve as a raft. Unfortunately, there are two people, A and B, who need it to survive and it will only bear the weight of one. It might be considered intuitively permissible for A to occupy the raft, thereby leading to B's death. Here, A prevents the prevention of B's death. Conversely, it might seem intuitively unjustifiable for A to save A's own life by directly creating a risk to B: for instance, suppose that A knows that if A drives to hospital for life-saving treatment, A's unsafe car will veer out of control and kill B, after which A will then be able to walk the remaining distance to the hospital. Nor would it be permissible for A to toss a coin in the second example and only drive to the hospital if A wins the toss. It seems unclear, however, whether the difference in these two situations is truly a difference between direct creation of risk and preventing the prevention of harm. Suppose that A knows that A's driving to hospital for life-saving treatment will dislodge a boulder that will kill B. Here A removes a barrier to the protection of B. The action still seems impermissible.[89]

If there is substantive normative unity between direct creation of risk and interference, and only linguistic awkwardness in subsuming the categories, it seems best to think of interference as a sub-species of creation of risk. As the discussion in the second half of the chapter has shown, there are non-obvious issues as to when a person's interfering conduct should trigger a duty, and these issues cannot be resolved directly by the concept of 'creation of risk'.

3. Conclusions

This chapter has focussed on two facts which are treated, or are in the process of becoming treated, in the current law as special facts which exceptionally generate P-duties. Under the version of the making worse versus not making things better distinction defended in Chapter 1, these cases do not involve genuine P-duties. In these cases, A is being required to take steps which are not likely to improve B's position compared to the position that B would be in had A and A's resources (and the causal effects of A and A's resources) not been present at the time of the conduct that generates liability. I have explained that these duties are indeed closely

[89] If this paragraph is incorrect, it would be necessary to recognise a distinctive enclave of liability rules concerning permissible competition between persons in need for unowned resources necessary to save a person's body from harm.

connected to general N-duties not to cause damage by creating unreasonable risk and not to cause damage by unreasonably interfering with harm-preventors. The main difference is simply temporal: the general N-duty requires risk-reducing measures to be taken before or at the time of the risk-creation, while the duties in this chapter require risk-reducing measures to be taken *after* the risk-creation.[90]

[90] For the same conclusion in relation to creation of risk, see A Beever, *Rediscovering the Law of Negligence* (Hart 2007) 324 (comparing cases where a defendant negligently creates an initial risk and where he negligently fails to reduce a risk already (innocently) created by him: the defendant is liable in both situations).

4

Assumptions of Responsibility: Part 1—The Law

Like contract, trust, and fiduciary law, tort claims to recognise legal duties that arise by choices to incur them. These duties are triggered by the special fact of 'assumption of responsibility'. At an abstract level, the idea seems relatively straightforward. On the one hand, there is an important value in each of us having the capacity to hold rights that others carefully assist us, since the preservation and promotion of our fundamental interests often depends upon the careful interventions of others. On the other, the objection that positive duties unduly interfere with freedom has a clear answer here: the duty-bearer *chose* to incur the duty. Such duties meet an important need, and do so in a way that is compatible with the freedom of others.

Yet while the basic normative logic of positive duties arising from choices is intelligible, it is far more difficult to pin down exactly when in tort a person will be said to have 'assumed responsibility', and, on analysis, doubts begin to emerge as to whether the law reflects the basic idea that the duties are 'chosen' rather than 'imposed'.[1]

The chapter seeks to demonstrate the existence of four strands of 'assumption of responsibility'.[2] What unites the strands is that a person has a certain measure of voluntary control over the circumstances which trigger the duty; the P-duty arises in each when they choose to do a certain action, such as making a promise or taking possession of another's thing. In this respect, these P-duties differ from those arising from innocent risks whose occurrence one could not reasonably prevent.[3] The importance of distinguishing the strands, however, is that each has importantly different requirements and a normative distinctiveness from the others.[4]

[1] On the possibility that there may not be a set of necessary and sufficient conditions for what counts as an assumption of responsibility, see R Bagshaw, 'Tort Law, Concepts, and What Really Matters' in A Robertson and H W Tang (eds), *The Goals of Private Law* (Hart 2009) 248.

[2] The general idea of deconstructing 'assumption of responsibility' is not new. For a different deconstruction, with a sceptical conclusion, see K Barker, 'Unreliable Assumptions in the Modern Law of Negligence' (1993) 109 Law Quarterly Review 461. See also *HXA v Surrey County Council* [2023] UKSC 52, at [90] (Lord Burrows and Lord Stephens): 'The precise ingredients of an assumption of responsibility appear to vary according to the general context in which it is being used.'

[3] See Chapter 3.

[4] Compare Barker (n 2). For a view that sees considerably more unity in the law on 'assumption of responsibility', see D Nolan, 'Assumption of Responsibility: Four Questions' (2019) 72 Current Legal Problems 123.

Omissions in Tort Law. Sandy Steel, Oxford University Press. © Sandy Steel 2024.
DOI: 10.1093/9780191898822.003.0004

Having described the four strands, the chapter considers two alternative, more unified, accounts of assumption of responsibility—the bare promise account and the taking on a task account. It rejects these. The next companion chapter considers various justificatory issues surrounding assumptions of responsibility.

1. Four Strands of Assumption of Responsibility

(i) Assumption of Responsibility as an Instantiation of *Innocent Risk* or Interference

In some cases, when 'assumption of responsibility' is invoked, the P-duty which arises can be explained simply on the basis that the promise creates a foreseeable risk of physical harm. By inducing another person reasonably not to take protective measures in relation to a risk, a promise can be a dangerous act. In this way, the P-duty can be explained by the *Innocent Risk* or *Interference* principles examined in the last chapter: by making a promise, one person creates a risk that the addressee of the promise will not take protective measures which the addressee otherwise would have done in relation to right-protected interests. This can be more accurately expressed in the following two principles:

> Principle 1 ('P1'): If A promises B that A will take steps to prevent the materialisation of a risk of harm to B protected by a general right, and A knows or ought to know that there is a substantial possibility that B will act on the basis that this promise will be fulfilled and thereby not take steps to prevent the materialisation of the risk, then A will have a duty to B to take reasonable care to fulfil the promise, or otherwise take care that B is not in a worse position than had the promise not been made.[5]

> Principle 2 ('P2'): If A promises C that A will protect B from a risk of harm protected by a general right, and A knows or ought to know that there is a substantial possibility that C will act on the basis of this promise being fulfilled and thereby not take steps to protect B, then A will be under a duty to B to take reasonable care to fulfil the promise, or otherwise take care that B is not in a worse position than had the promise not been made.

[5] For a similar articulation of a central strand of assumption of responsibility, see P Sales, 'Pure Economic Loss in Tort' in K Burns and others (eds), *Torts on Three Continents* (OUP, 2024); A Fagan, 'The Contract-delict Interface and Harm-causing Omissions' (2021) Acta Juridica 203.

Consider P1.[6] *Welsh v Chief Constable of Merseyside Police* is illustrative.[7] A Crown Prosecution Service (CPS) solicitor agreed with the claimant's solicitor to inform the Magistrates' Court that the claimant's charges had earlier been considered in sentencing in the Crown Court. In reliance upon this assurance, the claimant did not attend his bail hearing for those offences in the Magistrates' Court and was consequently arrested. It was held to be highly arguable that the CPS solicitor was under a duty to take care to inform the Magistrates' Court, in virtue of the assurance that they would do so.[8] Here, then, there was a promise to take steps whose effect would foreseeably be to prevent the risk of imprisonment, and a reasonable person would know that the effect of this promise was likely to be that the claimant would not seek to take risk-prevention measures himself. Similarly, in *Parramatta City Council v Lutz*, the Supreme Court of New South Wales held that a local council was under a P-duty to take reasonable steps to prevent the occurrence of a fire nearby the claimant's property, when it had assured her that it would imminently do so and that she need not take such steps herself.[9] She recovered damages for the cost of reinstating her property which was damaged by the fire.

Under this principle, the P-duty which arises is a duty to take reasonable care to protect the claimant from worsening of their general right-related interests. This can be discharged by performance of the promise, but also by taking care that the promise being made does not have this effect.[10] Suppose, for instance, that the council in *Lutz* had, seconds after assuring the plaintiff that it would perform the works, informed her that it would not in fact be doing so. In these circumstances, there would be no risk reasonably attributable to the promise that the promise would make the plaintiff worse off in relation to her general right-protected interests. If, however, the only way in which the promisor can prevent the promisee

[6] A 'promise' is held to constitute a sufficient 'undertaking' under §42 ('Duty Based on an Undertaking') in the *Restatement of Torts (Third): Liability for Physical and Emotional Harm*, vol 2 (American Law Institute 2010), but this only gives rise to liability when the promise is relied upon or creates a risk: §42(b).

[7] [1993] 1 All ER 692.

[8] ibid 703.

[9] (1988) 12 NSWLR 293. This was the basis of the decision adopted by Kirby P and Mahoney JA; McHugh JA based the decision on 'general reliance'. If there is an agreement between the parties whose terms make clear that A is not promising to take reasonable care in relation to matter, then this disapplies P1: see, eg, *Great Lakes Reinsurance (UK) plc v RAV Bahamas Ltd* [2024] UKPC 11.

[10] In some cases, the promisor will be required to take care to continue performance of the promised service if resiling from performance will make the promisee worse off than if the promise had not been made. Reasonable care does not entail a guarantee of continued performance, however: the promisor's interests may sometimes justify non-continuance and payment of compensation instead. Essentially the same problem arises in deciding when a promise to confer a proprietary interest will be enforced under the doctrine of proprietary estoppel, albeit the law has taken the view that enforcement is possible even when this is not necessary fully to protect the promisee from being worse off than if the promise had not been made: *Guest v Guest* [2022] UKSC 27, [2022] 3 WLR 911. The minority view of Lord Leggatt is essentially a version of P1.

being worse off is by performing the promised service, there is in principle a duty to do so.[11]

Consider now P2. The British Columbia case of *Goodwin v Mainroad North Island Contracting Co* is illustrative.[12] The defendant highway (A) contractor assured the police (C) that A would send out a crew or contact the local council about a report of black ice on a highway. A did nothing and the claimant, B, was physically injured when her car slid off the road due to the ice. The Court of Appeal for British Columbia held that A was under a P-duty to B in virtue of the assurance to C since 'having said it would dispatch a crew to Quinsam Road, it must be taken to have known the RCMP would not call the District and that users of the road could be harmed if it simply did nothing and alerted no-one'.[13]

The same principle appears to be relied upon in English law in *Sherratt v Chief Constable of Manchester Police*.[14] It will be recalled that the police assured the deceased's mother, who had called 999, that the police would immediately attend the deceased's house and arrange, if necessary, her daughter's transfer to hospital. The daughter committed suicide. King J held that a duty of care arose by virtue of an assumption of responsibility for the deceased's welfare coupled with detrimental reliance by her mother, who did not seek to check on her daughter herself or otherwise seek alternative means of transferring her daughter to hospital.[15] The promise made by the police (A) to the mother (C) created a risk that the latter would not take measures to prevent physical harm to her daughter (B).

It might be tempting to say that P1 and P2 are entailments of a single, broader principle, P3:

> Principle 3 ('P3'): A is under a duty to take reasonable care owed to B, to fulfil a promise made by A (whether to B or C), whenever the failure to fulfil the promise will foreseeably increase the probability that B will be worse off than if the promise had not been made.

But P3 is clearly too broad as a descriptive matter. It implies, for instance, that the parties to an employment relationship have a duty of care to each others' families to fulfil their contract so as to protect the family members from economic loss. This is not the case. More generally, it fails in cases of so-called relational economic

[11] In *Lejonvarn v Burgess* [2017] EWCA Civ 254, the view is stated that a tortious assumption of responsibility cannot generate a positive duty to provide a service, on pain of trespassing on contract [88]–[89]; there is no trespass, however, when the duty arises as means of preventing the right-holder from being worse off than if the promise had not been made.

[12] (2007) 237 BCAC 129 (CA), 2007 BCCA 81.

[13] ibid [30].

[14] [2018] EWHC 1746 (QB), [2019] PIQR P1. See also the discussion in Chapter 3, section 2.

[15] [2018] EWHC 1746 [80], [84]: 'the assurances given to the Mother and reliance by the Mother in leaving it thereafter to the police, in particular as regards getting her daughter to hospital if necessary, as she had been told, was sufficient to impose on the police a duty of care for the welfare of her daughter, owed to the daughter.'

loss when A breaches a promise made to C, with negative effect on the finances of B, who is in a legal relationship of some kind with C. Generally, A does not owe B a duty in these circumstances.[16]

The explanatory failure of P3 in certain cases of pure economic loss is instructive. It supports the view that P1 and P2 are entailments, not of P3, but of the general tort N-duties in relation to bodily injury, psychiatric injury, and property damage. That is, P1 and P2 identify cases in which *Interference* or *Creation of a Risk* apply. In *Goodwin*, for instance, Newbury J observed: 'In reliance on this statement, the RCMP reasonably assumed it was not necessary to call anyone else, i.e., the District of Campbell River . . . In this sense Mainroad may be said to 'have increased the risk' to which members of the driving public such as Ms. Goodwin were subject.' Similarly, *Sherratt* can reasonably be considered a special case of the *Interference Principle*, since the promise made to the mother is simply one way in which the police could interfere with the aid that would otherwise have been provided to the daughter.[17] For instance, a duty should also arise if the police had arrested the mother and knew that this would prevent her from helping her daughter; this shows that a promise is merely one way in which a person can endanger another.[18]

Notice that, under P1 and P2, there is no need for the duty-bearer to have actually commenced performance of their promise. The fact that the making of the promise foreseeably risks damage to a general right is sufficient. This is not necessarily inconsistent with the proposition that a mere promise to do a future act is unenforceable in tort.[19] It is the fact that the promise foreseeably risks harm to a general right-protected interest that generates the P-duty, not the promise alone. However, it is important to be clear that there is no requirement of 'entry' into performance of the promise under P1 or P2.[20] The statement that an assumption of responsibility always requires an undertaking of a service in the sense of a commencement of a performance for another, coupled with an undertaking that the service will be performed with care (a promise that care will be taken), is not correct.[21]

It might be objected that P1 and P2 are still too broad as statements of the existing law since neither draws a contrast between 'informal' or 'social' promises and promises made in a 'professional' context. In the context of damage to *general*

[16] Such a duty may exceptionally arise when *the purpose* of A's promised conduct to C is to confer a benefit upon B: *White v Jones* [1995] 2 AC 207.

[17] See Chapter 3 (especially section 2) on interference.

[18] For a structurally parallel case in which A promises C that A will attend to B, with the result that C does not, giving rise to liability, see *Brown v District of Port Edward* [1996] BCJ No 2465 (SC).

[19] For this proposition, see section 2(iii) below.

[20] See also W Seavey, 'Reliance Upon Gratuitous Promises and Other Conduct' (1951) 64 Harvard Law Review 913, 919–21.

[21] For a modern statement which sometimes implies that commencement of performance is necessary, see *N v Poole BC* [2019] UKSC 25, [2020] AC 780 [88]; see further below p. 106.

right-protected interests, it is not clear that such a requirement exists or would be justified, however.[22] So long as a person ought reasonably to know that their promise endangers another's person or property, this ought to trigger a P-duty. If you promise to look after a child for a moment while their parent goes to the bathroom, it should not matter for the purposes of P2 that this is a 'social' occasion—your promise, absent care, endangers the child.

Finally, it should be noted that there is a version of P1 which, unlike P3, does hold in cases of pure economic loss, and which is not, then, explicable as a particular instantiation of a general right. This version requires that B reasonably believe, due to A's conduct, that A is inviting B to rely upon A's promise to take reasonable care in relation to a task, and that A ought reasonably to know that the failure to behave carefully poses a risk of B's being worse off than if the promise had not been made.[23] The existence of a promise *between A and B* or an invitation to act on the basis that another B will do an act carefully generates an entitlement *in B*, but not others, to act on the basis that reasonable care will be taken in relation even to economic interests.[24]

(ii) Assumption of Responsibility as a Duty incurred by Occupation of a Special Relationship with Another

Special relationships are typically described as a source of P-duties in tort.[25] The relationship between 'special relationships' and assumption of responsibility is unclear. Sometimes the ideas are equated such that all special relationships are forms of assumption of responsibility.[26] It is suggested that there is a distinctive strand, however, of 'assumption of responsibility' where A chooses to occupy a relation with B and this itself creates P-duties owed by A to B. Importantly, while A *may* promise B, by choosing to occupy the relation, that A will take reasonable care to protect B from harm, this promise is probably unnecessary—and, even if required, there need not be a change of position on the basis of the promise by B or others.[27]

[22] In relation to pure economic loss, see *Lejonvarn* (n 11).

[23] *Hedley Byrne v Heller* [1964] AC 465 (HL) esp 528–29 (Lord Devlin). See further P Benson, *Justice in Transactions* (Harvard UP 2019) 69–73.

[24] See, again, for an exception, n 16 above.

[25] See, eg, *Hedley Byrne* (n 23) 486 (Lord Reid), 511, 529 (Lord Hodson), 528–29 (Lord Devlin), 539 (Lord Pearce); *Michael v Chief Constable of South Wales* [2015] UKSC 2, [2015] AC 1732 [100] (Lord Toulson); N McBride and R Bagshaw, *Tort Law* (6th edn, Pearson 2018) 87–88.

[26] See, eg, P Giliker 'Is there a Duty to Prevent Harm in Tort? A Common Law Perspective' (2021) 12 Journal of European Tort Law 116, 121–25. Special relationships should also sometimes be considered, not as sources of a P-duty, but as enhancing the stringency of duties that arise from other facts. For instance an employer might be required to do more under the *Innocent Risk Principle* than a stranger.

[27] Consistently with this, the Third Restatement of Torts (n 6) treats 'Duty Based on a Special Relationship' (§40) as a separate category from 'Duty Based on an Undertaking' (§42). Section 40 non-exhaustively lists the following 'special relationships': '(1) a common carrier with its passengers, (2) an innkeeper with its guests, (3) a business or other possessor of land that holds its premises open to the public with those who are lawfully on the premises, (4) an employer with its employees who, while at

Further, these relationships tend to be characterised by the feature that, although entry into the relationship and its constitutive duties is a matter of choice, the content of the legal duties that are incurred are fixed independently, or partly independently, of the parties' choice.

In *Michael*, Lord Toulson gave a 'not exhaustive' list of 'relationships in which a duty to take positive action typically arises: contract, fiduciary relationships, employer and employee, school and pupil, health professional and patient'.[28] It is submitted that the P-duties in these relationships are not entirely explicable by P1 and P2 and constitute a different 'strand' of assumption of responsibility.[29]

(a) School and Pupil

Consider the example of school and pupil, specifically the relation between a teacher employed by a school and a pupil. It is clear that teachers are under P-duties to pupils, both in relation to immediate dangers to the pupil's physical health that arise during school and the identification of educational needs.[30]

It is not impossible to construct an argument based on P2 for a teacher's P-duties. Although individual teachers do not normally make a promise to parents or children, the school, when it accepts a child as a pupil, plausibly thereby promises to take care of the child in relation to the provision of education. It is foreseeable, as a general matter, that parents will rely upon this promise by entrusting the child's safety to the school each day.

Suppose the school *knew*, however, that a child's parents had no interest in the child's welfare and showed no concern about the child's safety. It is hard to accept that this child would *not* be owed a duty since the parents did not change their position on the basis of the school's promise. The courts are unlikely to entertain the argument that the school's promise did not ultimately worsen the child's position. The simple fact that the child has been accepted as a pupil of the school is taken to justify a P-duty owed to the child in relation to the provision of education.

work, are: (a) in imminent danger; or (b) injured or ill and thereby rendered helpless, (5) a school with its students, (6) a landlord with its tenants, and (7) a custodian with those in its custody, if: (a) the custodian is required by law to take custody or voluntarily takes custody of the other; and (b) the custodian has a superior ability to protect the other.'

[28] *Michael* (n 25) [100].

[29] This is clearest, of course, with contractual P-duties: there is no requirement of foreseeable reliance for a contractual promise to be binding.

[30] *Hippolyte v Bexley London Borough Council* [1995] PIQR 309, 314 (Steyn LJ): 'it has long been recognised that there is a special relationship between a teacher and a pupil which may potentially give rise to a duty on a teacher to take positive steps to protect the pupil from physical harm'; in the case, a P-duty to respond appropriately to a pupil's asthma attack was accepted; *Phelps v Hillingdon London Borough Council* [2001] 2 AC 619, 666–67 (Lord Nicholls).

(b) Parent and Child

Consider another relationship which is normally considered to belong on the list of P-duty-creating special relationships: the relationship between parent and child.[31]

Precisely who constitutes a 'parent' and 'child' for tort law purposes is unclear. Biological parenthood is unnecessary and likely insufficient. It is unnecessary because, if biological parents ever owe P-duties, an adoptive parent or foster parent must also owe P-duties to the child.[32]

It is likely insufficient, too. In *Hahn v Conly*, the High Court of Australia were in agreement that the mere blood relationship between a grandfather and grandchild was not a source of P-duties.[33] Biological parenthood could itself be argued to trigger the *Innocent Risk* principle: by being causally responsible for the child's existence, one innocently causes the child to face worldly risks of harm, and therefore one owes a duty to protect the child against such risks. Sometimes the biological role a person plays in a child's creation may be highly indirect, however; suppose a person's sperm sample is mistakenly used. As we have seen, not all persons who are innocently causally responsible for a risk come under duties. A doctor who saved the mother's life prior to pregnancy would not by that fact be under duties to the child, despite being causally involved in the child's exposure to worldly risks.[34] The very act of taking a child home from hospital, however, will trigger both *Innocent Risk* and *Interference*: by removing the child from the care of others, and being in present custody of the child, one risks making the situation worse than if one had not done so.

A parent, in the sense that generates tort P-duties to a child, is likely a person who has accepted a wide-ranging responsibility to care for the child's welfare, and entered into performance of that accepted responsibility. Being a parent in this sense may often trigger other grounds of P-duties. For instance, when a parent takes a young child near a swimming pool, the parent creates an innocent risk of harm in such a way as to trigger a P-duty. In controlling access to the child, a parent will frequently trigger *Interference*: by exercising control over the child, others will be dissuaded from meeting the child's basic needs.

It seems likely, however, that a person who is currently occupying a parental care-giving role in relation to a child has a P-duty that is distinctive from P1, P2, or *Interference* more generally. Suppose that Parent 1 is looking after Child one

[31] See, eg, *Hedley Byrne* (n 25) 509 (Lord Hodson); see also *Phipps v Rochester Corp* [1955] 1 QB 450 (QB) 461, 465 (Devlin J). Parents have positive duties of assistance that potentially give rise to criminal liability: see, eg, *R v Morby* (1882) 8 QBD 571 (a parent's failure to seek medical assistance for a child; had causation been proven, a manslaughter conviction could have been upheld).

[32] *Surtees v Kingston upon Thames Borough Council* [1992] PIQR P101 (finding no breach); *S v Walsall Metropolitan Borough Council* [1985] 1 WLR 1150.

[33] (1971) 126 CLR 276.

[34] The steps that may be legally and morally required to be taken by a parent also seem likely to be more onerous than innocent creators of risk in general: see S Bazargan-Forward, 'The Identity-Enactment Account of Associative Duties' (2019) 176 Philosophical Studies 2351.

afternoon, while Parent 2 is supposed to be at work. Parent 1 takes Child on a shopping trip over lunchtime. Unbeknownst to Parent 1, Parent 2 is having an affair and by coincidence the pursuit of this affair brings Parent 2 to the same area. Parent 2 sees Child wandering down the street, having eluded Parent 1's control. Parent 2 is concerned about his affair being observed by Parent 1 and so decides not to intervene. The child is seriously injured by a car. Here Parent 2 cannot be said to have a P-duty to intervene on the basis of present custody of the child or creation of risk. An argument based on P1 or P2 seems strained: even if one can identify a promise made by Parent 2, it is difficult to identify any specific instance of reliance in the circumstances. Parent 1 and Child were unaware of Parent 2's presence, and others in the vicinity had no reason to believe that Parent 2 was connected to Child. Yet it seems highly likely that Parent 2 would have a legal P-duty to intervene here. The reason is that Parent 2 assumed a relatively wide-ranging responsibility for the child by accepting a parental care-giving role in relation to the child. This fact itself generates a P-duty to take reasonable care to intervene.[35]

Notably, this has effectively been recognised in *HXA v Surrey County Council*, wherein it is accepted in the partly analogous context of social services taking a child into temporary care that it 'appears not to be a necessary feature of an assumption of responsibility in this area that there is reliance, in any real sense, by the claimant. For instance . . . where one has a vulnerable young child with learning difficulties, it would be inappropriate to insist on specific reliance by the child in order to find that there was an assumption of responsibility triggering a duty of care during the respite period.'[36]

(c) Employer and Employee

An employer owes a duty to employees to provide a reasonably safe system of work, exercise reasonable care in the selection of fellow employees, exercise reasonable care in the provision of equipment, and provide training to allow employees to be reasonably safe.[37] To a significant extent these duties can be understood as N-duties to protect against risks created by employment-related activities; they are

[35] The idea that a parent who has accepted a wide-ranging responsibility for a child's care is thereby under a P-duty to act was accepted by North P in *McCallion v Dodd* [1966] NZLR 710; Turner and McCarthy JJ took the view that there would need to be an assumption of specific responsibility for the child at the relevant time. For discussion, see C McIvor, 'Expelling the Myth of the Parental Duty of Easy Rescue' (2000) 12 Child and Family Law Quarterly 229.

[36] *HXA v Surrey County Council* [2023] UKSC 52 [108]. It is true that this does not exclude reliance being constituted by *the parent(s)* entrusting the child conditionally upon a promise to take care of the child, and there is some evidence of this being a requirement ([107]). However, the better view is that the assumption of responsibility is constituted by the acceptance of (temporary) parental responsibility without more. It cannot be right that a child who is accommodated by a local authority because no one had parental responsibility for the child is not owed a P-duty. In some cases, even an 'acceptance' may not be strictly required, as when a court order is made vesting parental responsibility in the local authority under s 31 of the Children Act 1989.

[37] *Wilsons & Clyde Coal Company* [1938] AC 57.

duties to take care not to render an employee worse off with respect to their physical safety in relation to the employment.

It is difficult to find concrete evidence in the authorities that an employer would, simply by virtue of the relationship, owe a P-duty to protect a physically ill employee when the illness does not arise in some way from the workplace activity itself.[38] Suppose an employee suddenly has a stroke at work. In many cases, an employer will owe a duty to seek assistance on the basis of *Innocent Risk* even if the stroke was not caused by an employment risk. This is because it will be unclear whether the employment was a significant cause of the employee's illness. The employee's stroke might be the result of strenuous activity involved in the employment. So long as there is a reasonable ground to believe that there is a significant risk of this, the employer has a duty to take reasonable steps. In other cases, the employment will have the effect of secluding the employee from the assistance of others. For instance, if an employee has a stroke while operating a crane at a great height on behalf of his employer, his employer's activity has isolated him from the assistance of others, and this triggers a duty to act.

In the United States, the employer's duty seems to extend to risks not created by the employment. The Third Restatement of Torts, §40 lists, as generating such a P-duty, the relationship of 'an employer with its employees who, while at work, are: (a) in imminent danger; or (b) injured or ill and thereby rendered helpless'.[39] Suppose an employee is stung by a bee at work, and this bee-sting is unconnected to the purposes for which the employee is employed. Suppose the employee has a severe allergic reaction and needs urgent assistance. There appears to be no direct authority on this point, but if the statements in the authorities that the relationship generates P-duties are taken seriously, then this P-duty—a P-duty to take care to provide assistance when an employee is (a) in imminent danger or (b) injured or ill and thereby helpless—is plausibly understood as part and parcel of the employment relationship.[40]

A person spends on average 80,000 hours of their life at work.[41] If they do not work at home, they are dependent upon the assistance of relative strangers to meet such unexpected urgent needs. Since the reason for their physical presence at the workplace or on work-related activities is for the benefit of the employer, the employer makes use of their agency, and, finally, given the minimally onerous nature of this P-duty, it is submitted that it could reasonably be attached to the employment relationship.[42]

[38] In *Barrett v Ministry of Defence* [1995] 3 All ER 211 the duty arose when the employee was being cared for by another employee, not seemingly simply by virtue of the relationship.

[39] *Third Restatement of Torts* (n 6) §40.

[40] This would be consistent with the tenor of *Kasapis v Laimos Bros* [1959] 2 Lloyd's Rep 378 at 381; *Smith v Howdens Ltd* [1953] NI 131 (in which a duty arose in respect of a cut from a steel cable provided to the employee).

[41] See <https://80000hours.org> accessed 16 July 2024.

[42] See further Chapter 5, section 2.

(d) Health Professional and Patient

When a person is accepted as a patient by a hospital, this triggers a P-duty on the part of the hospital.[43] Any on-duty hospital doctor could be required by this duty to provide care to a patient.[44] This relationship could arise by mutual consent. It could also arise unilaterally by the consent of the hospital when a patient does not have the capacity to consent (suppose that an unconscious person is accepted as a patient).

It might be contended that hospitals have a P-duty to *accept* a person as a patient, and so a P-duty to take reasonable care of the person does not arise by virtue of their becoming a patient. Suppose that a seriously injured person is dropped off on the hospital forecourt in front of the Accident and Emergency ward. It might seem absurd to suggest that the hospital has no tort P-duty to assist here, but the point is non-obvious in a system which rejects a duty of easy rescue and treats public authorities as subject to the same rules as private individuals.[45] It might be said that people rely upon an expectation, engendered by the customary behaviour of public hospitals, of the hospital's being willing to help in these circumstances, and those who dropped off the injured person made an assumption to that effect. Even if this argument is accepted, however, it does not follow that being accepted as a patient has no independent significance.

(e) Occupier and Visitor

The fact that one has people on one's land by one's permission is usually considered to be a source of duties to the visitor.[46] This could be explained on the basis that giving permission is normally reasonably taken as involving a promise to have taken reasonable care in relation to risks on the land and the visitor relies upon this promise in entering the land. This would make the occupier's duty to a visitor an N-duty instantiation of P1. The Third Restatement suggests, however, that an occupier who permits the public to enter land also has a P-duty in relation to risks that are not obviously covered by such an implicit promise. It gives the example of a person who, having fallen seriously and obviously ill in a shop, is ignored for fifteen minutes by the staff and holds that the business as occupier has a P-duty to intervene.[47] In English law, it is at least arguable that such a duty arises by virtue of the occupier's invitation, and perhaps even to helpless trespassers.[48] This would

[43] *Gorringe v Calderdale London Borough Council* [2004] UKHL 15 [38] (Lord Hoffmann): 'the existence of a common law duty of care is based simply on its [a public hospital's] *acceptance of a professional relationship* with the patient no different from that which would be accepted by a doctor in private practice' (emphasis added).

[44] cf *Egedebo v Windermere District Hospital Assn*, 1991 CanLII 1921 (Supreme Court of British Columbia).

[45] There would likely be a duty to accept as a patient under the Human Rights Act in certain circumstances. See further Chapter 8.

[46] See, eg, the Occupiers' Liability Act 1957, s 2(2). See further Chapter 6, section 2(iii).

[47] Third Restatement of Torts (n 6) §40 ('Duty Based on a Special Relationship').

[48] The Occupiers' Liability Acts are restricted to 'dangers due to the state of the premises or things done or omitted to be done on them' (see s 1(1) of the 1957 Act) and this is interpreted to require the

not be an unreasonable burden to impose upon those who invite others onto their premises, however. The central freedom-based objection to P-duties has less force: the law would be attaching a P-duty to an act of choice—the permission.[49]

(f) Familial Relations

It is unlikely that a mere blood relationship, even a close one, is necessary or sufficient to trigger a P-duty for reasons given above. If a family member assumes a care-giving role in relation to another family member, however, this is likely to trigger a P-duty.

Anyone seeking a simple formula for when these relationship-based P-duties arise in tort is likely to be disappointed. They are united by the duty arising in virtue of a choice: unlike the N-duties not to assault or falsely imprison, these duties arise by virtue of an act, and normally an act that involves a choice to incur at least a moral responsibility to another person. The law's decision to enforce P-duties arising from certain relationships, or to attach P-duties to such relationships, involves a balancing of various considerations: 'No algorithm exists to provide clear guidance about which policies in which proportions justify the imposition of an affirmative duty based on a relationship.'[50] The next chapter examines these considerations.

(iii) Assumption of Responsibility as Taking Charge of a Person or Another's Thing

A third strand of assumption of responsibility comprises cases in which A takes B or B's thing into A's custody.

(a) Things

Consider, first, taking charge of another's thing. If A and B agree that A will take care of B's thing, and B entrusts the thing to A, then A owes a P-duty to B to take care of the thing: a bailment arises.[51] P-duties in bailments arising by mutual consent can generally be justified by P1: the bailor would not have entrusted the thing to the

risk to arise in some way from the premises. It seems to be assumed, however, that occupation may serve as a distinct source of P-duties at common law. For helpful discussion, see S Bailey, 'Occupiers' Liability: the Enactment of "Common Law" Principles' in TT Arvind and J Steele (eds), *Tort Law and the Legislature: Common Law, Statute and the Dynamics of Legal Change* (Hart 2013) esp 207–10.

[49] Allan Beever argues that the duty in *Depue v Flatau* should be understood as based on an assumption of responsibility, in the sense that it is attached to the invitation to enter premises: A Beever, 'The Basis of the Action in *Hedley Byrne*' in K Barker, R Grantham, and W Swain (eds), *The Law of Misstatements: 50 Years on from Hedley Byrne v Heller* (Hart 2015) 95–96. On *Depue*, see Chapter 8.

[50] Third Restatement of Torts (n 6) §40 cmt h.

[51] *Coggs v Bernard* (1703) 2 Ld Raym 909, 90 ER 107.

bailee but for the bailee's express or implied promise to take care of the thing. The P-duties of a sub-bailee—a person to whom the bailee bails the thing—can similarly be justified by P2: but for the sub-bailee's (A) promise, the bailee (C) would foreseeably not have sub-bailed, and so the sub-bailee's promise threatens to make the bailor (B) worse off than if the promise had not been made.

This analysis does not work, however, in relation to purely unilateral instances of taking charge of a thing, such as persons who find another's goods. If A finds B's lost goods and takes them into A's possession, A has been said to incur two P-duties: (1) a P-duty to take reasonable care of the goods, and (2) a P-duty to take reasonable steps to make known the discovery of the goods, with the aim of re-acquainting them with the owner.[52] This is not promise-based: when I pick up your goods, even with the intention of re-acquainting you with the goods, I am not *ipso facto* promising you anything.[53] Further, a finder may proclaim to the heavens that she promises no care whatsoever will be taken of the object, but this surely makes no difference. It follows that 'taking charge of a thing' constitutes a separate strand of assumption of responsibility in these cases.[54]

Consider (2). The basis of A's duty to B can be explained as follows. In order for A's non-consensual possession to be consistent with B's entitlement to the thing, A must hold the thing for certain purposes.[55] In order for A not to commit trespass or conversion in relation to the goods, A must hold the goods for a reason the law recognises as justifying non-consensual possession of another's goods. Plausibly, one such purpose should be re-acquainting the owner with the goods. The justification of the P-duty of reasonable steps towards re-acquaintance then is that, absent such action, the possessor will wrongfully possess the goods. In addition, by taking the goods away from their initial location, the finder will foreseeably increase the probability—typically—that the goods will not be found by their owner; this triggers the *Interference Principle*.

Consider (1). It might be possible to justify the P-duty of care on a similar basis: a person's non-consensual possession is non-wrongful only if it is sufficiently beneficial for the right-holder. This requires more than merely that the possession

[52] *Parker v British Airways Board* [1982] QB 1004 (CA), 1017 (Donaldson LJ) (a person who finds 'abandoned or lost' goods is under a duty to take reasonable steps 'to acquaint the true owner of the finding and present whereabouts of the chattel and to care for it meanwhile'). Donaldson LJ's statements are *obiter*. For an argument that (2) does not truly exist as a matter of law, see R Hickey, *Property and the Law of Finders* (Hart 2010) 75ff.

[53] Similarly, J Beale, Jr, 'Gratuitous Undertakings' (1891) 5 Harvard Law Review 221, 224: '[B] finds A's pocket- book in the street, and takes it up for the benefit of the owner; it is absurd to say that B promises the unknown owner, in consideration of being allowed to pick it up, to find him.'

[54] It is worth noting that, in many cases, there is no need to identify a P-duty on the part of a possessor in order to generate liability: an N-duty will do. For instance, if I find your Ming vase and while transporting it, I drop it, I will potentially breach an N-duty not to carelessly *damage* your property. The failure to take a positive step is likely to be an *impure* omission.

[55] For an illuminating analysis of the law's general treatment of powers held for the benefit of others or certain purposes, see L Smith, *The Law of Loyalty* (OUP 2023).

does not render the right-holder worse off: one cannot justify one's possession of another's thing merely on the basis that one is not making the other worse off. Perhaps conformity to a P-duty of care is required. Given, however, that the finder acts gratuitously for the benefit of right-holder, fairness supports a relatively non-demanding standard of care.[56] A different justification is *Interference*: the interference with others' protective steps is caused by the act of holding the goods. This assumes that there is a general foreseeable prospect that others would have intervened and protected the goods with reasonable care. This is a contingent matter, but still of relatively general application.

(b) Persons

Now consider taking charge of a *person*. There is an overlap here between assumption of responsibility and 'control', which is examined in Chapter 6. In many cases, if one person has control over a vulnerable person, and transfers custody of that person to another, it will be clear from the context that the recipient is promising to look after the person, and the transferor is relying upon that promise in making the transfer. This is like bailment of a person.

The last paragraph described a voluntary transfer of custody of a person. It is also possible for a person *unilaterally* to take charge of a person, with resultant P-duties. This person is akin to the finder, who unilaterally takes possession of goods. If a local authority takes a child into its care, through exercising its statutory powers, it will be said to have 'assumed responsibility' for the child's welfare.[57] The P-duties of the authority have three sources, here. First, because the authority secludes the child from the potential of protective interventions by others, it will be under a P-duty to take care of the child's basic needs. In this way, the P-duty arises by virtue of *Innocent Risk* or *Interference.* Second, the authority unilaterally assumes a responsibility to take care of the child's welfare, and to stand as a parent to the child; this unilateral assumption of responsibility is not wholly explicable by P1 and P2, since there may be no particular person who foreseeably relies upon a promise made by the authority. Third, if a person chooses to exercise substantial non-consensual control over another person, this plausibly in itself justifies a P-duty to exercise that control in a way that protects the interests of the other. The exercise of wide-ranging power over another person can only be justified if it is exercised in a way that benefits them (at least in expectation). In short, the moral permissibility of the exercise of parental power is conditional upon the power being exercised generally for the benefit of the child.[58]

[56] In German law, the finder is liable only for intention and gross negligence: §968 BGB.

[57] *Poole* (n 21) [81] (Lord Reed).

[58] cf P Vallentyne, 'Rights and Duties of Childbearing' (2003) 11 William & Mary Bill of Rights Journal 991.

(iv) Assumption of Responsibility as Duties Attached to a Chosen Role

In some cases the law attaches a P-duty to the choice to occupy a particular role, without the role-holder having agreed to enter a relationship with a particular person. Consider *ABC v St George's Healthcare NHS Trust and Others*.[59] The claimant's father killed her mother. The father's doctors suspected that he had a genetic neurodegenerative disorder. The claimant attended family therapy sessions in connection with the death of her mother. Some medical professionals also treating her father's condition were involved in these sessions. The clamant became pregnant. The doctors treating her father, who insisted upon confidentiality in relation to his degenerative disorder, did not inform her of the risk that she had the gene for this disorder. The gene carried a 50% chance of transmission to a child; she alleged that, informed, she would have terminated her pregnancy. Mrs Justice Yip held that the doctors treating her father's genetic condition owed her a P-duty to take reasonable care to inform her of her likelihood of carrying the gene and transmitting it to her own child. This duty was not based on C's being the recipient of family therapy provided by the defendant. The P-duties created by this were only P-duties in relation to family therapy after her father's killing her mother. Nor, in the judge's view, did her father's doctors assume responsibility to her. While they were aware of her existence, and the likely impact of not informing her, she was not their patient.[60]

It is clear from the judge's reasoning that the issue at stake was whether there was a 'professional' obligation to disclose to which a legal duty attached.[61] Consequently, it is clear that if a non-medical-professional stranger to the claimant discovered the information about her father's genetic condition, the stranger would have no legal duty to disclose it to the claimant. Here, then, it is the occupation of a certain role—doctor—which is considered to be an important part of the justification of the duty. Clearly, however, the doctor's duty in this case was not one that a reasonable person would have understood the doctor to be *promising* to the claimant by virtue of treating her father.

Mrs Justice Yip excludes the P-duty from the category of 'assumption of responsibility', so it might be objected that I am needlessly adding to the diversity of notions grouped together under that label. In other situations, however, the law has described the choice to engage in a certain kind of activity as an 'assumption of responsibility' that triggers a P-duty to those with whom one is not yet in any kind of special relation. The P-duties of those who exercise 'public callings' arguably

[59] [2020] EWHC 455 (QB), [2020] PIQR P13. For a structurally analogous US example, see *Tarasoff v Regents of the University of California* 17 Cal 3d 425 (1976), 551 P 2d 334. For the imposition of a duty of rescue upon a doctor seemingly in virtue of the doctor's assumed role, see *Lowns v Woods* (1996) Aust Torts Reports 81–376.

[60] *St George's* (n 59) [154].

[61] See, eg, ibid [165], [170].

also belong in this category.[62] This category refers to duties that attach to persons who engage in certain kinds of activity for gain. It traditionally included solicitors, inn-keepers, surgeons, farriers, and doctors.[63] If I present at a public inn, the inn generally has a duty to provide me with shelter if they have room and I am able to pay.[64] The inn will only be relieved of the duty if they remove their sign communicating the intention to offer accommodation to those who seek it.[65]

Now, it is arguable that these are instances of A making a promise to everyone of the form 'if you present here, we promise to accept your custom (under certain conditions)', and A can reasonably foresee that people will act to their detriment on this promise. If so, A must take steps to ensure that no such person does in fact suffer a detriment. This will typically be discharged by accepting their custom. Thus, the common callings are instances of P1. But it is not difficult to envisage cases in which it is clear that B will be no worse off if A refuses B's custom—for instance, if there is another inn next door which will accept B—and yet the duty still exists.[66] Hence the prospect of detrimental reliance is not a condition of the duty arising. Further, the duty is to perform the promise unless there is good justification for not doing so; it is not a duty to protect against detrimental reliance.

The existence of this category of P-duty attached to particular roles creates a tension in the law. In *Michael*, the police were held not to have a P-duty to assist others whom they know to be in imminent danger, absent the application of P1 or P2 and, possibly, absent the existence of a promise to a specific individual to intervene.[67] If a doctor has a P-duty to a non-patient, whose fundamental interests will be affected without the provision of some assistance, then why should the police not have a P-duty in relation to an endangered person to whom they have not made a specific promise or entered into a special relation? The *Michael* decision was not discussed in *AB* and it might be argued that *AB* is simply inconsistent with it. At any rate, it is not obvious how this line of authority can be reconciled with *Michael*, except by arguments about a different balance of the positive and negative consequences of holding the role-holder to be subject to compensatory liability in

[62] See generally P H Winfield, *The Law of Quasi-Contracts* (Sweet & Maxwel 1952) ch 3 (perspicaciously entitled 'pseudo-quasi-contracts') 30–34; R Stevens, *Torts and Rights* (OUP 2007) 12–13; *Lane v Cotton* (1688) 12 Mod 484, 88 ER 1458 (Holt CJ): 'If on the road a shoe fall off my horse, and I come to a smith to have one put on, and the smith refuse to do it, an action will lie against him, because he has made profession of a trade which is for the public good, and has thereby exposed and vested an interest of himself in all the King's subjects that will employ him in the way of his trade. If an innkeeper refuse to entertain a guest, when his house is not full, an action will lie against him; and so against a carrier, if his horses be not loaded, and he refuse to take a packet proper to be sent by a carrier; and I have known such actions maintained, though the cases are not reported.'

[63] Winfield (n 62).

[64] *Constantine v Imperial Hotels* [1944] KB 693 (KB), [1944] 2 All ER 171.

[65] Winfield (n 62).

[66] *Constantine* (n 64).

[67] *Michael* (n 25); *Robinson v Chief Constable of West Yorkshire Police* [2018] UKSC 4, [2018] AC 736. For the facts of *Michael*, see Chapter 1, p. 8.

the two contexts, and yet arguments of this character were not considered central to the absence of a P-duty in *Michael.*[68]

(v) Assumption of Responsibility, Bare Promises, and Taking on a Task for Another

(a) Promises Beyond P1 and P2

Some authors claim the existence of another promise-based principle in English law:[69]

> Principle 4 ('P4'): If A promises B that A will *x*, A will owe a tort duty to B to take reasonable care to *x*, if this promise would have been contractually enforceable if consideration had been provided.[70]

The distinguishing feature of P4 is that, under P4, a P-duty may arise independently of the foreseeable prospect of B's acting on the basis of the promise, or B's in fact acting on the basis of the promise.

Robert Stevens has defended the existence of P4.[71] He draws attention to cases in which a P-duty arises by an act of choice, and yet there is no foreseeable prospect of reliance—for instance, the P-duties of a finder or a hospital doctor treating an unconscious patient. In response to the objection that such P-duties are inconsistent with the law's general refusal to enforce gratuitous promises, Stevens points to differences in the mode by which the law enforces gratuitous assumptions of responsibility compared to contractually enforceable promises. For instance, the breach of a P-duty arising by an assumption of responsibility is only actionable upon proof of consequential loss, unlike a contractual promise whose breach is actionable *per se.*[72]

There are indeed cases which support Stevens' view. Apart from the unconscious hospital patient, consider *Calvert v William Hill.*[73] The claimant was a pathological gambler who requested the defendant, William Hill, a bookmaker, to exclude him from making telephone bets. The defendant promised the claimant that his bets

[68] See *Michael* (n 25) [97]–[100], [121], though Lord Toulson does envisage the relevance of a 'mixture of policy considerations' in determining whether to extend the law on P-duties: [102].

[69] See, eg, Stevens (n 62) 33; Beever (n 49).

[70] This might seem straightforwardly supported by Lord Devlin's speech in *Hedley Byrne* (n 25), which refers to a duty arising when there is a relationship 'equivalent to contract' (at 528–29). *Hedley* is complicated, however, by the fact that the claimant altered their position on the basis of the advice provided. It does not provide clear support for the enforceability of a bare promise.

[71] Stevens (n 62).

[72] ibid 34.

[73] [2008] EWHC 454 (Ch), [2008] LLR 583. The decision was not questioned on this point in the Court of Appeal: [2008] EWCA Civ 1427, [2009] Ch 330 [27].

would not be accepted for a six-month period. Briggs J held that this gave rise to a duty of care to implement the exclusion:

> the claimant presented himself as a problem gambler in need of help, asked for specific help, and was assured that he would be given it.
>
> In my judgment those facts disclose a sufficient voluntary assumption of responsibility by William Hill to exclude the claimant from telephone gambling with the company for six months to give rise to a duty to take care to implement that exclusion.[74]

It is difficult to identify any act of reliance taken on the basis of this assurance. Briggs J did not seek to do so. At most, it can be said that the claimant was led to believe that the assurance would be fulfilled, and possibly did not take alternative steps to reduce his gambling addiction in the future.

The weakness of the case for the existence of P4 is three-fold, however. First, P4 has been explicitly rejected in several authorities. In *Coggs v Bernard*, Holt CJ rejected the idea that a mere agreement or promise to do an act in the future is enforceable: 'assumpsit does not only signify a future agreement, but in such a case as this, it signifies an actual entry upon the thing, and taking the trust upon himself. And if a man will do that, and miscarries in the performance of his trust, an action will lie against him for that, though no body could have compelled him to do the thing'.[75] Similarly, in *Wilkinson v Coverdale*, A promised to obtain insurance for B, proceeded to acquire a policy, but acquired an invalid one with the result that B was worse off than if valid insurance had been acquired.[76] The mere promise was held insufficient to give rise to a duty to take care to perform the promise without more: 'But though there was no consideration for one party's undertaking to procure an insurance for another, yet where a party voluntarily undertook to do it, and proceeded to carry his undertaking into effect by getting a policy underwritten, but did it so negligently or unskilfully, that the party could derive no benefit from it, that in that case he should be liable to an action.'[77]

The Supreme Court recently affirmed this position in *N v Poole*.[78] Lord Reed explained that an assumption of responsibility requires that 'the defendant undertakes the performance of some task or the provision of some service for

[74] [2008] EWCA Civ 1427, [2009] Ch 330 [175]–[176].

[75] (1703) 2 Ld Raym 909, 90 ER 107, 113. For a modern statement, see *The Zephyr* [1985] 2 Lloyd's Rep. 529, 538 (Mustill LJ): 'the fault of the brokers lay in a continuing failure to perform a positive undertaking. Once any contractual background is subtracted, I do not see how such a right of action can be sustained without holding that if the relationship between the parties is of the right kind, the law of England recognizes the enforceability of a gratuitous promise. On the face of it, this would be inconsistent with fundamental principle.'

[76] (1793) 1 Esp 75, 170 ER 284.

[77] ibid 285.

[78] *Poole* (n 21).

the claimant with an undertaking that reasonable care will be taken'.[79] The word 'undertaking' means two different things in this sentence. The first time it means 'enter upon the doing of an action or service'. The second time it means 'promise'. Therefore, *a mere promise to take care* is insufficient. According to Lord Reed, it is necessary that there be an undertaking in the sense of an entry into performance *and* an undertaking in the sense of a promise to take reasonable care in the performance.

Second, some of the cases on assumption of responsibility simply do not involve a *promise*, and so cannot support P4. As noted above, a finder's P-duty is not based upon the finder's *promise* to take care of the goods.

Third, it is too quick to assert the consistency of P4 with the doctrine of consideration simply because gratuitous assumptions of responsibility are not actionable *per se*. If the concern reflected by the doctrine of consideration were only live when promises are enforced without loss, then all promises (when there is an intention to create legal relations) should be actionable when there is loss—that is, when the promisee is worse off than if the promise had been performed. But that is clearly not the law. A promise to pay £10 is not enforceable without more.

In summary, here are two conclusions about P4. First, P4 is not a complete explanation of the law on assumption of responsibility, since not all cases involve promises, notably the finder. Second, P4 is too broad—in (i) applying to all promises, and (ii) dispensing with any requirement of foreseeable reliance—to be consistent with recent authoritative statements of the law, and with the general law on the enforcement of gratuitous promises.

(b) Taking on a Task for Another

Donal Nolan has argued that what unifies invocations of the concept of assumption of responsibility is that 'A has taken on a task or job for B'.[80] When A takes on a task for B, according to Nolan, the law presumes, absent a good reason, that A 'implicitly undertak[es] to exercise due care'.[81] Nolan's view strongly resonates with Lord Reed's statement in *Poole* in employing the twin notions of 'undertaking'.[82]

This view is argued by Nolan to cover: (i) the P-duties of a bailee,[83] (ii) the P-duties of a person who takes on the management of a person's financial affairs,[84] (iii) the P-duties of a medical professional who commences treatment of another

[79] ibid [88].

[80] Nolan (n 4) 129.

[81] ibid 135.

[82] *Poole* (n 21) [88]; see also Lord Morris' reference in *Hedley Byrne* (n 25) to 'situations in which one person voluntarily or gratuitously undertakes to do something for another person and becomes under a duty to exercise reasonable care' (at 497).

[83] Nolan (n 4) 130.

[84] See, eg, *Henderson v Merrett Syndicates Ltd (No. 1)* [1995] 2 AC 145 (see especially Lord Goff at 186).

in a hospital or as part of an emergency response,[85] and (iv) the P-duty of a person who takes on the care of an unconscious drunken colleague.[86] It also helps to explain cases in which A intends to perform a task for the benefit of C not B, and is held not to owe B a duty grounded in an assumption of responsibility.[87]

Although Nolan distinguishes his view from a *promissory* account of assumption of responsibility, his view is, in truth, in part a promissory account. A undertakes a task for B, and this is taken by the law to involve an implicit undertaking (ie promise) to take reasonable care in doing the task. Nolan's view is thus that assumption of responsibility involves undertakings-*to*-within-undertakings-*of*. It is this apparently promissory aspect of the duty to take care which allows Nolan to explain certain alleged features of the law—namely, the ability of the undertaker to disclaim the duty of care[88] thereby cancelling the presumption that there is a promise to take care, and the ability of the undertaker to shape the standard of care and determine who acquire rights by virtue of the undertaking.[89]

Nolan's claim, then, is that this principle largely fits the law on assumption of responsibility:

> *Taking on a Task*. If A takes on a task for B, in circumstances in which A expressly or impliedly promises that A will perform the task with reasonable care, then A incurs a legal duty in tort to B to perform the task with reasonable care.

I now argue that *Taking on a Task* does not explain the entirety of the law on assumption of responsibility. I then argue that *Taking on a Task* and P1 and P2 can both explain cases that might be thought especially to support the former principle, but that P1 and P2 provide a superior justification.

There are at least two reasons why *Taking on a Task* does not explain the entirety of the law on assumption of responsibility. First, the duties that are attached to special relationships need not involve A taking on a task for B. An employer might not take on the task of protecting the physical safety of an employee performing work and yet still be under a P-duty to take reasonable care owed to the employee. Second, the P-duties of a person who takes another person or a thing into their custody are also unlikely to be open to disclaimer. If I find your goods and take them into my possession, it is not open to me to continue possession *and* disclaim

[85] See, eg, *Barnett v Chelsea and Kensington Hospital Management Committee* [1969] 1 QB 428 (QB), [1968] 2 WLR 422.

[86] See, eg, *Barrett* [1995] 1 WLR 1217.

[87] See, eg, *Banco Nazionale del Lavoro SPA v Playboy Club London Ltd* [2018] UKSC 43, [2018] 1 WLR 4041. cf *White v Jones* [1995] 2 AC 207 (HL), [1995] 2 WLR 187; *Spring v Guardian Assurance Plc* [1995] 2 AC 296 (HL), [1994] 3 WLR 354; *Smith v Eric S Bush (A Firm)* [1990] 1 AC 381 (HL), [1989] 2 WLR 790.

[88] *Hedley Byrne* (n 25).

[89] *Banco Nazionale* (n 87); *Williams v Natural Life Health Foods Ltd* [1998] 1 WLR 830, [1998] 2 All ER 577.

the P-duty. These differences are suggestive of different underlying justifications for these P-duties.

Consider the following cases that apparently support the existence of *Taking on a Task*:

> *Doctors*. A doctor who accepts a person as a patient owes P-duties to the patient.[90]
>
> *Barrett v Ministry of Defence*.[91] The defendant's officer tended to the claimant, another officer, on army barracks when the claimant became unconscious due to intoxication. The claimant was placed in his bunk and then not properly attended to. By placing the officer in his bunk, the defendant's officer was held to have assumed responsibility, thereby incurring a duty to take reasonable care.
>
> *Morcom v Biddick's Estate*.[92] Biddick (B), an 80-year-old man, told Morcom (M) that B that would keep the latch to the loft hatch in B's house in the closed position by holding it in place with a pole while M was carrying out work on the hatch from inside the loft. B stopped doing this for a few minutes to answer his phone. M fell through the hatch and suffered injuries. B was held to be under a P-duty on the ground that he assumed responsibility to M. B's assumption of responsibility was said to be constituted by his 'undertaking to ensure that the latch remained closed'. This raises the ambiguity of 'undertaking' again. It is not entirely clear whether the assumption of responsibility was constituted by a *promise* to ensure that the latch remained closed or simply by the *taking on of the task* of holding the latch closed for B. The latter is, however, suggested in this passage: 'Once Mr Biddick took upon himself the task of ensuring that the latch remained closed it seems to me that he assumed a duty to perform that task carefully.'[93] Further, this assumed duty arose 'even if Mr Morcom did not see Mr Biddick's role as an element in his own safety'.[94]

These cases provide support for *Taking on a Task* as distinct from P1 or P2 since, in each case, there is no emphasis placed upon the foreseeable prospect of reliance by others on a promise. In *Morcom*, there was no actual reliance by B upon the promise to hold the pole in place and the emphasis was simply upon the prospect that failing to hold the pole in place would increase the risk of physical harm to B.[95] In *Barrett*, no attention was drawn to the fact that, by tending to the officer,

[90] *Robinson* (n 67) [26] (Lord Reed); *Phelps v Hillingdon LBC* [2001] 2 AC 619 (HL), 655 (Lord Slynn). On doctors who happen upon would-be patients, see *Hedley Byrne* (n 25) 494–95 (the doctor would be under a duty to take all reasonable care in treating the person) (Lord Morris); compare *Capital and Counties plc v Hampshire County Council* [1997] QB 1035 (Stuart Smith LJ) (a doctor who commences treatment in these circumstances only comes under a duty 'not to make the victim's condition worse').

[91] *Barrett* (n 38). See further R Bagshaw, 'The Duties of Care of Emergency Service Providers' [1999] Lloyds Maritime and Commercial Law Quarterly 71, 78.

[92] [2014] EWCA Civ 182.

[93] ibid [53].

[94] ibid; see also [50].

[95] ibid.

this created a foreseeable risk that others would rely upon the assisting officer continuing to care for him. Similarly, in the case of hospital doctors, there is simply no discussion of the possibility of reliance by the patient or others. In the case of incapacitated patients, there will be no reliance upon a promise made specifically to the patient. The only possible reliance arguments are that (a) other people relied upon a hospital's promise to the public to treat patients with care in bringing the person to hospital, or (b) that the incapacitated person relied, prior to their incapacitation, upon a promise to the public made by the hospital by failing to make arrangements for alternative treatment, and those alternative arrangements would have been triggered in the circumstances of their incapacitation. In each case, however, the emphasis is mainly upon the fact that one person has taken on a task for another person, with no inquiry into the foreseeable reliance of the person who suffers harm or others.

On the facts of *Barrett* and *Morcom*, it seems highly plausible that the duty-bearer's conduct created a foreseeable prospect of reliance, so the results, at least, could be squared with P1 and P2. The rule that an accepted patient is owed P-duties by a hospital could in principle be explained on the basis of P1 and P2. The most plausible argument is that hospitals, by their nature, make a promise to everyone that, if a person is brought to hospital, that person will be treated with reasonable care.[96] People rely upon this promise by (a) entrusting themselves to the hospital for treatment, (b) bringing people to hospital upon the basis that the hospital promises to treat patients with reasonable care, and (c) by not making alternative arrangements for health care. So, the promise made to the world at large creates a risk of foreseeable reliance upon the performance of the promise: it thereby creates a foreseeable possibility that the unconscious person will not receive aid that they would otherwise have received from another hospital. Of course, it will be hard to say whether the promise will as a matter of fact have rendered the person worse off in this way, but if there is more than a far-fetched *foreseeable possibility* that the promise to the world will make people worse off, this is enough to trigger a duty of care to take steps to prevent this being the case under P1 and P2.

More generally, it is suggested that P1 and P2 can generally explain the principle that, if A takes on a task for B in circumstances in which A is promising that the task will be done with reasonable care, then A will owe B a P-duty in respect of the task. The reason is that it will normally always be reasonably foreseeable that B will rely upon the promise, even if B does not *in fact* do so. It is the reasonable foreseeability of a risk of right-related harm that generates a duty to act, not whether a person *actually* acts on the basis of the promise.

In summary, in terms of explaining some situations in which a P-duty arises, *Taking on a Task* scores better in terms of fit with judicial reasoning, but P1 and P2 can still explain the results in these cases. Nonetheless, it would be better to

[96] See, eg, *Poole* (n 21) [80] (Lord Reed).

re-orient understanding of these situations as based either on P1 or P2, or on the basis that agreeing to incur a P-duty to promote another's interests sometimes generates such a duty. This re-orientation would be preferable because the normative rationale for *Taking on a Task* is obscure. If the rationale is promissory, then the requirement that one has actually commenced performance—'undertaken the task'—is otiose. The promise should give rise to a P-duty whenever there is a prospect of foreseeable damage to a general right. If the rationale is not promissory, but simply that one has *done*, or is doing, something to benefit another, it is unclear why this generates a P-duty.[97]

2. Conclusion

In light of the analysis above, it would be better to recognise that 'assumption of responsibility' refers to a set of distinct principles. These different principles can overlap, with the result that a person could be subject to a duty on multiple grounds. Here are the different principles:

> Principle 1 ('P1'): If A promises B that A will take steps to prevent the materialisation of a risk of harm to B protected by a general right, and A knows or ought to know that there is a substantial possibility that B will act on the basis that this promise will be fulfilled and thereby not take steps to prevent the materialisation of the risk, then A will have a duty to B to take reasonable care to fulfil the promise, or otherwise take care that B is not in a worse position than had the promise not been made.
>
> Principle 2 ('P2'): If A promises C that A will protect B from a risk of harm protected by a general right, and A knows or ought to know that there is a substantial possibility that C will act on the basis of this promise being fulfilled and thereby not take steps to protect B, then A will be under a duty to B to take reasonable care to fulfil the promise, or otherwise take care that B is not in a worse position than had the promise not been made.
>
> P1 and P2 are, ultimately, not genuine P-duties, but instantiations of general tort N-duties in relation to bodily injury, psychiatric injury, and property damage; they identify cases in which *Interference* or *Creation of Risk* applies.[98]
>
> Custody or Possession of a Person or Thing: If A takes custody of a person without that person's valid consent, or possession of a thing without permission of the right-holder, then A has a P-duty to take care of the person or thing, and

[97] This last point is developed in Chapter 5, section 3.

[98] On P-duties in relation to pure economic loss arising because of induced reliance, see section 1(i).

in the case of a thing a P-duty to take reasonable steps re-acquaint the thing with its rightful owner. This duty arises independently of a promise or representation. It arises as a means of rendering the possession of the person or thing consistent with rights of the right-holder, and in order to protect against the risk of the possession rendering the right-holder worse off than if the possession had not occurred.

Relationships and Roles: A P-duty may arise independently of custody or possession, and independently of the prospect of detrimental reliance, when a person enters into a special relation with another or, arguably, occupies certain roles. The following examples were given: (a) parent–child, (b) medical professional–patient, (c) employer–employee, (d) school–pupil, (e) occupier–visitor. The next chapter seeks to identify general features of these relationships.

5
Assumptions of Responsibility: Part 2—Normative Issues

The previous chapter, Chapter 4, aimed to establish that the current law recognises different strands of assumption of responsibility, and that confusion is likely to ensue if these strands are not disaggregated. This chapter, which is closely connected to Chapter 4, moves from analysis of the positive law to central normative questions about the duties that arise by virtue of assumptions of responsibility.

First, what, if anything, justifies the duties currently arising by virtue of assumptions of responsibility? Second, to which roles and relationships should the law attach legally enforceable P-duties to take care to protect the interests of another? Third, should the law accept that taking on the task of assisting another person generates P-duties to take care in the provision of that assistance by virtue of an assumption of responsibility? Fourth, can the not entirely consistent decisions on the assumption of responsibility by public authorities be reconciled?

1. Justifications for P-Duties Arising by Virtue of an Assumption of Responsibility

We can identify two kinds of justification: (i) general rights, and (ii) rights created directly by a choice to enter a role or relationship.

(i) General Rights

The general rights each person has in relation to their body, property, and mind justify duties to respond to endangerments to those interests by the person who endangers. As we have seen, even innocent endangerment is generally considered a sufficient basis for such duties.[1]

One way in which these interests can be endangered by others is through promising. Promising invites another's trust and, in circumstances in which the promise will foreseeably lead another not to protect a person's general right-protected

[1] Chapter 3.

Omissions in Tort Law. Sandy Steel, Oxford University Press. © Sandy Steel 2024.
DOI: 10.1093/9780191898822.003.0005

interests, this may generate a duty to take reasonable steps in relation to those interests. Here promising is merely one way in which a person can foreseeably endanger another's interests. If I promise that I have taken reasonable care in servicing your fire alarm, this promise, in normal circumstances, will endanger you if you believe in the state of affairs asserted by the promise, and reasonable care has not been taken. In short, one justification of some of the duties, which the current law classifies as P-duties travelling under the label 'assumption of responsibility', is that these are entailments of a person's general right that others take care not carelessly to endanger their interests. In fact, such duties are general N-duties (and not genuine P-duties), since they are duties to take care not to make worse off. As Stephen Perry argued more than thirty years ago, albeit as an account of the whole terrain of assumption of responsibility, the duty to perform a service that one has intentionally induced another person to believe that they may safely rely upon one to perform is explicable as 'an obligation falling under the general tort principle that one ought not to cause certain kinds of harm to other'.[2]

In one way, the promise is incidental to the justification of the duty to act here. It is incidental in the sense that it is merely one amongst many ways in which a person's action can trigger an N-duty by endangering another's right-protected interest. This can also occur, for instance, by taking possession of a person or thing. If I take possession of your thing, I may expose it to risks to which it was previously not subject. If a police officer takes custody of a child's mother, the officer may endanger the child, thereby incurring a duty to act.

However, it is overstated to say that the promise is entirely incidental. In promising to do something, one is generally, if not always, indicating an intention that the promisee believe that the promisor may be relied upon to do the promised act (and to do it with reasonable care, unless the contrary is communicated). In this way, the promisor *invites* the promisee to believe that they may safely rely upon the promise. This makes it appropriate to attribute the promisee's conduct to the promisor when it would not otherwise be appropriate. Generally, our choices not to act to protect ourselves or others from harm are ones for which we bear sole responsibility as autonomous beings. However, when another person deliberately induces us to believe that we may trust them to act in some matter, this default position is shifted: our action taken in response to such a promise can be attributed, at least in part, to the inducer.[3] Furthermore, in cases of pure economic loss, the promise does not merely create a risk to a general right—there is no general right not carelessly to be caused pure economic loss—it grounds the special right that reasonable care be taken.

[2] S H Perry, 'Protected Interests and Undertakings in the Law of Negligence' (1992) 42 University of Toronto Law Journal 247, 286. See also E Weinrib, 'Causal Uncertainty' (2016) 36 Oxford Journal of Legal Studies 135, 162–63.

[3] For a similar observation, see Perry (n 2) 289.

A person's general rights have a further, separable, role in justifying what are really N-duties travelling under the label of 'assumption of responsibility'. In Chapter 4, it was suggested that a person may incur a duty as a condition of avoiding a wrong. If a finder chooses to possess another's goods without permission, this permission plausibly comes with strings: the finder is required to take re-acquaintance steps otherwise their possession is inconsistent with the rights of the owner (or person with better title). In doing an act which is normally inconsistent with a person's general rights, one may only justify one's conduct if one takes on certain duties in relation to the right-protected subject matter. Arguably, a similar logic applies more generally so as to justify P-duties on persons exercising authority over a person's right-protected interests. Whenever a person exercises an authority over another that is prima facie inconsistent with their general rights, that exercise can only be justified on condition that it is employed for the benefit of the other.

(ii) Rights Directly Created by Choices

When we think of rights that arise by choice in law, the first thought is contract. Contractual rights are rights that arise partly by virtue of a communicated intention that such rights arise. In justifying such rights, it seems difficult to avoid appealing to the contribution to autonomy made by being able jointly to create rights and duties by communicating an intention to do so. Furthermore, given that each of us rightly has limited enforceable P-duties to each other, if there were no mechanism by which we could be granted enforceable P-duties beyond that minimum, life would be much harder.

In some cases, however, there would be a significant moral problem if a person could only acquire a right to another's positive assistance by virtue of assenting to another's communicated conditional intention to generate such a right (the condition being the assent of the other). Persons who lack capacity, such as very young children, cannot give such assent, and conditioning the existence of a P-duty on their assent is not likely to serve their interests. In such instances, one solution to the moral problem is for *everyone* to have a duty to look after persons who lack capacity. Another solution, however, is for duties to take care of such persons to be conditioned upon the voluntary entry into a role which assigns the duties to the role-holder. In these cases, a person can acquire a special right, non-contractually, to another's protection by the other's (a) occupying certain roles and (b) occupying certain relationships with them. What justifies *the duty-bearer* being under the duty is generally their choice to occupy the role or relationship. This is a distinct issue from what justifies the content of the duties that one acquires by assuming the role or relationship. For instance, parental duties are grounded primarily in the child's well-being (including their interest in developing capacities for an autonomous life), and the parent being asymmetrically (in the case of young children) well-placed to provide it.[4] What justifies *a particular person* being subject to the parental duty is their choice to occupy the role.

The explanation in the last paragraph is intended to justify a person's being able acquire a positive right, without the assent (or consideration) required under the law of contract. The explanation rests upon the idea that it must be possible to acquire rights independently of one's assent when there is no opportunity to provide assent and conditioning the existence of a right on assent would substantially impair the interests of the beneficiary. This helps to explain why children, the incapacitated, and unconscious persons could become the beneficiaries of rights to another's care in tort when the other, as part of their role, designates them as a beneficiary of that role's function (or when the role itself designates the person as the beneficiary).

But what about the various special relationships described in the last chapter where the law appears to recognise a P-duty, but the beneficiary is not a person lacking capacity in this way? For instance, if A and B agree that A will act as B's lawyer in relation to a matter, A incurs a duty to take care of B's interest in the matter, even if no consideration is provided. Now, in virtually all cases, B will owe such a duty by virtue of a principle akin to P1: by inviting B to rely upon the promise to take care in the performance of a service, and the foreseeable prospect of B's so relying, A will have a duty to take reasonable care to perform or prevent B from being worse off by virtue of relying. As explained, this is not a genuine P-duty, but an N-duty. But it is strongly arguable that A will have a genuine P-duty to B independently of whether A's failure to take reasonable care will risk making B worse off than if A had not agreed to act. Just as a doctor comes to owe a non-contractual P-duty when they accept a person as their patient, a lawyer can be said to owe a non-contractual P-duty when they accept a person as their client. Should there be non-contractual legal P-duties of this kind—ones formed by agreeing with a person that one will perform a task for a person, absent consideration and the prospect of detrimental reliance?

It seems clear that a *moral* responsibility is being assumed in the case of the lawyer and the doctor. By agreeing to act as your lawyer in some matter, I do not merely communicate my intention to do some act for you in the future, I am accepting at least a moral obligation to perform the service for you and to do so carefully. If I agree to act as your lawyer, even absent consideration and reliance, and simply forget about filing your case, you have a moral complaint against my conduct. Things are different if, immediately upon accepting this obligation, I purport to terminate the relationship. Perhaps, unless I have or will render you worse off,

[4] For the view that parents' interests matter to the justification of parental rights and duties (other than in so far as they serve the child's interest), see M Clayton, *Justice and Legitimacy in Upbringing* (OUP 2006).

I should be entitled to do so, without incurring a further moral responsibility beyond an explanation and (depending on the circumstances) an apology.

The difficult issue is when such an assumed moral responsibility should generate legal liability in the absence of reliance. It is too quick to answer: 'only when something is provided in return'. As we have seen, there is a case for legal liability when one person takes on the role of providing care for a particularly vulnerable person, who is incapable of assenting to the acquisition of a right to reasonable care. A person who agrees to act, and is appointed, a trustee is exposed to liability for a failure to act, absent consideration and the prospect of detrimental reliance.[5] Gratuitous promises are binding when contained in a deed.[6]

It is suggested that there is a reasonable case for legal liability for breach of gratuitously assumed moral obligations to perform a task with care when this is unlikely to reduce the supply of beneficial assumptions of such responsibility, and when enforcement is unlikely to undermine the formation or sustenance of valuable kinds of intimate relationship. In cases in which the assumption of moral obligation is made in a professional context, when liability insurance is likely to be in place, both of these considerations are likely to be in the background. This is not to say that the typical presence of insurance is what positively justifies the defendant's liability in these cases. The assumed moral responsibility is the positive justification of the P-duty and its associated liability. The likely presence of insurance reduces the concern of depleting the supply of gratuitous aid in this context. The potential unfairness of a person being stuck with a demanding P-duty for which they receive no *quid pro quo* can be mitigated, as the current law appears to do, by allowing unilateral rescission of the obligation to perform the service, subject to the other party being compensated for any detrimental reliance.

2. Which Relationships and Roles?

The Third Restatement of Torts, §40 gives this non-exhaustive list of 'special relationships' that give rise to a P-duty with respect to risks that 'arise within the scope' of the relationship:

[5] See *Moyle v Moyle* (1831) 2 Russ & M 710, 715 (Lord Brougham): 'A man may renounce a trust, or he may refuse to undertake it, but having once accepted it, whether as executor or as trustee, he must discharge its duties, so long as his character of trustee subsists; for, by consenting to assume the office, he prevents other persons from being appointed, or accepting, who might have more time and leisure to devote to it. It is no excuse, therefore, that the parties are volunteers; for they are greatly to blame in consenting to act, if they really have not.' This carries the suggestion that a trustee's duties are explained by the *Interference Principle*: the trustee 'prevented' another from assuming the office. But this issue is never investigated in determining a trustee's liability.

[6] On non-contractual voluntary commitments more generally, see R Stevens, 'Borders: Contract, Torts, Property, Equity, "Unjust Enrichment"' (forthcoming).

(1) a common carrier with its passengers,
(2) an innkeeper with its guests,
(3) a business or other possessor of land that holds its premises open to the public with those who are lawfully on the premises,
(4) an employer with its employees who, while at work, are: (a) in imminent danger; or (b) injured or ill and thereby rendered helpless,
(5) a school with its students,
(6) a landlord with its tenants, and
(7) a custodian with those in its custody, if: (a) the custodian is required by law to take custody or voluntarily takes custody of the other; and (b) the custodian has a superior ability to protect the other.[7]

Lists of this kind are perplexing.[8] The main reason is that it is unclear what justifies the inclusion of any particular entry on the list.[9] What justifies P-duties arising from a special relationship? The bare idea of a 'special relationship' does not itself provide the answer: a special relationship, in at least one sense, is simply the obtaining of facts between two persons which do not obtain between everyone. One then wants to know *what facts* of that kind justify P-duties, *and how*. Not all do: 'being taller than' or 'being physically proximate to' are relations that may obtain between particular persons, but these do not ground P-duties in the current law. The world is full of relationships that one person has with another but not with everyone. Not all of these relationships should give rise to legally enforceable P-duties. Similar points can be made in relation to 'roles'.

It is suggested that there is a useful distinction between cases in which the relationship simply triggers a special fact that exists independently of the relationship and cases in which the relationship itself grounds the P-duty.

In the former—triggering—case, the relationship has legal significance as an authoritative determination that, when people stand in that relationship, the special fact is triggered. For instance, a prison custodian's duties to a prisoner can, at least in part, be understood as grounded in the risks which imprisonment creates to the person. The inclusion of 'prison guard and prisoner' on lists like the one above is simply an authoritative determination that the relationship triggers the special fact of creation of risk.[10]

[7] On its 'non-exclusive' nature, see the Third Restatement of Torts, §40, *Comment o*.

[8] For such a list in English law, see Chapter 4, section 1(ii).

[9] Another reason such lists are perplexing is that it is natural to think that it is the *value* of being in a particular relation with another which justifies their being under P-duties; in this way, the relationship can *justify* the P-duty. Yet some of the relationships on the list above are not relationships that it is valuable, or at least intrinsically valuable, to stand in: being involuntarily in another's custody is not such a relationship. I return to this below.

[10] The focus on the relationship as a source of risk may distract attention, however, from more specific actions done by parties to the relation which create risk, and give the misleading impression that a special relationship is required for there to be liability in relation to risk creation. cf *Abrahart v*

There is a further way in which the relationship may be relevant to the triggering of a special fact. It can determine who ought to be understood as creating the relevant risk. In an employment relationship, the authority held by the employer over the employee may justify the conclusion that a risk in the course of the relationship was created by the employer. The relationship in which the parties stand may thus give content to special facts that apply, in principle, between strangers.

Similarly, if the two parties stand in the relationship of friendship, this may be relevant to construing the undertakings they make to each other, for the purposes of the P1 and P2 principles. In *Farwell v Keaton*, the Supreme Court of Michigan held that a friend, Siegrist, owed a P-duty to another friend, Farwell, when the latter had been severely beaten up after following two girls to a bar.[11] Farwell and Siegrist drove around for a couple of hours after the beating and Farwell fell asleep in the back of Siegrist's car. Siegrist parked the car at Farwell's grandparents' house and left without notifying anyone. Farwell was found by his grandparents in the morning, but later died in hospital of an epidural hematoma. The basis of the majority's ruling was that the two were 'companions on a social venture' and that this joint activity involved an 'understanding that one will render assistance to the other when he is in peril if he can do so without endangering himself'.[12] Here the basis of the P-duty seems to be a specific assumption of responsibility, made on the occasion of the venture, with the friendship informing the content of that assumption rather than being a distinct reason for it. The idea is possibly that when *friends* go on such a venture, there is an implicit exchange of promises that assistance will be rendered in such an instance. If so, the decision is, in principle, unproblematic: the fact that two people are friends can reasonably inform the interpretation of a promise made by one to another.[13]

Now consider cases in which the relationship has an independent significance beyond triggering a special fact that applies regardless of whether the parties are in a relationship. If Chapter 4 is correct, this is true at least of employment, a school with its students, and parents and children. A further distinction, borrowed from John Gardner, is useful here. The distinction is between 'loosely' relational duties and 'strictly' relational duties.[14] A duty to take care not to injure another when imposing risk is 'loosely' relational in the sense that, though it is

Bristol University (County Court) [2022] 5 WLUK 260; the negligence issue was not analysed on appeal: [2024] EWHC 299.

[11] (1975) 396 Mich 281.

[12] ibid.

[13] An alternative, even more straightforward, basis for the decision is the *Interference Principle*: it seems not unlikely that Siegrist's conduct made Farwell worse off than if Siegrist had not driven Farwell away from his initial location.

[14] J Gardner, *From Personal Life to Private Law* (OUP 2019) 23–24.

'owed to' the beneficiary, being in the relation of risk-imposer to risk-imposee is not normally intrinsically valuable. Similarly, the relation of 'trespasser' to 'occupier', or 'prison custodian' to 'prisoner', is not intrinsically valuable. In so far as the law attaches P-duties to relations that there is no value as such in occupying, the relation merely identifies a set of circumstances in which there is some other reason for the imposition of a P-duty and the usual objections to P-duties do not have sufficient force.[15] An occupier's duty of humanity towards a dying trespasser is like this: having a person on one's land without one's permission is not a relation of intrinsic value, but the fact that the P-duty is only owed to those on one's land reduces the scope of the duty, and the situations in which one could be called upon to assist another.[16] By contrast, a moral P-duty of friendship plausibly could arise from the intrinsic value of the relationship itself—certain actions are required as an appropriate response to that value.[17] In short, the relationship between the parties can have a negative justificatory significance—it defeats the usual objections to P-duties—or a positive significance: it is part of the positive case for the P-duty in the first place.

Suppose that we focus in, then, on the question of which relationships justify P-duties that are not merely triggers of special facts that apply independently of a relationship (such as creation of risk). Here a further set of distinctions is useful between *bilateral voluntary associations* (such as friendship), *unilateral voluntary associations* (such as parents to young children), and *non-voluntary associations* (such as child family members to other child family members). In the first two cases one can, obviously, say that the existence of the P-duty is partly justified by the *choice* to incur it, whereas *non-voluntary* associations (setting aside creation of risk, etc) face a further justificatory hurdle. But this still does not answer the question of *which* bilateral or unilateral voluntary associations between people should be P-duty triggering.

It seems doubtful that there is a single unifying thread defining when a relationship ought to give rise to or be recognised as having P-duties to protect from a risk within the scope of the relationship. However, the following, non-exhaustive, observations are pertinent.

[15] There may still be an intrinsic value in certain of one's legal duties only arising when one is in the relation. But that is consistent with the relation itself having no intrinsic value. This seems to me a possible response to Christopher Essert's suggestion, contra Gardner, that being a 'neighbour' in the *Donoghue v Stevenson* [1932] AC 562 sense is a relation of intrinsic value: C Essert, 'The Value of the Neighbour Relation' in H Psarras and S Steel (eds), *Private Law and Practical Reason* (OUP 2023). There may be an intrinsic value in one only having duties to one's Atkinian neighbours (which is consistent with Gardner's view), but that is also consistent with the relation itself not being intrinsically valuable (as Gardner contends). These are different claims.

[16] On the occupier's duties, see Chapter 6.

[17] For one version of this view, see J Raz, 'Liberating Duties' (1989) 8 Law and Philosophy 3, 20: 'The justification of the duties of friendship is that they make, or are part of, a relationship which is intrinsically valuable.'

(i) Motivation-Dependent Value

Some relationships are valuable, at least in part, in virtue of the attitudes and motives with which persons in those relations act towards each other. This has two relevant consequences for legal enforcement. First, in many such cases, there is a real risk that legal enforcement would spoil the significance, and so value, of acts within the relationship. If friends, for instance, had legally enforceable duties to provide minor favours on request, this would diminish the communicative value of such acts, by clouding the transparency of the motive with which the acts are done.[18] One does not want one's friend to remember one's birthday because the law says so. Second, by enforcing the duty, in some cases, the law will not respond appropriately to the value that justified the duty. Damages for breach of the duty to acknowledge sympathetically one's friend's recent illness are unlikely to serve the value of friendship.

This concern has less force in relation to P-duties to protect one's friends from a grave physical danger at low cost.[19] Indeed, some of the moral duties of parenthood are motivation-dependent, but this does not provide a compelling argument against legal P-duties of parenthood to protect the child from physical harm (albeit the clouded-motives concern is not present with young children during their childhood). If, however, friendship is construed as involving an assumption of a status that carries with it P-duties to take reasonable care to protect one's friends from grave, physical, harm, there is still a substantial risk of the law spoiling the value of friendship. If these are P-duties to take *reasonable care*, then inquiries into one's friends' health could be construed as attempts to mitigate one's risk of liability. A further difficulty is that friendship comes in many forms and gradations of closeness, and it may often be unclear when a person amounts to another's friend.[20]

(ii) Benefit

Francis Bohlen argued that all P-duties in tort arise from 'a benefit to him on whom they are being imposed'.[21] This explained why there is a P-duty to the invitee present on the occupier's premises for the latter's business purposes, but not to

[18] C Barry and E McTernan, 'A Puzzle of Enforceability: Why Do Moral Duties Differ in their Enforceability?' (2022) 19 Journal of Moral Philosophy 229, 250: 'The presence of a norm permitting enforcement [of duties of friendship] might make us second guess why we do things for one another.'

[19] Plausibly, friends have special moral duties, beyond a duty of easy rescue, towards their friends. On duties of easy rescue, see Chapter 9.

[20] See generally E J Leib, 'Friendship & the Law' (2007) 54 UCLA Law Review 631 (see especially Section I). For an analysis of 'friendship' for the purposes of the trust law rules on certainty of objects, see *In Re Barlow's Will Trusts* [1979] 1 WLR 278, 282.

[21] F Bohlen, 'The Basis of Affirmative Obligations in the Law of Tort' (1905) 53 University of Pennsylvania Law Review 209, 237.

the trespasser.[22] As a justification of the current law, this is difficult to sustain: parental P-duties constitute a counter-example and (now) a trespasser may be owed minimal positive protection. Still, benefit has justificatory significance. Even if a trespasser is owed minimal positive protection, more is owed to a person whom one invites for one's own purposes. For instance, a nightclub might have a P-duty to its clients to take care to protect them from deliberate wrongs by others on the premises.[23]

It is very doubtful whether the fact that one benefits from a person or a thing can *alone* serve as a ground of a P-duty.[24] Suppose one's neighbour's apple trees overhang onto one's land and one is given permission to take the apples that fall on the land. It is doubtful, under the current law, that this benefit triggers a P-duty to take steps if the trees are about to collapse and cause damage to one's neighbour or others. Benefitting needs to be coupled with something else.

The significance of benefitting is also relevant in relation to the duties of adult children to their parents. Children can of course trigger duties to their parents in the same way as strangers, for instance by creation of danger, interference, control over their property, and assuming a caregiving role. In some jurisdictions, adult children are liable to maintain their parent financially when the parent is unable to meet their own basic needs, the child is able to provide for them, and the parent has not abandoned the child or been abusive or neglectful—subject to the consideration of the parent's responsibility for their situation.[25] One justification of this resides in the benefit conferred on the child by the parent's adequate discharge of the parental role. In so far, however, as these P-duties are grounded in a sincere expression of *gratitude* for the benefit intentionally conferred, they are again subject to the objection that legal enforcement cannot effectively enforce such duties.[26]

(iii) Vulnerability and Need

Young children are vulnerable in the following sense: without others providing sustained positive assistance to them across a broad range of environments and activities, they will likely suffer harm to their basic interests.[27] Others are vulnerable

[22] ibid 233–34.

[23] *Everett v Comojo (UK) Ltd* [2011] EWCA Civ 13, [2012] 1 WLR 150.

[24] This would also be inconsistent with the law of restitution's position that *mere receipt* of a benefit is not a liability-generating event.

[25] Maintenance of Parents Act 1995 (Singapore); strictly, parental abuse or neglect is a relevant consideration, rather than decisive: s 5(4).

[26] On different justifications of filial duties, see S Keller, 'Four Theories of Filial Duty' (2006) 56 Philosophical Quarterly 254.

[27] For an argument that 'vulnerability' underlies all special duties, see R Goodin, *Protecting the Vulnerable: A Re-Analysis of Our Social Responsibilities* (University of Chicago Press 1985).

in this sense, too, but not everyone needs sustained positive assistance in virtually every domain of their life in order to avoid serious harm.

As noted above, this vulnerability poses a moral problem. Children will face serious harm unless others have P-duties towards them, but no one can reasonably be required without more to bear these P-duties given their autonomous status. A reasonable solution to this moral problem is that each of us can be required to bear the P-duties if we *choose* to occupy the role of parent, guardian, or carer. The choice to take control of a vulnerable person typically involves a choice to occupy one of these roles with its attendant P-duties.

Notice that vulnerability (especially lack of capacity) is a reason for the law to create a status or role which persons can voluntarily choose to occupy, in a similar way to the law's role in creating the role of executor, tutor, or ward.[28] Urgent moral needs whose satisfaction requires positive conduct on the part of others, more generally, are reasons for the recognition of legal roles that serve these needs. A child's fundamental human right to be educated is a reason for the creation of legal roles that assign P-duties to specific duty-bearers towards specific children. This itself provides a justification of a school's P-duty towards pupils: the voluntary acceptance of a pupil crystallises the role P-duty upon the specific school and pupil.

(iv) Incorporation into One's Agency

The law provides a means by which one person's act is attributed to another, typically a legal, person. In this way one person's agency is incorporated into another's. This is a beneficial option for the person who is able to count another's conduct as their own, even if this does not always work to their overall benefit. It then seems unjust for the person who so incorporates another—and employs them for their own purposes—not to take on any minimal P-responsibility for the other in the course of the activity carried out on their behalf. If an employee suddenly becomes incapacitated in the workplace, even if not due to a risk of the employment, the fact that the employee is acting on behalf of the employer makes it just that the latter have a responsibility to protect them.

(v) Voluntary Control over the Entry into the Duty

Occupiers can decide whether to invite people to their land and delimit the domain in which permission is granted. The law can reasonably attach relatively

[28] Here I am using 'status' and 'role' interchangeably to refer to legally constructed or recognised constellations of rights, duties, and powers which a person can become subject to by doing legally specified acts. See generally M Hardimon, 'Role Obligations' (1991) 91 Journey of Philosophy 333.

non-onerous P-duties on an occupier partly for this reason. Employers choose to enter the relation of employment. More generally, a person can choose whether or not to provide a service to another for a specific purpose. Relatedly, it is generally straightforward to determine whether a person has been invited on the land so one can readily predict when one will come under the P-duties. Other relationships, such as friendship, have less clear entry and exit points.

(vi) The Choice to Occupy a Role Makes One Particularly Well-Positioned to Protect from Harm

Certain relationships or roles bring one into contact with special information, or an environment, which makes them particularly well-positioned to protect from certain harms. An occupier is well-placed to protect against dangers on the premises.

Sometimes the law simply appears to attach a duty to take care to take low-cost steps to particular roles when (a) the nature of the role makes it likely that the role-holder will be uniquely or particularly well-placed to provide assistance as compared to others or the beneficiary, (b) a person's fundamental interests are at stake, (c) the required steps are not particularly onerous, (d) the role is chosen, and (e) the imposition of the duty is not likely to do more harm than good.

Each of these conditions was arguably satisfied in *ABC*.[29] The doctor knew that the claimant's fundamental interests were likely to depend upon whether the doctor informed her or not. There is nothing about the character of their relationship which generates this duty; recall that the claimant was not the defendant doctor's patient. Compare the P-duty to report known cases of female genital mutilation in under eighteens to the police.[30] This duty attaches to regulated medical professionals and teachers.[31] This duty has a similar justification to the duty recognised in *ABC*: it targets persons whose role makes it likely that they will identify the problem, and be relatively well-placed to take some action, when a person's fundamental interests are at stake.[32]

Attaching P-duties to chosen roles in this way, in the absence of a relationship, is hard to reconcile, in English law, however, with the position the law has taken in

[29] [2020] EWHC 455 (QB), [2020] PIQR P13.

[30] Female Genital Mutilation Act 2003, s 5B. It is not asserted that this gives rise to civil liability. The point is simply about the justificatory basis of the duty.

[31] ibid.

[32] For similar reasoning, pointing to the asymmetric ability of a landlord vis-à-vis a tenant to protect against the risk of criminal assaults in an apartment block: *Kline v 1500 Massachusetts Avenue Apartment Corp* 439 F 2d 477 (DC Cir 1970), 480: 'No individual tenant had it within his power to take measures to guard the garage entranceways, to provide scrutiny at the main entrance of the building, to patrol the common hallways and elevators . . . to close the garage doors at appropriate hours, and to see that the entrance was manned at all times.' cf *Liverpool City Council v Irwin* [1977] AC 239 (HL).

relation to public authorities.[33] Conditions (a)–(e) could plausibly be satisfied in relation to a P-duty of easy rescue on a police officer, but no such P-duty exists at common law except in so far as the misfeasance in public office tort is made out.[34]

(vii) More Harm Than Good

The broader negative effects of legal recognition of certain P-duties arising from a role or relationship are, in principle, relevant, even if difficult to assess.[35] If tort liability on medical professionals for failing to assist when off duty significantly reduces the supply of medical professionals, then so much the worse the case for liability.

(viii) A General Objection

Before concluding this section, it will be apt to deal with an objection to the general idea of duties arising from special relationships. The criticism is that the idea is empty.[36] Part of the problem is that what makes a relationship *special* could be the existence of duties between the parties that are not owed by everyone to everyone. In other words, a 'special relationship' *just is* 'the existence of rights and duties between persons that are not owed by everyone to everyone'. But then it seems impossible for special relationships to be a *reason* for P-duties: deciding to create P-duties just is deciding to constitute the parties as in a special relationship. In short, 'special relationship' is the conclusion that a P-duty ought to be owed, not a reason for that conclusion. Another part of the problem is that, as we have seen, whatever one counts as a special relationship, not all of them should trigger P-duties in law.

In response, it can, however, be intelligible to invoke special relationships as reasons for legal duties when the relationship has some existence independently of law, or when it has a legal existence independently of the particular P-duty that the relationship is offered to justify. Friendship, for instance, is a relationship which does not owe its existence to law. The fact that two persons are friends can intelligibly be offered as a justification for legal duties even if the law ought, generally, not to enforce the duties of friendship through P-duties and associated liabilities. The fact that people stand in a legal relationship of employment can also be offered

[33] See Chapter 10.

[34] For a decision that still takes effectively this approach to the P-duties of the police, despite the clear conflict with the approach defined in *Michael* (see Chapter 10), see *Woodcock v Chief Constable of Northamptonshire Police* [2023] EWHC 1062.

[35] See Chapter 2.

[36] *Stockberger v US* (2003) 332 F 3d 479 (Posner J).

as a reason for new P-duties: the fact that the parties are already subject to certain duties may itself support further duties as a means, for instance, of enhancing compliance with the other duties. In other cases, the law's role is more constructive: its imposing P-duties is constitutive of a relationship which, in its inception at least, does not exist other than in law. None of this helps with the question of *which* relationships and roles ought to have P-duties attached to them, or which moral P-duties that part-constitute relationships independently of the law ought to be legally enforced: *to that extent*, the objection is correct. My point here is merely that invoking special relationships as a *reason* for P-duties is not inherently conceptually confused.

(ix) Summary

The focus of this section has been with which patterns of, primarily, chosen association with another person should attract legal P-duties. In many cases, the kind of association one has with another person will simply be a reliable trigger for one of the grounds of a P-duty discussed elsewhere in this book. For instance, the P-duties of *prisons* are explicable, in major part, simply by the fact that imprisonment triggers the *Interference Principle*. Many of an employer's duties to an employee can similarly be explained as involving a creation of a risk, with the relationship simply determining who the risk creator is: the employer's authority over the employee entails that risky action done for the employer is the creation of the latter. In these cases, talk of a 'special relationship' can be potentially confusing: it distracts attention from the underlying facts that explain the duty.

However, in other cases, the law attaches a P-duty to a chosen pattern of association between persons for reasons that go beyond *Creation of risk*, *Interference*, P1 and P2, or taking charge of a person or thing. In the case of parent and child, the parent's duty comes with the parental role, and the existence of that role is, in part, justified by the moral need to have persons to care for vulnerable beings. By accepting or continuing to occupy the role, one accepts the P-duty to take reasonable care in relation to the child's general rights.

The reader was warned to expect disappointment as to the level of specificity that can be offered on which relationships ought to trigger legal P-duties.[37] In the case of *triggering* relationships, there are as many of these as there are ways that voluntary interpersonal association can create risk by virtue of that association. In the case of relationships that *directly* create P-duties, an array of considerations are relevant to whether a pre-legal relation (such as friendship) ought to give rise to an

[37] See Chapter 4, p. 100.

enforceable P-duty, whether the law should attach a P-duty to the fixed package of duties that are already incident to certain legal relationships (such as employment), or whether the law should construct a relationship or role that persons can voluntarily occupy with its attendant P-duties. These include: (i) the extent to which the putative P-duty is justified a motivation-dependent value; (ii) whether the relationship is one from which profit is derived; (iii) whether the recognition of the role or relationship would provide an effective means of satisfying a basic human right or protecting the vulnerable, consistently with the freedom of the putative duty-bearer; (iv) whether the relationship or role is capable of relatively clear delimitation such that one can easily determine its entry and exit points; (v) the extent to which the relationship or putative role-holder is especially well-placed to deal with a risk of harm; and (vi) the broader consequences of recognising the enforceability of the P-duty.

3. Taking on Tasks and Rescues

Consider this example from Joseph Beale:

> A's sheep falls into the river; B, seeing it, undertakes to rescue it. Before the undertaking, B has no duty toward A in the matter; but as soon as he actually enters upon the task of rescue, he must perform it with proper diligence. Any negligence by which the sheep is injured would render him liable to A; so would a negligent abandonment of the rescue when it was almost certain to succeed.[38]

There are some statements in the authorities and literature that if a private individual, A, commences a rescue of B, that *simply* by taking on the task of rescue, A comes under a P-duty to perform the rescue with care.[39]

Modern English law does not accept this proposition without qualification, however: the mere taking on of a task for another is insufficient always to generate a P-duty.[40]

I now argue that English law is correct to reject the idea that *simply* commencing action intended to benefit another creates a P-duty to take care to confer the benefit. I proceed by ruling out possible justifications of such an idea.

[38] J Beale, Jr, 'Gratuitous Undertakings' (1891) 5 Harvard Law Review 221, 223. No authority is cited. Perry (n 2) agrees that Beale is mistaken.

[39] Beale (ibid); D Nolan, 'Assumption of Responsibility: Four Questions' (2019) 72 Current Legal Problems 123, esp 129–33 (and authorities cited therein).

[40] See the cases concerning taking on a task in Chapter 4, section 1(v), including *N v Poole BC* [2019] UKSC 25, [2020] AC 780.

(i) Promises, Again

It might be tempting to insist that the commencement of a task intended to benefit another is itself a promise. This view is implausible, however. A promise involves the communication of an intention to confer a right upon another. Simply picking up another's property, or starting to help someone, need not communicate such an intention. Suppose that I see a child swimming on a deserted beach. I start to monitor the child from my deck chair. I make a note in my diary that I will continue to monitor the child's activity. I have taken on the task of monitoring the child. It seems absurd to suggest that this itself is a promise or that it *itself* creates a P-duty. But it is taking on a task.

(ii) Careless Performance of a Task Commenced as an 'Impure' Omission

A different possible justification is that careless failure in the course of a chosen activity is more akin to an act, in the same way as careless failure to brake in the course of driving is akin to an act. When a person decides to rescue you, careless performance of the rescue is like failing to brake when driving. In important ways, however, it is not. First, impure omissions typically involve the failure to respond to a risk of one's own creation.[41] That is not necessarily the case when a person fails to carry through a rescue. If a rescuer's action *does* introduce a new risk, it should give rise to a duty to take care in relation to that risk, but this is a duty to respond specifically to that risk, not a P-duty to take care to improve the rescuee's pre-existing condition. Second, impure omissions involve failures which raise the likelihood that the person will be worse off than if the impure omitter had not been present. That, again, is not necessarily so in relation to careless performance of a rescue.

(iii) Choice as Defeating the Objection to Enforcement of a Moral Duty of Easy Rescue

If the central objection to P-duties is autonomy-based, then it might be thought that when a person *chooses* to become involved in a situation, their autonomy-based objection to being subject to a legal P-duty is weakened.

If we think, however, that individuals have a moral duty of easy rescue and this duty is morally enforceable by its beneficiary, then there is no such autonomy-based

[41] See Chapter 1.

objection to enforcement of a moral duty of easy rescue. There is no autonomy interest in not complying with one's moral duties. The content of one's moral duties already builds in a concern for one's autonomy. The fact that one has relatively *limited* P-duties compared to N-duties in morality is already a reflection of a concern for one's status as an autonomous being.[42]

Commencement of a rescue could be relevant to whether there *is* a moral duty of easy rescue in the circumstances. It could be so relevant if it entails that the costs to A of completing the rescue have become much lower than they were *ex ante*, and those costs are now at the level such that the rescue is an 'easy' one. While I am not morally obligated to wade through shark-infested waters risking my life to save yours, if I have successfully done so and am no longer at risk of harm, then I cannot turn back and fail to save you: the cost to me of the rescue is now sufficiently low that it is morally required and no longer supererogatory. This idea cannot justify the position that commencement of a rescue distinctively entails a P-duty. First, commencement will not necessarily make the rescue less costly so as to trigger a duty of easy rescue. Second, if the idea were that once a rescue is sufficiently advanced that it becomes trivial to complete, then there ought *pro tanto* to be a legal duty to make trivially costly rescues. That is not the law's position. It might seem morally repugnant not to recognise liability in a situation in which a person could trivially complete a rescue but devotes their attention elsewhere. It may well be, but it is hard to see why it is, *more* morally repugnant than the non-liability of a person who entirely fails to take an utterly trivial step to prevent serious harm to another.

(iv) Conclusion on Taking on a Task and Rescues

Ultimately, I am unable to identify a convincing justification for a general non-promissory taking on the task principle, though there may of course still be one. The most that can be said by way of justification is the following.

First, by becoming involved in a situation one will often reasonably foreseeably increase the probability that others will not intervene. In cases involving life-threatening risks, even a very small probability that one will have done so should trigger a P-duty to take care to continue the rescue by virtue of the *Interference Principle*.

Second, by taking on a rescue, one will often be positioned such that one is implicated in the creation of a risk to the person rescued. For instance, if a person rescues a small child by picking them up out of a pool of water, and then carelessly drops the child at the pool edge, the person is implicated in the creation of a further risk to the child: this may amount to the breach of an N-duty. This point also

[42] See Chapter 2, esp section 1(i).

deals with an example given by the Third Restatement, which claims that there is a genuine P-duty arising when a person takes on a rescue: 'once having secured the safety of the other, the rescuer may not then return the other to peril, even if the peril is no greater than that which existed at the time the actor initiated the rescue. Thus, one who rescues a drowning swimmer and brings the swimmer to shore may not leave the swimmer in the middle of a busy highway.'[43] The example in fact involves the breach of an N-duty to the swimmer stemming from the creation of a new risk to the swimmer (and, in addition, a likely breach of an N-duty to users of the highway). In these ways, there will be a robust, albeit still contingent, connection between taking on a task and incurring P-duties or triggering N-duties.

Third, certain actions of taking on a task amount, in certain contexts, to the choice to incur a role responsibility to a specific other. If a hospital takes a person into its charge, this itself amounts to a choice to incur a role responsibility to the person. If a person takes hold of a lost child's hand, this itself, by virtue of social conventions, amounts to a choice to incur a temporary role responsibility to the child.

4. Public Authorities and Assumption of Responsibility

The law on when a public authority, particularly an emergency service, will 'assume responsibility' is particularly complex. The following is relatively clear: if an emergency service—police, fire brigade, ambulance service—promises a specific individual to protect that or another specific individual from a risk, in circumstances in which it is reasonably foreseeable that the promisee will resultantly not take protective measures in relation to the individual at risk, this triggers a duty to take protective measures on the basis of an assumption of responsibility.[44]

Difficulties emerge when one considers the contrast between the following cases.

(i) P-Duties Recognised

If a paramedic, employed by a National Health Service Trust, commences treatment of an unconscious person as part of their employment, the paramedic will owe a P-duty to the person to do so carefully on the basis of an assumption of responsibility.

[43] Third Restatement of Torts (n 7) §44 cmt h.

[44] *Kent v Griffiths* [2001] QB 36 (ambulance); *An Informer v A Chief Constable* [2012] EWCA Civ 197, [2013] Q.B. 579; *Michael v Chief Constable of South Wales* [2015] UKSC 2, [2015] AC 1732 [69], [138] (police). The only room for doubt here is in relation to the fire brigade: no duty of care arose in *Capital and Counties plc v Hampshire County Council* [1997] QB 1004. But *Capital* did not involve a promise made to a specific person on which that person might foreseeably rely to their detriment. When P1 or P2 applies, if the fire brigade does not take reasonable care, it risks making the person worse off. This was accepted, as a general matter, to generate liability in *Capital*.

School teachers owe P-duties to pupils to take reasonable care to identify and accommodate learning difficulties.[45]

Educational psychologists working for local authorities owe P-duties to children referred to them for assessment by parents or schools.[46]

Doctors sometimes owe duties of care to identified non-patients to warn them of severe risks of harm, based on knowledge or constructive knowledge of these risks.[47]

(ii) P-Duties Not Recognised, Despite Commencement of an Activity within the Authority's Functions

If a fire brigade commences dealing with a fire, it owes no P-duty on the basis of an assumption of responsibility, simply in virtue of commencing the rescue towards persons who may be negatively affected by failure to do so carefully.[48]

If a police officer begins taking protective steps in relation to a risk, this does not itself create a P-duty carefully to continue this protection so as to prevent the materialisation of the risk.[49]

If a social worker arranges to have a specific child placed on a child protection register and monitors the child's home situation, they do not owe a P-duty to the child to take reasonable steps to protect the child from abuse on the basis of an assumption of responsibility.[50]

If a catchment board exercises a statutory power to repair a floodwall that protects the claimant's land, but conducts the repairs with careless delay, it owes no P-duty to the claimant.[51]

In my view, these distinctions cannot be fully justified. If it is accepted that a doctor may incur, by virtue of their assumption of a role responsibility, a P-duty to a third party when there is knowledge of a risk of severe harm to that particular third party, it is difficult to restrict this to the role responsibility of *doctors*.[52] A surveyor, for instance, who while acting for B discovers that neighbouring property occupied by C will soon collapse, unbeknownst to C or others, stands in a structurally similar position to the doctor in *ABC*. At any rate, this distinction cannot be

[45] *Phelps v Hillingdon LBC* [2001] 2 AC 619, 666–68.

[46] ibid 665–66.

[47] *ABC v St George's Healthcare NHS Trust and Others* [2020] EWHC 455 (QB), [2020] PIQR P13. See Chapter 4, p. 103.

[48] *Capital* (n 44).

[49] *Tindall v Thames Valley Police* [2022] EWCA Civ 25, [2022] 4 WLR 104.

[50] *Poole* (n 40). Even if it has been resolved that the child should be taken into care: *HXA v Surrey County Council; YXA v Wolverhampton City Council* [2023] UKSC 52.

[51] *East Suffolk Rivers Catchment Board v Kent* [1941] AC 74.

[52] For arguments against consequence-based distinctions between the liability of the police and other public authorities, see S Tofaris and S Steel, 'Negligence Liability for Omissions and the Police' (2016) 75 Cambridge Law Journal 128.

drawn without identification of competing consequence-based considerations in such a situation.[53]

In each of the no-P-duty cases, the law *could have* assigned a role-based P-duty to each of these entities.[54] Such a P-duty could rest upon the fact that the entity has been assigned the role of protecting people from certain kinds of harm. The duty would, then, rest upon the law's assignment of responsibility to certain public authorities. However, the fact that an authority has been assigned some harm-protective role is not considered to be sufficient on its own in the current law to justify a P-duty.[55] As the law stands, it is not an admissible argument, in relation to the 'role' strand of assumption of responsibility, that the public authority has a special role in protecting against the kind of harm suffered. Neither is it an admissible argument, in relation to the 'special relation' strand, that the public authority stands in the special relation of 'state to citizen or legal subject'. The relevant kind of 'assumption of responsibility' needs to be one which would generate a P-duty upon a similarly situated private individual. It is clear that private individuals would not be under P-duties merely by virtue of commencing the activities above in the last four situations. For instance, suppose that a concerned neighbour keeps a log of an abused child's activities and suspicious activity by the child's parents; if the neighbour fails to identify risks which a competent observer would have seen, this surely does not render the neighbour liable.[56]

Even if we set aside the idea that public authorities have special role or relational responsibilities that *ipso facto* constitute an assumption of responsibility to perform their role with care—an idea clearly rejected by the current law—it is not entirely clear why the position of a person being protected by the fire brigade or a child being monitored by a social worker is not analogous to an unconscious person being assisted by a doctor in hospital or a child being educated in a school. In these last instances, the law does not regard the defendant's conduct as merely the commencement of an activity; it is a duty-generating event.

The fundamental unifying thread in each case just mentioned is that a person takes on a task, as part of an organisational role, in order to protect another identified person from a harm or confer on that person a benefit; only in some cases, however, does the law affix a P-duty of care to the entry into performance of that task.

The differentiating feature cannot be that, in one set, the parties *agree* that one party will have a right to the careful performance of an act, whereas in the other set

[53] See, similarly, J Morgan, 'Nonfeasance and the End of Policy? Reflections on the Revolution in Public Authority Liability' (2019) 35 Journal of Professional Negligence 32, 52, identifying an essential role for 'policy' in determining the contours of assumed responsibilities.

[54] *Robinson v Chief Constable of West Yorkshire* [2018] UKSC 4, [2018] AC 736 [115] (Lord Hughes).

[55] See further Chapter 10.

[56] See further section 3.

they do not: the right may be acquired without agreement (as in the case of the unconscious patient or where a child's consent would not be valid).

Another possible distinction is between tasks done *for a person* and tasks done *for the public*. The task of fighting fire might be said to be conducted for the public as a whole, rather than for any particular person.[57] If doing a task 'for a person' is doing it, at least in part, with the aim of benefitting that person by doing the task, then this distinction does not map on to the cases: presumably, adopting a child protection plan is done with the intention of benefitting a child. And one can easily envisage cases of action by fire brigades that are intended to benefit specific persons: suppose a person is being removed from the wreckage of a car accident. If doing a task 'for a person' is doing the task in order to satisfy a request of that person, then, again, the distinction does not map on to the cases: a school does not provide education 'at the request of' a child, and conversely a fire brigade might provide a service in order to satisfy a request for rescue made by a particular person.

Perhaps the most plausible account of acting 'for a person' here is an account based on how a person's interests should figure in the performance of the task. Some tasks ought to be governed exclusively or predominantly by a concern for the promotion of the interest of a particular person or set of persons. Medical treatment ought to be governed by an exclusive or predominant concern for the interest of the patient. By contrast, fighting fires or protecting against flooding might be considered inevitably to involve trading-off the interests of multiple persons, such that it cannot be governed by an exclusive or predominant concern for the interest of a particular person. Indicatively, in relation to the prevention of fire or protection against flooding, no individual's consent to the task ought generally to be decisive, given the implication of multiple persons' interests. While a child's consent to education is not decisive, this is because of the child's lack of capacity. By contrast, a landowner's consent to repair of a floodwall may not be decisive regardless of their capacity: consent is not decisive because more than the individual's interest is at stake.

Still, this does not seem to give a robust distinction that maps onto the cases. In truth, even medical treatment *can* involve trade-offs between multiple individuals' interests. With scarce resources, devoting some medical resources to one patient may reduce the protection to another. True, stark instances where one person's interests are fundamentally set back to protect another are likely to be less frequent than in the context of protection against fires or floods. Nonetheless, a localised fire that affects a single isolated building posing no risks to others may not involve trade-offs between the interests of multiple individuals.

[57] See *Capital* (n 44) and Nolan (n 39).

A radical possibility for reconciling the cases—albeit only if we still set aside the P-duty of doctors to non-patients—would be to hold that a public authority only comes under a duty by assumption of responsibility if their promise foreseeably risks a person being made worse off, or if they take control of a person's body or property. Taking control is significant in so far as non-consensual interference with a person's body (as in the unconscious patient example) can only be justified if it promotes the interest of the right-holder. Duties to unconscious persons would be like the duties of finders of property: control in the former, like possession in the latter, is justified only on condition that it is for the benefit of the right-holder. In this way, a social worker would not generally be under a P-duty because it is not reasonably foreseeable that the beneficiary of the work or others would rely upon a promise made and, unless the child is taken into care, no control of the relevant kind is exercised. This broadly lines up the cases, but it would require the law to reject the idea that an assumption of responsibility can ever generate a duty absent control and foreseeable risk of detrimental reliance; Chapter 4 argued that assumption of responsibility goes beyond such cases.

Given the unifying thread, and the difficulty of identifying other distinctions between cases concerning when a public authority assumes responsibility, it is doubtful that the current law is entirely consistent. The unifying thread is A's entering into performance of a service, as part of A's organisational role as an authority, in order to protect B from physical harm or meet a fundamental need of B, and B agrees to this performance or B's agreement is irrelevant by virtue of B's incapacity.[58]

In summary, it is clear that the first strand of assumption of responsibility—P1 and P2—applies to public authorities. The second strand—based on role and relational responsibility—applies when the public authority is performing a task for which there is a private parallel, such as provision of medical care. The third strand—based on custody of a person—must also apply: when an authority's employee takes control of the body of a person, they owe that person P-duties, partly because of *Interference* and partly in order to justify the interference. The difficult cases are those in which the authority involves itself in the life of a person non-consensually, as may be the case with social work, since there is no clear private parallel (private relationships being typically formed by, or sensitive to, consent). In these situations, the law *could* construct a special role or relationship-based assumption of responsibility when the authority, as part of its role, agrees to provide protective services in relation to a person; however, this would be a special 'public' strand of assumption of responsibility. Since English law has firmly accepted the

[58] In some cases, a statutory scheme that regulates the relationship between A and B will make clear that A does not trigger a P-duty to B in such cases: see *HXA* (n 50) [97]. Indeed, a statute may itself be construed as setting out the conditions under which A assumes a responsibility to B, and this provides a reason against the common law defining an assumption of responsibility with a different content.

negative equality principle, which restricts an authority's duties in tort to those grounds that would apply against a private individual, such cases pose particular difficulties of coherence.[59]

5. Conclusion

If this chapter is correct, then some of the duties that travel under the label 'assumption of responsibility' can be justified as particular instantiations of the *Innocent Risk Principle*, with the promise creating a risk unless action is taken by the duty-bearer to avoid that risk. This is perhaps part of the reason why there is scepticism about the concept of 'assumption of responsibility': the fact that the duty can be understood, sometimes, as an instantiation of a general N-duty seems to make the concept dispensable.[60] Yet, as noted above, this point can be pushed too far. The specific duties to obviate risks one creates by one's promises are duties triggered by one's communicating an intention to create a moral obligation; they are, to that extent, chosen.

Other duties arising by virtue of an assumption of responsibility cannot be understood as manifestations of a general N-duty. This is the case with P-duties of voluntarily assumed roles, such as the role of parent, and with P-duties which the law attaches to relationships, such as employment. Here a person's choice to accept an obligation justifies their being the one to meet the interest or need which the obligation is designed to protect. It is a mistake to think that the only justifiable source of rights to another's careful action are those acquired contractually. It is appropriate to allow the assumption of enforceable legal obligations to persons without such persons' assent in cases where such persons cannot acquire rights by assent yet urgently need assistance. And limited non-contractual obligations to perform services carefully are justifiable enforcements of assumed moral responsibilities, in contexts in which legal enforcement will not undermine intimate relationships or deplete the supply of valuable forms of gratuitous aid.

59 For a rejection of the negative equality principle, see Chapter 10.
60 See J Stapleton, *Three Essays on Torts* (OUP 2022) 54.

6
Control

The idea that 'control' over a person, land, an animal, or a thing is a source of P-duties is well-established.[1] It is said that 'control imports responsibility', specifically a responsibility to act.[2] The nature of the control required and the justification of control as a basis for P-duties is, however, rarely examined. The question is interesting because, on one natural analysis, to have control of a risk is to have a reliable ability to prevent, or influence, the risk. Yet, this notion of control, if it generated P-duties, would contradict the general absence of a duty to intervene to prevent harm to others. Thus, if 'control' is significant simply in virtue of identifying persons reliably able to prevent harm, considerable tension is created in the law by the recognition of 'control' as a special fact.

The first two sections of the chapter analyse the current law. They make a simple, but often unarticulated, distinction between control as a source of duties to the controlled and control as a source of duties to third parties. The third section turns to justification.

Two overarching arguments are made. First, the situations in which control generates duties to the controlled can be reduced to other special facts: *Innocent Risk*, *Interference*, or assumption of responsibility; the relevant notion of 'control' is therefore to be determined by the conditions which trigger these principles. Second, control as a source of duties to third parties cannot be so reduced. In particular, an occupier's P-duty in relation to risks on their land is grounded in a variety of considerations connected with the enjoyment of a right to exclude.

1. Control as a Source of Duties to the Controlled

(i) Persons

In *Reeves v Metropolitan Police Commissioner*, an N-duty to take care not to provide a means by which a distressed prisoner could commit suicide was

[1] See sections 1–2.
[2] See, eg, *Home Office v Dorset Yacht Co Ltd* [1970] AC 1004 (HL) 1055 (Lord Pearson). For the view that 'power' or 'control' is the primary justification of legal duties to act, see M Shapo, *The Duty to Act* (Texas UP 1977).

Omissions in Tort Law. Sandy Steel, Oxford University Press. © Sandy Steel 2024.
DOI: 10.1093/9780191898822.003.0006

stated to arise from 'the complete control which the police or prison authorities have over the prisoner'.[3] The fact that control is held to justify an N-duty that would normally not exist—normally, there is no N-duty to take care not to contribute to a person's deliberately harming herself—strongly implies that it would also be held to justify an exceptional P-duty to the prisoner in this context.[4] It is difficult to believe, for instance, that a prison would have no P-duty of care in negligence to seek medical assistance for a prisoner who fell seriously ill.

A sufficient condition of the relevant kind of 'control' is likely to be that A is *detaining* B: A forecloses B's ability to access the external world. Normally, if A has non-consensually detained B, A wrongs B and has a duty to restore B's access to the external world. Since prison authorities have a permission and a duty to detain prisoners, this is obviously not possible. However, the fact that A is preventing B's ability to protect B's own right-protected interests justifies A's being under a duty to protect B's right-protected interests. This is justified by the *Interference Principle*: A, by detaining B, prevents B and others from being able to prevent harm to B.[5]

It is doubtful that this kind of control—detention – is necessary, however. A person can control another in myriad ways that should give rise to duties arising from *Interference*. A could control B by having brainwashed B such that B treats A's word as authoritative on all or some matters. A could control B by threatening B with sanctions if B does not act in accordance with A's directives. A could control B by exercising authority over B. For instance, if B is A's employee, then B is likely subject to a contractual duty to obey A's instructions in some domain. This fact can endanger third parties, but it can also endanger the employee: the employee is required to defer to the employer's judgement in relation to the employment.[6] In each of these instances, a duty should arise to the extent that the exercise of control creates a risk of harm to B. By exercising control in these ways, A can be said to be the creator of a risk to B when, normally, given B's status as an autonomous agent, the risk would be attributed solely to B.

[3] *Reeves v Commissioner of Police of the Metropolis* [2000] 1 AC 360 (HL) 369 (Lord Hoffmann).

[4] eg §40 of the Third Restatement of Torts lists 'custodian with those in its custody' as a special relationship triggering a P-duty: *Restatement of Torts (Third): Liability for Physical and Emotional Harm*, vol 2 (American Law Institute 2010).

[5] Detention need not involve *physical* constraint: a person may, for example, be fearful of the consequences of disobeying another if they move from a location, or treat the other as an authority on whether they should leave: see generally *Rabone v Pennine Care NHS Foundation Trust* [2012] UKSC 2, [2012] 2 AC 72 [29] (Lord Dyson).

[6] Christine Beuermann justifies the vicarious liability of the employer by reference to the employer's authority, on the basis that this creates risk to third parties: C Beuermann, *Reconceptualising Strict Liability for the Torts of Another* (Hart 2019) 69–71.

(ii) Land and Things

If A has possession of B's thing, it seems that A will owe a duty to B to take care of the thing, regardless of whether B has permitted A to be in possession or not. Of course, in this case the duty is not literally *to the controlled*, but to a person whose land or thing is subject to the control of another.

If A agrees to take possession of goods at B's request, whether for reward or otherwise, then this will likely constitute a bailment; it is then clear that A has a duty to take care of the goods.[7] A possible justification is the P1 principle: A impliedly promises to take reasonable care of the thing and in reliance upon this B gives up possession to A.[8]

If A finds B's goods and takes possession, then A has a duty to take care of the goods and to take steps to re-acquaint the owner with the thing.[9] If A *wrongfully* takes possession of B's goods, it seems unlikely that A will stand in a better position than a finder; a wrongful possessor cannot reasonably complain that they are subject to the same duties as a non-wrongful possessor.

In what sense must A have possession of B's goods in order for A to owe a duty to B? There appears to be a link drawn between a person's right to exclude from the thing and the existence of a duty: if there is control sufficient to give rise to the right, there is a duty.[10] In principle, however, it should also suffice if there is control which (i) secludes the thing from the care of others (triggering the *Interference Principle*), or (ii) amounts to an agreement to look after the thing which the transferor relies upon (triggering an assumption of responsibility in the sense of P1 and P2).[11]

[7] *Houghland v RR Low (Luxury Coaches) Ltd* [1962] 1 QB 694 (CA).

[8] As to which, see Chapter 4.

[9] *Parker v British Airways Board* [1982] QB 1004 (CA) 1017 (Donaldson LJ). For the link to *Interference*, see further Chapter 4, section 1(iii). See also L Rostill, *Possession, Relative Title and Ownership in English Law* (OUP 2021) 133–34 (locating a basis for the possessor's right to exclude on its function in facilitating their taking care of the goods for the benefit of the true owner).

[10] See ibid, esp *Parker* at 1017. This is also implicit in *Kowal v Ellis* (1977) 76 DLR (3d) 546, 548–49 (Manitoba Court of Appeal) (O'Sullivan J).

[11] See further, section 3(i)–(ii). In *Scarborough v Cosgrove* [1903] 2 KB 805 (CA), a lodger in a lodging-house was owed a P-duty by the keeper of the lodging-house when the arrangement in the house was that the key to the lodger's room had to be handed over to the owner when the lodger went out. The owner had 'custody' of the lodger's goods, and this custody generated a P-duty to take care in relation to access to the goods. Lord Collins MR held that '[t]he general control of the house must be in the keeper. By the nature of the arrangement itself the custody of the lodger's effects must be in him when the lodger is not in his room' (at 813). Both Lord Collins MR (at 813) and Romer LJ (at 815–16) also drew attention to the fact that the custody was obtained in the course of a business. This could be understood as involving an implied agreement to take care of the goods when the lodger handed over the key.

(iii) Voluntary and Involuntary Control

Clearly, the person controlled need not have chosen to be subject to the control: prisoners are the obvious example. A more difficult issue is whether the *controller* must have chosen to exercise the custody, charge, or possession over the person or thing. In almost all cases there will be an act whereby the controller chooses to take a person or thing into their control. Even in cases of so-called 'involuntary bailment', there is normally an act whereby the involuntary bailee takes the thing into their possession. For instance, in *Newman v Bourne & Hollingsworth*, a customer accidentally left a brooch behind in the defendant's shop; a clerk put the brooch in a desk drawer from which it was stolen.[12] The defendant was held liable as an involuntary bailee. The clerk's act of picking up the brooch can be said to trigger the duty, however.[13]

In principle, however, if A physically encloses B from the external world, and in that sense has 'control' over B, then A may come under a duty by virtue of *Interference*, even if this physical enclosure did not arise from A's choice. For instance, if A finds B, a trespasser, locked in A's garden shed, and the trespasser is about to die, it is arguable that A has a duty to B to call for assistance. The fact that A's property physically encloses B from the external world substantially raises the probability that others will not assist B. Similarly, if a lorry driver discovers that a refugee has secluded himself in the back of his lorry, the lorry driver cannot leave the refugee trapped in lorry: the fact that the lorry driver has the right to control access to the lorry, which is preventing others accessing the refugee, generates a duty.

Although such duties travel as P-duties under the current law, they are in fact N-duties; 'control' in this context breaks down entirely to *Interference* or *Innocent Risk*, which involve making B worse off than if A or A's resources did not exist.[14]

2. Control as a Source of Duties to Third Parties

This section is concerned with situations in which A has control, in some sense, over C, who is a source of risk to B, and C causes damage to B. There is some overlap with the cases discussed in the previous section, namely, when A has control over *both* C and B. However, the focus of the decisions here is on the control which A has over C, rather than control over B, the person to whom the duty is owed.

[12] (1915) 31 TLR 209.

[13] *York Products Pty Ltd v Gilchrist Watt and Sanderson Pty Ltd* [1970] 1 WLR 1262, 1268 ('the *taking of possession* in the circumstances involves an assumption of responsibility for the safe keeping of the goods' (emphasis added)) (Lord Pearson).

[14] See Chapters 1, 3, and 4.

(i) Control Over a Natural Person

If A has control of C, a young child, then A seems to have a P-duty to anyone who might foreseeably be injured by a failure to exercise that control carefully.[15] Here 'control' must involve more than a reliable ability to intervene to modify the child's behaviour: otherwise, the 'control' principle would, again, contradict the absence of a general P-duty to intervene to prevent harm to others when one could easily do so. That said, anyone who has accepted a young child into their care is likely to trigger the principle; this paradigmatically involves exercising authority over the child by determining the child's location, access to the child, and its activities. This conduct indicates that the person accepts the role of caregiver in relation to the child.

If C is an adult lawfully detained by A, then A has a duty to take care to prevent A's escaping and causing harm to general rights, but this duty only seems to be owed by A to persons who are especially endangered by C's escape from that detention. This is the effect of the House of Lords decision in *Dorset Yacht v Home Office*.[16] Borstal officers had borstal detainees in their custody on an island near to the claimant's property. The officers carelessly failed to supervise the detainees properly. Seven of them resultantly escaped at night, boarded the claimant's yacht, and damaged it by casting it adrift. The officers were held to be under a duty to take care to control the detainees to prevent damage to the claimant. It was accepted that there is no general duty to prevent a person being damaged by the deliberate wrong of another. A special circumstance is required. Lord Morris described this special circumstance as follows: 'There was a special relation in that the officers were entitled to exercise control over boys who to the knowledge of the officers might wish to take their departure and who might well do some damage to property near at hand'.[17] This suggests that the *right* to exercise control suffices to create the P-duty. Lord Diplock's judgment imposed a further condition, that 'there be some relationship between the custodian and the person to whom the duty is owed which exposes that person to a particular risk of damage in consequence of [the] escape'.[18] Those in physical proximity to the island were subject to this 'particular risk'.[19]

Lord Diplock's additional condition, beyond control between A and C, has been subsequently accepted.[20] The additional condition does not require physical

[15] *Carmarthenshire County Council v Lewis* [1955] AC 549 (HL), [1955] 2 WLR 517 (though note that 'control' is not used to justify this duty by the court: it is based on creation of risk). See also *Vicar of Writtle v Essex County Council* [1979] 77 LGR 656.

[16] *Dorset Yacht* (n 2). See also *Palmer v Tees Health Authority* [2000] PIQR P1, [2000] PNLR 87.

[17] ibid 1038–39.

[18] ibid 1070.

[19] ibid.

[20] *Palmer* (n 16); *Thomson v Scottish Ministers* [2013] CSIH 63, 2013 SC 628; *Couch v Attorney-General* [2008] NZSC 45, [2008] 3 NZLR 725.

proximity between A and B. It suffices if A ought to be aware that C's escape from custody would impose a particular risk on B.[21]

The meaning of 'control' for the purposes of generating a P-duty to take care to prevent a person under one's control causing damage to another is not entirely clear.

In *Dorset Yacht*, there was (i) detention, or actual custody, of the person at a particular point in time, (ii) a statutory duty to hold the person in custody, and (iii) a statutory permission to hold the detainee in custody. It is suggested that a mere permission to detain a person and a statutory duty to do so cannot be sufficient under the current law.

Point (iii) itself—a permission—is insufficient: if I see a dangerous criminal imminently about to kill a person, I have a permission to detain them at least temporarily to prevent the attack, but I clearly do not owe a legal P-duty to do so.[22] It might be said that while I have the permission to prevent the attack using force, I do not have the permission to detain. Presumably, however, depending on the facts, if detention is necessary to prevent violation of another's bodily rights, it may be permissible for a private person to do so for a period of time. It is true that public bodies have *special* permissions to detain going beyond those of private individuals. But the fact that public authorities have *special* permissions or powers has been held to be insufficient to justify their having more extensive P-duties: if the mere existence of such a special permission were sufficient for a P-duty, this would be inconsistent with *Michael*, in which the police had a right to control the wrongdoer and yet no P-duty arose.[23]

However, there are statements in the authorities which support the following principle: if A has the legal power to detain C, and A owes a P-duty to C in virtue of the relationship between A and C, then A will owe a duty of care to B either to detain C or to warn B if C is not detained, if A knows or reasonably ought to know that C will pose a particular risk to B's general rights if the power is not exercised. In *Palmer v Tees HA*, C was being treated as an outpatient in A's hospital, having been discharged as an in-patient. During his initial admission to hospital, he said that he would murder a child after being discharged. He later did. Stuart-Smith LJ suggested, without holding, that A *might* have a duty to warn a person at special risk from C, for instance, a child in C's household.[24] In *Griffiths v Chief Constable*

[21] *Couch* (n 20). See also *Griffiths v Chief Constable of Suffolk* [2018] EWHC 2538 (QB) [451] referring to *Palmer Tees* (n 16) as authority that it was necessary that the identity of the potential victim(s) could be established 'as distinct from general members of the public' to ensure that adequate steps can be taken in response to the duty imposed, for example to warn the victim (but this was not made out on the facts of the case: [455], [457].

[22] On the permission to detain, see, eg, s 24A of the Police and Criminal Evidence Act 1984 (civilian power to arrest to stop or prevent an indictable offence). On the absence of a legal P-duty to detain, see generally Chapters 1 and 2.

[23] See *Michael v Chief Constable of South Wales* [2015] UKSC 2, [2015] AC 1732.

[24] *Palmer* (n 16) [32]. At [31], Stuart-Smith LJ held that this was necessary, but did not express a view on whether it would be sufficient.

of Suffolk, C's psychiatric condition was being assessed by A, who had the power to detain him under the same legislation. Ouseley J held that, during C's assessment, A had sufficient control to trigger a P-duty. This was on the basis that A would have been able to prevent C from leaving and A had the legal power to do so.[25] Had B been identifiable by A as at distinctive risk of harm by C, A would have had a duty to warn B of C's release.[26]

The idea that A could have a P-duty in tort towards B to exercise a power to detain C, or a P-duty to warn B if that power is not exercised, is difficult to reconcile with the general absence of a P-duty to take care to protect others from harm. It is abundantly clear that the mere fact that a person has a special ability to help another is not itself sufficient to generate a P-duty to take care to do so.[27] This being so, the fact that a person has a special power to detain or special knowledge of a risk should alone be insufficient to trigger a P-duty. As noted above, if 'control' means 'especially well-placed to protect from a risk' then it cannot be reconciled with the absence of a general P-duty of easy rescue.

Point (ii) itself is also insufficient: it is clear that under the current law a statutory duty to do X does not itself entail a private law duty to (take care to) do X.[28]

Consequently, the references in *Dorset* to the idea that a statutory duty or entitlement to hold in custody justifies a P-duty cannot be reconciled with the modern position that special (public) powers or entitlements do not alone justify P-duties. If *Dorset* is to be reconciled with the proposition that the mere existence of a statutory duty or power does not itself entail a P-duty of care, there must be 'control' in some sense beyond the existence of a statutory duty and a permission to hold a person in custody.

One possibility is that it involves having a person *in one's custody* at a point in time. This does not mean that the wrongdoer must be in the custody of the person at the time of the wrong, but that the person failed to exercise care to retain the person in custody.[29] Yet it is not obvious why one should draw the line at custody. If custody simply signifies a reliable ability to prevent the harm, then it is arbitrary to insist upon it. Suppose that I have brainwashed a person into doing exactly as I say. If this person, on their own account, comes up with the plan of killing someone, I could easily prevent them by virtue of the authority I have over them. Yet I clearly

[25] *Griffiths v Chief Constable of Suffolk* [2018] EWHC 2538 (QB) [454]. A psychologist would have such a P-duty in Californian law, as a result of the decision in *Tarasoff v Regents of University of California*, 551 P 2d 334 (Cal 1976).

[26] *Griffiths* (n 25) [454]–[455].

[27] *Michael* (n 23) [2015] UKSC 2, [2015] AC 1732. See generally Chapter 10 on public authorities. See, eg, *HXA, SXA (A protected party by her litigation friend Andrea Webb) v Surrey County Council* [2021] EWHC 250 (QB) [35]: in rejecting the existence of a P-duty arising from control, Deputy Master Bagot QC held that 'here there was no such control over *or* right to control the wrongdoers' (emphasis added).

[28] *Gorringe v Calderdale MBC* [2004] UKHL 15, [2004] 1 WLR 1057.

[29] cf, eg, *Dorset Yacht* (n 2) 1069 (Lord Diplock regarding factual custody of the detainee at the time of the tortious act as inessential).

have no P-duty under the current law to do so simply because it is easy for me to help.

There seem to be three rational possibilities. First, it could be the fact that custody is itself risk-creating, and this generates a duty by virtue of the *Innocent Risk Principle*. Bringing offenders to an island without the usual protection of prison walls is a dangerous enterprise. By conducting it, one imposes a significantly greater risk upon nearby persons than those persons would be subject to were the prisoners not there. It is the *imprisonment* which creates the danger. Consequently, if a serial killer who attacks victims with red hair is carelessly allowed to escape, there would be no duty to red-haired persons *generally*, as their risk of harm is not increased by the imprisonment. By contrast, there would be a duty to nearby persons with red hair, whose risk has been increased by the presence of the prison nearby. This, though, does not provide support for a genuine P-duty, but rather an N-duty not to make worse off stemming from the *Innocent Risk Principle.*

Second, it could be argued that custody matters in so far as it involves placing persons who would otherwise be endangered by an offender in a position of safety, such that the careless release of the criminal amounts to re-endangering the person. It is like reducing a blazing fire to a low glow, and then allowing it to regain its initial blazing strength. But it is difficult to see how *reducing a risk* itself can be a ground of a P-duty.[30] It would be different if a prison guard deliberately assisted a prisoner's escape: here the guard would be directly implicated in the danger to the person.[31]

Third, when the state, through prison authorities, imposes a lawful sentence of imprisonment on a person, this could be understood as an assumption of responsibility to persons foreseeably endangered by that person, to protect them from that risk. This is plausible, but it would be the law's construction of a role responsibility on prison authorities based on their statutory duties and powers. For reasons given in Chapter 10, such an argument is defensible, but difficult to reconcile with the general position the current law has taken on public authorities. That position holds that assumption of responsibility requires something more particularised vis-à-vis the claimant.

(ii) Control Over a Legal Person

The exercise of control over a company may generate duties to the employees of the company and to others damaged by the careless failure to exercise that control reasonably.

[30] *Dorset* has a different structure to the cases in Chapter 10, where one person is currently providing protection from a risk, and the only way that protecting can be removed is by directly harming another.

[31] This would then be akin to the cases in Chapter 10.

Clearly, it cannot be a requirement that the company be in the 'custody' of the person. The issue is whether A exercises control over the company's (C) operations either generally or in relation to some particular activity. This has been described, more specifically, as whether A exercises 'de facto management' of the company or a particular activity.[32] In *Vedanta v Lungowe Resources*, Lord Briggs described one important instantiation of the kind of control that is sufficient when A is C's parent company: '[A] takes active steps, by training, supervision and enforcement, to see that they [policies of a group of companies] are implemented by relevant subsidiaries.'[33] Presumably, another manifestation would be, as in the case of natural persons, where A has authority over C, such that C takes A's directions as determinative of what C does in some matter; if A instructs C to do some act, in such circumstances, the risk created by C can also be attributed to A. Arguably, 'control' simply functions here as displacing the normal presumption that the companies are separate and autonomous legal persons, such that the parent cannot usually be described as the creator of risk by the subsidiary. If, however, A has sufficient control over some domain of C's activity, then A *can* be said to have created the risk of harm to B *through C*.

Lord Briggs also considered that it would be sufficient if a parent company held itself out as exercising control over subsidiaries in this way, even if it did not in fact do so: 'its very omission may constitute the abdication of a responsibility which it has publicly undertaken.'[34] Surely, however, this would not be a duty arising in virtue of control which, by hypothesis, does not exist. It would need to be a duty arising in virtue of an assumption of responsibility. As has been explained, however, the mere fact of promising to X does not normally generate a tortious duty to do X unless there is a foreseeable prospect that failure to do X will make another worse off, with respect to their bodily integrity or property, compared to what would have happened if the promise had not been made.[35] That will, however, often be true in relation to promises to supervise a company that affect the safety of others within a group of companies. For example, the subsidiary company employees might rely upon the promise of implementation of a safety policy by the parent and fail to take precautionary measures as a result.

(iii) Control Over an Environment

'Occupation is associated with control and is a ground of liability.'[36]

[32] *Okpabi v Royal Dutch Shell Company* [2021] UKSC 3, [2021] 1 WLR 1294 [147] (Lord Hamblen).
[33] [2019] UKSC 20, [2020] AC 1045 [53].
[34] ibid [53].
[35] See Chapter 4.
[36] *British Railways Board v Herrington* [1972] AC 877 (HL) 929 (Lord Pearson). See also *Commissioner for Railways v McDermott* [1967] 1 AC 169 (PC) 186: 'occupation of premises is a

(a) Visitors

Consider first an occupier's duty to visitors to take reasonable care that the state of the premises is safe for the purposes for which the visitor is invited to be there.[37] This duty can clearly require positive acts, such as fencing or warnings, to be done.[38]

An occupier's duty to visitors has been held to extend beyond dangers due to the physical state of the premises. In *Everett v Comojo*, the Court of Appeal held that a hotel is under a P-duty to its visitors to take care to regulate access to the hotel bar, and to remove dangerous persons.[39] This was justified partly on the basis that '[t]he management is in control of the premises. It can regulate who enters, who is refused entry and who is to be removed after entry', partly on the basis that guests come to the venue to relax and so may be said to let down their guard, and partly on the basis of the economic benefit the club obtained from its relationship with its guests.[40] The mere fact of control of a space seems to be considered an insufficient justification of a P-duty in relation to risks presently posed by the deliberate wrongdoing of a third party on the space, however. As in *Everett*, the benefit which the duty-bearer gains from granting access to the space is relied upon, as is the fact that the nature of the activity conducted by the right-holder on the space is one that is particularly protection-worthy (such as one's ability to enter one's home safely, if one lives in an apartment block).[41]

(b) Trespassers

Consider next an occupier's P-duty to a trespasser.[42] The duty owed to a trespasser appears to be less onerous than that owed to a visitor and is sensitive to the personal circumstances of the occupier, in virtue of the fact that the occupier does not choose to permit the person onto the land.[43] Suppose that there are concealed pits

ground of liability . . . because it gives some control and knowledge of the state of the premises' (Lord Gardiner LC).

[37] Occupiers' Liability Act 1957, see esp s 2(2).

[38] For warnings, see, eg, Occupiers' Liability Act 1957, s 2(4)(a).

[39] [2011] EWCA Civ 13, [2012] 1 WLR 150. See also *Bullock v Tamiami Trail Tours, Inc* 266 F2d 326 (5th Cir 1959), discussed in Chapter 3, section 1(i)(c).

[40] *Everett* (n 39) [31] (Smith LJ). cf *Modbury Triangle Shopping Centre Pty Ltd v Anzil* [2000] HCA 61, in which the High Court of Australia refused to impose a duty of care upon the occupier of a car park to provide lighting to discourage third parties from committing assaults there. Gleeson CJ and Hayne J reserved their view on whether a duty would exist to remove a malefactor from occupier of premises.

[41] See, eg, *Kline v 1500 Massachusetts Avenue Apartment Corp* 439 F2d 477 (DC Cir 1970). cf Hayne J in *Modbury* (n 40) [112]: 'The occupier of land has power to control who enters and remains on the land and has power to control the state or condition of the land. It is these powers of control which establish the relationship between occupier and entrant "which *of itself* suffices [sic.] to give rise to a duty . . . to take reasonable care to avoid a foreseeable risk of injury"' (emphasis added).

[42] Occupiers' Liability Act 1984, s 1(3).

[43] See, eg, *Herrington* (n 36) 898–99: 'an occupier does not voluntarily assume a relationship with trespassers. By trespassing they force a "neighbour" relationship on him. When they do so he must act in a humane manner—that is not asking too much of him—but I do not see why he should be required to do more' (Lord Reid).

on rural land near a busy public beach and that, if a person falls into a pit, this will certainly cause death. These circumstances are likely to trigger a duty to act on the part of the occupier.[44] Absent the grant of permission to enter the land, and given that the danger is posed—let us suppose—by the natural condition of the land rather than something added by the occupier, the argument that the occupier creates the risk of harm to the trespasser is less plausible. In these circumstances, the role of 'control' cannot simply be to identify who creates a risk.

(c) Persons Not on the Land

Consider now an occupier's duty to those not on the land. An occupier of land owes a P-duty in relation to risks of physical harm that arise on the land to others foreseeably endangered by the risks, even if those risks are not created by the occupier.[45] The P-duty is a duty to take reasonable steps to protect others from the materialisation of those risks. The duty is described as a 'measured' duty, which means that the duty's requirements are sensitive to the personal circumstances of the duty-bearer.[46]

The stringency of the duty, when the performance of the duty only benefits the right-holder, is also relatively minimal. *Lambert v Barratt Homes Ltd* is illustrative.[47] The defendant council was 'not in the slightest degree responsible' for the cause of flooding on the claimant's nearby land. The flooding had been caused by the negligence of a developer which had blocked up a pipe on its land. The only way of preventing the flooding, however, was to build a new catch pit and drainage pipe on the council's land. The Court of Appeal distinguished *Sedleigh-Denfield v O'Callaghan* where 'a simple and inexpensive act on the part of the occupier' would have abated the nuisance.[48] Here, the cost of the work would likely have been 'considerable'. The only action required of the defendant was to permit access to enable the catch pit to be constructed and to provide reasonable assistance in obtaining necessary consents for the drainage to be laid.[49] When the defendant is being required solely to benefit another, then the cost required is minimal.[50]

44 See, eg, ibid 938 (extending, *obiter*, occupiers' duties to dangers 'due to the natural condition of the land' (Lord Diplock)); see also *Goldman v Hargrave* [1967] 1 AC 645 (PC) 661–62, recognising 'a general duty upon occupiers in relation to hazards occurring on their land, whether natural or man-made' (Lord Wilberforce).

45 *Goldman* (n 44).

46 ibid 663. This contrasts with the normal, more objective, position which applies when a person chooses to create a risk: see *Nettleship v Weston* [1971] 2 QB 691.

47 [2010] EWCA Civ 681, [2010] BLR 527.

48 ibid [21] (Sir Anthony May).

49 ibid. See, similarly, *Coope v Ward* [2015] EWCA Civ 30, [2015] 1 WLR 4081 [76]–[77] (defendant not liable where not responsible for the damage and would not benefit from abatement of the hazard. cf *Abbahall Ltd v Smee* [2002] EWCA Civ 1831, [2003] 1 WLR 1472 where the benefit of repair of a common roof was shared); *Holbeck Hall Hotel Ltd v Scarborough Borough Council* [2000] QB 836 (CA) (defendant not required to undertake costly geological investigation of hazard and not liable for damage which could not have been foreseen without it).

50 cf *Abbahall* (n 49).

An occupier of land or possessor of a thing is likely also to have P-duties in relation to defamatory or privacy-invading content that is attached to the land or thing by a third party. In *Byrne v Deane*, a lampoon concerning the plaintiff was attached to a golf club noticeboard by a third party, without the consent of the club secretary.[51] The plaintiff alleged that defendants, directors, owners, and occupiers of the club were liable in respect of the posting. By a majority, the Court of Appeal held the statement was not defamatory. In *obiter dicta*, there was general agreement that a person could be liable in respect of a statement despite the absence of a positive act. The judgments are ambiguous, however, as to whether this depends upon inferred consent to the statement's remaining there, endorsement of the statement, or whether a person is constituted a publisher of the statement simply in virtue of control over the environment, knowledge of its presence, and its being reasonably easy to remove.[52] In principle, a person should not be permitted to allow their resource to become an instrument of wrongful harm to others. Although initially not voluntarily implicated in that harm, their resource facilitates its continuation, and this justifies a minimal duty to protect the subject of the statement.[53]

A person counts as an 'occupier' for the purposes of these duties if the person has control over the land or some part of it.[54] Precisely what this means is not clear, however. It has been stated that the occupier's duties 'can be understood as arising from his exclusive right of possession'.[55] It seems, however, that such a right is neither necessary nor sufficient, at least in relation to certain duties. For instance, a theatre company that occupies a theatre during a performance period may count as an 'occupier' for the purposes of the Occupiers' Liability Act 1957, without having the right to exclusive possession of the theatre.[56] A contractor working for a period on the 'tween deck of a ship owes a duty to another contractor, its invitee, even in relation to dangers not created by a positive act.[57]

[51] [1937] 1 KB 818.

[52] See Greer LJ at 829–30 (perhaps leaning towards the latter); Greene LJ and Slesser LJ appear to require inferred authorisation, endorsement, or association with the statement. For discussion, noting the ambiguity, see T Keren-Paz, *Egalitarian Digital Privacy* (Bristol UP 2023) 32–33.

[53] cf *Restatement (Second) of Torts*, §577(2): '[o]ne who intentionally and unreasonably fails to remove defamatory matter that he knows to be exhibited on land or chattels in his possession or under his control is subject to liability for its continued publication'. For discussion of the extent to which this represents US law, see B Zipursky, 'Online Defamation, Legal Concepts, and the Good Samaritan' (2016) 51 Valparaiso University Law Review 1, 21–22.

[54] *Sedleigh-Denfield v O'Callagan* [1940] AC 880 (HL) 905: 'responsibility . . . attaches to the occupier, because he has possession and control of the property' (Lord Wright); *Wheat v Lacon* [1966] AC 552, 579 ('any degree of control over the state of the premises' (Lord Denning)); see also *Cocking v Eacott* [2016] EWCA Civ 140, [2016] QB 1080 [25]: 'An occupier . . . will normally be responsible for a nuisance even if he did not directly cause it, because he is in control and possession of the property' (Vos LJ).

[55] *Robinson v Chief Constable of West Yorkshire Police* [2018] UKSC 4, [2018] AC 736 [7] (Lord Reed).

[56] *Wheat v Lacon* [1966] AC 552, 583 (Lord Morris discussing an example from Lord Wright). The US position is the same: see, eg, *Alcaraz v Vece* (1997) 14 Cal 4th 1149; *Simpson v Big Bear Stores Co*, 652 NE 2d 702, 704 (Ohio 1995) ('It is fundamental that to have a duty to keep premises safe for others one must be in possession and control of the premises.'); *Restatement (Third) of Torts*, §49 (though a person with the right to possess will have a duty if there is no person with actual control).

[57] *Hartwell v Grayson Rollo and Clover Docks Limited, and Others* [1947] KB 901.

The sufficiency of the right to exclusive possession is also a matter of doubt. In *Ibrahimi v Commonwealth of Australia*, a ship carrying migrants from Indonesia was headed towards Australia but tragically was destroyed on rocks near Christmas Island during a storm, with approximately fifty people losing their lives.[58] By virtue of section 261A of the Migration Act, the vessel was subject to automatic statutory forfeiture to the Commonwealth upon entering Australian territory. Consequently, ownership in the vessel vested in the Commonwealth. This was argued to generate a P-duty to take care to come to the assistance of the people on board on the basis of occupation. The New South Wales Court of Appeal rejected this on the ground that ownership did not give the Commonwealth 'control of the relevant risk of harm'.[59] This is consonant with Lord Pearson's observation in *Wheat v Lacon* that the 'foundation of occupier's liability is occupational control, ie, control associated with and arising from presence in and use of or activity in the premises'.[60] This must surely be more, however, than having 'power to take the measures that are necessary to prevent or eliminate' a particular risk.[61] It cannot be sufficient that a person has a factual ability to remove, warn, or prevent the materialisation of a risk, on pain of contradiction with the general position on the absence of P-duties without a special fact.[62]

(iv) Control of Online Content

The discussion has focussed on control of a physical space or thing. Similar principles are in the process of development in relation to online content.[63] The decision in *Byrne* has been held to support Google's potential liability in relation to allegedly defamatory comments made on a blog hosted by Google on its blogging platform, after notification of a complaint by the subject of the comments.[64] Although website operators obviously do not have a legal right to exclusive possession of a space, they have an authority to alter the content of the website, which

[58] [2018] NSWCA 123.

[59] ibid [242].

[60] [1966] AC 552, 589.

[61] *LE Jones (Insurance Brokers) Ltd v Portsmouth City Council* [2002] EWCA Civ 1723, [2003] 1 WLR 427 [11] (Dyson LJ).

[62] See §51 in the *Restatement* (n 4), comment *e*: 'The current possessor is the only person with the legal authority to eliminate or ameliorate the risks.' Strictly, this is not true as sometimes a risk may be so grave that others have legal permissions to enter the land to quell the risk: cf *Burmah Oil Co v Lord Advocate* [1965] AC 75 (HL) 165 (Lord Upjohn), recognising permissions to trespass to land but limiting them in light of the role of modern state emergency services; see more generally the law on public necessity in the context of property rights (eg *Rigby v Chief Constable of Northamptonshire* [1985] 1 WLR 1242, [1985] 2 All ER 985).

[63] For an instructive discussion of the US position, which immunises internet service providers, platforms, and users for omissive liability (and re-publication liability), see Zipursky (n 53).

[64] *Tamiz v Google* [2013] EWCA Civ 68, [2013] 1 WLR 2151. See also *Oriental Press Group Ltd v Fevaworks Solutions Ltd* [2013] HKFCA 47, (2013) 16 HKCFAR 366.

others do not have, and which it would be considered conventionally inappropriate for anyone to use; a person's website, as a matter of social reality, is considered something over which they have a justified claim to control and prevent others from altering its content without permission. Clearly, difficult questions arise as to the precise responsibilities of operators, platforms, and internet service providers.[65] In so far as any purport to exercise an authority to determine what happens in relation to a virtual space, the analogy with an occupier has some force, however; a raft of factors may then differentiate the stringency of the P-duties each owes.

(v) Temporary Control of a Danger without Possession of the Space on Which It Arises

There are situations in which it is natural to speak of a person having 'control' over a danger, and yet this control does not give rise to a P-duty. These are situations in which A takes on the task of preventing the materialisation of a risk which A did not create, A has performed the task in such a way that the risk could now be easily averted by A, but A then abandons the task or completes it in a careless way, with the result that the risk is not averted. For example, if a fire brigade attends a fire and has almost succeeded in quelling the fire, this does not seem to trigger a P-duty to take care in the completing the task.[66] Similarly, if a police officer performs a breathalyser test upon a person whom they suspect of drunk driving, but the officer misreads the breathalyser and wrongly sends the driver on their way, with the result that the driver kills a third party, this does not generate a P-duty.[67] This is so despite the fact that the officer could be described as having 'control' over the risk posed by the driver. If the police attend an accident caused by black ice on the surface of a road, set up a warning sign, but then remove that sign without taking further steps, this does not generate a P-duty based on 'control' of a risk.[68] These examples show that 'control', in so far as it generates a P-duty, requires more than physical proximity to a risk and an ability to intervene easily.

3. Justifying Control-Based Duties

This section considers the justificatory significance of control. It proceeds by showing that 'control' can almost always be understood as a trigger for the

[65] For analysis, see Keren-Paz (n 52).
[66] *Capital and Counties Plc v Hampshire County Council* [1997] QB 1004 (CA).
[67] *Ancell & Ancell v McDermott* [1993] RTR 235, 244 (Beldam LJ).
[68] *Tindall v Thames Valley Police* [2022] EWCA Civ 25, [2022] 4 WLR 104 [54(iii)], [71]–[72].

operation of some other ground of a duty, such as *Innocent Risk*, *Interference*, or assumption of responsibility. The difficult cases for this reduction strategy are the duties of occupiers to trespassers and to persons not on the land. These duties are justified, I suggest, partly in virtue of the innocent implication of a person's resources in a risk, their choice to accept a right to which the law attaches a management responsibility in relation to a space, the fact that they benefit from a right whose enjoyment justifiably creates a risk that others will not intervene, and a circumscribed duty of easy rescue.

(i) Control as Creation of Risk or Interference

In many cases, exercising control over a person, land, or thing involves the creation of a risk or interfering with alternative means of harm-prevention.

The decision in *Dorset Yacht* itself can be justified as part of the 'category of exposing others to risk through the deeds of third parties'.[69] This gains support from Lord Diplock's emphasis on the special risk imposed on nearby persons by the detention on the island.[70] It also gains support from cases involving young children who 'escape' from schools near busy roads, resulting in third parties being injured; here the emphasis is on the risks imposed by running a school near a road.[71] The created risk of escape attempts creates dangers to those who might become embroiled in those escapes. In short, in detaining people one may substantially increase the risk to others from harm-causing escape attempts. This is especially so when one takes prisoners to an island without the normal security provided by physical barriers.[72]

If this is correct, however, then *Dorset Yacht* would not justify liability when the risk which materialised is not a risk resulting from the escape itself. For instance, if a serial killer escaped due to a prison guard's carelessness, and having gotten free later killed a person not in the vicinity of the prison, there would be no liability on the basis of risk creation since this risk was not created by the detention itself. By contrast, if the serial killer killed a person or damaged their property in order to effect the escape, there would be liability since this risk is created by the detention.

This might seem to generate an implausibly narrow liability on the part of custodians of dangerous adults. However, it is not obvious how this result can be avoided under the current law, on pain of inconsistency with the general position

[69] A Ripstein, *Private Wrongs* (Harvard UP 2016) 96.

[70] See nn 18–21 above and related discussion.

[71] *Lewis* (n 15). There is even an analogy to *Rylands v Fletcher* [1868] UKHL 1, (1868) LR 3 HL 330, here—bringing the imprisoned to an island is like bringing large quantities of water to an artificial reservoir—though *Dorset* does not, of course, impose strict liability.

[72] For an endorsement of this analysis of *Dorset*, see *Mitchell v Glasgow City Council*, 2008 SC 351, 358 (Lord Reed).

on public authorities. If *Dorset* is held to create a P-duty to anyone who is foreseeably endangered by a careless failure to maintain the person in detention, this goes beyond a duty based on creation of a risk. Compare the situation of a prison providing protection to the public against the risks posed by dangerous criminals to the police putting up a warning sign on a dangerous road. If the police put up such a sign, they protect the public from a risk. It is clear, however, that the police have no duty to continue this protection (unless they have created a misleading impression that the protection will be continued); if they remove the sign for no good reason, they are not liable.[73] The question arises, then, as to why one should be liable for the careless removal of protective custody of a risk—which would be the effect of holding prisons liable for negligent failure to continue detention—but not for removal of those other forms of protection from risk.[74]

As noted above, it might be tempting to appeal to the notion of assumption of responsibility here: prison authorities *assume responsibility* to maintain dangerous criminals in custody, whereas the police do not assume responsibility to continue protection on a highway. But the facts which would justify this different conclusion about assumption of responsibility are unclear: the law would have to choose to attach certain P-duties to the occupation of roles such as prison authority, but not to attach these to other roles such as police officer. It may be argued that there are good reasons for this, such as the role of a police officer involving discretionary decisions in the public interest, whereas the role of a prison officer has a more operational character. This would imply, however, that police officers should have limited P-duties in relation to 'operational' matters, which is not the current law's position.

The upshot is, if English law seeks coherence with the position firmly established by *Michael*, it should restrict *Dorset* to cases in which the detention creates a new risk. Such a duty would not be a genuine P-duty, but rather an N-duty based on *Innocent Risk*. If, however, it seeks to develop the law on public authorities in a more expansive direction, as Chapter 10 argues is justified, *Dorset* need not be so restricted.

The cases in which a parent company (A) exercises control of a subsidiary (C), or an activity of C, seem to be rationalisable on the basis of *Innocent Risk* and *Interference*. When A takes charge of C's activity, then A or A *and* C will typically create a risk. The control simply identifies 'who' the risk-creator is at

[73] *Tindall* (n 68).

[74] There is a possible *Interference* argument when a prison employee makes a person worse off than if that employee had not been there. For instance, suppose that a prison guard mistakenly releases a serial killer, mistaking their identity. But for the presence of the employee, the harm would not have occurred. This would imply, however, that if two police officers, D1 and D2 turned up to an accident scene, and one placed a warning sign down, and the other removed it, the police would be vicariously liable for the remover's action, even though the act does not make things worse than if *the police* had not become involved. It seems extremely arbitrary that liability would hinge upon the presence of more than one officer.

a particular time, defeating the normal presumption that the other company is a wholly autonomous agent in virtue of its separate personality.[75] A person with control over land, in so far as that control gives rise to a right to exclude others, also typically raises the probability that others will not intervene to deal with problems on the land. When A displaces C's decision-making in relation to risk-alleviating measures, then A will typically have raised the probability that C will not intervene to protect a person (B) against a risk, thus triggering *Interference*.

The duty of care in relation to a prisoner's basic needs owed by a prison is also explicable on this basis: the prison prevents the prisoner from obtaining assistance. Similarly, the duty to protect against the risk of suicide is explicable on the basis of creation of risk: 'because the very fact of incarceration heightens the risk of self-harm'.[76]

It might be objected that this delivers an implausibly limited account of the duties of a prison—confined, again, to what are in fact N-duties based on *Innocent Risk* and *Interference*. Suppose it is known that, if B were not imprisoned, B would be immediately killed by a gang. The imprisonment does not prevent B from obtaining access to means to sustain himself, since B would be immediately killed were it not for the imprisonment. Nonetheless, surely the prison authority still owes a genuine P-duty to take care to provide for B's basic needs.

It will rarely be the case that there is a *certainty* that B will be unable to sustain himself but for the imprisonment, however. If there is even a small probability of the contrary, then this seems enough to trigger a duty under *Interference*. Furthermore, if prison does not take positive steps to assist B in these circumstances, the prison will be causally responsible for B's death: the duty can be understood as a duty that arises that requires action on the part of A, so that A will avoid being causally responsible for B's death. Finally, it is plausibly a condition of the permissibility of restricting a person's liberty for the purposes of punishment, that the limits on their liberty are necessary and proportionate to that aim; absent positive steps of various sorts, including meeting a prisoner's basic needs, this condition is not met.

The significance of control goes beyond identifying who created a risk. The duties of an occupier extend to the risks posed by third parties or natural events which, on ordinary principles, the occupier could not be said to have created and in respect of which it will often be speculative whether the occupier's right to exclude prevented others dealing.[77]

[75] 'Control' arguably functions in a similar way in the context of vicarious liability; it identifies to whom a risk is to be attributed: see, eg, *Cox v Ministry of Justice* [2016] UKSC 10, [2016] AC 660.

[76] *Rabone* (n 5) [101] (Baroness Hale).

[77] For risks posed by third parties, see generally section 2. For risks posed by natural events, see generally n 42–44 and related discussion.

(ii) Control as Assumption of Responsibility

Given the analysis in Chapter 4, justifying 'control' in terms of 'assumption of responsibility' requires us first to identify the relevant notion of 'assumption of responsibility'.[78]

Consider, first, an account of assumption of responsibility in terms of P1 and P2, the principles based upon a promise being made with foreseeable reliance upon the promise. Not all cases of control-based duties involve a promise. It is fictional to suppose that a promise justifies the P-duty of the occupier in *Goldman*.

Duties to children and prisoners can also be explained by the 'taking charge of' strand of assumption of responsibility: in these cases, the taking charge either creates a risk of harm or prevents a means by which harm could be prevented. It is also plausible that the exercise of certain forms of control over a child is itself to assume the role of 'parent'. If a person exercises a wide-ranging authority over a child—the exercise of a power to determine permissible conduct of the child and permissible interactions with the child—this itself amounts to an assumption of the role of parent and its attendant P-duties.

The choice to permit someone to access one's land for a purpose will also typically involve an implied promise or representation that care has been taken in relation to the premises, so that the premises are reasonably safe for the purposes for which permission is given. Just as a hotel which agrees to provide a room for a customer implicitly agrees to provide a bed in the room, the hotel which permits a guest's stay, by default, impliedly promises that the premises are reasonably safe for use as a hotel.[79]

It is suggested that this is one reason why a person who does not have a right of ownership of land or a thing can be under a duty to a person whom they invite to use the land or thing.[80] At least in a business context, if a person has continuous use of land for a business purpose, an invitation by that person will normally carry with it an assurance that the land is reasonably safe for the purposes of the invited use. This does not hinge upon whether the 'occupier' has an exclusive right of possession.

One could, in principle, describe an 'occupier' as a 'role' which triggers duties and explain the P-duty of an occupier to trespassers and persons not on the land in this way.[81] But the label 'role' does not itself do any justificatory work. It remains

[78] For a judicial statement that the categories of assumption of responsibility and control 'overlap', see *Selwood v Durham County Council* [2012] EWCA Civ 979, [2012] PIQR P20 [49] (Smith LJ).

[79] *Thomson v Cremin* (1953) 2 All ER 1185, 1191–92: 'The duty of the invitor towards the invitee . . . he *warrants* . . . that due care and skill to make the premises reasonably safe for the invitee have been exercised' (Lord Wright, emphasis added).

[80] See section 2(iii)(a).

[81] See, eg, S Tofaris and S Steel, 'Negligence Liability for Omissions and the Police' [2016] 75 Cambridge Law Journal 128, 141 (identifying the duties of occupiers as arising from their 'status' as occupiers).

to be explained why an occupier should be singled out as a role which attracts P-duties.

(a) Occupier P-Duties to Persons Not on the Land, and Non-Visitors

If the analysis in this section is so far correct, it is possible to justify the duties that arise by virtue of control to the controlled (or the owner of the controlled thing or land) by reference to *Innocent Risk, Interference*, or a strand of assumption of responsibility. In addition, the P-duties that arise in virtue of control to third parties can partially be so justified: *Dorset*, for instance, is explicable as a creation of risk case. As explained along the way, although such duties travel as P-duties under the current law, they are generally explicable as N-duties not to make worse off.

The particularly difficult cases in which control appears to have an irreducible role are the P-duties of an occupier of land to trespassers and to others not on the land. The difficulty resides in identifying a justification for such P-duties which does not contradict the law's conclusion that there is an absence of P-duties in other domains. For instance, the justification relied upon in some cases that an occupier is typically well-placed by virtue of their control to deal with risks on the land could equally apply to public authorities whose statutory powers make them particularly well-placed to deal with certain risks. No P-duty arises, however, simply in virtue of their being well-placed because of their statutory powers.[82]

The law could, of course, be inconsistent here: it might be that 'being particularly well-placed' to prevent or monitor a risk is a sufficient justification for a P-duty, and the law should be modified to reflect this. It is not, however, a sufficient justification in relation to private individuals. The sole fact that a person could easily deal with a risk not of their own creation does not alone entail that it is reasonable to *require* this of them: this fails to show due concern for the freedom and non-instrumentalisation considerations that underpin the distinction between N and P-duties.[83]

More can, however, be said in favour of these P-duties beyond the fact that the occupier is typically especially well-placed to deal with risks on the land.

Implication

If your arm unexpectedly begins to spasm nearby others, you have a duty to take reasonable steps to protect others from your arm. It is tempting to say that, just as your body's being implicated in a risk triggers a duty to protect others from the risk one did not choose to create, your property's being implicated in a risk triggers a duty to protect others from the risk one did not choose to create. So, if a tree on one's land unforeseeably poses a risk to neighbouring land, one has a duty to take reasonable steps in relation to it once the risk becomes foreseeable. Or if one

[82] See Chapter 10.
[83] See Chapter 2.

acquires title to land on which the predecessor has built an infringing, trespassory, structure, one has a duty to remove the structure if one is able to do so.[84] If one's land becomes a 'base' from which wrongful incursions are made into adjacent properties, one's land is providing assistance to those wrongs.[85] The explanation of the P-duty here is simply that your resources are implicated in, or constitute, the risk. In *Goldman*, it might be said that since your tree is providing fuel for the fire, this implicates your resources in the risk. And sometimes the law holds a person with ownership rights to have P-duties independently of occupation.[86]

Although this seems intuitive, it is unsatisfactory to rest the explanation of these duties simply on the proposition that 'it's yours'. One wants to know *why* something being one's resource generates a responsibility in relation to risks that one did not choose to create. Part of the explanation may, again, be simply that generally the owner is in the best position to protect others. Beyond that, however, one can say that this allocation of responsibility is in the interest of the owner in so far as it prevents the need for overly intrusive monitoring of their resources by others. And, in the property case, unlike the body case, by taking ownership, one can be understood to choose the management responsibility that the law assigns to the owner, for the reasons just given. Admittedly, the justificatory force of this 'choice' depends on the extent to which one can avoid such a choice. In relation to dangerous animals or even non-dangerous pets, one could reasonably hold that the choice to acquire such an animal can fairly be burdened with special responsibilities in relation to the risks posed.

Benefits and the Right to Exclude

Robert Stevens points to the fact that the right to exclude is a benefit made possible by law and, as a matter of fairness, it is legitimate for the law to attach conditions to the enjoyment of this benefit, including P-duties.[87]

As stated, however, this does not provide an argument for the specific P-duties we find in the law. One could equally say, on the basis of this kind of argument, that the right to exclude justifies P-duties to pay tax, for example. Two further considerations support the occupier's P-duties specifically. First, the fairness of imposing duties in return for benefits, *in conjunction* with the fact that the occupier is generally best-placed to deal with the risks on the land, supports the P-duties in question. Second, the enjoyment of a right to exclude others itself requires that others generally neither take responsibility for nor intervene too excessively in managing

[84] *Manchester Ship Canal Company v United Utilities Water Ltd* [2022] EWCA Civ 852 [93].

[85] See *Lippiatt v South Gloucestershire Council* [2000] QB 51; *Smith v Littlewoods Organisation Ltd* [1987] AC 241.

[86] Defective Premises Act 1972, s 4. A landlord who retains a right to repair has a duty towards persons who may suffer personal injury or property from non-repair of a defect in the property.

[87] R Stevens, *Torts and Rights* (OUP 2007) 16: 'The rights we have against landowners that they take positive steps to protect us are the quid pro quo for the law's protection of their rights to exclusive enjoyment.'

risks on the land. Unless there is a P-duty upon the part of the occupier to deal with risks on the land, there would need to be more extensive qualifications upon the right to exclude permitting more wide-ranging entry upon the land by others, and this would undermine the value of such rights to the right-holder. Without the primary responsibility for dealing with a risk on the land being allocated to the occupier, others would need to be more widely permitted to enter onto the land to avert dangers. Consequently, part of the quid pro quo for having such an extensive right to exclude is the existence of a P-duty to deal with risks that arise on the land.

An objection to this justification of an occupier's P-duty to trespassers and persons not on the land is that 'occupation' is not equivalent to having ownership or a right to exclude.[88] If the occupier enjoys no rights, then there is no *quid* for the *quo*. This objection has no purchase against the adverse possessor who acquires a right to exclude. Licencees constitute the other category of person who may occupy without a right of exclusion. Clearly, not all licencees are 'occupiers'; if I pass through a supermarket every day, I do not occupy it. What distinguishes a person's repeated physical presence on a space from 'occupation'? It seems to me that the answer is that the occupier takes charge of, or exercises authority over, the space, even if that authority is not exercised against everyone. Even this limited ability to determine what goes on in the space can reasonably be understood as a benefit to the person who has it, and as potentially dissuading others from intervening.[89]

Acceptance of a Management Responsibility

A person who voluntarily takes charge of a space can reasonably be expected to take steps to protect others from risks that arise in connection with that space. In taking charge of the space, the law may reasonably attach a role-based P-duty, which a person accepts by taking the role. This management responsibility for the space is coupled, as a default, with acquisition of the right to exclude, but it can go beyond situations in which there is a right to exclude.

Localised Easy Rescue

A further justification of the P-duties of occupiers in relation to trespassers and persons not on the land is that these duties involve the limited recognition of a duty of easy rescue, or a duty akin to one of easy rescue. Such a duty is not to take reasonable care in relation to a risk, but a minimal duty to take a low-cost measure when one knows that another is in imminent grave danger of losing their life or suffering a harm of similar magnitude.

88 See above pp. 147–148.

89 See Lord Nicholls of Birkenhead in his dissenting speech in *Stovin v Wise* [1996] AC 923 at 931, stating that '[t]he right to *occupy* can reasonably be regarded as carrying obligations as well as rights' (emphasis added).

In *Herrington*, the House of Lords emphasised that an occupier's duty towards a trespasser is not the ordinary duty of care, but a duty of 'ordinary humanity':

> if the occupier knows or as good as knows that some emergency has arisen whereby the trespasser has been placed in a position of imminent peril, ordinary humanity requires further steps to be taken.[90]

It is clear that the demandingness of this duty is lower than the ordinary duty of care.[91] The role of 'occupier' here merely delimits the general moral duty of easy rescue, and obviates the supposed concern that the duty has far-reaching consequences for personal freedom, as well as concerns pertaining to detrimental activity level effects.[92] Whereas the other justifications point to some fact about occupation that serves as a positive justification for a P-duty, such as being particularly well-placed to assist or one's implication in the risk, this justification treats occupation merely as a condition for the application of a more general P-duty.

This justification would imply that there should be a P-duty in the following situation. Suppose that your front garden is adjacent to a public footpath. A person collapses due to a heart attack on the footpath and falls into your front garden. On the easy rescue justification, if you, the occupier, know of this person's situation, you have a duty to provide minimal assistance such as calling for an ambulance. This is not in virtue of your implication in the risk or the fact that you are especially well-placed to deal with the risk to the person (suppose that any passer-by can see the person's plight). It is simply that the boundaries of your land provide a clear demarcation of the boundaries of your duty of easy rescue.

Summary

In the final analysis, then, an occupier's P-duty to non-visitors and persons not on the land in relation to risks not created by their own activity is justified by (i) the innocent implication of their resources in the existence of a risk, (ii) their choice to accept a right which makes them typically well-placed to deal with a particular class of risk, (iii) the fact that the benefit enjoyed by the right to exclude involves others reasonably deferring (to some extent) to the owner's authority to deal with risks, and (iv) in relation to risks in which (i) and (ii) is not the case, by a circumscribed duty of easy rescue.

[90] *Herrington* (n 36) 923.

[91] ibid (n 36) 925: 'It would be unfair if trespassers could by their misbehaviour impose *onerous* obligations on others' (emphasis added).

[92] See Chapters 2 and 9.

4. Conclusion

Although the general idea that 'control' generates special responsibilities is intuitive, it is not always clear what kind of control is relevant, nor why control has this normative impact.

This chapter has explained that control is relevant to the duties owed to the controlled (or owners of the thing or land controlled), and to those not subject to the control.

In relation to the controlled, it has shown that control generates duties by virtue of *Innocent Risk* (when the control displaces the controlled person's autonomy to assess or respond to risk independently), *Interference* (by preventing access to the external world, or other means of assistance more generally), and assumption of responsibility (taking control may amount to a promise that creates a risk of detrimental reliance, or the assumption of a role responsibility).

In relation to those not subject to the control, it has shown that control can similarly generate duties by virtue of *Innocent Risk* (when controlling persons is a risky business, as with prisoners), *Interference* (when others are reasonably dissuaded from dealing with a source of risk because of the controller's position), and assumption of a role responsibility. In the last case, this may arise when a person takes on a management responsibility of a space. By default, a person takes on this responsibility when they accept ownership rights over a space, but the responsibility can be taken on through occupation too.

7
Statute

'Statute' is not a special fact in the same family as creation of risk, assumption of responsibility, or control. Statute refers to the source of a legal duty, not to the justifying substantive reason for its existence, or at least not to a justifying reason which implicates the duty-bearer's responsibility. The social fact that the legislature has imposed a duty is normally taken as a reason for the action mandated by the duty, but it is not a substantive normative justification for it. So there is an element of illogic in having a chapter on 'Statute' alongside those on the special facts already considered (imagine the chapter was entitled 'Common Law'). Nonetheless, it seems important to consider whether the statutory P-duties that give rise to rights to compensation diverge significantly from the common law P-duties. If the statutory law on P-duties cannot be justified in terms of the special facts we have already identified, then there is potentially a conflict between the common law's commitments as to the scope of justifiable P-duties and that recognised by statute.

The first section of the chapter considers express statutory rights to compensation for breach of P-duties. A central example is the liability to compensate for breach of P-duties under the Human Rights Act (HRA) 1998. It is shown that these P-duties cannot be fully rationalised as situations in which a special fact recognised by the common law is in place. The argument will show that, if the liability to compensate for breach of P-duties under the HRA 1998 is justified, then the absence of certain special P-duties at common law cannot be justified on *substantive* grounds. This lays the foundation for Chapter 10's consideration of the extent to which tort law should recognise more extensive actionable P-duties against public bodies.

The second section of the chapter considers the extent to which the tort of breach of statutory duty has been recognised to give rise to actionable P-duties beyond the special facts recognised by the common law. The overall argument is that the situations in which a statutory P-duty has been held to be civilly actionable can generally be rationalised as situations in which a special fact recognised by the common law is already in place. What the statute adds to the common law, in these situations, is a concretisation of the relevant P-duty: it makes some vague duty to act more specific. Conversely, the situations in which a P-duty has been rejected are typically those in which no special fact exists. In short, in the absence of express provision, it is suggested that the statutory law's provision of compensatory rights for breach of P-duties generally follows common law entitlements. In the

Omissions in Tort Law. Sandy Steel, Oxford University Press. © Sandy Steel 2024.
DOI: 10.1093/9780191898822.003.0007

final, concluding, section of the chapter, I suggest that this is justifiable so far as the statute concerns private persons, but not in relation to public bodies.

1. Express Statutory Rights to Compensation for Breach of P-Duties

Statute imposes innumerable P-duties and empowers persons to create P-duties. These range from P-duties that apply to a broad class of duty-bearers, such as duties to pay tax[1] or duties upon drivers to stop and provide information after being involved in a vehicle accident,[2] to more narrowly circumscribed duties that apply to particular classes of person or the holders of particular roles, such as duties upon public bodies to report children at risk of abuse[3] and duties on professionals to report suspected cases of female genital mutilation.[4] The following are examples in which P-duties are rendered expressly actionable in damages by the statute.[5] It is shown that the actionable statutory P-duties of public authorities and public undertakers go beyond those recognised at common law.

(i) Public Authorities under the HRA 1998

The HRA 1998 aims 'to give further effect to rights and freedoms guaranteed under the European Convention on Human Rights' (ECHR).[6] It does so, in part, by conferring a power upon 'victim[s]' of a public authority's unlawful act, when the act is unlawful in virtue of being incompatible with a Convention right, to bring proceedings.[7] The Act empowers courts in such cases to award damages in civil proceedings and sets conditions under which such a determination is made.[8] The precedential effect of judicial decisions awarding damages for breach of Convention rights has effectively created a duty on the courts to award such damages in certain cases.

In some cases, the duty owed by an authority under the HRA 1998 is concurrent with a duty arising by a special fact at common law.[9] For instance, prison

[1] eg the Local Government Finance Act 1992, s 4 (council tax).

[2] Road Traffic Act 1980, s 170.

[3] Social Services and Well-being (Wales) Act 2014, s 130.

[4] Serious Crime Act 2015, s 74.

[5] For other examples of this, see K Stanton, *Breach of Statutory Duty in Tort* (Sweet and Maxwell 1986) 9–12.

[6] HRA 1998, introductory text.

[7] Ibid s 7; s 6(1).

[8] Ibid s 8(1). Section 8(4) requires the court to consider the principles applied by the European Court of Human Rights in determining whether to make an award and on the quantum of an award.

[9] For a general treatment of P-duties under the ECHR, see V Stoyanova, *Positive Obligations under the European Convention of Human Rights* (OUP 2023).

authorities are held to owe duties to prisoners under Article 3 of the Convention in virtue of having 'assumed responsibility' for their welfare.[10] It is clear, however, that the civilly actionable P-duties under the HRA 1998 extend beyond those at common law. Consider, for instance, the state's duty to protect endangered life under Article 2 of the Convention. In *Osman v UK*, it was held that, when the authorities know or ought to have known of a 'real and immediate risk to the life of an identified individual or individuals from the criminal acts of a third party', there is a duty to take reasonable preventative measures.[11] This duty is triggered simply by virtue of knowledge or constructive knowledge of a certain kind of risk of harm by a person who is not necessarily in control of that risk. None of the special facts at common law, as currently interpreted, justifies such a duty: there is no creation of risk, assumption of responsibility, control, or right to exclude. Thus, in *Michael*, the Supreme Court held that the common law claim for negligent failure to respond timeously to an emergency call could not succeed, but that the claim under the HRA 1998 should proceed to trial.[12]

If the civilly actionable P-duties under the HRA 1998 cannot be completely rationalised as grounded in the common law special facts, then there is a divergence between the common law and the entitlements to compensation for breach of P-duties under the HRA 1998. If the HRA 1998 is arriving at the normatively correct result in relation to duties to compensate for breach of P-duties, then it follows that the common law can only be defended on the basis that it would be an inappropriate judicial extension of the common law to expand the suite of P-duties beyond the existing special facts in order to protect human rights. A defence of the common law cannot, in other words, appeal to the substantive injustice or undesirability of P-duties on public bodies being civilly actionable—that is off the table if it is assumed that the HRA 1998's position is justified—instead, it must appeal to institutional arguments about non-legislative extensions of the law on civilly actionable P-duties of the state.

For instance, a defence of the common law position could appeal to the argument that the judicial recognition of a public status-based P-duty would be a non-incremental, illegitimate, legislative development of the law. As will be seen in Chapter 10, this is not typically how debates about the common law position are conducted. Instead, arguments tend to focus on the *substantive merits* of P-duties being owed by public authorities beyond the common law special facts. This is akin to arguing against punitive damages in private law on the basis that punishment is unjustifiable. If it is accepted that punishment is justifiable *sometimes*, it follows that any argument against punitive damages *in private law* must take on

[10] *Angelova and Iliev v Bulgaria* (2008) 47 EHRR 7, para 92.
[11] *Osman v UK* ECHR 1998-VIII 3124, esp para 166.
[12] [2015] UKSC 2, [2015] AC 1732.

a more local character. So, too, arguments against civilly actionable P-duties of public authorities, if it is accepted that such duties are sometimes justifiable.[13]

It might be objected that comparing liability to pay damages for breach of a Convention right and liability to pay tort compensation is comparing apples and oranges. In *Dobson v Thames Valley Utilities*, the Court of Appeal stated that:

> The Convention serves principally public law aims; the principal objective is to declare any infringement and to put a stop to it. Compensation is ancillary and discretionary. The interests of the individual are part of the equation, but so are those of the wider public.[14]

Laws LJ described liability under HRA 1998, section 8 as 'often a closer neighbour to our public law than our private law'.[15] In short, on this view, liability under the HRA 1998 is properly conceptualised as a public law liability for breach of a duty owed to the public as a whole, akin to the duties imposed upon officials by virtue of the rules that ground judicial review.[16]

If this is correct, then it is flawed to think of there being a problematic divergence between the common law and statutory liabilities of public authorities: unlike the common law, the Act does not impose P-duties owed to particular persons, but public P-duties owed to everyone as a collective.

This is not correct, however.[17] First, considerable weight needs to be given to the simple fact that the Act is, well, the Human *Rights* Act—an Act about the rights of humans, rather than the public as a whole—and that the courts regularly describe the nature of unlawfulness under the HRA 1998 as the violation of the *victim*'s right, and the victim being owed a duty by the public authority to do a specific act. Second, only the victim has the power to bring a claim for damages; the element of exclusive control over enforcement of the duty's incidents is further evidence of the right-based nature of the claim.[18]

The only qualification to the foregoing is that the interests protected under the Convention may *sometimes* generate non-relational duties as well as relational duties. For instance, states are under a P-duty to punish 'life-endangering offences'.[19] Yet it has been explicitly denied that the right to life 'entail[s] the right for an applicant to have third parties prosecuted or sentenced for a criminal offence'.[20]

[13] Arguments of the form that 'x is illegitimate *in private law*' tend to dangle in the air unless it is explained why x is illegitimate in private law but not elsewhere.

[14] [2009] EWCA Civ 28, [2009] 3 All ER 319 [42].

[15] *R (Sturnham) v SOSJ* [2012] EWCA Civ 452, [2012] 3 WLR 476 [15].

[16] For critical discussion of these, see J Varuhas, *Damages and Human Rights* (Hart 2015) 169–70.

[17] See again ibid (n 16) 169–70.

[18] Under the Equality Act 2006, s 30, there is a power for the Equality Commission to bring a claim when there is a victim, but no claim can be had for damages.

[19] *Öneryildiz v Turkey* (No 2) (2005) 41 EHRR 20 [96].

[20] ibid.

Thus, the better view is that the HRA 1998 gives rise to both relational and non-relational duties.

It might be argued that the reference to 'rights' in the Act means 'interests sufficient to ground duties', and not duties owed to others correlating with a claim-right.[21] Rights, in this sense, are 'inputs', while rights in tort law are 'outputs' or conclusions about what duties a person has to another. The view which more accurately describes the current position, however, is that *both* senses of rights are used in relation to claims under the Act. A person's Article 2 right (in the 'input' sense put by this objection) grounds specific 'output' claim rights, including the claim right to reasonable assistance when one's life is endangered.

In summary, the HRA 1998 recognises relational P-duties whose breach gives rise to a right to compensation even when no special fact is recognised. If the HRA 1998 is justified, then the common law's non-recognition of special P-duties on public authorities cannot rest on substantive grounds. The absence of recognition of such P-duties may only be justified, if at all, on grounds of institutional legitimacy in the development of the common law.

(ii) Public Utility Undertakers

In relation to gas, electricity, and sewage undertakers, elaborate statutory schemes exist to provide compensation orders in the event of breach of statutory requirements, or specific orders made by regulators.[22] In some cases, specific statutory P-duties are made civilly actionable. Under section 52 of the Water Industry Act 1991, an undertaker is placed under a duty to provide a supply of water to any domestic premises or to maintain a connection between a water main and a service pipe by which such a supply is provided. This duty is 'owed to the consumer' and enforceable by a claim for damages.[23] These duties reflect a judgement that the state, or persons operating on behalf of the state, have a duty to provide basic necessities in the interest of individuals and to compensate when such duties are breached.

(iii) Highway Authorities

Prior to 1961, highway authorities had been held to be under common law N-duties (for misfeasance), but not under P-duties (for nonfeasance). This position

[21] This has been put to me in conversation by Robert Stevens.

[22] See, eg, the Gas Act 1986, s 30G (consumer redress orders); the Electricity Act 1989, s 27G (consumer redress orders); and the Water Industry Act 1991, s 52 (duty to supply water owed to consumer).

[23] Water Industry Act 1991, s 54.

was changed by statute; other statutes establish similar duties of maintenance on the operators of public transport systems.[24] As Lord Hoffmann explained in *Gorringe*:

> . . . the duty to take active steps to keep the highway in repair was special to the highway authority and was not a private law duty owed to any individual. Thus it was said that highway authorities were liable in tort or misfeasance but not for nonfeasance. Sometimes it was said that the highway authority was 'exempt' from liability for nonfeasance, but it was not truly an exemption in the sense that the authority had a special defence against liability. The true position was that no one had ever been liable in private law for non-repair of a highway . . . But all this was changed by section 1(1) of the Highways (Miscellaneous Provisions) Act 1961. The public duty to keep the highway in repair was converted into a statutory duty owed by the highway authority to all users of the highway giving a remedy in damages for its breach.

This explanation suggests that at common law a highway authority could not be said to be under a P-duty in relation to the repair of the highway. Apart from the purely historical argument that the inhabitants of a parish, who were initially responsible for the repair of the highway, were never made liable for nonfeasance, the argument must be that the authority does not have sufficient *control*, or has control of a different kind, over the highway to make it analogous to an occupier of land. Thus, in *Buckle v Bayswater Road Board*, in rejecting a common law P-duty on road authorities in Australia, Dixon J said:

> The purpose of giving the road authority property in and control over the road is to enable it to execute its powers in relation to the highway, not to impose upon it new duties analogous to those of an occupier of property.[25]

There are at least two disanalogies between the road authority and the occupier of private land.[26] First, the highway authority does not have the same power to exclude from, or set terms of entry to, the highway as a private occupier; the public has a common right to enter upon and pass along the highway. Second, the rights held by the highway authority do not accrue to the benefit of the highway

[24] See, eg, *Roe v Sheffield City Council and Others* [2004] QB 653, holding that ss 25 and 28 of the Tramways Act 1870 give rise to a claim for breach of statutory duty.

[25] [1936] HCA 65. The position was changed in *Brodie v Singleton Shire Council* [2001] HCA 29.

[26] See also the judgment of Hayne J in *Brodie* (n 25) [292]: 'The imposition of a duty on a private occupier to act to avoid foreseeable risk of injury owes much to the control which the occupier has not only over the state of the land, but also over whether (or over the terms on which) a person may enter and remain on the land. An authority will often not have that latter kind of control over its facilities even if it does have the former. Indeed there will be cases where it has neither'; and at [303]–[304].

authority; they are held, as Dixon J points out, purely for the specific purpose of management of the highway.[27]

The relation between a highway authority and highway users is more like the relation between an occupier and a trespasser, in the sense that the highway authority comes under a duty regardless of whether the authority chose to accept a person onto the highway. These P-duties have at least a common law echo, then: the highway authority's P-duty is akin to, in its conditions of existence, the common law duty of humanity owed by an occupier to a trespasser.

(iv) Defective Premises Act 1972

Section 1(1) of the Defective Premises Act 1972, entitled a 'duty to build dwellings properly', provides that:

> (1) A person taking on work for or in connection with the provision of a dwelling (whether the dwelling is provided by the erection or by the conversion or enlargement of a building) owes a duty—
> (a) if the dwelling is provided to the order of any person, to that person; and
> (b) without prejudice to paragraph (a) above, to every person who acquires an interest (whether legal or equitable) in the dwelling;
>
> to see that the work which he takes on is done in a workmanlike or, as the case may be, professional manner, with proper materials and so that as regards that work the dwelling will be fit for habitation when completed.

Section 2A(1) extends this beyond work in provision of dwellings to persons who 'in the course of a business, take[s] on work in relation to any part of a relevant building'.[28] Section 38 of the Buildings Act 1984, when brought into force, will make civilly actionable breaches of building regulations which impose various requirements on the nature of buildings.

It is difficult to describe the Defective Premises Act 1972 as concretising a common law duty. The builder does not assume responsibility (in the sense of P1 or P2) to all and only persons having an interest in the dwelling. If the builder creates a risk by building, and then fails to take reasonable measures in relation to that risk, the duty would be owed to all foreseeably affected, not simply persons with an interest in the dwelling. And why should the duty be limited to *dwellings* if the basis is creation of risk: building commercial properties with, for instance, insufficient

[27] This distinguishes the case of the private company tasked by statute with the management of a resource and empowered to charge for its use: cf *The Mersey Docks and Harbour Board Trustees v Gibbs* (1866) LR 1 HL 93, 123.

[28] This was inserted by the Building Safety Act 2022.

fire precautions is also risky in the same sense? Further, the duty is 'to see that the work' meets a certain standard; it is not merely a duty 'to take reasonable care' that this is done.

However, although the Defective Premises Act 1972 goes above and below a conceivable parallel common law duty, in so far as it imposes duties to take certain actions for the benefit of others, it seems that these duties can virtually always be understood as duties not to commit *impure* omissions. Failing to install sufficient fire escapes is a failure to respond to a source of risk that is *partly* of one's own creation: the building itself. This rationale covers any case in which building regulations impose duties in order to protect against risks inherent in the building itself.

2. P-Duties Actionable in the Tort of Breach of Statutory Duty

In determining whether there is civil compensatory liability for breach of a statute in the absence of express provision in the statute, the legal question is conventionally described as whether the legislator intended for the statutory duty to be civilly actionable.[29] Rarely, however, does the statute contain an express statement of such an intention. In the face of legislative silence, the courts apply a set of presumptions of intention.

The first presumption usually applied is that civil liability will exist 'where upon the true construction of the Act it is apparent that the obligation or prohibition was imposed for the benefit or protection of a particular class of individuals, as in the case of the Factories Acts and similar legislation'.[30] Further, the more detailed the remedial or enforcement provisions in the statute for breach of a duty, the less likely an intention to create civil liability.[31]

As has often been pointed out, the criterion of a 'particular class' struggles to account for the decisions reached.[32] If the employees in a factory constitute a 'particular class', it is not obvious why the persons endangered by the absence of adequate water pressure in a fire hydrant do not constitute such a class. Yet in *Atkinson v Newcastle and Gateshead Waterworks Co*, there was held to be no tort action for breach of a statutory duty to maintain the water pressure in a fire hydrant.[33] In *O'Rourke v Camden LBC*, there was likewise held to be no action for

[29] *Campbell v Peter Gordon Joiners Ltd* [2016] UKSC 38, [2016] AC 1513 [35] (Lord Toulson): 'The conventional jurisprudence is that the court's function is to ascertain as a matter of interpretation whether Parliament intended that there should be civil liability.'

[30] *Lonrho Ltd v Shell Petroleum Co Ltd (no 2)* [1982] AC 173, 185 (Lord Diplock). See *Campbell* (n 29) [7], [12], [37]–[42].

[31] See, eg, *Morrison Sports Ltd v Scottish Power Plc* [2010] UKSC 37, [2010] 1 WLR 1934 [29].

[32] G Williams, 'The Effect of Penal Legislation in the Law of Tort' (1960) 23 Modern Law Review 233, 244–45.

[33] (1877) 2 Ex D 441.

breach of a statutory duty to provide housing to the homeless in a particular area.[34] Conversely, in *Monk v Warbey*, a claim for breach of statutory duty was recognised for failure to ensure that a person using a motor vehicle held insurance; such a duty was ultimately held to be owed to anyone who was injured by the vehicle's driver.[35] If the focus is simply upon the idea of a 'particular class', it is difficult to explain these divergences.

(i) Statutory Duties and Civil Liability

An alternative explanation of when a statutory duty is held to be actionable focusses on whether the duty can be understood to 'concretise' an existing private law duty.[36] The idea is that the statutory duty to do *x* amounts to an authoritative determination of what the pre-existing private law duty requires in the circumstances.

This neatly explains why employers' statutory safety duties have traditionally been considered unproblematic.[37] These duties simply give concrete content to the employer's pre-existing duties not to impose unreasonable risks of physical harm to employees, or specify what P-duties an employer will assume by occupying the relationship of employer to employee. Thus, the statutory duty to fence machinery, held to be civilly actionable in *Groves v Winborne*, is simply an authoritative determination that not fencing constitutes a breach of a general duty not to impose an unreasonable risk of physical harm. Similarly, it explains why there is an action for breach of section 10 of the Education Act 1944, which requires school premises to conform to safety regulations designated by a Minister, but no action for section 8 of that Act, which requires local authorities to ensure 'sufficient' provision of primary schools in their area.[38] The first duty is essentially to protect against risks related to the state of the premises recognised at common law, the second is a P-duty with no common law equivalent.

Further, this view explains why there appear to be few civilly actionable statutory P-duties in the absence of a special fact. As we have seen, in *Atkinson v Newcastle and Gateshead Waterworks Co*, there was held to be no action for breach of a statutory duty to maintain adequate water pressure in its system, with the alleged result that the plaintiff's house and workshop had burnt down in a fire.[39] By

[34] [1998] AC 188.

[35] [1935] 1 KB 75.

[36] See E Thayer, 'Public Wrong and Private Action' (1914) 27 Harvard Law Review 317. For a development of the same idea, see J Robert, S Pritchard, and A Brudner, 'Tort Liability for Breach of Statute: A Natural Rights Perspective' (1983) 2 Law and Philosophy 89.

[37] See now, however, s 69 of the Enterprise and Regulatory Reform Act 2013, which reverses this position in relation to many statutory safety duties owed to employees.

[38] *Reffell v Surrey CC* [1964] 1 WLR 358; *Keating v Bromley LBC* [1995] 2 AC 633; *Phelps v Hillingdon LBC* [2001] 2 AC 619.

[39] (1877) LR 2 Ex D 441.

contrast, in *Read v Croydon Corporation*, it was held that the duty to provide pure water, contained in the same legislation, was actionable.[40] Similarly, in *Dawson & Co v Bingley Urban District Council*, the statutory duty was to mark the location of hydrant points on a water line. The mark was placed inaccurately with the result that the fire brigade were delayed in finding the hydrant, resulting in greater damage than would have occurred if the duty had been correctly performed. It was held that this breach was civilly actionable.[41] *Atkinson* was a case of pure omission with no special fact. By contrast *Read* and *Dawson* are both cases in which the authority's failure arguably made things worse than if they had not acted at all.[42]

Three objections may be made to this concretisation explanation of the authorities. First, the statutory duty is often a strict duty—to *ensure* that machinery is fenced, for instance. In this way, the duty goes beyond a reasonable determination of what the duty of *reasonable care* requires. In response, however, it might be pointed out that the objectivity of the duty of reasonable care entails a refusal to countenance excuses that the duty-bearer might have; to that extent, there is some strict liability at common law, too.

Second, there are some actionable statutory duties which clearly go beyond the pre-existing common law duties. *Monk v Warbey* is a well-known example.[43] The defendant was held liable in tort for breaching his statutory duty not to permit another to drive a motor vehicle uninsured, with the result that, when the claimant was physically injured by the driver's negligence, they were unable to obtain compensation from the driver. Since this breach was not legally causative of the claimant's physical injury, the loss in respect of which the defendant was held liable was effectively the economic loss in not receiving compensation for physical injury. Had the driver been insured, this loss would not have been suffered. This being so, this is an example of liability for pure economic loss in the absence of the typical requirement of an assumption of responsibility. While an assumption of responsibility is not a necessary condition of a duty of care in respect of pure economic loss, it is certainly not easy to reconcile *Monk* with the common law view as to the justifiable scope of duties in respect of pure economic loss. The most that can be said is that the floodgates concern which has clearly influenced the development of the law on pure economic loss is not present in *Monk*: the duty to compensate for economic loss will only be triggered by the driver tortiously injuring another.

Third, an alternative explanation to the concretisation theory might point, instead, to the existence of countervailing considerations pertaining to the negative

[40] [1938] 4 All ER 631.

[41] [1911] 2 KB 149.

[42] For a more recent refusal to recognise an actionable P-duty when no special fact at common law existed, see *Health and Safety Executive v Thames Trains* [2003] EWCA Civ 720 (no liability for breach of safety regulation possibly requiring inspection of works, with the alleged result that thirty-one people were killed).

[43] [1935] 1 KB 75.

consequences of liability, rather than the absence of a special fact, to explain the absence of actionability. For instance, in *X v Bedfordshire*, in concluding that section 2(2) of the Child Care Act 1980, which required a local authority to take certain children into care, was not civilly actionable, Lord Browne-Wilkinson adverted to the 'peculiar sensitivity' of the welfare sector, which involves 'very difficult decisions how to strike the balance between protecting the child from immediate feared harm and disrupting the relationship between the child and its parents'.[44] Perhaps the underlying concern here is that the imposition of liability will have a detrimental impact upon the performance of the statutory duty. Similarly, the absence of actionability in *Atkinson* might be explained on the basis that there would otherwise be a floodgate of claims against public utility providers.[45]

This alternative view struggles to explain, however, the contrast between *Atkinson* and *Dawson*: the floodgates risk is not materially different between cases of misfeasance and nonfeasance. And in cases in which the floodgates concern seems particularly obvious—the liability of highway authorities for failure to repair—this has not prevented the legislature from expressly imposing civil liability.[46]

(ii) Civilly Actionable Statutory P-Duties that Go Beyond the Common Law?

The instances of P-duties in the tort of breach of statutory duty that go beyond the duties at common law appear to be relatively few and far between. As has already been argued, the duties in the cases in the previous sub-section can be rationalised as giving concretisation to a common law special fact.

Here is one potential exception. In *Solomons v R Gertzenstein Ltd*, a majority of the Court of Appeal held that section 133 of the London Building Acts (Amendment) Act 1939 gave rise to civil liability for its breach.[47] This section required the 'owner' of a building to keep and maintain in position a means of escape in the event of fire. The claimant, who worked for one of the tenants occupying a floor in a building in Soho, suffered injuries when a fire broke out and the ladder leading to the roof was not in its customary position. Ultimately it was held that the defendant, an agent for the mortgagee of the landlord, was not within the Act's definition of 'owner', but the duty in section 133 was held to give rise to a civil right to damages.

44 [1995] 2 AC 633, 747.

45 See *Atkinson* (1877) 2 Ex D 441, 445–46: 'the company would virtually become gratuitous insurers of the safety from fire . . . of all the house within the district over which their powers were to extend.'

46 See section 1(iii).

47 [1954] 2 QB 243.

It might be contended that this is a P-duty—to maintain an effective means of escape—with no common law parallel. It certainly could not be said that the P-duty attached to a landlord–tenant relation: the claimant was not a tenant. Nor could it be said that the owner necessarily created the danger. If an owner builds a high-rise building without a fire escape, this might be considered an unreasonable interference with an ability to protect oneself from a risk. Clearly, however, the owner may not be the builder. At best, an analogy can be drawn to *Goldman v Hargrave*: the fact that a person has the right to exclude from a space justifies their being under certain P-duties in relation to risks that arise on the space, even if those risks were not directly created by the right-holder.

3. Breach of Statutory Duty and P-Duties: The Future

Is the current position in which statutory P-duties civilly actionable in the tort of breach of statutory duty rarely outstrip common law duties desirable?[48]

Consider, first, the liability of private persons. As we have seen, the central moral objection to more extensive P-duties on the part of natural persons is rooted in their freedom.[49] This objection obviously applies regardless of whether a judge or a legislator is imposing the P-duty. In this respect, there ought not to be a significant divergence between actionable statutory P-duties and common law P-duties.

What statute can usefully add is concretisation to P-duties that arise by virtue of special facts. For instance, statute might clarify that an employer's P-duty of reasonable care to an employee extends to calling for emergency services if the employee suffers an emergency in the workplace not due to the inherent risk of the work. In addition, statute may creatively attach relational P-duties to particular choice-based roles. In this way, it permissibly goes beyond the common law. In these circumstances, the legislature is usually better equipped to make the empirical judgement as to whether the imposition of a P-duty will do more harm than good. As we have seen, whether to attach a P-duty to some chosen role often turns on this issue.[50] In these cases, the freedom objection is met by conditioning the P-duty on a particular role. Statutory concretisation of the P-duty may be even more effective at obviating the freedom objection, by making clearer what duties come with particular roles.

Consider now the liability of public authorities and persons tasked with the provision of public services. In these cases, there is no intrinsic freedom objection to liability, or the freedom objection is met by conditioning liability on the choice

[48] For a defence of the continued existence of the tort of breach of statutory duty, see N Foster, 'The Merits of the Civil Action for Breach of Statutory Duty' (2011) 33 Sydney Law Review 67.
[49] Chapter 2.
[50] Chapter 5.

to occupy a role carrying special duties.[51] As we have seen, the current law recognises more extensive actionable statutory P-duties on public authorities and public undertakers than at common law. The main example are the P-duties rendered actionable by the HRA 1998. If these instances are justifiable, then the common law position on public authorities, which requires a special fact for P-duties to be triggered, can only be justified on institutional competence grounds. In short, if this is correct, the only good reason for the restrictive common law position on the P-duties of public authorities is that judicial development of the law on public authorities is *institutionally*, not *substantively*, illegitimate.

How should courts proceed in the absence of express statements in the legislation that a P-duty creates civil liability? Clearly, it is possible for legislation impliedly to create civil liability, or impliedly to exclude it, for instance when a remedy created by the legislation would be inconsistent with ordinary civil liability. In cases in which there is no express statement, however, it must generally be the case that the legislation should be interpreted in a way that it is consistent with the legal principles underpinning extant common law P-duties. Absent an express indication or by necessary implication, one would not expect the legislator to be departing from the law's existing scheme.

Consequently, it is suggested that, in the case of private persons, the courts ought to understand the statute's contribution to the law in line with the most justifiable understanding of the basis of tort law P-duties. This involves asking in cases of private persons: 'Can the statutory duty be understood as a crystallisation or reformulation of an existing P-duty, given the special facts currently recognised?' If so, it should be held to be actionable.

In cases involving public authorities, or persons tasked with a public function, there is less justification for this approach: the common law position on P-duties is generally modelled around the moral position of private persons, and this is inapt in relation to public authorities when it comes to the question of *additional* P-duties beyond those owed by private individuals.[52] If one insists that the duty or liability to compensate exists by virtue of legislative intention, then there is no basis for presuming that legislative intention is to mirror the common law special facts and go no further in this context. Instead, in the absence of express statement or necessary implication, the issue should be whether the P-duty represents a coherent extension to the suite of P-duties that are owed distinctively by public authorities. For instance, if the statute can be understood as giving concretisation to a fundamental human right, then it could represent a coherent extension of the existing suite of actionable P-duties under the HRA 1998.[53]

[51] See Chapter 10 on public authorities.
[52] See Chapter 10.
[53] See Chapter 10, section 4.

In some cases, the courts have adopted strained understandings of the justificatory basis of particular statutory duties in the absence of an express legislative intention. For instance, in *X v Bedfordshire*, Lord Browne-Wilkinson described the scheme of statutory child protection duties, including duties to take steps to investigate the risk of abuse to a particular child, as creating an 'administrative scheme designed to promote the social welfare of the community'.[54] Similarly, in *O'Rourke*, Lord Hoffmann described the Housing Act 1985 as

> a scheme of social welfare, intended to confer benefits at the public expense on grounds of public policy. Public money is spent on housing the homeless not merely for the benefit of people who find themselves homeless but on grounds of general public interest: because, for example, proper housing means that people will be less likely to suffer illness, turn to crime or require the attention of other social services. The expenditure interacts with expenditure on other public services such as education, the National Health Service and even the police. It is not simply a private matter between the claimant and the housing authority.[55]

The idea that the specific duty to protect a child whom one believes to be at risk of abuse is primarily justified by 'social welfare', at best, misses a fundamental part of the moral case for such a duty.[56] It treats child protection legislation as akin to clean air legislation. The latter is justified by the sizeable aggregate benefit to everyone in having clean air—its contribution to social welfare (perhaps we have individual moral *rights* to clean air against the state up to a threshold, but legislation requiring particular levels of air quality likely goes beyond any individual right). The duty to take a particular child into care is primarily justified by the moral importance of that particular child's life and the harm to which the child will otherwise be subject without assistance; children are not units of social welfare.[57] This is not to say that there necessarily ought to be rights to compensation in such cases: the legislator might justifiably exclude such liability. However, when legislation imposes a duty to do an act to protect another specific person from harm, the person's interest provides a sufficient justification for that duty, and the interest protected is particularly fundamental, it would be a reasonable default rule to understand the statute as crystallising a basic right against the state.[58]

[54] [1995] 2 AC 633, 747.

[55] [1998] AC 188, 193.

[56] See, similarly, R Carnwath, 'The *Thornton* Heresy Exposed: Financial Remedies for Breach of Public Duties' (1998) Public Law 407, 415 (in relation to homelessness legislation).

[57] On homelessness and rights, see C Essert, 'Property and Homelessness' (2016) 44 Philosophy & Public Affairs 266.

[58] See further Chapter 10.

4. Conclusion

It has been observed that legislation is often unjustifiably set aside in theorising tort law.[59] A similar observation applies in relation to the normative basis of statutory duties that give rise to civil liability. 'The legislator has made it so' is no more of an answer to the question of what justifies these duties than 'the doctrine of precedent has made it so'. This chapter has argued that, so far as private individuals are concerned, the justified role of statute is concretisation of interpersonal duties that are justifiable independently of the statute. On the assumption that the common law grounds of P-duties in relation to private individuals represent a just scheme of such grounds, then civilly actionable statutory P-duties should ideally not significantly diverge from those at common law. In relation to public bodies, statutory P-duties should more readily diverge from those at common law, in so far as the common law grounds of P-duties are justified by reference to the position of private persons.

[59] J Goudkamp and J Murphy, 'Tort Statutes and Tort Theories' (2015) 131 Law Quarterly Review 133.

8
Current Protection from a Risk

Unlike innocent creation of risk, interference, assumption of responsibility, control, and statute, the law does not explicitly refer to this brief chapter's subject matter as a distinctive ground of positive duties. However, in some cases, a person who is currently providing protection to another from a risk is under a P-duty to take care to continue to provide that protection. For instance, adjoining landowners are under duties not to withdraw the support their land provides to the other's land, and there are arguably circumstances in which one is required to allow a person to continue to use one's property in circumstances in which one's property is currently protecting them from a grave risk.

The chapter is in three sections. The first section begins by explaining that current protection from a risk is insufficient to trigger a P-duty. The second considers two situations in which current protection does appear to give rise to P-duties, and what distinguishes them. The third part considers the extent to which a general principle can be formulated that explains the scope of P-duties that arise when protection is currently being provided.

1. Current Protection from Risk Insufficient on its Own

There are many situations in which a person commits no legal wrong in removing the protection from a risk which they are currently providing. Suppose that I have an alarm system which visually monitors both my house and, unbeknownst to you, your house. If the system detects a burglar at either house, it calls the police. My system protects you from a risk. Clearly, however, I have no duty to take care to continue this protection. If I choose to discontinue the protection, even purely out of spite, I commit no wrong.

Furthermore, in some situations, the fact that my body or resources are *about to* provide protection to you does not create a P-duty to allow myself or my resources to be used to benefit you. If a plague of locusts is headed towards my farm to eat my crops, I am permitted to repel them onto your adjoining land under the common enemy rule in private nuisance.[1] I am not required, here, to allow my land to be harmed to save yours from the same harm. And, presumably,

[1] *Grevensteyn v Hattingh* [1911] AC 355.

Omissions in Tort Law. Sandy Steel, Oxford University Press. © Sandy Steel 2024.
DOI: 10.1093/9780191898822.003.0008

if a bullet is headed towards me, an innocent person, I am permitted to duck out of the way to avoid being killed, even if I know that this will expose you to the bullet.[2]

These appear to be implications of the general rule that I have no duty to improve your position relative to the position you would be in had my body and resources not been present at the time of the impugned conduct.[3]

The provision of protection can, however, itself create risk and, on this basis, trigger a P-duty.[4] In *Bird v Pearce*, the Court of Appeal held that by removing the warning lines it had previously painted on a road, a council had created a risk of harm to road users, and had a P-duty to take reasonable care to avoid that risk by repainting the lines or taking other risk-avoiding measures.[5] Eveleigh LJ reasoned:

> the authority had . . . created a potential source of danger that did not exist before it placed white lines upon the roads. Up to that moment drivers had no justification for relying on anything other than their own appreciation of the road situation. Once the authority in the exercise of its power created a pattern of traffic flow, drivers could be expected to rely to some degree upon it. Thereafter the authority was under a duty of care to all road users to take reasonable care to see that the system it had imposed would not be allowed to deteriorate so as to create a hazard.[6]

The risk is constituted, here, by the absence of warning lines against the background of a pattern of warning lines across the traffic system put in place. Given the presence of warning lines elsewhere in the vicinity, in similar circumstances, a reasonable person could mistakenly infer that the absence of a warning meant the road was in one respect safer than the other similar roads. Strictly, liability should only be established if it is shown that the risk which materialised was a risk due to acting upon the misleading appearance created, and there is perhaps some doubt as to whether that was the case in *Bird*.[7]

[2] On this philosophical favourite, see Chapter 2, p. 36.

[3] See Chapter 1.

[4] And when it amounts to the acceptance of a professional relationship, or a care-giving role for a vulnerable person, it may trigger an assumption of responsibility: Chapters 4 and 5.

[5] [1979] RTR 369.

[6] ibid.

[7] In *Gorringe v Calderdale LBC* [2004] UKHL 15, [2004] 1 WLR 1057 Lord Hoffmann said (at [43]) that this 'may be an artificial assumption', but endorsed the general principle that 'if a highway authority conducts itself so as to create a reasonable expectation about the state of the highway, it will be under a duty to ensure that it does not thereby create a trap for the careful motorist who drives in reliance upon such an expectation'. For a summary of the application of this principle in cases involving provision of street lighting, see *McCabe v Cheshire West and Chester Council* [2014] 6 WLUK 795.

2. Current Protection from Risk as a Source of P-Duties

Consider two situations in which the law imposes P-duties when one person or their resources are providing protection to another: (1) rights to the support of adjacent or subjacent land, and (2) rights to continue one's use of another's property.

(i) Rights to Support of Adjacent or Subjacent Land

An owner of land is entitled to the support provided by adjacent or subjacent land to the natural condition of the land.[8] It has been stated that this is merely a negative right, requiring the adjacent or subjacent owner not to *act* in such a way as to remove the support:

> A negative right not to have the support removed cannot accurately be expressed in terms of a positive right to have the support maintained.[9]

In terms of the analysis in this book, however, the right can justifiably be characterised as positive. It is a right that another not act so as to discontinue the benefit they are providing: the adjacent or subjacent land is providing a benefit in that it improves the position of the other land relative to the position it would be in were the land not there. If A's land is subjacent to B's land, and B's land cannot exist without the support of A's land, then but for the presence of A's land, B's land would not be at all usable. Even if negative rights are understood in terms of the act-omission distinction as rights against an *act*, it is likely that a landowner may be required to take minimal positive steps in circumstances in which they become aware, or could reasonably become aware with minimal oversight, that the support provided by their land is likely to be discontinued with harmful effect to the right-holder.[10]

(ii) Rights to Continue One's Use of Another's Property

Some jurisdictions recognise duties not to withdraw the protection one is currently providing another through one's property. It is true, as with duties of support, that these are duties not to *act* in certain ways; the peculiarity is that one's act will not make the person worse off than if one's body or resources had not been present at the time. In this way, these duties are positive in nature. As Alan Brudner puts

[8] See, eg, *Bower v Peate* (1876) 1 QB 321. There is no natural right to the support of a building: *Dalton v Angus* (1881) 6 App Cas 740.

[9] *Byard v Co-operative Permanent Building Society Ltd* (1970) 21 P & CR 807, 821 (Megarry J).

[10] By virtue of the P-duties of the occupier: see Chapter 6. See, eg, *Holbeck Hall Hotel Ltd v Scarborough BC* [2000] QB 836.

it, these cases stand for 'a [limited] legal duty not to withhold one's goods from a stranger if he has already laid hold of them'.[11]

Consider the Vermont decision, *Ploof v Putnam*.[12] It was alleged that a 'violent tempest' arose while the plaintiff was sailing on a sloop with his wife and their two minor children, and that the plaintiff moored his boat to the defendant's dock to protect them from a substantial risk of death or serious injury. The defendant's employee unfastened the boat, with the result that the plaintiff's wife and children suffered serious injuries and their property was destroyed. The court held that this allegation disclosed an actionable wrong on the part of the defendant. The plaintiff's interference with the dock was justified by necessity, and it was wrongful for the defendant to interfere with this justified use in such a way as to endanger the plaintiff's life without sufficient reason.[13]

Depue v Flateau is similar.[14] The plaintiff was invited to inspect some furs at the defendant's home. Having bought the furs, he stayed for dinner and then fell seriously ill, in such a way as to be unable to care for himself. He requested to stay the night, but was instead assisted into his cutter to make his way home. He was found nearby almost frozen to death the next day, and his fingers had to be amputated. The court said:[15]

> We do not wish to be understood as holding that defendants were under an absolute duty to entertain plaintiff during the night. Whether they could conveniently do so does not appear. What they should or could have done in the premises can only be determined from a full view of the evidence disclosing their situation, and their facilities for communicating his condition to his friends, or near neighbors, if any there were.

The implication is that, if it were convenient to do so and there were no other means of ensuring his safety, their duty would have been to accommodate him for the night.[16] In *Southwark LBC v Williams*, the Court of Appeal held that necessity could not justify the trespass committed by squatters, in desperate need of housing, on vacant council property.[17] The privilege being asserted by the squatters in *Southwark* was far more extensive than that in *Ploof*—essentially a privilege to remain indefinitely on another's property.

[11] A Brudner, *The Unity of the Common Law* (2nd edn, OUP 2013) 278.

[12] 81 Vt 471, 71 A 188 (1908).

[13] Note that, despite the apparently positive act taken by the defendant's employee in unfastening the boat, the case remains one of a failure to benefit the claimant as it cannot be said that the former's actions made things worse: see generally the discussion of *Ploof* in Chapter 1, section 4.

[14] 111 NW 1, 100 Minn 299 (1907).

[15] ibid 305–06.

[16] For a more recent example, see *Kmart Corp v Lloyd* 155 Or App 270, 963 P 2d 734 (1998) (holding that K-Mart had a duty to render aid to an ill customer rather than ejecting her at closing time; the basis of the duty was said, however, to be the special relationship).

[17] [1971] Ch 734.

It might be argued that these cases are truly concerned with the limits on a right-holder's right to enforce their rights without a court order—that is, their rights of self-help—and not genuine *duties* on the part of the owner to allow the use of their resource.[18] This understanding cannot explain, however, why the court in *Ploof* understood the unfastening as a wrong to the plaintiff nor the reference to 'duty' in the reasoning in *Depue*. This is unsurprising: in so far as the reason why one's privilege of self-help is limited is the disproportionate or unnecessary effect upon the person interfered with, this involves a breach of a duty to that person.[19]

Suppose your garden is severely flooded and the garden fence is protecting your neighbour's property from being severely damaged by the floodwater. If you open the garden gate, the water will escape and cause this damage. The limitation on the common enemy rule, that one cannot deflect a threat which has already caused damage to one's land, applies here.[20] One would have a duty not to open the gate, or a more limited duty not to offload all of the water onto one's neighbour in order to prevent one's own land suffering further damage; this is a P-duty since it requires one not to do an act that will prevent the other from being better off than if one's land had not been present.[21] Even if one treats this as a purported exercise of the privilege of self-help (which is somewhat awkward as one is not seeking to repel or counteract an invasion of one's *rights* by another *person*), it is still a *wrong* to the neighbour.

Allan Beever makes the interesting suggestion that the P-duty in *Depue* arose by virtue of the defendant's invitation, and the limited assumption of responsibility for his welfare thereby constituted:

> The defendant ... was entitled to turn the plaintiff away from the beginning, but having invited the plaintiff into his house, became responsible for him in a way he was not previously responsible ... The obligation arose because of the defendant's invitation to the plaintiff.[22]

It is plausible that inviting someone to one's property involves this kind of assumption of responsibility.[23] However, this view struggles to explain *Ploof*, which makes clear that the duty is not contingent upon the person being on the property initially by invitation. The initial entry may be justified simply because of necessitous

[18] For the view that *Ploof* reflects a limit on the privilege of self-help, see J Goldberg, 'Inexcusable Wrongs' (2015) 103 California Law Review 467, 483.

[19] It is otherwise when the privilege is impermissible for other reasons, eg the effect on third parties. In such cases, the exercise of the privilege may be wrongful vis-à-vis third parties, but not necessarily the person against whom it is exercised.

[20] On this limit, see *Whalley v Lancashire and Yorkshire Railway* (1884) 13 QBD 131.

[21] As in *Whalley* (n 20), where the defendant cut trenches in their embankment, allowing water to damage the plaintiff's land.

[22] A Beever, 'The Basis of the *Hedley Byrne* Action' in K Barker, R Grantham, and W Swain (eds), *The Law of Misstatements: 50 Years on from Hedley Byrne v Heller* (Hart 2015) 96.

[23] See Chapter 4, section 1(ii)(e).

circumstances, and thus the owner is duty-bound not to repel the user despite the absence of any initial invitation.

3. Conclusion: A General Principle?

It is tempting to analyse the duties that exist in current protection cases simply as instantiations of the general duty to take care not to be a cause of damage to a person's general right-protected interests through positive action, but with the special feature that the only way of complying with that duty involves allowing a person to use one's resource.

If that analysis were correct, these cases would still be distinctive, but not in relation to what grounds the existence of a *duty*. Instead, the special feature would pertain to the *standard* of the duty in question: since one is being required to allow use of one's right-protected resource, one may be entitled to privilege one's own interests to a greater extent than usual. One's general duty loses its normal stringency, and becomes more akin to a duty of easy rescue in terms of the cost it requires one to bear.[24]

The difficulty with this suggestion is that it would imply a problematic conclusion about *Cancellation*, where one's charity payment was *about to* prevent another's death, but one cancelled it before it did so. In this case, the overwhelming likelihood is that there is no duty to take care not to cancel the payment. It seems that there is no general duty to take care to ensure that one does not deprive another, by one's positive act, of access to one's resources, even when this would foreseeably result in damage.

The better view is that one has a special duty, when one's resources are *currently* providing protection from a risk, to take care not to remove that protection, when the only way of removing the protection is by doing an act which will expose a person who was reasonably safe from risk to danger—but the demandingness of this duty can be relatively minimal, precisely because one is being required to allow use of one's resources. In *some* right of support cases, the duty may be more stringent since there is a distinctive unfairness involved in the refusal to continue to support when the other party's land is supporting one's own land:[25] the reciprocity of support involved may make the duty more demanding.[26] However, in *Depue* and *Ploof*, where the current protection is wholly for the benefit of the persons in need, the duty is less demanding. One is not required to accommodate seriously ill strangers indefinitely in one's property.

[24] On such duties, see Chapter 9.

[25] The parallel case involving human beings would be the duties owed by conjoined twins to each other. Each has a duty to contribute to the preservation of their shared bodily resources.

[26] Not all cases have this feature: my subjacent land may support yours, without yours supporting mine. In such a case, there is a reasonable case that the duty should be less demanding.

It may be objected, as a normative matter, that the principle described in the last paragraph is too broad and too narrow. It is too broad, so the objection goes, in so far it applies to the current protection provided by *any* resource. But is one really required to allow a person to continue to use one's *body* for protection? Judith Thomson famously gave the example of a person who goes to a musical concert, falls asleep, and awakens to find that a violinist has been 'plugged in' to their body and will die unless one maintains the connection for nine months. Thomson's claim was that in these circumstances one *may* discontinue protection since the duty here was positive in character and so relatively undemanding; one might be required to provide minimal assistance, but not to provide the use of one's body for this duration.[27] Surprisingly, such cases do not populate the law reports. Still, it seems too difficult to draw a sharp line here between body and property. Suppose a variant of *Ploof* where the plaintiff needed to grasp the defendant's ankle momentarily in order to hoist himself to safety. The difference is simply that the costs one can be expected to bear in relation to the use of one's body are very minimal.

The narrowness objection is that it is arbitrary to distinguish between cases in which one's resource is *currently* providing protection and cases in which it is *about to* provide protection. In one respect, this objection is correct as a normative matter: in some cases, as Chapter 9 argues, one should be under a duty to provide protection (and thus, in some cases, a duty not to interrupt protection that one was about to provide). However, it will typically be true in cases involving current protection that the only way to discontinue this protection is by dislodging a person from their present safety. Other things being equal, it seems worse to disrupt a person's established security from their prospect of security in the future[28]

[27] J Thomson, 'A Defense of Abortion' (1971) 1 Philosophy & Public Affairs 47. Hence, Thomson argued, a pregnant woman could sometimes permissibly cease to provide protection of a foetus by aborting it.

[28] See T Honoré, 'Are Omissions Less Culpable?' in P Cane and J Stapleton (eds), *Essays for Patrick Atiyah* (OUP 1991) 41–42.

9
Easy Rescue

This chapter is concerned with a P-duty not recognised by the current tort law in England and most common law jurisdictions: a duty of easy rescue owed by all persons. The term 'duty of easy rescue' normally refers to a general duty to provide assistance to another when there is an imminent high risk of death or serious damage to their body, in circumstances in which the assistance needed would not involve significant cost to the duty-bearer, and when the failure to assist will not make the person subject to the risk worse off than if the duty-bearer had not been present. The duty is general in that it applies to all persons, or all persons with sufficient capacity to assist.

The topic has been examined extensively by many authors.[1] Broadly, we can identify the following positions in the literature:

(1) If A fails to conduct an easy rescue of B, A breaches a moral duty, but this duty is *not* justifiably enforceable in *law*, for *non-instrumental* reasons.[2]
(2) If A fails to conduct an easy rescue of B, A breaches a moral duty, but this duty is *not* justifiably enforceable in *tort law*, for *non-instrumental* reasons.[3]
(3) If A fails to conduct an easy rescue of B, A breaches a moral duty, but this duty is *not* justifiably enforceable in *law*, for *instrumental* reasons.[4]
(4) If A fails to conduct an easy rescue of B, A breaches a moral duty which is justifiably enforceable in tort law.[5]

[1] See, eg, J M Ratcliffe (ed), *The Good Samaritan and the Law* (Anchor Books 1966); J Kortmann, *Altruism in Private Law: Liability for Nonfeasance and Negotiorum Gestio* (OUP 2005); E Weinrib, 'The Case for a Duty to Rescue' (1980) 90 Yale Law Journal 247; C Fabre, 'Good Samaritanism: A Matter of Justice' (2002) 5 Critical Review of International Social and Political Philosophy 128; A Ripstein, *Private Wrongs* (Harvard UP 2016) ch 3; J Feinberg, 'The Moral and Legal Responsibility of the Bad Samaritan' in J Feinberg (ed), *Freedom and Fulfilment: Philosophical Essays* (Princeton UP 1994); L Murphy, 'Beneficence, Law and Liberty: The Case of Required Rescue' (2001) 89 Georgetown Law Review 605; R A Epstein, 'A Theory of Strict Liability' (1973) 2 Journal of Legal Studies 151, Section III; N Gray and J Edelman, 'Developing the Law of Omissions: A Common Law Duty to Rescue?' (1998) 6 Torts Law Journal 240 (specifically in relation to a doctor's duty to rescue). In relation to the criminal law, see A Ashworth, 'The Scope of Criminal Liability for Omissions' (1989) 105 Law Quarterly Review 424.

[2] See R Stevens, 'Private Rights and Public Wrongs' in M Dyson (ed), *Unravelling Tort and Crime* (CUP 2014) 536.

[3] Ripstein (n 1); Murphy (n 1).

[4] N J McBride, *Humanity of Private Law: Part 1: Explanation* (Hart 2018) 120–23 (though the discussion is focussed on a general duty to protect others from 'harm' when one is well-placed to do so).

[5] Weinrib (n 1), though Weinrib now rejects this view.

Omissions in Tort Law. Sandy Steel, Oxford University Press. © Sandy Steel 2024.
DOI: 10.1093/9780191898822.003.0009

My intention is to argue that either (3) or (4) is true, and give some reasons for preferring (4) over (3). It follows that the primary purpose of the chapter is to show that, at a foundational moral level, there is no in principle objection to the enforcement in tort law of duties of easy rescue. The normative action is primarily in the instrumentalist weeds: if the expected bad consequences of enforcement of duties of easy rescue outweigh the expected good consequences, this speaks against tort liability. In short, I argue that duties of easy rescue are 'owed to' the beneficiary in the sense relevant to generate justified compensatory liability. It is a further question whether the bad consequences of legal enforcement of that moral liability justify non-enforcement.

The reason for the focus of the chapter is that influential Kantian normative theories of private law have changed the argumentative battleground in relation to legal duties of easy rescue.[6] It has typically been accepted that if I see you drowning in a shallow pool of water, with no one else around, I morally owe it *to you* to help if I could do so without significant cost, for instance by calling for help.[7] The legal issue then becomes an instrumentalist one: would legal enforcement in tort law do more harm than good? Here is where appeals are made to the legal uncertainty of such duties, the possibility of reducing the available numbers of rescuers, sapping altruistic action, and so on.[8] The Kantian literature generally argues *in principle* against a tortious duty of easy rescue, *before* one reaches the question of balancing the pros and cons of legal enforcement in tort. It does so by arguing that duties of easy rescue are not the right kind of duty for enforcement in tort as they are not *owed to* the beneficiary.

In the first section of this chapter, I briefly explain the English law position. In the second section, I make a two-pronged case for a limited, enforceable, duty to use one's resources to protect others from death or grave injury. One prong is a consistency argument: it says that, if one accepts a P-duty to allow others to use one's property in situations of dire need, then it is difficult to resist a P-duty of easy rescue on foundational moral grounds (even if practical considerations against it can still be mounted). The other prong is more direct: it is the argument that the best explanation of the moral intuition that one must help in situations of easy rescue is an enforceable relational duty to do so. The section then considers a variety of arguments against tortiously enforceable duties of easy rescue which posit distinctive moral problems with the enforcement of such duties in tort law specifically. The third section considers, and largely rejects, alternative justifications for a duty of easy rescue.

[6] See generally A Ripstein, *Force and Freedom: Kant's Legal and Political Philosophy* (Harvard UP 2009); R Stevens, *Torts and Rights* (OUP 2007) 337–40 (although this last author explicitly denies that a strict Kantian analysis of the issue is necessary: 329).

[7] See, eg, A P Simester, 'Why Omissions are Special' (1995) 1 Legal Theory 311, 317–18, 332.

[8] For some preliminary discussion of these, see Chapter 2, esp sections 3–4.

1. English Law: No General Duty of Easy Rescue

In 1867 Willes J said, *obiter*, that 'no action will lie against a spiteful man who, seeing another running into a position of danger, merely omits to warn him'.[9] One hundred and thirty years later, Lord Keith added his own variant of a man 'who sees another about to walk over a cliff with his head in the air, and forebears to shout a warning', concluding that no duty would exist.[10] Then, in 2020, Lord Reed, re-emphasising the general rule of no liability for pure omissions, mentioned these as 'commonly given examples' of pure omissions: 'someone who watches and does nothing as a blind man approaches the edge of a cliff, or a child drowns in a shallow pool'.[11] These are plausible examples of situations in which a moral duty of easy rescue would be triggered.

Notice, however, that the law's accepting that there is no general duty or liability in relation to a pure omission is not equivalent to a rejection of a general duty of easy rescue. This point is sometimes overlooked.[12] It would be logically possible to accept that there is no general tort duty in relation to pure omissions, while accepting that there is a general duty of easy rescue. This is because a duty of easy rescue is a duty to avoid a particular kind of pure omission: one in which a person's life or other fundamental interests are known to be at imminent risk of destruction or damage, when it is possible to intervene at low cost to prevent that destruction or damage. This is consistent with the position that one does not have a general duty not culpably to pure-omit when others' interests are at stake. If the distinction between acts and pure omissions in English law, however, is understood as the proposition that there is no duty in respect of *any* pure omission unless a special circumstance, beyond one's mere existence, obtains, then acceptance of this proposition does rule out a general duty of easy rescue. The important point is that the law can accept (1) an important distinction between acts and pure omissions by ruling out a general duty to act to promote others' interests, and (2) still accept a general duty of easy rescue. This, as we shall see, is the position in French and German law: general duties to rescue exist, but there is no general tort duty to act for the benefit of others.

[9] *Gautret v Egerton* (1866–67) LR 2 CP 371, 375 (*obiter* because the case concerned at most a careless omission).

[10] *Yuen v Attorney-General of Hong Kong* [1988] AC 175 (PC) 192.

[11] *Robinson v Chief Constable of West Yorkshire* [2018] UKSC 4, [2018] AC 736 [72].

[12] It was recognised by Lord Goff in *Smith v Littlewoods Organisation Ltd* [1987] AC 241, when his Lordship comments (at 271) that abandoning the common law's approach to pure omissions would not provide a simple resolution of the problem in that case; his point was that one would still need to treat pure omissions as a special category, even if one abandoned the general rule in relation to pure omissions.

2. A Defence of Duties of Easy Rescue

This section first offers the consistency prong of the argument for duties of easy rescue—or more precisely, for the absence of a foundational moral objection to duties of easy rescue. The section then advances the second prong of the argument, which seeks to identify a normative basis for enforceable moral duties of easy rescue.

(i) The Consistency Argument: Duties to Allow Others to Use One's Property

Some jurisdictions recognise duties not to withdraw assistance one is currently providing another. It is true that these are duties not to *act* in certain ways; the peculiarity is that one's act will not make the person worse off than if one's body or resources had not been present at the time. In this way, these duties are structurally akin to duties of easy rescue.

The argument begins with *Ploof v Putnam*, which was discussed in the last chapter.[13] In this case, the court held that it was wrongful for the defendant to prevent the plaintiff's current use of the defendant's property, when this use was justified by necessity.

Consider, now, a variation on *Ploof*:

> *Ploof 2*. A sees that B's boat has become endangered by a sudden, violent, storm. B shouts to A that he needs to anchor on A's dock. A wants to avoid any damage to his dock that might be caused by B's boat anchoring on it. A presses a button which coils up the dock so that B cannot anchor there.

It is suggested that the distinction between *Ploof* and *Ploof 2* is difficult to sustain. If you should have a duty not to unfasten the anchor, you should also have a duty not to press a button preventing the anchoring. If that is true, then property right-holders should have some kind of legal duty not to prevent their property being used by others in situations of dire need, in order to protect their lives.[14] The only difference in the two cases is between prevention or interference with *current* use, and prevention of an *immediately imminent* use. It is hard to see why that temporal difference could bear this stark moral significance, even if it has some significance.

Consider now:

[13] 81 Vt 471, 71 A 188 (1908). See Chapter 8, p. 177.

[14] If there were several dock-owners, and all coiled up their dock to prevent its use, each should be said to be in breach of a duty to allow their dock to be used. cf *Cancellation* and surrounding discussion (see generally Chapter 1) where removal of one's resources does not seem subject to any kind of general duty.

> *Ploof 3.* A sees that B's boat has become endangered by a sudden, violent, storm. B shouts to A that he needs to anchor on A's dock, but cannot reach it. A could press a button which extends the dock so that B can save his life. A wants to avoid any damage to his dock that might be caused by B's boat anchoring on his dock and does not press the button.

If there is a duty to press in *Ploof 3*, this is indistinguishable from a standard duty of easy rescue. Consequently, there is an argument of consistency for such a duty if the distinction between *Ploof 2* and *Ploof 3* cannot be sustained.

The obvious distinction is that a duty in *Ploof 3* would require an *act*—pressing the button—while a duty in *Ploof 2* only requires the absence of an *act*. If we accept the force of examples like *Cancellation*, there is an objection to being required not to act so as to fail to confer a benefit upon another through one's resources. If we also think that whatever is objectionable about that is what explains the objection to duties to act, then the act–omission distinction cannot distinguish *Ploof 2* and *Ploof 3*. In other words, if the central objection to a duty of easy rescue is the idea that a person's ends or the ends to which their resources are put, will be solely determined by another's ends, then the law has, effectively, already rejected that objection by recognising the duty in *Ploof* and, its close cousin, *Ploof 2*. There would have to be some further objection to a duty to act—beyond the sense in which such duties involve a requirement to use one's resources to benefit others—for the cases to be distinguishable at a foundational level.

Here is a further way in which the duty in *Ploof* is part of the same family as duties of easy rescue. Consider another variation on *Ploof*:

> *Ploof 4.* As in *Ploof*, except A's life is also endangered, and the only way in which A can protect himself from a substantial risk of death is by unfastening B's anchor, and attaching A's own anchor to the dock.

Here it seems permissible for A to unfasten B's anchor, even though this risks B's death. But this is generally impermissible: generally, I am not permitted to shift a substantial risk of death away from myself onto another innocent person.[15] The distinguishing feature of *Ploof 4* is that the means of protecting A from a substantial risk of death is A's property. This tends to suggest that duties not to prevent others from being assisted by one's own property are normatively special, in that these duties can be permissibly infringed by one's own substantial self-interest, even when another's life is at stake. In this way, these duties have a similarity to moral

[15] Suppose that a person's only way of receiving life-saving medical treatment at hospital is by running over and killing an innocent person to get there. For arguments against views which accord a 'prerogative' to agents to kill innocent others in certain situations, see V Tadros, *To Do, To Die, To Reason Why: Individual Ethics in War* (OUP 2020) 197–200.

duties of easy rescue: one's moral duty of easy rescue is highly sensitive to personal cost. Even if another person's life is at stake, one is permitted not to save them, even when what is at stake for oneself is substantially less important than the preservation of the other's life.

(ii) The Direct Argument for an Enforceable Relational Duty of Easy Rescue

The aim of this section is to defend the existence of a relational enforceable moral duty of rescue. To do so, it will be useful to have a running example:

> *Drowning Child.* A, an able-bodied adult, is walking past a shallow swimming pool in a park while on a morning stroll. A sees B, a small child, in serious distress, gasping for breath, in the pool. A knows that no one else is around. A could reach into the pool and lift B to safety. [16]

A first argument is based on intuition. The existence of a moral duty of easy rescue in cases like *Drowning Child* 'seems to be one of our most firmly-held moral intuitions'.[17] It might be objected that the intuition can be explained as being based on the bad character that A displays in failing to save, or A's failure to behave virtuously. Judith Thomson describes such a person as 'self-centered and callous, indecent in fact, but not unjust'.[18] For Thomson, the wrongness of the non-intervention is not a right-related wrongness: the drowning child has no moral *right* to assistance. Yet, this fails to capture other features of the situation which point towards a right-based interpretation. For a start, B, or someone on B's behalf, could surely *demand* and *insist* that A help; the aptness of demands by or on someone's behalf is an indication of a claim of right (compare the inaptness of a *demand* that another be generous). Further, B's situation, and the fact that A could intervene at minimal cost, do not seem to provide A only with a vanilla other-regarding *reason* to intervene. It would be odd for A to believe that A has a discretion whether to act on this reason. B's situation should operate as a peremptory demand on A's practical reason.[19]

A second argument begins from the general proposition that our duties to do or not do an act are determined by the balance of (i) certain kinds of reason to do that act, and (ii) permissions not to act on that reason.[20] For instance, I have a reason

[16] For this kind of example, see P Singer, 'Famine, Affluence and Morality' (1972) 1 Philosophy & Public Affairs 229, 231.

[17] D Miller, 'The Nature and Limits of the Duty of Rescue' (2019) Journal of Moral Philosophy 1, 2.

[18] J J Thomson, 'Rights, Restitution, and Risk: Essays' in William Parent (ed), *Moral Theory* (Harvard UP 1986) 14.

[19] In this way, it is not merely that A has an excellent moral reason to intervene.

[20] See T Pummer, *The Rules of Rescue* (OUP, 2022) ch 1.

not to impose a 1% risk of death on you, but if the cost to me of not imposing that risk is certain death, I am not *required*—that is, I am not under a duty not to impose the risk. On this general view about duties, their more fundamental determinants are the balance of certain kinds of reason.

Now, the idea that duties are determined by a balance of certain kinds of reason does not imply a simple comparison of the relative effects on welfare of the duty-bearer and the counterparty. Since each of us is not purely an instrument for the benefit of others, we have permissions not to act so as to benefit others all of the time. This was part of the explanation given in Chapter 2 for the existence of a general distinction between positive and negative duties. It was also pointed out there, however, that the scope of this permission need not rule out *all* P-duties. This is because it is not plausible that one is treated merely as an instrument for the benefit of others if one is required to bear only minimal costs to prevent them suffering grave harm. The fact that one is only required to bear minimal cost (compared to the harm which will be suffered if one does not intervene) already guarantees that one is not so treated.

So here is the argument more succinctly:

(i) Duties to X are determined by a balance of reasons to X and reasons permitting a person not to X.
(ii) There is a reason to protect other people from serious harm.
(iii) The reason to protect others from serious harm is not outweighed or cancelled by the permission grounded in one's free, independent, moral status, when the costs of acting on it are sufficiently low.
(iv) Absent a permission not to act upon the reason to protect others from serious harm—grounded in a person's free, independent, moral status, when the costs of acting on it are sufficiently low—there are no other reasons sufficient to outweigh the reason.
(v) Therefore, there is a duty to protect other people from serious harm when the costs of acting on this reason are sufficiently low.

It might be objected that I have overlooked the possibility that some reasons, even if they are genuine reasons to do an act, simply do not rise to the level of generating *duties*. For instance, if I see a stranger next to me in a café, struggling to identify the missing piece of a jigsaw puzzle, and I can see the missing piece, I probably have a reason to tell them the location of the piece. And it would be more or less costless for me to tell them. But do I act *wrongfully* in failing to tell them about the jigsaw piece? Presumably not. Even if this is true, however, the reason to protect another person from losing their life seems unlikely to be within this category, given the stakes to the person affected.

It might further be objected that the only reasons which ground duties, or duties owed to others, are reasons grounded in others' *authority interests*. On this view, the only basis on which my conduct will breach a duty is when the conduct is inconsistent with the other's authority over their resources. Wrongness is exclusively grounded in one person arrogating an authority over another which is not theirs to exercise.[21] In failing to save, one does not arrogate authority over another, and so there can be no duty to do so.

Here are five responses. First, it seems false that all right-related wrongness is grounded exclusively in the wrongful exercise of authority. It is possible to violate the right of another person who is incapable of exercising authority over their body (such as a very young infant). Nor is it clear why we should think of the wrong of negligently damaging a person's body as a wrongful exercise of authority. Negligently damaging the person's body was not a decision made for the right-holder by the duty-bearer.

Second, if this view is true about *all* duties, it is difficult to justify duties to support institutions in protecting others from serious harm that is not directly caused by any particular individual. A duty to contribute to the state's alleviation of poverty through taxation, for instance, will be unjustifiable since no individual arrogates authority over another in failing to contribute.

Third, it seems that the expected harmfulness of conduct on a person's welfare affects the costs that each of us can be expected to bear to abstain from the conduct. The costs I can reasonably be expected to bear to prevent you suffering a broken toe by my act are different from the costs I can reasonably be expected to bear to prevent you being paralysed by my act. If the effects on a person's welfare can have this kind of moral significance, it is not clear why they can never positively generate a duty to protect welfare.

Fourth, if the motivation for the authority view is that no one can be required to fulfil the ends of another, but only to respect their capacity to set ends, this motivation does not support the absence of a duty of rescue. In being required to protect another in dire need, one is not being required to fulfil their ends. One is being required to preserve their capacity to set ends.

Fifth, if the motivation for the authority view is that wrongness is concerned with standing in an unequal relation to another free person, this motivation does not rule out a duty of easy rescue. One of the reasons not to allow a person to die when one could assist them at small cost is that this instantiates a relation between you and that person which bespeaks the inferiority of that person's moral significance in relation to you.

(a) Relationality

If it is accepted that there is a *duty* of easy rescue, it is difficult to resist the further claim that this duty is 'owed to' the beneficiary.

[21] This is the view taken of relational duties of right in Ripstein (n 1).

First, if a duty is owed to a person when that person's interests justify the act subject to the duty, then the duty of easy rescue is owed to the beneficiary. Their interest—be it in their continued capacity to set ends or welfare—justifies the duty. Second, if a duty is owed to a person when that person has a distinctive moral complaint when the duty is breached, then this is also true of the beneficiary of the duty of easy rescue. It is to this person that apology, explanation, and feelings of remorse are owed or aptly directed. I consider the objection that the duty is not owed to the beneficiary, because the duty is a public duty of citizenship, below.[22]

(b) Enforceability

There are various reasons why a moral duty may be inapt for legal enforcement.[23] Broadly we can distinguish 'in principle' unenforceability and 'instrumental' unenforceability. The former purports to identify some inherent feature of a duty that makes it inapt for legal enforcement. The latter purports to identify some practical considerations that render the duty unfit for enforcement.[24] This sub-section focuses upon issues relating to enforceability in principle; practical considerations relating to the enforcement of P-duties in general were considered in Chapter 2.

Rights

Consider this argument: [25]

(i) Tort law enforcement should require the breach of a primary moral duty correlated with a primary moral right.
(ii) Moral duties of easy rescue do not correlate with primary moral rights.
(iii) Therefore, tort law enforcement of moral duties of easy rescue is unjustified.

Consider (i). This claim seems false since there are enforceable moral rights to compensation that do not depend upon the breach of a primary moral duty correlated with a primary moral right.[26] For instance, if A permissibly damages B's property to save A's body from harm for which B is not responsible, B is arguably still entitled to compensation from A.

Suppose (i) is accepted, (ii) should nonetheless be rejected. There is *an important sense* in which duties of easy rescue are correlated with moral rights. They

[22] See section 3(iii). If a duty is owed to a person when their interests ground an individual complaint to any principle that permits the conduct mandated by the duty, then duties of easy rescue are also relational on this basis. See RJ Wallace, *The Moral Nexus* (Princeton University Press 2019) ch 6.

[23] See, already, Chapter 2.

[24] Labelling all non-enforceable moral duties or reasons as duties or reasons of virtue is unhelpful as there are various reasons—not much connected—why duties are unenforceable in law.

[25] See also Murphy (n 1).

[26] See A Slavny, *Wrongs, Harms, and Compensation: Paying for Our Mistakes* (OUP 2023) chs 3, 5, 6. At least if one understands rights and duties as all-things-considered notions.

are grounded in the beneficiaries' interests, are demandable by the beneficiary, and *ex post* moral reactions are appropriately directed towards the beneficiary.

Another definition of a 'right-based' duty is a duty which is 'waivable by the person to which it is owed'.[27] It's not clear why tort law enforcement should require such a duty, however. There seems to be nothing problematic about people being able (as they currently are) to enforce compensatory claims in tort on behalf of young children who are unable to waive duties of non-interference.[28]

No Duty to Compensate for the Breach of a Duty of Easy Rescue

A different argument for tort law to steer clear of enforcement of moral duties of easy rescue is this:

(i) Enforceable tort law duties to compensate should require the existence of a moral duty to compensate.
(ii) Breach of a moral duty of easy rescue does not give rise to a moral duty to compensate.
(iii) Therefore, tort law should not recognise enforceable duties to compensate for breach of moral duties of easy rescue.

Let's grant (i) and consider (ii). One argument for (ii) is that, in situations in which a person breaches a moral duty of easy rescue, the counterparty of the duty will be dead or so severely injured in such a way that compensation will have no beneficial impact upon the person's welfare. Even granting the assumption that one has a duty to compensate only if compensation will have some welfare-impact, it is false that compensation will *never* be welfare-improving in circumstances in which the duty applies. It just depends.

A different argument for (ii) begins with the observation that duties of easy rescue are duties to protect people *only in so far as the costs to yourself are low*. Compensation is often *not* low cost. Indeed, it seems likely that, given the nature of easy rescue situations, the costs of effective compensation (eg twenty-four-hour care for a person who suffers brain damage from being left to drown) are likely to be very high. If the duty of easy rescue only required a small cost to be borne *ex ante* for the sake of another—in order to comply with the duty—the thought goes, it cannot require *a very high cost* to be borne *ex post*, after the duty has been

[27] Stevens (n 2) 118: 'It is a characteristic of rights-based duties that the rightholder has control over whether to enforce the right'.

[28] See, eg, V Kurki, 'Rights, Harming and Wronging: A Restatement of the Interest Theory' (2018) 38 Oxford Journal of Legal Studies 430. Cecile Fabre considers it important to establish that the duty of easy rescue is a duty of justice, where justice is the domain of morality that regulates allocation of scarce resources (see Fabre (n 1) 134–35). The connection between norms that have this subject matter and enforcement in tort law is obscure, however.

breached. In short: the stringency of a secondary duty to compensate is the same as the stringency of the primary duty from it derives.

This equivalence-in-stringency thesis appears to be false, however. The stringency of a duty seems to be sensitive to whether one had a reasonable opportunity to avoid breaching the duty. While one has no reasonable opportunity to avoid incurring a *primary* duty of easy rescue, one can, given the nature of the primary duty, easily avoid a secondary duty to compensate for its breach—simply by avoiding breach. Hence the stringency of the secondary duty to compensate may be greater than the stringency of the primary duty of easy rescue. It is difficult to say *how much more* stringent. Helen Frowe gives the example of a selfish person who, for no good reason, fails to move out of the way of a person who is fleeing an attacker across a bridge.[29] The only way the person can avoid the attacker is by pushing the selfish person off the bridge. Frowe claims that the culpable, wrongful, failure to move out of the way of the person in flight renders the selfish person liable to be killed. I'm not sure: but it does seem correct that the burdens that can be permissibly imposed upon the person who deliberately breaches a duty of easy rescue with no justification can become significantly higher than the initial burden that the person was required to bear.

More Appropriately Enforced in Public Law

Arthur Ripstein asserts that '[i]n those countries—notably France—in which there is tort liability for failure to rescue, the liability always follows the breach of a public law provision requiring rescue'.[30] The fact that these systems incorporate the duty of rescue by relying upon other legal regimes is said to illustrate 'how foreign' the idea of a duty of easy rescue is to tort law.[31]

Assessing Ripstein's claim will be a useful way of better understanding the duties of easy rescue in these and other legal systems, and considering the claim that such duties, in some way, do not belong in tort. The claim can be contested in a number of respects.

Firstly, some legal systems do establish duties of easy rescue within their civil liability provisions—Czech law is one.[32] Ripstein is right, however, that most European systems recognise such a duty in their criminal laws.[33]

Second, in French law, it is strongly arguable that a private law duty of easy rescue arises independently of Article 223-6 of the Criminal Code simply by virtue

[29] H Frowe, *Defensive Killing* (OUP 2014) 76. For further discussion of the connection between the stringency of primary and secondary duties, see Slavny (n 26) 69–73 and S Steel, 'Culpability and Compensation' in J Goudkamp, M Lunney, and L McDonald (eds), *Taking Law Seriously: Essays in Honour of Peter Cane* (Hart 2022).

[30] Ripstein (n 1) 60.

[31] ibid.

[32] See §2901 Czech Civil Code of 2012.

[33] See J M Smits, *The Good Samaritan in European private law: on the perils of principles without a programme and a programme for the future* (Inaugural Lecture, Maastricht University 2000).

of Article 1240 of the Code Civil. Geneviève Viney and Patrice Jourdain report that it is 'beyond doubt' that an omission motivated by an intention to harm 'always' constitutes *faute*.[34] Admittedly, the example cited by these authors is a complicated one. The example is that of a Jewish husband who intentionally refuses to deliver the *get*, which dissolves the religious marriage and permits re-marriage.[35] An English lawyer might argue that this is an example of a duty arising from a special relationship—albeit one which pertains to its dissolution.

Similarly, the *Branly* decision, which is most often claimed to illustrate the reduced significance of the distinction between acts and omissions in French tort law, is not a straightforward example either.[36] In *Branly*, Albert Turpain wrote a history of the development of radio communication without mentioning Edouard Branly. Branly, who had a state funeral, was recognised in France as having made an important contribution to its development; Marconi had sent the first cross-channel message to Branly, acknowledging Branly's contribution.[37] Turpain was himself a physicist convinced of his own contribution to the development of radio communication; in his history, he attributed Branly's invention to another person. Branly's son sought to hold Turpain liable under Article 1382 (now Article 1240), on the basis that the omission to refer to Branly was a *faute* which had caused (presumably reputational) damage. The Court of Appeal had rejected the claim on the basis that Turpain had not intended to damage Branly's reputation, but had honestly expressed his opinions. The decision was struck down by the Cour de Cassation.

The Cour de Cassation characterised the case as one involving omission (*abstention*), and observed that an omission can give rise to liability under Article 1382 (now Article 1240) without an intention to harm, when the omitted action 'should be done pursuant to a statutory, regulatory, customary obligation, or also, in virtue of a professional obligation, in particular, in relation to a historian, the requirements of objectivity'. For an English lawyer, the case is striking, but not because it imposes liability for an omission. The striking feature of the case is the legal regulation of the production of information in an academic context; the decision seems to involve an astonishing invasion of free speech. It was immediately criticised by Jean Carbonnier, in a famous case note, on precisely this ground.[38] Setting this aspect of the decision aside, however, it seems analysable as a case of an *act* or *impure* omission: by writing the history without mention of Branly, the author was effectively communicating either that 'Branly was mistaken about his involvement' or 'Branly lied about his

[34] G Viney and P Jourdain, *Traité de Droit Civil: Conditions de la Responsabilité* (LDGJ 1998) §455.

[35] See Civ 2e, 13 December 1972, D 1973, 493 note Larroumet. It is not always clear what exactly the *dommage* is in these cases.

[36] Cass Civ, 27 February 1951, D 1951, 329.

[37] One can visit the quai Branly in Paris, and the Musée du quai Branly.

[38] J Carbonnier, 'Le Silence et la gloire' (1951) XXVIII Chronique 119.

involvement' (or some related proposition). In some circumstances, the act of saying something without saying something *else* can communicate something more than what is explicitly said.[39] Turpain's conduct clearly either did make or risked making Branly's reputation *worse* than it would have been had Turpain not published the history. So the decision could be rationalised as one concerning impure rather than pure omission. This distinction is also recognised in French doctrinal writing, which distinguishes between *abstention dans l'action* and *abstention pure et simple*.[40]

Although the *get* cases, and *Branly*, could conceivably be analysed in these ways—as a special relationship and an impure omission case, respectively—this is not their conceptualisation in French law. The *get* cases typically refer to the more general doctrine of abuse of rights, rather than any relationship-based consideration, to justify the duty to deliver the *get*; the reasoning in *Branly* is not based upon the notion of an impure omission.

Third, although German law gives effect to the duty of easy rescue by way of incorporation of the criminal law duty in §323c StGB, it is important to note the basis on which this incorporation occurs. The basis of the incorporation involves a determination that the criminal law duty is a *Schutzgesetz*—that is, a 'legal norm, which according to its purpose and content serves to protect individuals or a class of individuals against the infringement of a particular right-related interest'.[41] And, indeed, the courts have held that §323c StGB is indeed a *Schutzgesetz* for the purposes of §823 II BGB. While the duty aims to respond to the general social interest in solidarity, it *also* aims to protect an individual's right-related interests when they are endangered in the way envisioned in the provision.[42] Hence §323c StGB is not 'treated in the same way as other criminal law requirements imposed as parts of systems of mandatory social cooperation', such as a failure to pay one's taxes.[43] In one case, four persons were held liable in damages for non-pecuniary loss under §823 II BGB for standing outside a car knowing that a woman was being raped without doing anything about it.[44]

[39] See the law on 'misleading' statements in England in the context of property and commercial acquisitions, eg, Property Misdescriptions Act 1991, s 1(5): 'a statement is misleading if... what a reasonable person may be expected to infer from it, *or from any omission from it*, is false' (emphasis added); see also *ACL Netherlands BV v Lynch* [2022] EWHC 1178 (Ch), applying the Financial Services and Markets Act 2000, s 90A and Sch 10A: 'a combination of statements or omissions might create an overall impression which could found a claim' (describing the liability of issuers of security for 'a misleading statement or dishonest omission').

[40] Viney and Jourdain (n 34) §456.

[41] See BGH 24 May 2013, VI ZR 255/11 (Federal Court of Justice).

[42] ibid [8] (referring to the legislative debates, which had stated the reason for criminalisation as also being 'Versäumung einer wirklichen Chance zu erfolgreicher Schadensabwendung').

[43] Ripstein (n 1) 61. See, for a helpful overview, Cees van Dam, *European Tort Law* (2nd edn, OUP 2013) 521–23.

[44] OLG Düsseldorf, 26 July 2004, NJW 2004, 3640 (Higher Regional Court of Dusseldorf).

Fourth, it is likely that tort liability for *intentional* failure to effect an easy rescue would arise under §826 II BGB for intentional conduct causing loss contrary to *good morals*.

Ultimately, these facts about other jurisdictions cannot settle the normative issue, but they at least undermine the idea that these other jurisdictions conceive of liability for failing to rescue as radically external to ordinary tort liability.

More Harm than Good

If the tort law enforcement of a primary legal duty of easy rescue had no impact upon rescuers, it could still be justified.[45] Even if it did not incentivise more rescues, the enforcement would provide a means by which wrongdoers' secondary duties could be enforced for the benefit of those wronged.[46]

There is a risk, however, that the tortious legal enforcement of the duty of easy rescue will backfire by causing people to avoid situations in which their duty will be triggered when these people might otherwise have intervened to rescue, or encourage dangerous rescues. In Chapter 2, I argued that these kinds of risk are relevant to the question of whether the duty of easy rescue ought to be legally enforced. Against this risk, one needs to weigh the probability that legal enforcement will prevent harm that otherwise would arise.[47] David Hyman, on the basis of reported incidents, concludes that 'confirmable instances of non-rescue are actually an extraordinary rare event, occurring about 1.7 times per year in the entire United States during the past decade'.[48] Only a few States have introduced easy rescue statutes. This is evidence that the introduction of the duty would not prevent a great amount of harm. Further, on the basis of analysis of rescue statistics in states which have had almost a century of easy rescue statutes, he concludes: 'the available data provides no indication that imposing a duty to rescue has any effect whatsoever'. If this is true, there still may be undefeated reason to introduce the duty: it would assist right-holders to enforce their secondary rights to compensation.

The Problem of Rational Limits

Drowning Child has the standard feature of cases discussed in relation to duties of easy rescue in tort law: physical proximity between the duty-bearer and right-holder. Physical proximity often tracks facts of moral relevance. First, physical proximity may affect one's ability to see what is going on and this normally allows one to assess more readily whether a person is in fact in great danger. Second, it is often more costly to intervene when one is at a distance than when in physical

[45] D Hyman, 'Rescue without Law: An Empirical Perspective on the Duty of Rescue' (2006) 84 Texas Law Review 653, 658–61 seems to presuppose the contrary.

[46] See further S Steel, 'Deterrence in Private Law' in H Psarras and S Steel (eds), *Private Law and Practical Reason: Essays on John Gardner's Private Law Theory* (OUP 2022).

[47] For a sceptical view, see Hyman (n 45) Section III.

[48] ibid 665.

proximity. Third, physical proximity often singles a person out as the only person able to help in the circumstances, such that the duty of easy rescue falls clearly upon that person.

These are clearly contingent connections between physical proximity and facts of moral relevance. Suppose that a person has hacked into a person's web-camera and witnesses that person being viciously strangled by their partner.[49] If the hacker knows the person's location, then they are able to help by phoning the police, and this is no more costly than if the hacker lived next door. Further, the hacker is the only person aware of the situation and so is uniquely able to help. It seems clear that the hacker is under a moral duty to call for assistance.[50] So, physical proximity cannot be a necessary condition of the duty arising, as a moral matter.[51] Notably, no legal system that recognises a duty of easy rescue seems to limit such a duty by considerations of physical proximity.[52]

Once physical proximity is set aside, however, it becomes unclear why we are all not under legally enforceable duties to provide assistance to people in other countries whom we could assist at low cost by providing relatively small monetary payments with life-saving effects.[53] The most plausible view is that we are, but that the state should not enforce this duty through tort law.[54] Hence the permissibility and duty of the state to use taxation to provide international aid. The absence of such liability within tort law is justifiable on the same basis as the absence of tort liability for failure to pay tax. If there were only one person in the rest of the world, tort liability for breach of a duty of easy rescue to that person might be a good idea. When millions of persons are the right-holders of duties owed by millions of duty-bearers, and when satisfaction of the duties is likely to require substantial coordination between duty-bearers, or their states, tort liability is an unsuitable vehicle for the enforcement of these duties.

[49] This example is complicated by the privacy violation. It may be that by violating the person's privacy one comes under special obligations to them.

[50] Compare the Kitty Genovese case: see generally M M Gallo, '*No One Helped*': *Kitty Genovese, New York City, and the Myth of Urban Apathy* (Cornell UP 2015). For digitally witnessed crimes, see generally Z D Kaufman, 'Digital Age Samaritans' (2021) 52 Boston College Law Review 1117.

[51] For the view that physical proximity *does* intrinsically matter morally, see F M Kamm, *Intricate Ethics: Rights, Responsibilities, and Permissible Harm* (OUP 2007) ch 11. For the opposite view, see, eg, V Igneski, 'Distance, Determinacy and the Duty to Aid: A Reply to Kamm' (2001) 20 Law and Philosophy 605.

[52] See, eg, Article 223-6 *Code Pénal*; §323c StGB; §253 Danish Criminal Code.

For a useful (though somewhat out-of-date) catalogue, see A W Rudzinksi, 'The Duty to Rescue: A Comparative Analysis' in Ratcliffe (n 1). For a superb online catalogue, see Z D Kaufman, 'Bad Samaritan Laws' (*Zachary Kaufman*) <http://www.zacharykaufman.com/projects/bad-samaritan-laws?sortAsc=true&sortByDate=true> accessed 2 August 2022.

[53] Epstein thought that recognition of the duty would entail that the state had a duty to provide a welfare system and so the duty must be rejected: R A Epstein, *Takings: Private Property and the Power of Eminent Domain* (Harvard UP 2009) 324.

[54] GiveWell estimates that roughly every \$3,500–\$5,500 given to the most effective charities saves one life, for instance through the delivery and provision of malaria nets. For affluent individuals this is likely to come within 'easy' rescue.

3. Alternative Accounts of the Duty of Easy Rescue

In this section, I briefly discuss and critique alternative foundations of a duty of easy rescue. This will also serve to respond to a further objection that the duty is not owed to the beneficiary.

(i) Consequentialism

It might seem that the duty of easy rescue is easily explained by a consequentialist morality. Peter Singer suggests that the intuition in *Drowning Child* is evidence of a commitment to the following broader principle, which might appear to be consequentialist in character: 'if it is in our power to prevent something bad from happening, without thereby sacrificing anything of comparable moral importance, we ought, morally, to do it.'[55]

It is clear, however, that consequentialism does not explain common intuitions about the scope of the moral duty of easy rescue. First, the duty only seems to be triggered with bads of a certain threshold of moral importance: if I could prevent a person from having a cold, by giving them a warning, I do not seem duty-bound to do so. If we have a duty to maximise the good, however, this threshold is difficult to explain. Similarly, suppose I could save five billion people from a mild, temporary, headache, or save the child's life: intuitively, I should save the child. Second, suppose that two people are in danger and the only difference between them is that you find one of them physically attractive, and so it will provide you with more pleasure to save that person. This seems a morally irrelevant consideration in deciding whom to rescue; yet, if the basis of the moral duty were the maximisation of good states of affairs, this is difficult to explain. Third, intuitively, we do not think morality is so demanding: it does not seem to be the case that we are morally bound to suffer, say, paralysis in order to save a stranger's life. Fourth, suppose that if you allow the child to drown, it will be possible for the child's organs to be used to save five other people's lives. Nonetheless, you are duty-bound to save the child. Fifth, more controversially perhaps, suppose that you encounter the drowning child on the way to a business meeting whose success (which cannot be achieved without your presence) will allow you to give £100,000 to a highly effective charity that will save the lives of five children. Nonetheless, you seem duty-bound to stop and help the child, even if this means you cannot attend the meeting, and there will be more deaths overall.[56]

[55] Singer (n 16) 231.
[56] For this sort of example, see Miller (n 17) 5–6.

Possibly some of these intuitions can be debunked as stemming from certain well-known psychological biases.[57] For instance, we might be tempted to think, in relation to the last example, that the visibility of the drowning child compared to the five non-visible children is what drives the intuition. Suppose instead that the other five children were in another shallow pool of water beside the drowning one, and you could rescue those five. Here it seems much less clear that you should rescue the one. So, perhaps visibility and physical distance, which are intuitively morally irrelevant on their own, are clouding our intuitive judgements.[58] Yet, this strategy seems not fully persuasive. In the fourth example, where you leave the child to drown so that her organs can be taken for the benefit of five others, my intuition is wholly unchanged when the five others are present at the scene.

(ii) Constrained Deontology

On this view, there is a background moral duty to maximise the good, which is limited by constraints on using people in certain ways and permissions not to maximise the good. These permissions are justified in so far as one cannot exist as a separate individual, with some reasonable control over one's life, if one has a standing duty maximise the good. If these constraints and permissions are not applicable, however, we might think that we should be maximisers. On this picture of morality, there is a kind of default moral position of consequentialism, which gets hemmed in at the edges when necessary. If that picture is correct, then the duty of easy rescue seems explicable as the form that the duty to maximise the good takes once we have built in the necessary constraints and permissions.

This view could explain why you have a duty to save the child even though the child's organs would be useful to save the lives of five others: the omission would involve treating the child as a mere means, and so violate a deontological constraint.[59] It also helps to avoid the demandingness objection: one has a moral permission not to maximise the good so far as is necessary to allow one to live a separate, individual, life. This requires freedom from duties to bear immense personal costs for others absent some special fact, but not freedom from duties to bear minimal costs.

This view is nonetheless problematic. First, it does not explain why you have duty to save the child rather than prevent five billion people from having a headache.

[57] For a powerful set of arguments to this effect, see P Unger, *Living High and Letting Die: Our Illusion of Innocence* (OUP 1996).

[58] For the issue of physical distance specifically (which the author *does* consider to matter morally), see Kamm (n 51) ch 11.

[59] The example shows that one can omissively treat a person as a mere means, see KH Ramakrishnan, 'Treating People as Tools' (2016) 44 Philosophy & Public Affairs 133 (see especially the *Guinea Pig* case).

Second, it struggles to avoid the irrelevant reason—physical attractiveness—problem. Third, it struggles to explain the threshold of moral seriousness that must be reached before another person's welfare becomes something you must promote. Fourth, it struggles to explain why it would make sense to rescue a person who has collapsed in water due to a heart attack in preference to a person who is drowning because of a high-risk dive, which they undertook knowing that it carried a serious risk of death. The root problem here is that this view is still objectionably consequentialist: it treats human beings as sites of value, rather than as having a distinctive moral status.

(iii) Citizenship Duties

It has been suggested that the duty to intervene in *Drowning Child* is a moral 'civic' duty, akin to a duty to pay taxes.[60] Ripstein, for instance, claims on this basis that a person may legitimately be held to account by the state for breaching a duty of easy rescue, but not by a private individual.[61]

The civic duty view could take at least two forms. One form is that one owes the duty to intervene only to one's fellow citizens in virtue of some special relation one enjoys with them, and this special relation determines the beneficiaries of the duty in particular cases. This view is too narrow. If a non-citizen child is drowning in front of you, the duty surely applies too; while citizenship may ground special duties to other citizens, the minimally demanding duty to protect another's life does not seem to be one owed in virtue of citizenship.

In the other form, the duty is owed to other citizens in virtue of a special relation with other citizens, but that relation need not exist in a particular case for the duty to be triggered. Perhaps 'doing one's fair share' in society normally requires one to pay a fair share of taxes, but occasionally requires us to step in to deal with problems that are, in some sense, social problems that are normally the responsibility of the state.

This view has three problems. First, it is too narrow: morally, the duty simply does not seem to depend upon being a citizen. If I, not a citizen of Italy, see a small child gasping for their last breath in the Trevi fountain at 3am, I must act. Second, it is unclear why intervening to save a non-citizen stranger is really an incident of 'good *citizenship*'.

A third problem common to both versions is that, if true, the central moral complaint would be one of *unfairness* in relation to other citizens in general: a person who fails to pay their taxes might be accused of free-riding on others' efforts, wronging everyone in society but no one in particular. Ultimately, this is a

[60] See, eg, A Ripstein, 'Three Duties to Rescue: Moral, Civil, and Criminal' (2000) 19 Law and Philosophy 751; L Valentini, 'Social Samaritan Justice: When and Why Needy Fellow Citizens Have a Right to Assistance' (2015) 109 American Political Science Review 735.

[61] Ripstein (n 1) (arguing that liability for failing to rescue should be considered a crime, not a tort).

distortion of our moral reaction to *Drowning Child*—at best the 'social' wrong is a secondary phenomenon. The primary moral complaint is a culpable failure to respond to the special value of another human being's life.

Laura Valentini has offered a nuanced version of the view which seeks to avoid these objections. Her view begins with the idea that people who live under a common system of freedom-constraining rules have a duty, as a matter of justice, to 'guarantee a roughly equal sphere of sovereignty to all those subjected to them'.[62] Valentini's conception of 'sovereignty' (or, equivalently, 'right to freedom') is not an austere Kantian one, which only requires a person not to damage or use another's resources without permission; it includes access to certain valuable opportunities.[63] A legal system which 'leaves the needy unassisted, when reasonable assistance could be provided at reasonable cost to others is one that foreseeably and avoidably places unjustifiable constraints on the freedom of some: it is unjust'.[64] This is the source of the state's justice-based duty to assist others in need. When the state cannot discharge this duty, emergency services being unable to be omnipresent, well-placed citizens may acquire obligations which they must carry out 'on the state's behalf'.[65] So, in *Drowning Child*, one would have a duty to intervene to fulfil the state's justice-based duty of assistance. In breaching this duty, one would wrong the particular individual, upon whom the state's justice-based duty becomes focussed. In this way, Valentini seeks to avoid the objection that the wrong is not a wrong against the individual. She accepts that the duty of justice is not owed to non-citizens, but accepts that a generally non-enforceable duty of beneficence would require intervention. That duty is, in fact, morally enforceable in emergency situations, but at the cost of wronging the person who is forced to act. So her account appears to deliver the result that one has an enforceable duty of assistance to citizens and non-citizens, but the duty-bearer would be wronged by the enforcement in the latter case.

Here is an objection to Valentini's account. It is unclear why the state has a duty of justice to assist people in dire need, *in virtue of coercively enforcing a common set of rules*, when the existence of their need is causally unrelated to that enforcement. In one of Valentini's examples, a person's need arises because of a financial crash: one could plausibly argue that, here, the state has a duty of justice to intervene to help because the crash is a causal upshot of the operation of coercively enforced legal rules that constitute the market. This is not so in relation to harms to a person that do not arise from the operation of the coercive rules. So Valentini's account seems to me not to justify what it purports to justify: a *general* duty of easy rescue even between co-citizens.[66]

[62] Valentini, 'Social Samaritan Justice' (n 60) 741.
[63] This is implicit in ibid.
[64] ibid.
[65] ibid.
[66] For a similar objection, see Fabre (n 1), 131.

(iv) Other Kantian Arguments

Kant considered the duty of beneficence to be an imperfect duty, which gave one a kind of latitude as to when and how to satisfy it. The implication that one could permissibly choose not to rescue in *Drowning Child* has seemed unacceptable to some modern Kantians, however, even if other forms of beneficence are more discretionary in some sense.[67] Here are two lines of argument that have been offered by some modern Kantians for a duty of easy rescue.

The first is that one could not rationally will without contradiction that no one conduct easy rescues as a universal law for everyone. Assessing this would require us to enter into thorny territory about what kind of contradiction is relevant here. The prospects of making this kind of argument work seem bleak to me, however. There would be no logical contradiction in such a law. Nor would there necessarily be the kind of instrumental self-defeatingness that arises when a liar seeks to justify lying by reference to a universal maxim: if everyone were permitted to lie, then no one could trust any communication, and the liar's aim in lying could not be achieved. The willingness of others to conduct rescue is not a necessary condition of the success of not-rescuing. Success in not-rescuing is not dependent upon the presence of other rescuers. Nor would it necessarily be prudentially irrational to agree to a universal law that did not contain a requirement of rescue. If you are able-bodied, strong, and isolated from others, perhaps it would not be irrational.

The second is that the duty of easy rescue is an entailment of a more general duty not to be *indifferent* towards another person, in the sense of treating her ends as something 'not worth factoring into my plans'.[68] Karen Stohr proposes that, in certain circumstances, a failure to assist another person will express indifference in this sense; it will express the attitude that the other person's ends are not worthy of any weight in my deliberations.[69]

Stohr's proposal seems on the right track, but it seems objectionable in three respects.

First, presumably a person behaves in breach of a duty even if the person gives *some* weight to a person's ends, but radically undervalues their importance. Suppose that I would intervene to rescue the drowning child if only I didn't have my favourite shoes on. Here I recognise the child's claim upon me, but radically undervalue its importance.

[67] On 'discretionary' or imperfect duties of beneficence, see generally T E Hill, Jr, *Dignity and Practical Reason in Kant's Moral Theory* (Cornell UP 1992) 155. Violetta Igneski is one author who considers the duty to aid owed to a drowning child to be a perfect duty: V Igneski, 'Perfect and Imperfect Duties to Aid' (2006) 32 Social Theory and Practice 439.

[68] K Stohr, 'Kantian Beneficence and the Problem of Obligatory Aid' (2011) 8 Journal of Moral Philosophy 45, 61. Compare Nicholas McBride's similar concept of the wrong (or 'harm') of being treated 'like a dog' in N J McBride, *The Humanity of Private Law Part II: Evaluation* (Hart 2019) 134–45.

[69] Stohr (n 68).

Second, I am not sure that objectionable indifference is restricted to a concern for other people's *ends*. One could be concerned with another's ends by supporting particular ends. One could be concerned with another's ends by supporting the possibility of their being able to have ends at all. But one could simply be concerned with a person's well-being independently of a concern for their particular ends or their capacity to set ends. A person who stands by while a car slowly reverses over a screaming kitten behaves objectionably because he fails to recognise, or radically undervalues, the well-being interest of a being with some moral status. In my view, objectionable indifference extends across a failure to recognise the reason-giving force of people's ends, their capacity for setting-ends, *and* their well-being. The non-Kantian inclusion of well-being need not lead us back to the consequentialist problems identified above: the concern is not with well-being in the abstract, but the interest in well-being of existing particular people.

Third, the expressivist dimension of Stohr's proposal seems unnecessary. The positive ground of the requirement to prevent serious harm is the beneficiary's interest in the avoidance of serious harm, not their interest in being recognised in a person's deliberations or others expressing certain attitudes towards them.

4. Conclusion

This chapter has argued that the moral foundations of the duty of easy rescue make it apt in principle for enforcement in tort law. Many questions about legal duties of easy rescue remain unanswered by this chapter.[70] I have not attempted to provide a statement of the ideal form such a legal duty should take. However, I hope to have shown that common law materials—and, indeed, the position in civilian jurisdictions—provide more support for such a duty than is usually recognised, and to have dispelled some important moral objections in the recent literature.

[70] For instance, whether a duty to compensate should be owed by the beneficiary to the duty-bearer, when the duty-bearer suffers harm in the course of the rescue. If we think compensation ought to be paid when a person permissibly damages another's property in order to protect their life, even if the property-owner had a duty to allow the use of the property, then it is plausible that compensation is sometimes due. In both cases, a person (the damaged property-owner, the rescuer) bears a cost that they are required to bear solely for the benefit of another. The current law sometimes allows a person to deduct their expenses in complying with an imposed duty to assist. One example is attachment orders against employers for the payment of an employee's judgment debts under CPR r 89.7: under the Attachment of Earnings (Employer's Deduction) Order 1991, SI 1991/356, an employer is entitled to deduct £1 in administration costs for each deduction made from the employee's salary in response to the order.

10
Public Authorities

Public authorities have P-duties which individuals do not have, and their having such duties is one major reason for their existence. All sorts of things need to be done when people live together which it would be inappropriate legally to require individuals to do on their own. In some cases, this is because the burden of some P-duty cannot justly be imposed on an individual without more, given the limited general duties of assistance each person has to others. In other cases, it is because living together generates harms for which no individual is justly individually responsible. In so far as each of us engages in permissible (market) transactions, for instance, whose collective effect is the foreseeable risk of others being in dire need, we are required by a collective version of the *Innocent Risk Principle* to coordinate our conduct, by establishing relevant institutions to counteract the harmful effect of those permissible transactions.[1] In yet other cases, it is because we are required to have institutions with certain features that other P-duties necessarily arise. For instance, in so far as the state employs coercion to enforce its directives, or those directives otherwise have substantial impact on people's lives, it has a P-duty, for instance, to take steps to ensure that people are able to understand and respond to those directives.

The breach of the legal P-duties that crystallise these (and other) underlying justifications does not necessarily give rise, however, to tort liability. This chapter considers when public authorities owe tort P-duties, and whether the rules determining when public authorities owe such P-duties ought to be identical to those that apply to private individuals.

The first section of this chapter is focussed on the current law. It explains that the law can be understood as accepting what I call the '*Positive Equality Principle*', according to which a public authority ought to be under a P-duty if it triggers a special fact that would apply to a private individual.[2] It further explains, however, that the law's endorsement of the '*Negative Equality Principle*'—according to which a public authority is *only* under a P-duty when a special fact that applies to a private individual—is piecemeal, albeit importantly recognised in the tort of negligence. The tort of misfeasance in public office renders public law P-duties actionable in

[1] See E Weinrib, *Reciprocal Freedom* (OUP, 2022) ch 5.

[2] See P Cane, 'Damages in Public Law' (1999) 9 Otago Law Review 489, 490 (distinguishing two 'limbs' of the 'equality principle'; in Cane's formulation the principle applies to duties, powers, immunities, and liabilities, though he rightly notes that it is rarely endorsed in such a broad form).

Omissions in Tort Law. Sandy Steel, Oxford University Press. © Sandy Steel 2024.
DOI: 10.1093/9780191898822.003.0010

tort, some civilly actionable statutory P-duties are based on public status, and there is sometimes liability in public nuisance for the breach of a public P-duty.

The second section assesses the equality principle, focussing on the negative aspect, which prevents more expansive tort P-duties on public authorities compared to private individuals. It begins by responding to a wide range of arguments that have been offered, or might be offered, for the negative principle. In most cases, it rejects these arguments. The fundamental problem with most such arguments is that they entail unsustainable conclusions about the duties of public authorities *in general*—that is, beyond tort law. In other cases, the section accepts the force of the argument, but denies that it entails rigorous adherence to the *Negative Equality Principle*.

The third section aims briefly to outline a positive case for compensation for breach of certain P-duties beyond the equality principle. It argues that some P-duties on the part of public authorities should be considered to correlate with primary rights in such a way as to justify rights to compensation for their breach.

Finally, the chapter concludes with some more concrete reflections on how the state P-duties which should give rise to liability should be determined.

1. The Equality Principle

The equality principle has two limbs: (i) a negative, necessity, limb, which holds that a special fact that would generate a P-duty for a private individual is generally necessary for a P-duty to arise, and (ii) a positive, sufficiency, limb, which holds that such a special fact is generally sufficient for a P-duty to arise.

Consider the negative limb. This is supported, for example, by the Supreme Court decisions in *Michael v Chief Constable of South Wales Police* and *N v Poole Borough Council*.[3] In both decisions, the Supreme Court rejected the existence of a P-duty of care on the part of the police and social services, respectively, on the basis that there was no assumption of responsibility by their representatives to the victims, nor any other special fact applicable to private individuals.[4] In *Poole*, Lord Reed clearly implied the need for a special fact in relation to public authorities:[5]

> Like private individuals, public bodies [do] not generally owe a duty of care to confer benefits on individuals, for example by protecting them from harm.

[3] *Michael v Chief Constable of South Wales Police* [2015] UKSC 2, [2015] AC 1732; *N v Poole Borough Council* [2019] UKSC 25, [2020] AC 780. See also *Gorringe v Calderdale MBC* [2004] UKHL 15, [2004] 1 WLR 1057 [17], [38] (Lord Hoffmann).

[4] See *Michael* (n 3) [101]; *Poole* (n 3) [65].

[5] *Poole* (n 3) [28] (Lord Reed).

Further, in *Robinson*, his Lordship observed that: 'In the absence of such circumstances [*ie special facts*], however, public authorities generally owe no duty of care towards individuals to confer a benefit upon them by protecting.'[6] The reference to 'generally', rather than 'universally', may be a reflection of the possibility of a statutorily created tort P-duty of care that is not triggered by a special fact, for instance a highway authority's actionable P-duty to maintain the highway.[7]

Consider now the positive limb. This is the proposition that, if a special fact is shown, nothing *further* needs to be shown for a P-duty to arise. It is supported by general statements such as this: 'if conduct would be tortious if committed by a private person or body, it is generally equally tortious if committed by a public authority'.[8] It is also supported by the focus in decisions upon whether a special fact exists; the assumption is that such a fact would be sufficient to trigger a duty.[9] It is true that there may, exceptionally, be a statutory exclusion of a tort duty; but absent clear deprivation of a common law right that would otherwise apply, a duty will very likely arise.

It is also true that, in claims against public authorities, there will sometimes be an issue of whether the claim is 'justiciable'.[10] This is not necessarily an additional hurdle that pertains to the existence of a P-duty, however; the issue of justiciability can logically relate to any issue in proceedings that is not apt for adjudication, not only 'duty' issues.[11]

Finally, it is also true that there is an association between immunity rules and public functions: judicial immunity and combat immunity are examples.[12] Strictly, these do not constitute exceptions to the *Positive Equality Principle* in so far as that principle relates to primary legal *duties*: the duties may be the same, even if one type of defendant is immunised from *liability*. More fundamentally, however, the consideration that is typically invoked to justify immunity rules is also invoked against private individuals—that the enforcement of one duty will lead to misperformance of another more important duty, or worsen compliance with the conduct standard imposed by the duty overall.[13]

We have already considered at several points how special facts apply to public authorities, without necessarily drawing specific attention to the public nature of

[6] *Robinson v Chief Constable of West Yorkshire Police* [2018] UKSC 4, [2018] AC 736 [35].

[7] Highways Act 1980, s 41.

[8] *Robinson* (n 6) [33].

[9] For instance, it is clear that, if there *had* been an assumption of responsibility in *Michael*, a duty would have been owed.

[10] See *Smith v Ministry of Defence* [2013] UKSC 41, [2014] AC 52 [110]–[117] (albeit treating this as negativing a duty of care); *Connor v Surrey County Council* [2010] EWCA Civ 286, [2011] QB 429.

[11] It is more likely, however, that the determination of breach will be 'unmuddied' by policy: see *Connor* (n 10) [104]–[109].

[12] See *Mulcahy v Ministry of Defence* [1996] QB 732 (combat immunity).

[13] For instance, in relation to the now rejected immunity of barristers, one argument was that liability would conflict with the advocate's duty to the court: *Rondel v Worsley* [1969] 1 AC 191, 251 (Lord Morris).

the defendant.[14] However, it may be questioned whether it is possible in every case to set aside the public nature of the defendant in determining whether a special fact is made out.[15] In some cases, the fact that a defendant is known to be under a legal duty not owed by a private person seems to be relevant to whether their conduct creates a risk of harm or prevents others from intervening. It is not the *mere fact* that the defendant is under a duty which is important here—relying upon the mere existence of a statutory duty imposed specially upon a public authority to generate a private law P-duty would offend the *Negative Equality Principle*—but the fact that legal subjects may *know* that authorities have legal duties to intervene, which may discourage them from taking harm-preventative steps.

This is the structure of arguments for public authority liability for failure to act based on 'general reliance': in virtue of the fact that authorities are legally bound to intervene to protect the public from harm in certain situations, this may engender a general reliance that they will do so.[16] In essence, this involves a version of the P1 and P2 principles of assumption of responsibility discussed in Chapter 4: when legislation imposes a P-duty on an authority, this amounts to a commitment by the state, through the authority, to take an action, and it is foreseeable that others will rely upon that commitment. Legislation that constitutes, empowers, and renders duty-bound public authorities is a kind of assumption of responsibility by the state. Now, the content of that assumption of responsibility should be determined by the objective meaning of the legislation. If, properly construed, it does not amount to the creation of a duty to the individual, then the individual does not gain a right directly from the statute. But even if such a statutory duty is not *owed to* the specific individual, but to the public as a whole, it may be reasonable for the individual to rely upon the performance of the duty. At least presumptively, surely it cannot be unreasonable for members of the public to rely upon the performance of duties owed to the public. In so far as a particular person can demonstrate that

[14] See the previous chapters on special facts.

[15] A related sceptical observation is that the equality principle cannot always be coherently applied because it is artificial to imagine a counterpart private person doing the same activity as a public authority (see J Morgan, 'A Riddle Wrapped in An Enigma: Assumption of Responsibility, Again' [2022] 81 Cambridge Law Journal 449, 451). However, the equality principle only asserts that a public authority's duties are to be determined by the same *reasons* or *grounds* as that of a private individual, not that there must be a realistic counterpart private activity.

[16] See *Sutherland Shire Council v Heyman* [1985] HCA 41 [28]–[29]; Mason J rejected the need for a specific alteration in the plaintiff's conduct; this goes beyond the principle in P1–P2, whose rationale is prevention of detrimental reliance. The idea that a 'general community expectation' that a statutory power will be exercised can generate a private law duty to exercise the power is rejected by Brennan CJ in *Pyrenees Shire Council v Day* [1998] HCA 98 [19]; general reliance is also rejected by Gummow J and Kirby J; cf McHugh J [103]–[110]. General expectations which are not based objectively in the construction of the relevant legislation or the authority's conduct are rightly not the source of P-duties: the mere fact that many people expect that a person will do something cannot itself *require* them to do it. For discussion of 'general reliance' in English law, see *Stovin v Wise* [1996] AC 923, 954; *Capital & Counties Plc v Hampshire County Council* [1997] QB 1004, 1027; *Watson v British Boxing Board of Control* [2001] QB 1134, 1151; *Thames Trains v Health and Safety Executive* [2003] EWCA Civ 720 [25], [48]; *A v Secretary of State for the Home Department* [2004] EWHC 1585 [36].

they reasonably believed that a public duty would be performed and changed their conduct to their detriment, thereby suffering harm to their general right-protected interests, in principle it is not clear why they ought not to succeed. If A promises C that A will protect B from physical harm, and A can reasonably foresee that this will cause C not to take harm-preventive measures, A has a duty to B, by virtue of *Interference*. When legislation imposes a statutory P-duty owed to everyone, it is as if the state promised everyone that the authority would intervene, and they may foreseeably change their position in relation to their right-protected interests on the basis of this. The problem with such arguments is not one of principle, but proof: demonstrating that one relied upon the authority's performance of the duty, and that one would have taken harm-preventative steps that would have avoided the harm suffered, is likely to be particularly difficult.[17]

(i) Departures from Equality

There are at least four departures from the *Negative Equality Principle* in relation to P-duties: (a) the tort of misfeasance in public office renders public law P-duties actionable in tort; (b) statutory P-duties based on public status, which are actionable in the tort of breach of statutory duty; (c) liability in public nuisance for the breach of a public P-duty; and (d) P-duties of public duty-bearers in private nuisance. Each is briefly explained in turn.

(a) Misfeasance in Public Office

The tort of misfeasance in public office operates as an exception to the equality principle: public defendants are treated specially by virtue of the tort's exclusive application to defendants subject to public law duties.

The tort is made out when a person with a public law duty (1) breaches that duty; (2) (i) intending to cause harm to another, or (ii) knowing that harm will result to another, or (iii) knowing that there is a risk of harm to another and being indifferent to this risk; (3) in the knowledge that, or reckless as to whether, their conduct is unlawful; and (4) the unlawful conduct causes harm to the other.[18]

Crucially, the relevant kind of 'unlawful' conduct includes conduct that is *not* a breach of a private law duty owed to the claimant.[19] The breach of a public law duty would be sufficient. Furthermore, it is clear that the tort applies to N-duties *and*

[17] The problem *is* one of principle in so far as the individual is not required to show a change of position. In such a case, the idea that the authority must act to prevent its making the situation worse cannot be the rationale of the liability.

[18] See *Three Rivers District Council v Governor and Company of the Bank of England (No 3)* [2001] UKHL 16, [2003] 2 AC 1.

[19] ibid 229.

P-duties: it covers purely omissive conduct by a public official.[20] In *Ashby v White*, to which the origins of the tort of misfeasance in public office are traced, the failure to allow a person to vote was itself a pure omission.[21] Other examples of pure omissions that have fallen within the tort include the failure to maintain a sea wall,[22] the failure to investigate a rape by another police officer,[23] and the failure of police officers to cooperate with an external investigation.[24]

In principle, then, the tort of misfeasance in public office provides rights to compensation for egregious pure omissions by public officials. For instance, if a police officer failed to intervene to protect a person being violently assaulted because the officer considered people of that person's ethnicity to be unworthy of protection, or because the officer decided to continue playing Pokémon Go instead of intervening, the victim would be entitled to compensation under the tort.[25] Failures to intervene, in the absence of subjective awareness of a risk of harm, will not suffice, however.

(b) Breach of Statutory Duty

The tort of breach of statutory duty applies, of course, to both public and private persons, depending on which duty-bearers are identified by the legislation. In this sense, it is not an exception to the equality principle: private and public defendants can come to owe P-duties by virtue of legislation. However, some statutes identify public authorities as exclusive duty-bearers, and when these duties are civilly actionable in the tort, the public authority has a tort duty which has no private counterpart. To this extent, the tort can operate as an exception to parity: the special fact triggering the duty may be one whose conditions of application single out only public authorities. As we have seen, the central example of this is liability for breach of a person's human rights under the Human Rights Act (HRA) 1998.[26]

(c) Public Nuisance

The breach of a public P-duty which causes special damage may be actionable by a private individual in the tort of public nuisance. A person who has ferry rights, for example—rights to exclusive operation of a ferry for the benefit of the public—is under a duty to keep the ferry in operation at reasonable times and to accept the custom of those wishing to travel.[27] The failure to conform to this duty, when it

[20] ibid 230: 'If there is a legal duty to act and the decision not to act amounts to an unlawful breach of that legal duty, the omission can amount to misfeasance for the purpose of the tort' (Lord Hobhouse).

[21] *Ashby v White* (1703) 2 Ld Raymond 928, 92 ER 126.

[22] *Henly v Mayor of Lyme* (1828) 5 Bing 91, 130 ER 995.

[23] *Garrett v Attorney General* [1997] 2 NZLR 332.

[24] *Odhavji Estate v Woodhouse* [2003] 3 SCR 263.

[25] 'Pokémon Go: Police fired for chasing Snorlax instead of robbers' (BBC, 11 January 2022) <https://www.bbc.co.uk/news/technology-59953330> accessed 12 January 2024.

[26] Chapter 7.

[27] *Gravesham Borough Council v British Railways Board* [1978] Ch 379.

causes special damage to a person wishing to use the ferry, is actionable in public nuisance. The ferry operator is not a public authority, but they hold a public duty.[28]

(d) Private Nuisance P-Duties

The preceding exceptions involve an enlargement of civilly actionable P-duties compared to those owed by ordinary private individuals. The House of Lords decision in *Marcic v Thames Water Utilities Ltd* is a possible example of a diminishment of the P-duties of a person acting subject to public duties.[29] The claimant's property was repeatedly flooded by sewage which overflowed from sewers operated by the defendant, Thames Water, a sewerage undertaker. Section 18 of the Water Industry Act 1991 provided an enforcement procedure for breach of a sewerage undertaker's duty under section 94(1) of the Act to provide an adequate system of public sewers, but preserved under section 18(8) any cause of action for an act or omission that amounted to a breach of a legal duty independently of its being a breach of a statutory requirement. Mr Marcic sued Thames Water in private nuisance, arguing that it had a P-duty at common law as an occupier of land to take reasonable steps to prevent the sewage overflow by constructing new sewers. This argument was accepted by the Court of Appeal on the basis of the positive equality rule:[30]

> The sewers form part of a system which Thames are operating as a commercial venture in order to make profits for their shareholders. Thames are in no more favourable position than a landowner on whose property a hazard accumulates by the act of a trespasser or of nature.

The House of Lords allowed the defendant's appeal. Lord Nicholls, with whom Lord Steyn and Lord Hope agreed, reasoned that the attempt to enforce a duty to create new sewers through private nuisance 'ignores the statutory limitations on the enforcement of sewerage undertakers' drainage obligations'.[31] It is not entirely clear, however, how this meets the point that section 18(8) of the Act preserved common law rights that existed independently of the statute: what is needed is an argument that there is no common law right in private nuisance to the construction of a new sewer by an occupier. Lord Hoffmann, whose speech also had the support of a majority, reasoned explicitly that no private law P-duty was owed in the circumstances because an occupier's P-duties are only appropriate 'between neighbouring land owners simply in their capacity as individual land owners'.[32] The essential point here seems to be that, in the latter context the court is 'performing

[28] See further Chapter 7 on statutory duties of public undertakers.
[29] [2003] UKHL 66, [2004] 2 AC 42.
[30] [2002] EWCA Civ 64, [2002] QB 929, 994 [83].
[31] *Marcic* (n 29) [35].
[32] ibid [33].

its usual function of deciding what is reasonable as between the two parties to the action', whereas with the positive duties of defendants like Thames Water, determining the content of the duty is far more complex and has been entrusted to the persons empowered by the legislation to determine.[33]

In substance, this could operate as a diminishment of the P-duties of occupiers subject to similar statutory schemes as the defendant in *Marcic* relative to the P-duties of 'ordinary' occupiers. As Chapter 6 explained, an occupier may come under a P-duty in respect of risks not of their own creation, but when the prevention of these risks primarily benefits others, the steps required are minimally costly. Suppose that one analogises the undertaker in *Marcic* to a purely private occupier whose land is subject to several easements, which permit neighbouring landowners to run pipes across the occupier's land. In the event that those pipes overflowed from the occupier's land onto neighbouring land, it is doubtful that the occupier would have a *stringent* P-duty to take mitigatory measures: the cost of remedying the problem would have to be shared amongst the persons who benefit. It might then be said that construction of a new sewer system is likely to exceed the level of cost an 'ordinary' occupier could reasonably be expected to bear for others. This analysis is contestable, however: as the Court of Appeal in *Marcic* observed, the undertaker operated as a commercial venture which does obtain benefits from the operation of the system; to the extent that a private occupier obtains a benefit from the operation of the system that leads to harm to neighbouring land, it is at least arguable that their ordinary P-duty as an occupier would extend to require significant expenditure to be made to prevent that harm.

2. Justifying the *Negative Equality Principle*

This section considers a wide range of arguments for the *Negative Equality Principle*.[34] The basic problem with many of these arguments is that they are too general in character: if true, they would imply implausible conclusions about the morally justified legal P-duties of public bodies in general. If the principle is defensible, it must be because the P-duties of public bodies which go beyond the P-duties of private individuals ought not to be enforceable *in tort law*. The problem with the standard arguments is that they entail that state entities have no enforceable

[33] ibid [62]. It has been made clear that the decision in *Marcic* does not preclude claims in private nuisance for the breach of the undertaker's common law N-duties, even though compliance with such decisions may also have a significant impact on the undertakers' budgets: *The Manchester Ship Canal Company Ltd v United Utilities Water Ltd* [2024] UKSC 22, [135]–[136].

[34] Parts of this section draw on S Tofaris and S Steel, 'Negligence Liability for Omissions and the Police' (2016) 75 Cambridge Law Journal 128. For an incisive critique of the equality principle as a 'ceiling' on the P-duties of public authorities, see E Chamberlain, 'Diceyan Equality and Public Authority Liability: Floor or Ceiling?' in A Robertson and J Nevers (eds), *Private Law and the State* (Bloomsbury 2024).

P-duties *at all*—in tort law or any area of law—beyond those which private individuals would have.

(i) Freedom

In *Stovin v Wise*, Lord Hoffmann said, 'it is less of an invasion of an individual's freedom for the law to require him to consider the safety of others in his actions than to impose upon him a duty to rescue or protect'.[35] As a justification for the absence of any P-duty of care being owed by public authorities beyond those owed by private individuals, this statement is problematic. A private individual has a life of their own. This fact alone probably generates an entitlement not to have very extensive P-duties to serve the interests of others.[36] In short, human persons have a moral status, in virtue of having lives of their own, which entitles them to a measure of normative protection from the needs of others. By contrast, the value of the state's freedom is purely instrumental: the state's freedom is valuable only in so far as it contributes to the fulfilment of its proper functions. The freedom argument, in so far as it is based upon a person's moral status as a being with their own life, simply does not have application to states or public authorities as such.

(ii) Crowding out Virtue

It has been argued that the moral significance of virtuous acts would be diminished if individuals are not legally free not to undertake those acts, but are instead duty-bound to do so.[37] Forced virtue is no virtue at all. It seems true that the value which triggers some moral reasons or duties can only be respected or aptly responded to by actions which are voluntary in a thick sense. Suppose that that is what is meant by 'matters of virtue'. Possibly, generosity is an example.[38] There are clear difficulties in applying this kind of argument to the P-duties of states, however. At the very least, it requires substantive argument to show that the careful provision of certain public services is a matter of 'virtue' in the sense just described. It is doubtful that this is typically the case: the value which principally justifies, for instance, the duties of police officers to intervene to protect subjects from risks to their lives, is the value of the lives of those individuals—which can be conformed to independently of any particular motivation on the part of the officer. Finally, if *the state* had special, enforceable, P-duties in tort, this need not entail parallel duties on

[35] *Stovin v Wise* [1996] AC 923, 943H (Lord Hoffmann).
[36] See Chapter 2.
[37] N J McBride and R M Bagshaw, *Tort Law* (5th edn, Harlow 2015) 217.
[38] See again Chapter 2.

private individuals, so the 'crowding out' concern need not be realised in the private sphere where it seems to matter most.

(iii) Erosion of Individual Responsibility

Another argument for limited P-duties is that we are primarily responsible for what we do and not for what others do; if we are held legally responsible for failing to prevent the actions of others, then we blur and potentially erode this moral distinction. The premise of this argument is correct: intuitively, we are primarily responsible for what we do rather than what others do; our responsibility for our own actions is a special one. It would indeed erode our sense of special responsibility and authorship over our own lives if there were unlimited moral responsibility for outcomes with which we are prima facie unconnected. But it is difficult to see how this supports the *Negative Equality Principle.* If the state had special P-duties not shared by private individuals, this hardly implies that the distinction between N-duties and P-duties will be left without any moral significance. Limited special P-duties on the part of the state do not involve wholesale rejection of this distinction. More fundamentally, this concern also seems particularly activated by the fact that a person has a life of their own, which would be undermined by very significant P-duties to others.

(iv) Why Pick on Me?

In *Stovin v Wise*, Lord Hoffmann also referred to the 'why pick on me?' argument for limited P-duties.[39] This argument states that it is unfair to single out one person for failing to take positive steps to protect someone when there are other people who similarly failed to do so.

The shortcomings of this argument in this context have often been pointed out. The essential problem is that there is special reason to single out a public authority in relation to some injury where the public authority's reason for being is to do that task. Serving the needs of others, *and only* others, is not the reason for being of an individual.

It might be responded that it is unfair to impose P-duties upon the state that are not owed by private individuals because 'it would be effectively punishing the state for trying to do good, and employees of the state for choosing a life of public service over one of self-interest'.[40] This objection has the striking conclusion, if valid,

[39] *Stovin* (n 35) at 944. Lord Hoffmann recognised the deficiency of the argument in relation to public authorities: 946.

[40] N J McBride and R M Bagshaw, *Tort Law* (6th edn, Pearson 2018) 201.

that there is always an unfairness in the state being subject to duties to which private individuals are not subject. If part of the moral justification of the state is the discharge of duties in respect of moral goals which no individual can reasonably be required individually to perform, but to which each individual can reasonably be required to contribute, then this objection fails. By choosing to occupy a position in an institution whose moral function is to perform duties which are not properly owed by any particular individual simply qua individual, one cannot reasonably object to being required to perform those duties. It is true that there may be unfairness, depending upon the nature of the breach, in requiring that individual to bear the total burden of the compensatory duty, but the solution to this is to reform the rules on vicarious liability, not to deny the existence of the duty. In practice, public employees are indemnified for negligent breaches of duty.[41]

(v) The *Rule of Law*

It has been argued, in light of the fact that private individuals enjoy the benefit of only being subject to P-duties when certain special facts apply, that the *Rule of Law* demands that public authorities must also be entitled to the benefit of this principle.[42] This typically relies on a conception of the *Rule of Law* which requires that 'every man, whatever be his rank or condition, is subject to the ordinary law of the realm and amenable to the jurisdiction of the ordinary tribunals'.[43]

It is, however, doubtful that the *Rule of Law* mandates the *Negative Equality Principle*. The *Rule of Law* does not prohibit differential treatment of the state and private individuals if there are normatively important differences between private individuals and the state which justify this. Such differences obtain in virtue of the special functions entrusted to public authorities, and the fact that public authorities are not individuals with a special moral status.

[41] Note the statutory removal of personal liability of certain public officials: see Local Government Act 1976, s 39; National Health Service Act 1977, s 125, modifying Public Health Act 1875, s 265. In relation to the NHS, see the NHS indemnity policy, <https://resolution.nhs.uk/wp-content/uploads/2018/10/NHS-Indemnity.pdf> accessed 17 July 2024. See also the position in German law, under Article 34 *Grundgesetz*: 'If any person, in the exercise of a public office entrusted to him, violates his official duty to a third party, liability shall rest principally with the state or public body that employs him. In the event of intentional wrongdoing or gross negligence, the right of recourse against the individual officer shall be preserved. The ordinary courts shall not be closed to claims for compensation or indemnity.'

[42] See B Feldhusen, 'Unique Public Duties of Care: Judicial Activism in the Supreme Court of Canada' (2016) 53 Alberta Law Review 955, 965: 'Unique public duties violate this idea of equality [before the law].'

[43] A V Dicey, *Lectures Introductory to the Study of the Constitution* (London 1885), 177–78. Dicey himself did not object to public officials being subject to special duties *going beyond* those of ordinary individuals, so references to the 'Diceyan' view here are better avoided.

(vi) Cost

There is a concern that extending public authority liability beyond N-duties will expose authorities to costs that are exorbitant, with the result that the authority will be hindered in the proper performance of its functions, or funding will be re-allocated from other public goods, or tax burdens will increase.[44]

Obviously, this cost concern cannot be ignored. The effect of compensatory duties on public authorities is potentially to put strain on the provision of other public goods, and there may be duties owed to provide these goods too. Even if the state's P-duties to rectify wrongs have some priority over the state's P-duties to provide other forms of assistance, other things being equal, this priority must be limited in character.[45]

Three observations are in order, however. First, the cost concern does not require a strict division between N-duties and P-duties. Complying with compensatory duties arising from the breach of N-duties, or duties arising from the assumption of responsibility, may be very costly for a public body. The negligent delivery of a child during labour by NHS staff can trigger compensatory liability reaching into millions of pounds. The costs of meeting the vicarious liability bill for the N-wrongs, and wrongs arising from assumed duties, of public officials impacts upon the total burden that needs to be met through taxation. The view that meeting the costs of compensation for N-duties, and assumed duties, has a strict moral priority over meeting the costs of compensation for other P-duties is not plausible. Sometimes such a duty—for instance to protect a person from being killed—is of considerably greater moral importance than an assumed duty, say, to take care to treat a person's broken arm. Second, the force of this concern depends upon the nature of the P-duty in question. The nature of the P-duty partly determines the probability of its being breached. If there is a low probability of breach, as would be the case if the P-duty was only breached by failure to take a non-costly and evident precautionary measure, then the total cost to the taxpayer may not be significant. Third, as has often been observed, the existence of an actionable P-duty does not itself trigger a right to compensation; further hurdles of breach, damage, and causal attribution need to be proven.

[44] See, eg, D Squires and D Fairgrieve, *The Negligence Liability of Public Authorities* (2nd edn, OUP 2019) [1.22]–[1.28].

[45] For some powerful arguments against *any* priority, see T Douglas, 'Should Institutions Prioritize Rectification over Aid?' (2010) 60 The Philosophical Quarterly 698.

(vii) Institutional Competence

A related concern is that creating special public authority P-duties actionable by compensation claims raises inherently politically controversial issues of distributive justice, concerning the allocation of public resources, that cannot be adjudicated upon by courts.[46] In discussing the idea that public authorities may be held to owe a P-duty to all members of the public to protect them from an (especially) dangerous person released on parole by adequate supervision, Hannah Wilberg writes that this requires courts to determine whether the:

> defendant authority, on behalf of the state and the community, owes an obligation to use its resources for the benefit of all individuals who have the relevant need, either for protecting them or for compensating them if they have failed to protect them. That, arguably, represents a broad distributive judgment which would be better left to the political branches.[47]

For this to serve as an objection to the judicial recognition of legal compensation claims for breach of P-duties, there must be some distinctive set of distributive justice issues that does not apply to state N-duties. It is doubtful that there is a distinction in kind here. In setting out the standards to be adhered to in conforming to N-duties, the law also causes wide-ranging distributive effects. If reasonable care by a hospital doctor now requires certain tests to be done, this impacts hospital budgets and so affects the health service's ability to treat other patients. The very decision to apply the doctrine of vicarious liability to the actions of public officials for breach of N-duties—a decision with truly enormous distributive implications—itself entails that a significant part of public bodies' budgets is absorbed by the costs of compensatory duties.[48]

We can imagine decisions about which state P-duties ought to exist which raise enormously complex, and politically controversial, issues (when, if ever, should there be legal rights to welfare assistance?), but so too can we imagine parallel decisions about N-duties (when is going to war a breach of an N-duty not to cause undue harm to rights?). This is not, of course, to say that the courts ought to adjudicate upon these questions. It is only to say that the *Negative Equality Principle* does not provide a neat demarcating line between 'non-justiciable' and 'justiciable'.

Notably, this is borne out by Wilberg's own analysis, which is that this kind of institutional competence argument does *not* rule out public authorities being

[46] See generally Squires and Fairgrieve (n 44) ch 2. See also, in relation to *Marcic*, section 1(i)(d) above.

[47] H Wilberg, 'In Defence of the Omissions Rule in Public Authority Negligence Claims' (2011) 19 Torts Law Journal 159, 186. Wilberg is considering a proposal made in the minority concurrence by Elias CJ in *Couch v Attorney-General* [2008] 3 NZLR 725.

[48] For a similar point, see R Alexy, *A Theory of Constitutional Rights* (OUP 2011) 344.

judicially recognised to be under P-duties not owed by private individuals, in virtue of their statutory powers and the particular vulnerability of a class of persons who are at *special risk* of harm.[49]

(viii) The Role of Legislation

Public authorities are typically created by legislation. When this is the case, it might be argued that the only source of additional private rights and duties, beyond those that apply to ordinary persons at common law, is the legislation. If the legislation, properly construed, creates a right to compensation for breach of a legislatively created P-duty, then the tort of breach of statutory duty is made out. If the legislation does not, on proper construction, confer such a right, then, it might be argued, the common law may not step in to create either a primary tort P-duty or a secondary legal duty to compensate, absent a legislative intention that such duties exist.

Let us distinguish two ways in which legislation can change normative incidents such as powers, duties, rights, etc. First, it can do so directly by communicating the legislature's intention that some legal incident be changed (call these the 'legislated norms'). For instance, in *Marcic*, it arguably impliedly expressed a restriction of the common law right to claim compensation in relation to the breach of certain duties.[50] Second, it can do so indirectly by virtue of the interaction of the legislated norms with other, existing, legal norms. If a public authority is created by statute and vested with various powers, those legislated norms may be relevant to the duties that public officials have in tort. If the failure to exercise a legislated power is done knowing that the failure is wrongful in public law, with the intention to harm the claimant, then the misfeasance tort may be made out. So, an official's potential liabilities under the misfeasance tort have been indirectly altered by the legislation.

The tort of breach of statutory duty is concerned with the first way in which legislation may change the law: by communicating an intention that a civilly actionable P-duty arise. In theory, however, the absence of a claim for breach of statutory duty need not, as a normative matter, exclude the possibility of another legal norm assigning compensatory duties for the breach of the statutory norm. The common law *could have* coherently developed, for instance, the idea that when a statutory norm articulates a fundamental right enjoyed by legal subjects to the provision of some good, that the breach of the legislative norm triggers a right to compensation, unless the legislation excludes such a right. By analogy, the duty to perform an express trust arises by virtue of communicating an intention to incur such a duty. The duty to pay compensation for breach of trust is the result of a background norm

[49] See Wilberg (n 47) 171ff.
[50] See section 1(i)(d).

that is triggered by a breach, whose existence is not dependent on the settlor's intention.

(ix) No Worse Off

In *Stovin v Wise*, Lord Hoffmann remarked:

> It is one thing to provide a service at the public expense. It is another to require the public to pay compensation when a failure to provide the service has resulted in loss. Apart from cases of reliance . . . the same loss would have been suffered if the service had not been provided in the first place.[51]

One way of understanding this is as the claim that, if the authority has not made things worse, it is unfair to require compensation. In response, it can reasonably be objected that this does not account for the existence of positive rights to careful performance of a public service. *If* there are such P-rights, then compensation ought to be payable for non-performance. Compare: it is no answer to a claim for breach of contract that the contract-breaker did not make things worse than if he had not been there in the first place, the right to performance requires a surrogate performance by way of compensation.

(x) Fairness between Victims of Harm

Compare these two victims of harm:

> *V1.* V1 suffers severe harm because a police officer, P, culpably fails to intervene to protect V1.
>
> *V2.* V2 suffers as severe harm as V1, but because of an unpredictable earthquake.

If V1 is entitled to full compensation for P's breach of duty, and V2 is restricted to rights to social security payments which do not provide full compensation, this might be thought unfairly to distinguish between V1 and V2. Both are effectively being compensated out of public funds, yet V1 is entitled to full compensation, while V2 receives partial compensation.

This is not simply the objection that the legal system unfairly discriminates between victims of pure accident who are entitled to limited social assistance, and victims of wrongs who are entitled to full compensation. That objection would have

[51] *Stovin* (n 35) 952.

force if, in operating tort law, the state was effectively creating a scheme by which the state *itself* pays full compensation specifically for the victims of private wrongs, to the exclusion of persons who suffer equally serious harm non-wrongfully. But this is (of course) not the kind of public assistance provided by the tort system. The tort system provides a public mechanism for enforcing the rights one enjoys against others. In providing such a mechanism, the state generally facilitates the enforcement of *others'* compensatory duties. It does not *itself* provide full compensation to the victims of wrongs.

However, when it comes to providing compensation for wrongs committed by public authorities, the position is different. Here the state is effectively providing full compensation, via the doctrine of vicarious liability, for wrongs committed by its representatives; this 'amounts to public provision of compensation'.[52] It might, then, be argued that the victims of harmful wrongs by public authorities ought, as a matter of justice, to stand in line and be treated on a par with the victims of non-wrongful harms in the queue for public resources.[53]

Of course, there may be various important instrumental benefits in attaching full compensatory duties to cases of public authority wrongdoing. It may be that it provides a useful incentive for compliance with primary P-duties, particularly in comparison to a system which vests enforcement entirely in the hands of other public regulators. In addition, compensation in cases of wrongdoing by public authorities likely contributes to public trust in authorities, by virtue of the knowledge that such authorities can be held accountable for the non-performance of their duties in the relatively demanding mode of accountability represented by tort levels of compensation. These instrumental benefits do not, however, amount to a case for according priority, *as a matter of justice*, to providing full compensation to the victims of public authority wrongs over the victims of comparable non-wrongful harms.

Tentatively, it seems to me that this objection of unfairness still fails to register that the breach of state P-duties may amount to a serious wrong to an individual, and that the presumptive moral response to wrongdoing—subject to countervailing considerations—is to correct its effects. If it is accepted that the state has morally justified positive primary duties to protect people from harm in certain cases, and that those duties may correlate with moral rights on the part of individual legal subjects, then the default moral response is corrective compensation. The ordinary moral logic of corrective justice requires wrongdoers to take steps to undo the effects of their wrongs. A failure to recognise this at least as a starting point involves a failure to take seriously the values that grounded the original primary duty. In a sense, a failure to impose legal duties of compensation on states

[52] T Endicott, 'The Public Trust' in E J Criddle and others (eds), *Fiduciary Government* (CUP 2018) 316.

[53] This kind of objection perhaps underlies part of the majority's reasoning in *Michael* (n 3) [130].

that violate positive moral rights involves privileging the state vis-à-vis individuals: ordinary individuals are held to their secondary moral reparative duties of justice through the private law, but not so states that lack secondary legal duties to repair their wrongs. More pragmatically, once it has been decided—as English law has—to require public resources fully to compensate the victims of N-wrongs by public bodies, it then becomes difficult, as a matter of consistency, to draw a strict line between such victims and the victims of P-wrongs. As noted above, it cannot be right that compensation for N-wrongs is *always* a greater moral priority than compensation for P-wrongs.

(xi) Incentive Effects

In *Hill v Chief Constable of West Yorkshire*, Lord Keith raised the concern that the imposition of negligence liability on the police might have negative effects on the performance of the police's primary function of investigating and suppressing crime.[54] It may encourage a defensive approach to that function, inhibiting police officers' ability to take difficult operational decisions and act in the public interest.[55] While in principle relevant, the basic problem with such arguments is the lack of empirical evidence to test the claim.[56] In jurisdictions which recognise special P-duties on public bodies in the tort of negligence, there appears to be no evidence that policing has been negatively affected.[57] Furthermore, the likelihood of detrimental incentive effects is presumably greatly dependent on the nature of the P-duty in question. P-duties that set relatively non-demanding standards and which can only be breached with significant culpability seem particularly unlikely to have such effects.

(xii) Tort Law as an Inept Regulator

Suppose it is accepted that (i) public authorities sometimes ought to have special P-duties beyond the *Negative Equality Principle*, and (ii) these P-duties ought to give rise to rights to compensation. It still might be said that it is not *tort law's* job to recognise such rights and duties.

[54] [1989] AC 53, 69.

[55] For an extended discussion on which this part draws, see S Tofaris and S Steel, 'Negligence Liability for Omissions and the Police' [2016] 75 Cambridge Law Journal 128, 133–36.

[56] See ibid. On their 'in principle' relevance, see Chapter 2.

[57] See, eg, *Doe v Metropolitan Toronto (Municipality) Commissions of Police* (1998) 160 DLR (4th) 697 (Ontario Court of Justice); *Hill v Hamilton-Wentworth Regional Police Services Board* [2007] 3 SCC 41 (Supreme Court of Canada); *Carmichele v Minister of Safety and Security* 2001 (1) SA 489 and 2004 (3) SA 305 (Supreme Court of South Africa).

One argument here is conceptual. By its nature, it might be said, tort law is the law which sets out and constitutes the rights and duties that each of us has simply by virtue of being legal persons.[58] As noted in Chapter 2, this view of tort law has to contend, for instance, with the existence of tort rights that exist by assumption of responsibility (rather than mere existence), other rights that arise by special facts, and the misfeasance in public office tort. Even if it is said that these aspects of tort law are excrescences from the core essence of tort law, this does not answer the normative question of whether it is justifiable to have these special sub-departments of tort law.

In the United Kingdom, a related argument is that state P-duties that correlate with rights ought to be the exclusive province of claims for damages under the HRA 1998, rather than tort. In *Michael*, Lord Toulson could find no 'orthodox common law principles' in favour of 'gold-plating' a person's human rights protected by the Act with common law claims.[59] If the HRA 1998 should be regarded as an exhaustive determination of what rights a person has against public authorities by virtue of their humanity, then this point would have force. But it is not obvious why the Act should be regarded as the legal system's exhaustive response to that question. The Act sought to provide domestic recourse for breaches of the UK's duties under the European Convention of Human Rights (ECHR). It is not obvious why that aim is inconsistent with a parallel or more extensive common law regime. The reasons that support the human rights recognised by the ECHR also provide reason for cautious judicial development of legal rights recognising human rights.

Whether the legal system treats liability under the HRA 1998, or a parallel common law regime that imposes special P-duties on public authorities owed to individuals coupled with a liability to compensate for breach, as 'tort' substantively depends on whether these P-duties ought to be regulated by principles that are currently recognised to govern torts. These principles include rules about fault standards, causation, remoteness, the measure of compensation, and limitation. Other things being equal, these principles should apply if the facts which make these principles apt in the tort context also exist in the context of special state positive duties. I suspect that there is no general truth about whether this is the case: it depends. Some state P-duties might be strict duties. Some are P-duties to take reasonable care to protect others. To the extent that the remedial rules applicable to a duty depend upon its nature, then, just as in tort, different rules should apply depending upon the nature of the duty.[60] However, there are some uniform rules,

[58] This view seems to be presupposed in some Kantian writing on tort law: see P Cane, 'Tort Law and Public Functions' in J Oberdiek (ed), *Philosophical Foundations of Tort Law* (OUP 2014).

[59] *Michael* (n 3) [125].

[60] Compare the different remoteness rules that apply in deceit, negligence, and in tort claims that arise concurrently with a breach of contract. In each case, a different remoteness rule applies; the justification for this variation is the different kind of duty at stake. There is a danger of fixating upon one part of tort law and finding it radically different from human rights law, when other parts of tort law provide

for instance, as to the basic measure of compensation. If the rationale of compensation in general is that it gives a surrogate effect to the initial right, this rationale suggests that the aim of compensation everywhere and anywhere should be to put the right-holder in the position they would have been in had the right not been violated, subject to countervailing considerations.[61]

In relation to causation, it has been argued that a different approach is justified in relation to compensation for violations of human rights by the state compared to tort law.[62] The essence of the argument is that (a) the nature of the rights is different, and (b) the vindicatory goals of human rights law will be better served by different causal rules.

As to (a), some rights against the state, it is said, are rights against *risk*—rights, for instance, that protective measures be taken in relation to risks to one's life, regardless of whether this causes harm. This risk-based orientation of the primary rights is said to justify a different approach to causation. Against this, it may be replied that the fact that the primary right may be breached by risk imposition simply justifies the conclusion that causation of harm is irrelevant to whether the primary right has been violated. If the right can be violated by allowing certain risks to occur, then causation of harm is simply not part of the content of the primary right. It is a different question whether, when assessing compensation for the violation of a risk-based right, the violation caused harm or loss. It is not clear why the mere fact that the defendant is a public authority could justify a different approach to whether their conduct was a factual cause of a person's harm. Whether two events are causally connected does not depend upon the legal nature of the defendant.

As to (b), the idea is that the need to vindicate rights through a substantial monetary award justifies a relaxed proof of causation. For example, it might be contended that if there was a *substantial chance* that a protective measure mandated by a P-duty would have made a difference, this should be sufficient proof. This allows the right-holder's right—not to be exposed to risk in breach of a P-duty—to be vindicated by a payment of substantial compensation. This serves the distinctive goal of 'vindication'.

This is not persuasive. If a person's risk-based right has been violated, there may be a case for substantial monetary damages in the name of vindication. This does not, however, support an alteration in the proof rules on causation. It is simply a matter of accurately characterising the right in question and responding

closer analogies. The same problem often arises in comparisons between law and equity; equity's distinctiveness is defended by focussing only on some parts of the common law or some parts of equity.

[61] For an extended argument that the same damages rules should apply under the HRA 1998 as apply in trespass torts, see J Varuhas, *Damages and Human Rights* (Hart 2016).

[62] G Turton, 'Causation and Risk in Negligence and Human Rights Law' [2020] 79 Cambridge Law Journal 148.

appropriately to violation of that right: the right does not *depend* upon any causal connection between a breach and harm, so there is simply no issue of proof of causation.[63]

In summary, it seems likely that some issues as to the regulation of breach of special P-duties and compensation claims for these should be treated in parallel with tort principles. Whether we want to classify these as 'tort' claims is mainly a question of whether we think it is important that those developing the law consider analogies from tort cases and aim to develop the law consistently with the principles recognised to apply to torts.[64] One reason to be careful in applying the word 'tort' to these rules is that it could risk the illegitimate extension of state P-duties onto ordinary individuals. Given the central freedom argument against extensive P-duties on individuals, and the absence of that concern (as an intrinsic objection) in relation to public bodies, cases involving state P-duties deserve some kind of special labelling within the law. 'Public torts' would likely serve this function.

3. A Positive Case for Actionable P-Duties beyond the *Negative Equality Principle*

The idea that the state, and persons who perform its functions, ought to have precisely the same legal duties as private individuals is false. If the state is justified, it is at least partly in virtue of its ability to take on tasks which no individual can reasonably be morally required to do, absent a choice to fulfil a role, but which there is a moral need to be done when people live together. This is the fundamental reason why many of the arguments against special P-duties upon public authorities fail: part of the very point of such authorities is their being subject to duties that it would be wrong to impose on individuals without more.

Yet this does not positively establish that there should be any actionable P-duties, going beyond those owed by private individuals, in tort. Accepting that public authorities ought to have special, primary, legal duties does not itself entail that individuals should have rights to enforce those duties by claims for compensation, injunction etc, determined by similar principles to those that apply in ordinary tort claims.

Consider this principle, typically described as a principle of corrective justice:

[63] A more plausible argument is that the proof rules of factual causation may justifiably be altered in relation to public defendants because of the relative costs of false positives and false negatives. Is it true that the moral cost of a false positive against a public defendant is equally regrettable as a false negative against an individual? If not, then there is a case for departures from the balance of probabilities standard.

[64] D Nolan, 'Negligence and Human Rights Law: The Case for Separate Development' (2013) 76 Modern Law Review 286.

> *CJ.* If A breaches a (justified)[65] duty owed to B, and this causes non-remote loss to B, then A has a *pro tanto* duty to compensate B for this loss.

This principle is generally accepted, even if there is disagreement as to precisely *why* it is true.[66] If the principle is justifiable, then, on the face of it, it applies equally to the special P-duties of public authorities. Consequently, if the state, through a public authority, breaches a (justified) legal P-duty owed to B in this way, then this should trigger a legal duty to compensate B.

There is a complexity here. Normally *CJ* is understood as a principle about moral duties. If A breaches a moral duty to B not to cause harm to B, then A has a moral duty to B to compensate for the harm. If A breaches a morally justified legal duty to B, then this results in a moral duty to compensate B. Conceivably, there are situations in which (i) A breaches a morally justified legal duty to B, (ii) A has a moral duty to compensate B, but (iii) the law is justified in not creating a *legal* duty upon A to compensate B. I will return to this possibility later. For the moment, let us proceed on the assumption that if A breaches a justified legal duty to B, thereby incurring a moral duty to compensate B, then A ought normally to be under a legal duty to compensate B too.

If *CJ* is valid, an important question, then, is whether state P-duties are ever *owed to* individuals.[67] It might be contended that state P-duties are 'public' duties that are owed to no particular person or sub-set of persons. In rejecting a common law P-duty on the police in *Michael*, for instance, Lord Toulson drew attention to the 'public' nature of the police duty to keep the peace: 'it is a duty owed to the public at large for the prevention of violence and disorder'.[68] More generally, the absence of rights to compensation in judicial review proceedings has been justified on the basis that the relevant public law duties are not owed to individuals.[69] In the United States, the 'public duty' doctrine is similarly invoked to reject claims for pure omission against authorities.[70] There is very little clarity, however, in the law itself on what makes a duty 'owed to' someone in particular, rather than to everyone as a collective or no one. These claims are simply asserted, leaving unease about what their basis might be, even if they sometimes have a measure of intuitive force.

[65] A morally justified duty. It might be a legal duty that is morally justified, or a purely moral duty. In what follows, I will make the assumption that the legal state P-duty is morally justified.

[66] For invocations of this or similar principles, see P Cane, 'Damages in Public Law' (1999) 9 Otago Law Review 489; T Cornford, *Towards a Public Law of Tort* (Routledge 2016) 7, 15–16, Principle I. For an articulation and defence of the general moral idea, see J Gardner, *Torts and Other Wrongs* (OUP 2020) ch 2.

[67] This issue is sometimes overlooked when corrective justice is invoked to justify public authority liability: cf C Harlow, *State Liability* (OUP 2004) ch 1. Cornford addresses it: Cornford (n 66) 24–25, ch 8.

[68] *Michael* (n 3) [33].

[69] See Varuhas (n 61) 199ff.

[70] See generally S Beswick, 'Equality under Ordinary Law' (2024) Supreme Court Law Review (forthcoming).

In the philosophical literature, there are two well-known kinds of accounts of when a duty is 'owed to' another person, normally understood as theories of rights: the interest theories and the will theories. Interest theories focus upon the role that a person's interest has in grounding the duty. If a person's interest is sufficient to justify the duty, then the duty is owed to that person.[71] The will theory focuses upon who has, or should have, certain powers in relation to the duty, such as *ex ante* powers of waiver, or *ex post* powers to hold accountable or enforce the duties that arise from its breach. On the *ex ante* view, if a person can consent to what would otherwise amount to a breach of the duty, then the duty is owed to that person.[72]

If we understand the will theory as stating that a duty is owed to the persons who should have the *ex post* powers of holding to account and enforcement of the duty, or duties arising from its breach including the duty to compensate, then a duty's directionality cannot be invoked to determine when a person ought to have a right to compensation. On this view, determining whether a duty is *owed to* a person just is to determine whether they ought to have the power to demand compensation from the wrongdoer upon breach. This view seems objectionable precisely for this reason: intuitively, the fact that a duty was *owed to you* is a reason for your being entitled to compensation for its breach, rather than the other way around.

Consider now the idea that a duty is owed to a person if and only if the person has, or should have, the *ex ante* power to waive the duty. It seems obscure why there should be a necessary (rather than a contingent, perhaps even robustly contingent) association between the ability to waive a primary right and rights of compensation. Who, if anyone, should have the ability to waive a primary duty is a different normative issue from who, if anyone, should pay for the harmful consequences of a breach of duty. The former issue pertains to whether the existence of a requirement to do or not do an act should be within someone's volitional control, not (directly) the justice of one person being required to compensate for violating a requirement.

Consider this example in which no one has the power to waive the primary duty, yet the person in breach has a duty to compensate:

> *Child.* Argento fails to look in the mirror when reversing his car and runs over a young child. The child's arm is damaged and needs costly therapy.

In this case it does not appear that anyone's consent could make a difference to whether the harm-causing conduct is permitted. No one has the moral power to

[71] See J Raz, 'Legal Rights' (1984) 4 Oxford Journal of Legal Studies 1, 4; J Raz, *The Morality of Freedom* (Clarendon Press 1986) 166.

[72] See H L A Hart, 'Bentham on Legal Rights' in A W B Simpson (ed), *Oxford Essays in Jurisprudence, Second Series* (Clarendon Press 1973) 171. Hart's view is more nuanced: he thinks that the will-theory captures one important invocation of 'rights', namely that in private law; he allows that there are rights independently of waiver in other contexts.

waive the primary duty not negligently to damage the child. Yet it still seems very plausible that Argento has a duty to compensate for the harm caused.

An explanation of this is that the child's interest in not being harmed was sufficient to justify the duty breached. The child's interest in not being physically harmed grounded a duty not to drive without due care. In virtue of that fact, the duty may be said to be owed to the child. As John Gardner put it, on this account, a 'duty counts as owed to another in virtue of the reasons for its existence'.[73] Consequently, a general duty to maintain, for instance, a public health system, would not be a duty owed to any particular individual since the interest of that particular individual, important as they are, is not sufficient to justify the existence of the entire health system. Such a duty would be owed to the collective in that it is the joint interest of many people that justifies the duty.

If a primary duty's being *owed to* a person is necessary for that person to be owed a secondary duty for the primary duty's breach, it seems that the interest theory provides a better account of the relevant sense of 'owed to' for this purpose. It would be hasty to conclude that, therefore, the interest theory is the best account of when a primary duty is owed to another. Perhaps another account of the directionality of duties does better. However, it seems plausible that, on any view, if a person's interest is sufficient to justify, or at least a major part of the justification of a duty, this provides a ground for there being a duty to compensate that person upon breach of the primary duty.

If this is correct, then a duty to compensate an individual for breach of a state P-duty should arise when that person's interest justified the duty. If, however, that is the criterion, it would initially seem that *legal* duties are never owed to a particular person. Isn't the decision to elevate a moral duty into a legal duty always justified, in part, by the *collective* interest? Given that legal institutions will have a duty to recognise and, normally, enforce a legal duty, the decision to create a legal duty necessarily involves reliance upon collective interests. And yet it seems possible for legal duties to be owed to specific individuals.

One answer to this conundrum is that a legal duty can be owed to a person if the underlying moral duty to which the legal duty gives effect is justified by that person's interest. This allows for the possibility that the legal duty is itself justified by a collective interest. So, the duty not to trespass against a person's body plausibly enforces a moral duty whose justification is (inter alia) a person's interest in controlling the use of their body; the collective interest in there being an institutional means of determining the content of that duty and having it enforced justifies its being a legal duty.

[73] J Gardner, *From Personal Life to Private Law* (OUP 2018) 56. Rowan Cruft defends the idea that the interest theory provides a sufficient condition for a moral duty to be owed to a person: R Cruft, *Human Rights, Ownership, and the Individual* (OUP 2019) 19–20, ch 7.

If this is correct, then it is hard to resist the view that some state P-duties are owed to particular individuals *in the sense relevant to trigger corrective duties.* Consider a state P-duty to provide public education for a particular child. There is a collective interest in the existence of well-educated citizens, and this may be sufficient to justify the existence of such a duty. But the interest of a particular child in an education is also sufficient to justify the duty to provide public education to that child. The main reason is that the ability of the child in most societies to have a minimally decent life is contingent upon such provision. When one considers states that fail to provide education to a child, the central moral complaint resides in the individual loss or wasted individual opportunity. This is different from saying that the duty to set up a public education system is *owed to* a particular child; a particular child's interest is unlikely sufficient to justify the entire system. But the child's interest is sufficient to justify an operational duty within that system.

Suppose that states have a P-duty to take reasonable steps to protect the lives of their subjects. This duty requires the creation of various institutions which assign powers and duties to role-holders in relation to the preservation of life. Plausibly, it requires a criminal justice system, to deter violations of the right to life. Plausibly, it requires a public health system. These are moral duties to set up (contribute one's fair share in setting up) institutions with particular legal duties. There are multiple possible configurations of these systems and more than one reasonable kind. However, there are some non-negotiable features of a state that is committed to respect for the value of life and has reached a certain level of resources. Such a state will require specialist officials to take reasonable steps to preserve life when the costs are trivial, for example. Even if it is denied that everyone should have a legally enforceable duty of easy rescue—is rejected, the case for an *official* duty of easy rescue, as a bare minimum, is difficult to resist, at least so long as the 'cost' of rescue is not restricted to individual cases, but considers the costs of a rule requiring easy rescue. And when, to the knowledge of public authorities, a particular individual is at risk of losing their life, this is sufficient to justify a duty to take reasonable steps *owed to* that individual.

Suppose, finally, that there is a state P-duty to take reasonable steps to provide everyone with the means to live a minimally decent life. This duty plausibly requires the creation of a public education system and a welfare system to address situations in which a person is at severe risk of harm to their life prospects (through no fault of their own). Suppose that this moral duty is legally concretised by establishing legal duties to provide welfare assistance in particular circumstances. Suppose then that an individual is denied welfare assistance due to a negligent failure to apply the criteria correctly, with the result that the person attempts to kill himself, suffering severe injuries. Can we say that the moral correlate of the legal duty to provide welfare payments in precise circumstances is owed to a particular individual? Again, the answer is 'yes, in the sense relevant to compensation claims': this duty is grounded in major part in each individual's fundamental interest in having the means to live a minimally decent life. It may of course be that their individual interest does not justify *that specific duty*. There is no natural (institution-independent) right to the payment of that precise amount of money from the state, but this does not mean that the individual's interest is not a ground of the P-duty.[74] It may also be that the P-duty is only morally owed when the state has a certain level of resources but, again, this does nothing to show that the P-duty, when owed, is not grounded in the particular individual's interests.

When is a state P-duty *not* owed to a person in the sense relevant for that person to have a right to compensation? The answer suggested by the above is 'when avoidance of the kind of harm suffered by the person is not what justified the underlying moral duty to which the legal duty gives effect'. I might foreseeably be very upset if a local authority does not provide housing to my homeless brother, pursuant to its duty to provide housing to those satisfying certain criteria which he satisfies, but my interest in not being very upset is not part of the rationale of the duty.[75]

(i) An Alternative View

Tom Cornford develops a different view. He essentially gives the common law of negligence's answer to the question of when a state P-duty is owed to an individual: when the authority ought reasonably to have the particular person or persons in contemplation as affected by its acts or omissions covered by the state duty (or power).[76]

This answer is, however, incomplete. It raises the question: who *ought* the authority reasonably to have in contemplation? It could be *anyone* who is foreseeably affected by the breach of the duty. If so, this account is overinclusive: I may be foreseeably upset by the breach of a duty, yet I am not entitled to compensation for this upset if the avoidance of upset is not part of the rationale of the duty.

Cornford's account also seems underinclusive. He writes: 'the effects of the Bank of England's power to fix interest rates are too widespread and diffuse for it to be plausible to say that the Bank should have in contemplation the interests of particular individuals when exercising the power'.[77]

It is not clear, however, why one should believe that the widespread effects of a breach of duty (or exercise of a power) point against it (or the duties that arise in its exercise) being owed to persons. If I am responsible for monitoring the UK's water

[74] See Cruft (n 73) 149–50.

[75] It is worth also noting that the connection between a state P-duty being *owed to* a person and that person having a compensatory right is not *itself* obvious. In some circumstances, it might be unfair for me to have to put up with the breach of a duty that was owed to another person, or owed to everyone, for instance, if I suffer special damage from the breach.

[76] Cornford (n 66) 25.

[77] ibid 25.

supply, the effects of my actions or omissions will be very 'widespread', yet this seems if anything to point towards my duty being owed to each person, in the same way that the common law duty of care may be owed to anyone who is foreseeably affected in relation to their general right-protected interests.

(ii) The Gap between Moral Duties and Legal Duties

As noted earlier, *CJ* is normally understood as a principle about the moral duties of individual persons. Two 'gaps' between the moral and legal might then be a concern. First, can *CJ* in principle apply to justified institutional moral duties? It can. Either an institution is a collective agent or it is not. If it is an agent, then it can have duties. A public authority might well satisfy the various criteria that have been suggested for collective agency.[78] If it is not, then its agential members can individually have duties. If the members breach those duties in the course of acting on behalf of the authority, and the authority is justified by the collective interest, then there is a case for legal subjects being liable to contribute, through taxation, for the reparative duties which individual members incur.[79]

The second gap is the following. We are assuming that states have, through constituent public authorities, special, morally justified, legal P-duties. If *CJ* holds, then states also have moral corrective duties upon breach. But this does not entail that states should also have *legal* corrective duties which correspond to and crystallise those corrective duties.

It could be that primary legal state P-duties are justified, and yet secondary legal corrective duties for the breach of those duties are not. We have already encountered various reasons that *could* make this so: for instance, the substantially greater cost of complying in some cases with secondary legal duties compared to primary legal duties, the associated potential negative impact on the ability to pursue the authority's function, and the potential overdeterrent effects of enforceable secondary duties.[80]

In principle, if state authorities incur moral duties to compensate from breach of a duty that was justifiably legally enforceable, the authority ought to be liable to compensate, just as a private individual is liable to compensate for such a breach (even though a private individual would not have the same primary duty as the state). In a sense, this involves treating public authorities and private individuals equally in one relevant respect: it holds public authorities to their right-correlated duties just as private individuals are held to their right-correlated duties.

[78] For discussion, see H Lawford-Smith, *Not in Their Name: Are Citizens Culpable for their States' Actions?* (OUP 2019) chs 3 and 4.

[79] See further S Steel, 'Justifying State Remedial Duties' in S Besson (ed), *Theories of International Responsibility Law* (CUP 2022).

[80] See section 2.

This starting point is defeasible, but it is unlikely that courts are well-placed to determine the empirical facts needed to know whether it is defeated. If that is true, there are two options. First, courts might adhere rigorously to the *Negative Equality Principle* and never hold public authorities liable to compensate for breach of special positive rights, unless legislation confers a right to such compensation. Second, courts might seek, incrementally, to give effect to the general principle that public authority P-duties that correlate with rights ought to be enforceable by compensation claims. Given the speculative nature of many of the arguments for the *Negative Equality Principle*, it seems difficult to justify *never* holding authorities liable for breach of positive rights in the absence of legislative intention.

4. Public Authority Liability for Breach of P-Duties: English Law

The arguments for the *Negative Equality Principle* are unpersuasive. I have also argued that there is a positive normative case for departing from it.

It might reasonably be objected, however, that this remains a relatively abstract and formal proposal. The proposal is that state P-duties which are owed to individuals ought to give rise to compensation claims, but beyond the point that the duties are grounded in an individual's interest, this does not tell us which duties these are nor how judges ought to identify them.

A significantly more concrete account would require a worked-out political theory of what positive legal rights persons ought to enjoy against the state, and what roles different institutions ought to play in the development of those rights. Unfortunately, such an account cannot be articulated in the confines of this chapter. At the risk of superficiality, such an account is likely to identify a number of basic interests which states must take positive steps to protect simply in virtue of the moral status of legal subjects. Any fully justified state will, for instance, recognise some legal P-duties grounded in persons' fundamental interest in life. Some of these duties will be matters of political controversy, raising complex distributive questions best resolved by legislatures, for instance, the appropriate general structure of the health care or welfare system. Others will be far less disputable matters, such as a duty on the part of certain public officers to take reasonable steps to protect life which they know to be endangered, when there is no sufficiently important competing demand on their role. Any fully justified state will need to recognise and enforce P-duties not to show sheer indifference to an individual's interest in life on the part of public officials.[81]

On the picture developed in the previous section, the P-duties imposed upon the state by the HRA 1998, and interpreted by the courts, are plausibly understood

[81] On different possible justifications of enforceable human rights, see N J McBride, '*Michael* and The Future of Tort Law' (2016) 32 Journal of Professional Negligence 14.

as duties whose primary rationale is to protect persons from harm to their fundamental interests. To the extent that these duties are grounded in, or aimed at protecting individual interests, it is justifiable, on the argument above, that they give rise to compensation claims. Obviously, it is not my claim that incorporated articles of the ECHR represent a morally ideal specification of the rights that persons ought to enjoy against states. It is that, given a central moral point of states—to protect urgent interests when individuals cannot reasonably be required to provide the protection—there ought to be a system of state P-duties of some kind, and in so far as these P-duties are justified by a concern to protect individual interests, they ground claims to compensation for their breach. Whether the content of these P-duties should be determined, primarily by judges (as it is under the HRA), or primarily by legislatures, is a further question.[82]

Beyond damages claims under the HRA 1998, English law recognises two further categories of civilly actionable state P-duties:

(i) The misfeasance in public office tort.
(ii) Breach of statutory duty, including P-duties on highway authorities and public undertakers, such as electricity and gas providers.

The tort of misfeasance in public office is notoriously difficult to rationalise.[83] On the one hand, it is said to generate liability for breach of a public law duty even when the duty does not correlate with a right, and rights are typically considered necessary to justify compensation claims.[84] On the other, it only does so when a

[82] My own view is that there is legitimate room for some judicial development of state P-duties in relation to fundamental rights, when the correlative duties concern a truly minimum core of respect for the value of human dignity. For a development of this kind of view, see E Weinrib, *Reciprocal Freedom* (OUP 2022) ch 6.

[83] See M Aronson, 'Misfeasance in Public Office' (Appendix B) in Law Commission, *Misconduct in Public Office: Issues Paper 1—The Current Law* (20 Jan 2016), 2, 19 <https://lawcom.gov.uk/project/misconduct-in-public-office/> accessed 12 January 2024: an 'oddity'.

[84] See R Stevens, *Torts and Rights* (OUP 2007) 242–43. For an argument that the tort can be understood as giving effect to a Hohfeldian claim-right, see E Chamberlain, 'The Need for a "Standing" Rule in Misfeasance in a Public Office' (2007) 7 Oxford University Comparative Law Journal 215. This is criticised by D Nolan, 'A Public Law Tort: Understanding Misfeasance in Public Office' in Barker and others (eds), *Private Law and Power* (Hart 2017) as involving a 'fuzzy' concept of rights. It is clear that it is conceptually possible for there to be a Hohfeldian claim-right that a public official not behave in the ways prohibited by the misfeasance tort. In describing the misfeasance tort as not 'right-based', some authors seem to have in mind some other criteria for when a duty correlates with a right (other than the courts simply declaring that it does). Perhaps it is whether the duty can be waived (although this is not a requisite of a Hohfeldian claim-right, so this presumably cannot be the reason for Hohfeldians denying its rights base). As I argued above, however, the normative significance of waiver to rights of compensation for breach is obscure. Perhaps it is the role of intention or mental states in the content of the duty which suggests to these authors that the interest of the claimant cannot be a ground of the duty (again, a non-Hohfeldian idea about rights); this would be mistaken, however. Some interests might only be sufficiently important to generate intention-sensitive duties, rather than duties that require care to be taken against invasions of the interest. *Possibly* the claim is that, if the duty correlates with a right, then the defendant's mental state alone changes whether the act is a right-violation, without this being explained by a difference in the importance of the claimant's interest. At any rate, it needs

high degree of culpability on the part of the office-holder is made out. Both features are often considered unusual within tort law: the absence of a right and the focus on a high level of culpability.[85]

Here are three possible views of its justification:

(i) The breach of a public law duty *pro tanto* grounds a duty to compensate for loss, but a general liability for breach of public law duties would have undesirable chilling effects, and so 'bad faith' is introduced to prevent the occurrence of those effects.[86]

(ii) An intentional abuse of a public power amounts to a 'privatisation' of a public office for a personal end. This constitutes an impermissible means of pursuing the office-holder's ends, even if the end is itself desirable.[87] The abuse amounts to a public law wrong and a private wrong.

(iii) The tort is justified by the need for public accountability for egregious abuse of public office, with the person targeted or disregarded given standing because they are particularly affected, and because of the desirability of a private mechanism for accountability for egregious misuses of public power.[88]

Each view has difficulties. The first needs an explanation why the breach of a duty gives rise to a duty to compensate anyone who suffers loss as a result, when this is not the generally accepted position in private law; normally the duty has to be 'owed to' the loss-sufferer. The second implies there ought to be no liability in misfeasance for pure omission, even when this amounts to breach of a public law duty. In such a case, the duty-bearer does not 'use' their office to pursue a private end. A police officer who stands by instead of assisting a person being attacked does not 'use' their office for an ulterior end; in such cases, the 'office' is not the instrumentality by which the officer harms the other. The third, in focussing on the need for public accountability, seems to miss the fact that the victim can reasonably claim to have a distinctive grievance against the duty-bearer. It also lacks a clear explanation why a right *to compensation* should arise on the part of the victim. If I breach a contract with you, with the intention of harming a third party, the law, at least, holds that I do not have a duty to compensate the third party. But if targeting another through the breach of a duty is sufficient for a right to compensation, it is not clear why this should be so.

further explanation why correlation with a Hohfeldian claim-right has normative significance for rights to compensation.

85 But see J Murphy, 'Misfeasance in a Public Office: A Tort Law Misfit?' (2012) 32 Oxford Journal of Legal Studies 51.

86 For this kind of justification, see P Cane, 'Mens Rea in Tort Law' (2000) 20 Oxford Journal of Legal Studies 533, 554.

87 This is Ripstein's view: A Ripstein, *Private Wrongs* (Harvard UP 2017) 183–85.

88 See Nolan (n 84).

Still, it seems to me that the tort can be justified in a piecemeal fashion. In cases in which the public duty breached correlates with an individual right not contained in the HRA 1998, the misfeasance tort identifies situations in which none of the concerns underlying the *Negative Equality Principle* should prevent judicial recognition of an entitlement to compensation. There is no risk of overdeterrence when liability is conditioned upon deliberate wrongfulness. Arguably, the risk of a negative impact on public officials' proper performance of their functions would be minimal were the tort extended to cases of gross negligence. In cases in which the public duty breached does not correlate with an individual right, the tort serves a useful function of providing an independent accountability mechanism for egregious public wrongs in the hands of private individuals. Furthermore, it is arguable that, even when the public duty does not correlate with a right, the highly culpable targeting of an individual by a person tasked with serving the interests of the public involves a distinctive wrong to that person. Being deliberately harmed by a person who ought to be serving your interest gives rise to a justified complaint in the victim.[89]

Finally, consider the cases of compensatory duties on public authorities arising in the tort of breach of statutory duty. When the statute can be understood as a concretisation of moral rights that each of us can demand against the collective and its representatives in virtue of our moral status or fundamental interests, then it naturally supports the existence of a duty to compensate for its breach. This suggests that there are two broad strands of legislation that should ideally inform our understanding of the tort of breach of statutory duty so far as it applies to public bodies. There are duties which are legal concretisations, by the legislature, of abstract moral duties that any just state owes. Legislation in this sphere has the same normative impact as laws specifying the contours of *mala in se*. The statute concretises the underlying moral duties. Legislation specifying duties of easy rescue of public authorities is like this.

By contrast there is legislation which ought to confer a legal right directly in virtue of the legislative intention to confer the right. It creates an entitlement because there is an intention to create such an entitlement, and there is a general value in the existence of such an entitlement-creating device (just as there is a value in there being an ability, through promising, to create private entitlements through one's communicating an intention to do so). Even in such cases, however, we can still ask whether the legislature was justified in creating such an entitlement. In Chapter 7, it was suggested that the highway authority's duty can be justified as an extension of the common law duties imposed upon occupiers, by virtue of the rights held over the highway and the highway being open for public use.

[89] For arguments that a person can have a justified complaint (in his terms, be 'wronged') without an antecedent primary right, see N Cornell, 'Wrongs, Rights, and Third Parties' (2015) 43 Philosophy and Public Affairs 109.

The duties of public undertakers are akin to those imposed on the 'common callings'. Arguably, such duties can be justified on the ground that the undertaker agrees to fulfil a basic need of particular individuals—that is, to provide access to the supply—and the duty is one from whose performance they are entitled to benefit.

5. Conclusion

This chapter has rejected the *Negative Equality Principle*. It proposed that the principle ought to be departed from when a public authority's P-duty is owed to a particular individual. At most, the *Negative Equality Principle* identifies duties which raise less starkly the kinds of consideration against special P-duties adverted to earlier in the chapter, and so marks out a line at which judicial caution in developing the law is particularly merited.

11
Beyond Duty Issues: Breach, Causation, Remedies

Almost all of this book has focussed on when a person has a P-duty, that is, on the *existence conditions* of a P-duty in tort. This penultimate chapter examines the extent to which P-duties involve, and should involve, distinctive rules in relation to other liability-related questions in tort. It considers three central matters: the *standard of the duty* (what the duty requires of the duty-bearer), *causation* (whether distinctive causal rules apply in relation to P-duties), and *remedies* (whether the P-duty/N-duty distinction bears on what remedies courts will order upon, or in anticipation of, breach).

1. Standards of Duty

In the tort of negligence, the duty-bearer must exercise reasonable care in relation to risks covered by the duty. This is determined by reference to the conduct of a reasonable person in relation to the risks. The default position is that the reasonable person standard is 'objective'. This means that, in determining what conduct is reasonable in relation to a risk, the duty-bearer's personal characteristics, so far as they diverge from an 'ordinary' reasonable person, have no or highly limited relevance.[1]

We can distinguish two different ways in which the standard is, in this sense, impersonal. First, it is *cost-impersonal.* A precaution costing £1,000 may be a trivial cost for a large company, but crushing for an individual. Generally, the law does not seek to measure the (welfare or autonomy) impact of a market cost to the particular person. Second, it is *ability-impersonal.* So long as the duty-bearer reaches some minimal standard of 'agency', their particular abilities to form accurate beliefs about risk and act appropriately upon those beliefs are irrelevant.[2]

These features of the reasonable person standard are normally illustrated by cases involving N-duties that apply when the duty-bearer has created a risk of right-related harm. For instance, in *Nettleship v Weston*, a learner driver was

[1] See generally J Goudkamp and D Nolan, *Winfield & Jolowicz on Tort* (19th edn, Sweet and Maxwell 2014) [6-002].

[2] See *Dunnage v Randall* [2015] EWCA Civ 673, [2016] QB 639.

Omissions in Tort Law. Sandy Steel, Oxford University Press. © Sandy Steel 2024.
DOI: 10.1093/9780191898822.003.0011

held to be subject to the standard of a reasonable, qualified, driver when taking driving lessons.[3] It is arguably the fact that the learner driver has chosen to create an exceptional risk of harm for their own purposes which justifies this demanding standard. The rationale, in other words, is essentially the same as one justification for strict liability for abnormally dangerous activities.[4] Driving around two tons of steel is already dangerous, but doing so with no acquired skills is especially so. In so far as one chooses to impose abnormally significant risk on others for one's own purposes, it is fair that one bears the costs of that excess risk materialising. This rationale for a strict standard is tied to the choice to create risk for one's own benefit: it is tied to N-duties regulating the creation of a risk for one's own purposes.

It is necessary to distinguish between duties that arise by assumption of responsibility and P-duties which do not; the standards of duty differ depending on the reason why the duty arises.

(i) Non-Choice-Based P-Duties

When a P-duty arises in relation to a risk which was not created by the duty-bearer, and the duty-bearer did not assume responsibility to protect from that risk, the standard of duty diverges from the default impersonal standard. An occupier's duty in relation to natural risks, not created by the occupation, is to take reasonable steps to protect persons foreseeably endangered by the risk.[5] However, in determining what reasonableness requires, the law takes regard of the fact that the occupier 'had this hazard thrust upon him through no seeking or fault of his own'.[6]

This is held to licence appeal to the personal (dis)abilities of the duty-bearer, including physical and mental disability, and their financial resources:[7]

> The criteria of reasonableness include, in respect of a duty of this nature, the factor of what the particular man—not the average man—can be expected to do, having regard, amongst other things, where a serious expenditure of money is required to eliminate or reduce the danger, to his means. Just as, where physical effort is required to avert an immediate danger, the defendant's age and physical condition may be relevant in deciding what is reasonable, so also logic and good sense require that, where the expenditure of money is required, the defendant's capacity to find the money is relevant.

[3] [1971] 2 QB 691.

[4] On fairness justifications of this kind for strict liability, see G Keating, *Reasonableness and Risk* (OUP 2022), ch 6; N Jansen, *The Structure of Tort Law* (OUP 2021), s 6.

[5] *Goldman v Hargrave* [1967] 1 AC 645, 663 (Lord Wilberforce).

[6] ibid.

[7] *Leakey v National Trust* [1980] 1 QB 485, 526–27.

The relevance of mental disability contrasts with the approach taken to general N-duties in relation to risk created by one's own conduct, where mental disability is set aside unless it eliminates agency.[8] In this way, the standard appears to involve a departure from the ability-impersonal and cost-impersonal properties of the default standard.

Beyond these features, the *stringency* of the duty, as we have already seen, is reduced when the risk was not created by the occupier—that is, the maximum level of cost one can be expected to bear to eliminate or mitigate the risk is lower in these cases.[9] Even in cases in which the risk of physical damage is substantial, all that may be required is a warning. In *Frost v Northern Beaches Council*, for example, the claimant's property was situated below a cliff on which stood a boulder on the defendant's land, 'like the sword of Damocles', its overhanging section weighing 55 tonnes.[10] It posed a 'very substantial risk' to both property and persons on the claimant's land.[11] The cost of mitigating the risk was likely to be between $264,000 and $683,000, far beyond the defendant's resources. In these circumstances, no injunction was awarded to require such works to be undertaken at the sole cost of the defendant. It was emphasised, however, that the risk was not created by the defendant: 'the hazard constituted by the boulder is entirely the work of nature and has not been at all increased or modified by any occupant of the land on which it stands'; reliance was also placed on the fact that the claimant's predecessor in title had chosen to build a residence at the foot of the cliff.[12] Had the boulder been brought on the land by the defendant, it seems clear that remediation works would have been ordered.

The question arises as to how far the 'measured duty' approach should extend. It could be argued that it should apply in cases of duties arising by virtue of the *Innocent Risk Principle*. The similarity between these cases and the P-duty of an occupier in respect of risks arising on the land is that the duty-bearer did not wrongfully or culpably create the risk. However, in cases in which an innocent risk materialises, which the duty-bearer chose to create through engaging in an activity that carries a reasonably knowable risk of harm, it would not be appropriate to apply the stringency discount reflected in the measured standard of duty to the same extent. In so far as it is true that the duty-bearer chose to enter into an activity with a known risk, and that risk materialised, this justifies the duty-bearer being subject to a higher level of cost to avert the risk than a person who did not create the risk at all. In short, a distinction should be drawn between different kinds of

[8] *Dunnage* (n 2).

[9] *Holbeck Hall Hotel v Scarborough Borough Council* [2001] QB 836 at [38]: 'the present is a case of non-feasance: Scarborough have done nothing to create the danger which has arisen by the operation of nature. And it is clear that *the scope of the duty is much more restricted*.'

[10] [2022] NSWSC 1214, [4].

[11] ibid [24].

[12] ibid [26].

Innocent Risk cases. On the one hand, there are risks which can be attributed to the creator's choice to enter into an activity. And within that category one might further distinguish between choices for one's own benefit and choices for the benefit of others. On the other hand, there are risks which emerge as an entirely unforeseeable consequence of an act and are unchosen. In such cases, the stringency threshold of the duty is justifiably lower.

(ii) Duties Arising from Assumption of Responsibility

The standard of duty in relation to duties arising from assumptions of responsibility is shaped by the content of the responsibility, relationship, or role assumed.[13]

In relation to an assumption of responsibility that arises by virtue of a promise that risks detrimental reliance, the standard of duty should, in principle, be dependent on what the duty-bearer must do in order to protect the right-holder from detrimental reliance. In some cases, this might require only a very minimal step: if the promisor makes clear, for instance, immediately after making the promise, that he is resiling, then a reasonable person could not rely upon the promise, and so there is no risk attributable to the promisor if the promisee continues to act on the basis of the promise. However, in other cases, the assumption of responsibility will only be discharged if the promisor lives up to the promised standard. The promised standard is significant in so far as it reflects what is needed to protect from detrimental reliance. If a friend tells their friend: 'Don't seek a professional architect, my plans are equally as competent as such a professional', the promisor friend will have a duty to behave as a professional architect in completing the plans on the assumption that the promisee friend would have otherwise gone to a professional architect, who would have behaved carefully. In this way, it is generally true that the standard should depend in principle upon what has been objectively communicated by the person making the promise.[14] A jeweller piercing ears is held to the standard of a reasonable jeweller, not a reasonable surgeon.[15]

It should follow that personal disabilities can be relevant if they are communicated by the duty-bearer and affect what can be understood as being promised. For instance, if I agree to look after your dog while you are on holiday, but tell you that, because of my bad back, I will not be able to run after the dog if it escapes, I will not be in breach if I fail to do so because of my back. On the other hand, if I do not communicate the existence of my disability prior to assuming responsibility,

[13] On the different kinds of assumption of responsibility, see Chapter 4.

[14] D Nolan, 'Assumption of Responsibility: Four Questions' (2019) 72 Current Legal Problems 123, 138 (n 75 and accompanying text).

[15] *Phillips v William Whiteley Ltd* [1938] 1 All ER 566.

a reasonable person would understand me to be promising to take 'ordinary' care, unless my disability was patent.[16]

In relation to assumptions of responsibility that arise without a promise being made to the right-holder, the standard of duty need not depend upon what is objectively communicated. For instance, what a parent objectively communicates to their child does not itself set the standard of care: if parent tells child that parent will only do the bare minimum to keep child alive, this is obviously irrelevant. Plausibly, certain basic standards are attached by the law to the parental role, and their content thus does not depend upon what is communicated. Similarly, if the law annexes a minimal P-duty in relation to the employee's physical well-being in the workplace, this P-duty could justifiably be made a non-excludable term of the relationship, just as certain implied terms in law cannot be excluded by agreement. Ultimately, the standard of duties in such cases should depend upon the reasons why the law attaches the P-duty to the role, fairness-considerations, including whether the role-holder could reasonably expect to be subject to the standard upon occupying the role,[17] and considerations pertaining to the consequences of a particular standard being attached to the relationship or role. For instance, if overly demanding standards deprive those in need of gratuitous assistance, this counts against standards of that kind. If taking the hand of a lost child imposed full-blown parental responsibility, which one could only avoid by putting the child up for adoption, this would discourage potentially valuable assistance.

In relation to persons who unilaterally take charge of another person or a thing for the benefit of the other, the position should, in principle, vary depending upon the precise basis of the P-duty. If a finder indicates to another, more skilled, person, that the finder will look after the goods, the finder ought to be under a P-duty to take the care that they have deprived the owner of receiving from the more skilled person. In the absence of such interference, a finder's P-duty should partly be determined by a judgement about what is required to make the possession consistent with the owner's entitlement. If the finder does not increase the probability that the owner will be worse off, then arguably it is sufficient that the finder take a relatively minimal, non-demanding, standard of care.[18] To avoid disincentivising valuable

[16] Nolan (n 14). The fact that a person agrees to do a task gratuitously may be relevant to the content of what is being promised: *Port Swettenham Authority v TW Wu & Co (M) Sdn Bhd* [1979] AC 580, 589 (Lord Salmon, PC). This is not necessarily inconsistent with *Houghland v RR Low (Luxury Coaches) Ltd* [1962] 1 QB 694, which rejects a strict division between gratuitous and other bailments. The gratuitous nature of the bailment is only *one* feature of the context that may be relevant in determining the standard of care promised.

[17] This is arguably the explanation of *Wilsher v Essex Area Health Authority* [1987] QB 730, which held a junior doctor to the standard of care of a reasonable person occupying that role. There is no conflict with *Nettleship*: the duty arises by virtue of an assumption of responsibility in *Wilsher*, and so this shapes its content; not so, in *Nettleship*.

[18] The fact that the finder acted for the benefit of another would be a relevant consideration in determining breach under the Social Action Responsibility and Heroism Act 2015, s 2.

assistance for property owners, there is also reason to condition liability in the case of good faith finders upon a relatively non-demanding standard of care.[19]

2. Causation and P-Duties

As we have seen, it is sometimes claimed that omissions cannot be causes at all, and that this fact underlies the moral and legal asymmetry between acts and omissions.[20] Clearly, the idea that omissions can never be causes is not the law's view. Still, it remains to be seen whether the law's approach to causation does, or should, vary depending upon whether the conduct is omissive or not.

This issue is considered in four parts, pertaining to (i) factual causation, (ii) proof of factual causation, (iii) legal causation, and (iv) apportionment of liability.

(i) Factual Causation

In determining whether a breach was a cause of damage or loss, the fundamental 'but-for' test applies regardless of whether the breach was of a P-duty or an N-duty.[21] In applying that test, the relevant counterfactual question is always 'but for the breach, would the outcome of interest not have occurred?' In all cases involving an allegation of breach of duty, one is counterfactually replacing conduct that constitutes a breach with duty-conforming conduct.

In doing so, it will typically be true that the counterfactual replacement will involve the duty-bearer *doing a certain act* in cases of P-duties, whereas it will involve the *not-doing of a certain act* in case of N-duties.[22] So, if the breach of the N-duty is touching-a-person-without-their-permission, then the counterfactual involves supposing that this act did not occur. If the breach of the P-duty is failing-to-refer-a person-to-hospital, the counterfactual involves supposing that, instead, there was an act of referral.

It does not follow that the counterfactual involves the duty-bearer doing *nothing at all* when the breach is of an N-duty: if the breach is driving-while-

[19] This is one major consideration underpinning reduced liability standards for good Samaritan interveners in the United States: see D Waisman, 'Negligence, Responsibility and the Clumsy Samaritan: Is There a Fairness Rationale for the Good Samaritan Immunity?' (2013) Georgia State University Law Review 609, 628–33; these statutes are overbroad in failing to distinguish between worsening and non-worsening interveners.

[20] Chapter 2, section 1(i).

[21] For its application in a case of pure omission, see, eg, *Barnett v Chelsea and Kensington Hospital Management Committee* [1969] 1 QB 428; *Vaile v Havering London Borough Council* [2011] EWCA Civ 246 [29]–[35]; *Richins v Birmingham Women's and Children's NHS Trust* [2022] EWHC 847 [132]–[153].

[22] It is only contingent because, as Chapter 1 showed, the difference between N-duties and P-duties is not simply the act/omission distinction.

using-a-mobile-phone, for instance, the counterfactual might involve the duty-bearer driving-while-concentrating. One complex act is counterfactually replaced with another.[23]

Might the difference be that with N-duties the counterfactual always involves *subtraction* from what actually happened, while with P-duties the counterfactual involves *addition* of a new act or course of conduct? There is an initial plausibility to this. For instance, suppose A punches a stranger, B, on the street for no reason, and B suffers a brain injury. It seems that all we need to do to test causality between the punch and injury is to subtract A's conduct from the world, without supposing what A would have done instead of punching. But this is true because it was wrong of A, in the circumstances, to interfere with B's bodily integrity at all. Contrast a situation in which A uses unnecessary force to defend himself against B's unlawful attack. Suppose A, a police officer, could defend himself using a taser or a firearm, and using a firearm is unnecessary. If we then wish to know whether the trespass to B constituted a cause of B's injury, we would then need to assess what would have happened had only necessary force been used. This (a case of breach of an N-duty) would involve substitution of shooting with tasering: one act would be *substituted* with another act.

(a) Overdetermination and Pre-emption

The law holds that a person's breach can be a cause of an outcome, even when the outcome would have happened had there been no breach.[24] These are cases of causal pre-emption (the causative breach did the causal work before another event which would have done the same) or causal overdetermination (the causative breach contributes to causing the outcome, but there are other events present which are sufficient to cause the outcome in its absence). Satisfying the but-for test is at most a sufficient, but not a necessary, condition of being a cause in the law.

The standard examples given of situations in which a breach can be causative despite failing the but-for test are of multiple breaches of N-duties.[25] For example, if D1 and D2 each carelessly fire a bullet at C, and each bullet strikes C's brain at the same time, each breach is considered a cause of C's death. Or, if D1, D2, D3 … D*n* all add effluent to a river such that a public nuisance is committed, each may be liable even if none of their contributions is necessary or sufficient for the nuisance, if each 'materially contributed' to its existence.[26]

Can a breach of a P-duty, or an omission more generally, be a cause, even if had the breach not occurred, the damage would have ensued in any event? It has

[23] See similarly T Honore, 'Necessary and Sufficient Conditions in Tort Law' in D Owen (ed), *Philosophical Foundations of Tort Law* (Clarendon 1995) 370–74.

[24] *Financial Conduct Authority v Arch Insurance (UK) Ltd & Others* [2021] UKSC 1, [2021] AC 649 [182]–[185].

[25] ibid.

[26] *Duke of Buccleuch v Cowan* (1866) 5 M 214.

reasonably been claimed that the answer to this question is less clear than in relation to breach of N-duties.[27] The reason for this, perhaps, is that in cases of multiple breaches of N-duties, intuitively, one can trace a physical process between each breach and the outcome. In the two bullets example, one can identify a separate causal process connecting each breach to the outcome. By contrast, in cases of multiple *omissions*, this connection seems absent. The only causal glue, so to speak, that might seem to link an omission to an outcome is *necessity*: the omission must make a difference to whether the outcome occurred.[28]

It is reasonably clear that the breach of a P-duty can sometimes be a cause, according to the law, even when the but-for test is not satisfied. For example, suppose that in breach of a P-duty, D fails to prevent a vehicle which exceeds a certain weight limit from entering onto a bridge. The bridge collapses due to the weight on the bridge. Suppose that, simultaneously, however, another vehicle was allowed onto the bridge which would have resulted in the same outcome in any event. Allowing the presence of the excess weight vehicle on the bridge would be said to *materially contribute* to the collapse of the bridge, even if this would have occurred at the same time in any event.[29]

Compare the decision in *Bailey v Ministry of Defence*.[30] The defendant's doctor in breach of a P-duty failed to provide appropriate post-operative care, resulting in the claimant being weakened further after her operation. Her weakened condition made her unable to clear vomit from her windpipe, with the result that she asphyxiated and suffered brain damage. Although it was impossible to determine whether the breach made a difference to the occurrence of the brain damage—her pre-existing weakness, non-wrongfully caused, may have been sufficient alone—it was held that the doctor's breach materially contributed to the extent of her weakness, and thereby to her brain damage. *Bailey* supports the view that an omission can be counted as a cause, even if the but-for test is not satisfied, when had the omission not occurred, there would have been an absence of an element of a positive causal process leading to the outcome.[31]

The harder examples are ones in which the breach of a P-duty does not alter the positive causal process by which damage occurred. A common example of this structure is when a person fails to provide a warning in breach of duty, and a third party or the right-holder would not have heeded the warning in any event. For

[27] Y Abrams, 'Omissive Overdetermination: Why the Act-Omission Distinction Makes a Difference for Causal Analysis' (2022) 49 University of Western Australia Law Review 57, 62. See also D Fischer, 'Causation in Fact in Omission Cases' (1992) Utah Law Review 1335.

[28] This appears to be the position in German law: an *omission* is only causative if the but-for test is satisfied, whereas a positive act may be causative in the absence of this: S Steel, *Proof of Causation in Tort Law* (CUP 2017) ch 1.

[29] For discussion of the recent law on material contribution to damage, see S Steel, 'Material Contribution to Damage, Again' (2022) 138 Law Quarterly Review 545.

[30] [2008] EWCA Civ 883, [2009] 1 WLR 1052.

[31] See J Stapleton and S Steel, 'Causes and Contributions' (2016) 132 Law Quarterly Review 363, and generally, J Stapleton, *Three Essays on Torts* (OUP 2022) ch 3, s V.

instance, suppose D2, a doctor, fails to consult the medical records of patient C, and those records did not contain material information due to D1's breach.[32] D2 performs an operation on C which should not have been done given C's prior medical treatment, resulting in serious injury. Had D2 consulted C's records, however, these would not have revealed C's prior treatment. And had D1 properly recorded, this would have made no difference as D2 failed to consult. In these circumstances, there is some support for the view that both D1 and D2 are liable in respect of C's damage. Since C would not have suffered the damage had D1 and D2 not breached their duties to C, and since C cannot satisfy the but-for test in relation to D1 or D2 individually, each is held liable; otherwise the presence of multiple wrongs would deprive C of an entitlement to compensation that would exist were there a single wrong.[33]

The proper causal analysis of these situations is not entirely clear. Jane Stapleton has argued that, if there is liability in situations of this kind, it ought to be considered an exceptional *non-causal* liability.[34] Consider:

> *Sprinkler.* D1 installs a water sprinkler on C's property. D1 carelessly fails to connect the sprinkler to the water supply, which has been constructed by D2. D1 reasonably does not recognise that the water supply system has been carelessly constructed by D2. A fire destroys C's property. The fire would have been extinguished if D1 and D2 had not breached their duties to C.

In *Sprinkler*, neither defendant's breach is a but-for cause of the fire damage. Furthermore, in contrast to the bridge example above, if a defendant had not breached its duty, the positive physical process by which the property was consumed would have been exactly the same. If the sprinkler had been connected, it would not have worked in any event, as the water supply system was not properly installed. According to Stapleton, D1 and D2 should be held liable in this kind of example, but on a non-causal basis. Part of Stapleton's argument is that holding that D1 or D2 was a cause in cases like *Sprinkler* generates deeply counterintuitive conclusions about causation in other cases. It would entail, for instance, that a person who fails to depress defective or non-existent brakes while driving is a cause of a person's death, even though the physical process by which the person died would have been identical but for the breach, that is, even if the brakes had been depressed.[35]

Carolina Sartorio makes the same causal claim about a case like *Sprinkler*, arguing that such cases are unusual instances of *non-causal* moral responsibility on

[32] This is based on *Elayoubi v Zipser* [2008] NWSCA 335.

[33] ibid [57]. See also *Wright v Cambridge Medical Group* [2011] EWCA Civ 669, [2013] QB 312.

[34] J Stapleton, 'An "Extended But for" Test for the Causal Relation in the Law of Obligations' (2015) 35 Oxford Journal of Legal Studies 697, 715–20.

[35] ibid.

the part of D1 and D2 for an outcome.[36] Sartorio's argument is similar to Stapleton's. It is essentially that, if one holds that D1 is a cause of the damage in such cases, one generates a strongly implausible proliferation of causes. For instance, suppose it is argued that D1 is a cause of C's damage in *Sprinkler* on the basis that, had D1 not breached D1's duty *and had D2 not breached D2's duty*, then the damage would not have occurred. The trouble with this extended counterfactual, as Sartorio says, is that if there are no principled limits on what can be counterfactually supposed, then we can generate any causal conclusion we like. For instance, suppose that a patient has an inoperable brain tumour which will not respond in any way to treatment, and their doctor carelessly fails to identify the tumour. If the doctor had identified the tumour, *and if the tumour had been operable*, then but for the doctor's breach, the patient would not have died. But it is surely wrong to conclude that therefore the doctor's breach was a cause of the patient's death.

If Sartorio and Stapleton are right, then there is no causation in cases in which the breach of a P-duty fails to activate a harm-preventive mechanism which would have failed in exactly the same way in any event due to the absence of another necessary condition of that mechanism's being operational. Granting causation in these cases entails an implausible proliferation of causality.[37]

The weakness in this position resides in the claim that accepting causation by D1 in cases like *Sprinkler* generates an implausible proliferation of causes. It needs to be shown that there is no consistent way of (a) holding that D1 is a cause in *Sprinkler*, but (b) denying that, for example, a doctor who fails to operate on an inoperable tumour is a cause of a person's death.

Sartorio does not consider the possibility that a sufficiency-based analysis of causation could provide a coherent stopping-point between (a) and (b). According to the NESS analysis, x is a cause of y if and only if x is necessary for the sufficiency of a set of antecedent conditions sufficient for y.[38] In *Sprinkler*, D1's failure is sufficient, along with the existence of the fire at a certain stage and the absence of other preventive mechanisms, for the fire damage. Further, D1's failure is necessary for the sufficiency of *a* sufficient set. Consider a set which includes the sprinkler system, it is not being connected to a water supply, and the fire. If the absence of a connection is set aside—by supposing that the sprinkler is connected—then the set is no longer sufficient for the damage: it may then be that the sprinkler *is* connected to an effective water supply, and so the damage may be prevented. By contrast, in Sartorio's brain tumour example, the doctor's failure to treat will not be a necessary element of a sufficient set: a set which includes the brain tumour at a certain level of progression will already be sufficient in the absence of a failure to treat, and so

36 C Sartorio, 'How to be Responsible for Something without Causing It' (2004) 18 Philosophical Perspectives 315.

37 See also M Moore, *Causation and Responsibility: An Essay in Law, Morals, and Metaphysics* (OUP 2009) 449–50.

38 R Wright, 'Causation in Tort Law' (1985) 73 California Law Review 1735.

the failure to treat is not necessary for its sufficiency. Arguably, then, the NESS view avoids the causal proliferation problem, and provides a coherent stopping-point between (a) and (b).

Even if this is rejected, there is a pragmatic resolution to the problem posed by cases of multiple breaches of P-duties, each of which does not alter the positive causal process by which the injury occurred because of the presence of the other breach. In cases in which the breaches are simultaneous, and the injury would have been avoided had the breaches not occurred, then it seems generally agreed that fairness demands that each defendant be liable, whether this be classified as causal or not. In cases in which the breaches are non-simultaneous, and the subsequent breach would be such as to enliven the rules on breaks in the chain of causation, these rules could be applied analogously to the situation, even if it is considered a non-causal liability.

(ii) Proof of Factual Causation

It has been stated that proof of causation in cases of 'positive act or misfeasance' is properly characterised as a question of 'historical fact', whereas in cases of 'omission or non feasance' it depends not on historical fact but on the answer to a 'hypothetical question'.[39]

This classification matters for two reasons: (i) it affects the relevance of counterfactual questions to liability, since if the historical fact view is correct, then a right-holder may succeed on causation without proving a counterfactual, and (ii) it has an impact upon whether an all-or-nothing threshold proof rule applies to the question or a chance-based approach.[40]

This view—that misfeasance distinctively does not require proof of a counterfactual—has sometimes been endorsed in cases concerned with whether a person relied upon a misrepresentation in entering a transaction.[41] The issue of 'reliance' is described as a historical question of fact that depends upon whether the misrepresentation was 'actively present' on the representee's mind, and not on the counterfactual of what would have happened had there been no misrepresentation.[42]

If the correct legal question in these cases is 'was a/the reason provided by the statement present in the person's mind?' then this is clearly a question of

[39] *Allied Maples Group v Simmons & Simmons* [1995] 1 WLR 1602, 1609–610 (Stuart-Smith LJ).

[40] This was the reason for the classification in *Allied Maples*. It is, however, clear that the mere fact that a counterfactual question is at issue does not trigger a loss of chance approach.

[41] See *BV Nederlandse Industrie van Eiprodukten v Rembrandt Enterprises Inc* [2019] EWCA Civ 596, [2020] QB 551 [32].

[42] ibid. For discussion of this issue, favouring a counterfactual requirement, see N Venkatesan, 'Causation in Misrepresentation: Historical or Counterfactual? And "But for" What?' (2021) 137 Law Quarterly Review 503, but note his qualification at n 56.

historical fact. Equally clearly, however, this is not a *causal* question. I can be aware of a reason for doing something, it can be present to my conscious mind, and that reason may have no causal impact upon what I do. Mere presence on the mind is insufficient for causality.

The better view is that the reason given by the statement must *causally influence* entry into the transaction. The question is then: what differentiates a reason that is *merely* 'present on the mind' but has no causal impact, from one that 'causally influences' a person to enter a transaction? A natural answer is that this depends upon a counterfactual: the causal reason is one of which it is true that, had the reason not been present, the transaction would not have occurred. In other words, the reason was necessary for my decision.

That answer cannot be right, however, if it is accepted that there can be multiple, independently sufficient, causal reasons for the entry into a transaction, none of which is necessary. Suppose I am falsely told that 'Sleepy Tea' is soporific by Person A, and calorie-burning by Person B, and I would still have bought the tea had it lacked one of these features. I can still truly report that I bought it for two reasons, even though neither was necessary for my decision.

Perhaps the 'historical fact' view about causation in misfeasance cases is motivated, implicitly, by the thought that one may be a cause in such cases without a but-for counterfactual being satisfied. In short, it is the possibility of overdetermination in misfeasance cases which underwrites the idea that causation here is a non-counterfactual issue of historical fact. As we have seen in the previous section, it is a controversial issue whether there is an asymmetry between P-duties and N-duties so far as the possibility of causal overdetermination is concerned, and there is a reasonable argument that this distinction does not hold. Moreover, even if a but-for counterfactual need not be satisfied in misfeasance cases, it still does not follow that the causal issue is a non-counterfactual, purely historical, one. It may be that a more complex counterfactual will need to be shown, such as whether the transaction would have occurred if only the reason given by the statement had been present—a positive answer to this would tend to show that, for instance, the calorie-statement was a cause of my entry into the transaction. More modestly, and conceding that the issue is strictly non-counterfactual, counterfactuals will still be evidentially relevant to demonstrating that an act is a cause.

It is suggested that the application of special causal proof rules, which allow causation to be proven despite the absence of proof on a balance of probabilities, should not turn upon whether the breach is of a P-duty or an N-duty.[43] In so far as such rules are justified by the impossibility of proving causation, a rule based on whether the breach is a pure omission or not will be problematically under and over-inclusive. It will be underinclusive as some acts give rise to extraordinary

[43] On such rules, see Steel (n 28), esp chs 4 and 5.

causal proof difficulties, as in cases of multiple exposures to asbestos through acts.[44] It will be overinclusive because it is often straightforward to assess counterfactuals in cases of pure omission. If I had not failed to water my plants, they would not have died when they did.

(iii) Legal Causation

It has been asserted that an omission cannot break the chain of causation.[45] Nicholas McBride and Roderick Bagshaw give this example as an illustration:[46]

> *Malice* pushes *Drunk* into a lake, where *Drunk* starts drowning. *Bystander* could very easily save *Drunk's* life, but does not do so.

They conclude that *Malice* cannot successfully argue that *Bystander's* omission breaks the chain of causation in relation to *Drunk's* death. This would be true, they claim, even if *Bystander's* omission were wrongful—that is, even if *Bystander* had been under a legal duty to save *Drunk*, for instance if *Bystander* had assumed a responsibility to *Drunk*.[47]

The authorities support the view that an omission is less likely to break the chain of causation, but the view that an omission can never break the chain is not supported.[48] Indeed it seems to be accepted, for instance, that the *gross omissive negligence* of a medical professional in treating a person injured by an earlier wrong *would* break the chain of causation.[49]

Against this, as a normative matter, it might be considered intuitively implausible that *Malice* should be relieved of responsibility in McBride and Bagshaw's example. It is suggested, however, that the force of their example can be accommodated while accepting that a pure omission can break the chain of causation. This is because the first actor is described as malicious—as intending to cause harm for no good reason. In these circumstances, the law has traditionally exposed the initial actor to responsibility in respect of a wider range of consequences.[50] It has been argued that the law on breaks in the chain of causation is also influenced by

[44] *Fairchild v Glenhaven Funeral Services Ltd* [2002] UKHL 22, [2003] 1 AC 32.

[45] N J McBride and R M Bagshaw, *Tort Law* (6th edn, Pearson 2018) 299. See also A Simester, 'Causation in (Criminal) Law' (2017) 133 Law Quarterly Review 416, 439–40.

[46] McBride and Bagshaw (n 45) 299.

[47] ibid.

[48] *Knightley v Johns* [1982] 1 WLR 349, 366.

[49] See *Wright* (n 31). See also *Miraflores (Owners) v George Livanos (Owners)* [1967] 1 AC 826 at 847 (Lord Pearce): 'it may be that the initial act was so slight or easily avoidable and the subsequent failure to take avoiding action so gross that the blame for the accident falls more largely or even (if the interval and opportunity for avoidance are sufficiently great) wholly upon the person who failed to avoid the consequences of another's negligence'.

[50] *Smith New Court Securities v Scrimgeour Vickers Ltd* [1997] AC 254.

a comparison in the moral (or legal) abnormality of the original wrongdoing and the intervening wrongdoing: when the initial agent behaves in a way that is *more* abnormal than the intervening factor, then the intervening factor does *not* break the chain of causation.[51] This view would predict that, if we replaced *Malice* with *Incompetent*, who accidentally knocks *Drunk* into the lake, *Incompetent* would be relieved of responsibility in respect of a subsequent, highly culpable, wrongful failure to protect. Suppose that a wheelchair user accidentally knocks a child into a lake by carelessly manoeuvring the chair, and the parent of the child watches the child drown instead of calling for assistance. Surely the user would not be liable in respect of the child's death.

Even if we want to insist that there is no break in the chain of causation in the *Incompetent* example, it is possible to argue that there is a *distinct* rule which relieves *Incompetent* of responsibility. McBride and Bagshaw consider the possible objection to their view that it cannot explain the law on mitigation, which cuts off a wrongdoer's responsibility for loss resulting from a victim's omissive failure to take loss-preventing steps after the wrong. For example, if the victim of a minor cut fails, for no good reason, to take any preventative action with the result that their arm becomes gangrenous and needs to be amputated, the victim is not entitled to compensation in respect of the loss due to the amputation. Yet this is a pure omission on the part of the victim. An objection to McBride and Bagshaw's view is therefore that it cannot explain why the victim is not entitled to compensation here: on their view, there is no break in the chain of causation. Their response is that the failure to conform to the duty to mitigate relieves the wrongdoer of responsibility *even though* the wrongdoer is causally responsible for the loss. The duty to mitigate is not, on their view, an application of causal principles. One could make the same argument, however, in relation to the conduct of third parties: even if their conduct does not defeat the conclusion that the original wrongdoer was a cause of the loss, as a distinct matter of fairness, their much greater culpability and responsibility for the loss justifies the subsequent wrongdoer being solely liable in respect of it.

(iv) Causative Potency

In apportioning damages between a tortfeasor and a person against whom the defence of contributory negligence applies, or between tortfeasors causally responsible for a damage, the courts consider the relative blameworthiness of causal factors and their causative potency. It is clear, for these purposes, that a

[51] J Knobe and S Shapiro, 'Proximate Cause Explained: An Essay in Experimental Jurisprudence' (2021) 88 University of Chicago Law Review 165.

pure omission can have causative potency.[52] Furthermore, if the purpose of the defendant's P-duty is to protect the claimant from an act of self-harm or the act of another, then the defendant may still be liable for a very substantial proportion of the claimant's damages, even if their conduct is purely omissive. In short, the mere fact that the defendant's conduct is *omissive* does not necessarily result in a substantial reduction in responsibility.[53]

A more difficult question is whether, all else equal, the fact that the defendant's conduct is *omissive* makes a difference to apportionment. It is difficult to construct such cases as it is often the case that the creation of a risk is more culpable than the failure to respond appropriately to a risk: all else is rarely equal.[54] An arguable example would be when one doctor carelessly prescribes an ineffective medication and another, equally qualified, doctor carelessly fails to identify that ineffective medication has been prescribed, despite having ample evidence of this. If there is a difference in responsibility here, it is intuitively a slender one.

3. Remedies

The law of remedies in respect of wrongs recognises a distinction between *mandatory* and *prohibitory* injunctions: [55]

> whereas a prohibitory injunction merely requires abstention from acting, a mandatory injunction requires the taking of positive steps, and may (as in the present case) require the dismantling or destruction of something already erected or constructed.[56]

This difference is considered to justify a more restrictive approach to the availability of mandatory injunctions compared to prohibitory injunctions.[57] Whereas

[52] See, eg, *CAR v Eljamel & NHS Tayside* [2021] CSOH 130 [44]. This provides an additional argument against the claim that omissions can never break a causal chain: if they have causal potency, then why *never* sufficient causal potency so as to amount to a break in the chain?

[53] See *Reeves v Metropolitan Police Commissioner* [2000] 1 AC 360.

[54] See, eg, *Widdowson v Liberty Insurance Ltd* [2021] CSOH 15, where the first defender had driven around a bend at high speed, causing life-threatening injuries to the deceased, who had then been subjected to careless omissions in hospital.

[55] The kind of involvement a person has in a wrong—omissive or otherwise—also has a relevance to duties of disclosure in relation to establishing facts relevant to enforcing rights. A person who 'through no fault of his own a person gets mixed up in the tortious acts of others so as to facilitate their wrongdoing . . . may incur no personal liability but he comes under a duty to assist the person who has been wronged by giving him full information and disclosing the identity of the wrongdoers': *Norwich Pharmacal Co v Customs and Excise Commissioners* [1974] AC 133 at 175. By contrast, a person not so involved cannot be so required prior to litigation. Innocent involvement in this way generates additional burdens, consonant with the *Innocent Risk* principle.

[56] *Shepherd Homes v Sandham* [1971] Ch 340, 348 (Megarry J).

[57] ibid 350.

a person is defeasibly entitled to a prohibitory injunction in respect of a past wrong when there is a risk of future repetition, there is no such presumptive entitlement in relation to a mandatory injunction.[58]

The distinction between mandatory and prohibitory is typically understood in terms of the distinction between doings and not-doings. This is slightly misleading, however, as what is truly at stake is the difference between doing and not-doing in relation to *conduct other than the payment of money*. Whatever objection there is to requiring a person *to do* something is routinely defeated in relation to monetary payments: an order to pay damages or to pay a debt is an order *to do* something. In that non-technical sense, an order to pay a debt is a 'mandatory injunction'. The distinction between mandatory and prohibitory, in this legal context, is rather a distinction between doings and not-doings in relation to non-monetary acts, or acts that go beyond payment of money.

There are two reasons to be wary of applying this distinction in the law of remedies. First, when a person is ordered to take positive steps to prevent some future occurrence, the person may be being ordered simply not to make the right-holder worse off than if the duty-bearer and their resources were not present. Although the order takes the form of a positive act, it is merely the implementation of a duty not to worsen the right-holder's position in some way.

Second, relatedly, the person subject to a mandatory order may well be under a P-duty to do the relevant act because of their prior or anticipated wrong. If the addressee of the order comes under a duty to do the act in virtue of their prior wrong, they can hardly object simply to being required to perform the duty. Importantly, in the law of remedies, the moral character of the situation is typically different to the issue of what primary duties a person does or should have: at the primary duty stage, a person can object to being subject to a P-duty to improve the position of others; at the remedial stage, when a wrong has been or is highly likely to be committed, the law is merely ordering the duty-bearer to take steps to prevent or correct the wrong. It does not follow, of course, that the P-duty should be enforced no matter the cost.[59] The law on specific performance of personal service P-duties shows that the cost of enforcement to the duty-bearer (and perhaps the legal system, more generally) of certain types of P-duty is thought to justify their non-enforcement by this means. If the defendant is subject to a P-duty by virtue of committing or threatening a wrong, however, their objection that they are being required *to do* something has already been met.

The contingent issue with mandatory non-monetary orders is that they can typically be more costly to comply with than a prohibitory non-monetary order.[60]

[58] ibid 351; *Redland Bricks Ltd v Morris* [1970] AC 652, 665 (Lord Upjohn).

[59] On necessity and proportionality as limits to the enforcement of remedial duties, see S Steel, 'Defensive and Remedial Liability' in J Oberdiek and P Miller (eds), *Oxford Studies in Private Law Theory Volume 2* (OUP 2022).

[60] See Chapter 2 on this general feature contingently distinguishing P- and N-duties.

Being required to tear down a building is more costly, typically, than being required not to build on one's neighbour's land. However, some care is needed here: the costs that can justifiably be imposed upon a person are sensitive to whether that person is responsible, by virtue of a breach of duty, for the fact that the costs have to be incurred. Even if some remedial measure involves a substantial cost, the duty-bearer may permissibly be required to bear that cost because they have brought about a situation, through wrongdoing, in which that cost must be borne by someone. The focus on the *costs* of the order on the defendant, rather than the distinction between doing and not-doing, has been rightly suggested as the primary concern: 'arguments over whether the injunction should be classified as prohibitive or mandatory are barren ... What matters is what the *practical consequences* of the actual injunction are likely to be.'[61]

4. Conclusion

This chapter has considered the extent to which P-duties attract special legal rules in relation to standard of duty, causation, and remedies. In relation to standard of duty, the answer depends on why the P-duty arises: assumed P-duties should be treated differently from non-assumed P-duties, and in relation to the latter, a distinction should be drawn between innocent risk cases and cases in which the duty-bearer is not responsible for the initial risk. In relation to causation and remedies, the chapter has argued against sharp distinctions being drawn between P-duties and N-duties.

[61] *National Commercial Bank Jamaica v Olint* [2009] UKPC 16, [2009] 1 WLR 1405.

12

Conclusion—Restating the Law on Pure Omissions

1. General Primary Tort Duties

A person has primary duties in tort by virtue of their existence as a person. These general duties are duties requiring the duty-bearer:

(a) Not to conduct themselves such that a person's right-protected interests are in a worse position than the position the interests would be in had the duty-bearer or their resources not been present at the time of the conduct.

These general duties are duties in respect of specific risks, either of one's creation, or to whose existence one substantially causally contributed, or in relation to which one interfered with preventive measures.

(i) Specific Duties Explained by section 1.

A person who innocently creates a risk to a right-protected interest comes under a duty to take reasonable steps to prevent the risk materialising or mitigate its effects, by virtue of these general duties. These duties are not truly positive, since the duty-bearer is not required to take steps to make the right-holder better off than if the duty-bearer or their resources had not been present.

A person's general N-duty not to make unauthorised interferences with another's body or property can require measures to be taken *ex ante* to reasonably ensure that unauthorised interferences do not occur. These measures are not strictly P-duties since they respond to the future risk that the duty-bearer will wrong the beneficiary by making an unauthorised non-consensual interference. Hence, at least some duties of disclosure prior to a bodily interference can be justified by reference to the risk that the duty-bearer will otherwise wrong the right-holder by making an unauthorised interference.

The content of the general duties also explains why a person is generally not under a duty to maintain the protection they would provide to another's right-protected interests even by abstention from an action, while they are under a duty

Omissions in Tort Law. Sandy Steel, Oxford University Press. © Sandy Steel 2024.
DOI: 10.1093/9780191898822.003.0012

not to interfere with the protection provided by others. Stopping one's highly effective charity payments is not generally a breach of a duty, but preventing others from helping may be.

2. Tort Primary Duties Arising from Special Facts

A person can become subject to a primary duty in tort by virtue of a special fact—a fact other than the person's mere existence. These special facts may trigger positive duties to conduct oneself such that a person's right-protected interests are in a better position than they would have been had the duty-bearer or their resources not been present.

The current law on special facts can be represented as shown in Table 12.1:

Table 12.1 Current law on 'special facts'

Innocent risk and interference	**Assumption of responsibility and special relationships**	**Control**	**Current protection from risk**	**Public authority**
eg Duties to correct innocent misrepresentations, duties to disclose risk prior to an interference, duties to respond to innocent harm creation	*eg Promises that risk harm-causing reliance; taking charge of persons and things; employer and employee*	*eg Occupation of land, spaces; exercise of authority over a person*	*eg Land which provides lateral support to other land; property which protects a person from an immediate risk*	*eg Public P-duties made actionable in the tort of misfeasance in public office; rights-based claims under the HRA 1998; statutory providers of public infrastructure*

Once we excise cases of innocent risk as non-genuine P-duties,[1] and re-allocate parts of the other categories which are simply specific instances of the general principle of innocent risk, and disaggregate the different strands of assumption of responsibility, we arrive at the following set shown in Table 12.2:

[1] See Chapter 3, p. 56.

Table 12.2 True special facts

Assumed responsibilities: (i) Special relationships (ii) Roles	Responsibility from right-holding ➢ The P-duty on owners of land, things, and spaces, unless the responsibility has been validly assigned to others	Current protection from risk	Public authority

Assumption of responsibility has been reduced to 'special relationships' and 'roles' because it is in these categories that the P-duties cannot be understood as entirely arising from innocent risk or interference. Recall that, in light of the general risk-creating features of promises, it is very frequently the case that promise-makers will incur duties to take care to act by virtue of having made a promise that risks harm to a person's general right. As Chapter 6 argued, 'control' almost entirely breaks down into creation of risk, interference, and entry into a role. The only situation in which this is not true is in relation to the P-duties of occupiers of land and owners, unless ownership and occupation is treated as a 'role'. Here the P-duty arises in virtue of the fact that occupation gives rise to rights of control. A property right-holder can also have P-duties in relation to land subject to the right unless the responsibility has been divested.[2] These are responsibilities that attach at least partly in virtue of having certain rights. By default, the law assigns the management responsibility of land or things to the person exercising the right to exclude.

If we wish to identify the fundamental grounds of the P-duties in English tort law, setting aside those based on innocent risk and interference, the most fundamental is choice. The P-duties that arise from special relationships are ones that arise when a person chooses to enter into the relationship, even if the content of the P-duty is not subject to their control. Likewise, roles are accepted as a package deal, with the P-duty arising by choosing to enter the role, even if one does not have control of the contents of the package. Even P-duties arising from rights are P-duties one acquires by an act of choice. Confusion ensues if one fails to distinguish between choice in relation to the *content* of one's duties (largely the domain of contract) and choice in relation to the *existence* of certain duties. The P-duties in tort largely depend for their *existence* upon acts of choice, even if their *content* does not.[3] Indeed, the *content* of P-duties is

[2] Defective Premises Act 1972, s 4.

[3] Parental duties are not necessarily an exception. It depends on which duties one is referring. 'Parental duties' needs considerable unpacking (see Chapters 4 and 5). Biological parents may have duties explicable by *Innocent Risk*. *De facto* parents have duties by virtue of *Innocent Risk* and *Interference*, and the authority exercised over the child. Persons who occupy parental roles have P-duties that can be justified by the choice to enter or remain in the role. Parents also plausibly have moral duties arising from the value of the kinds of shared interaction over time they have with their children, but these duties are not needed to justify the law's enforcement of certain basic P-duties, such as P-duties to provide for the child's basic needs. In this way, some parental duties are not choice-based, others are.

usually justified by considerations other than the duty being one that is valuable to choose to incur (for instance, protection of the interests of a vulnerable person).[4]

The outlier here are P-duties that exist when a person or their resources is currently providing protection to a person's general right-protected interests, and the only way of ceasing protection is by acting in a way that will directly damage the person's general right-protected interests. This is *Ploof v Putnam*: a person is using one's property in order to protect their life. One may not dislodge the person for no reason at all, even though their being there involves allowing them to benefit from the use of your property. This is a localised recognition of a basic duty to provide a minimal form of assistance to another person.[5]

3. Public Authorities

Chapter 10 explained that English law, by and large, within the four corners of tort law, accepts the positive and negative equality principles:

> *Positive Equality Principle.* If a public authority triggers a fact that generates a P-duty on a private person, then the public authority owes that P-duty.
>
> *Negative Equality Principle.* The mere fact of public authority does not amount to a special fact and does not alone justify P-duties beyond those applicable to private persons.

I largely took the justification of the *Positive Equality Principle* for granted. The basic case for the principle is relatively clear. Public authorities perform their tasks through their representatives. Those representatives are people like the rest of us, and their role does not itself work any moral magic: they continue to be bound by the general set of enforceable moral rights and duties that apply to everyone by virtue of being a human.[6] Prima facie, therefore, what grounds a duty on an ordinary person should ground a duty on a public official.[7] Moreover, by being public officials, they incur special duties to adhere to their ordinary, general, legal

[4] See, similarly, J Gardner, *Torts and Other Wrongs* (OUP, 2019) ch 11.

[5] See Chapter 9.

[6] See J Gardner, 'Criminals in Uniform' in R A Duff and others (eds), *The Constitution of the Criminal Law* (OUP 2013); S Steel, 'Public Authority for Failure to Protect from Harm' (2024) Journal of Tort Law (forthcoming). It is a further question why it is justifiable for citizens to foot the bill, ultimately, through vicarious liability when employees breach these duties in the course of their work. For an overview of different accounts (albeit in the context of wrongs against other states), see S Steel, 'Justifying State Remedial Duties' in S Besson (ed), *Theories of International Responsibility Law* (CUP 2022).

[7] Only prima facie; there may be reasons which justify immunising public officials in certain contexts.

duties by virtue of the *Rule of Law*, and that ideal also requires special scrutiny of immunities in relation to the ordinary duties of public officials.[8]

The focus of the attention in Chapter 10 was on the *Negative Equality Principle.* I argued that any justification of that principle which points to the general reasons for a restrictive approach to P-duties, such as freedom and the non-instrumental value of human beings, will be implausible. Moreover, it will need to deny the justifiability of the fairly extensive raft of civilly actionable P-duties that exist by virtue of the Human Rights Act 1998 and other legislation.[9] In addition, it was argued that there is a positive case for enforceable compensatory rights being recognised in relation to state P-duties, when owed to a person; the ordinary moral logic that underpins corrective duties in cases of N-duties applies to them.

4. Non-Duty Rules in Relation to Pure Omissions

(i) Standard of Duty

It was explained that the level of costs a person is required to bear ('the standard of their duty' in this sense) depends on the nature of their responsibility for a risk. Here is the overall picture in Table 12.3:

Table 12.3 Standard of duty

No initial causal responsibility for a risk	Innocent causal responsibility for a risk	Wrongful responsibility for a risk (with varying degrees of responsibility and culpability)
Minimal cost (duties of easy rescue; duties of an occupier of land in relation to non-created risks)	Greater than minimal cost	Increasing cost up to the maximum threshold for the duty

The maximum cost a person can be expected to bear to protect another from a risk depends, of course, not only upon a person's relation to the risk and its wrongfulness, but also the importance of the interests at stake. The costs one must bear are, in

[8] As noted in Chapter 10, it is perfectly consistent with the *Rule of Law* that officials are subject to *enhanced* P-duties, just as it is consistent with the ideal for children and adults to be treated differently. However, *in so far as* the reasons for legal duties attach simply by virtue of a person's rational capacity (as is the case with most general N-duties), the *Rule of Law* demands that these duties be owed by public officials, too (those officials having rational capacity). It is because there are further, distinguishing, normative considerations, which permit (and require) public officials to have special P-duties.

[9] Chapters 7 and 10.

part, a function of the level of benefit (or harm prevented) by a precaution. However, one important variable—which is missed by simple cost-benefit formulations of the standard of care in negligence—is that the extent to which a person is responsible for a risk alters the nature of the measures they must take to avoid the risk.[10]

(ii) Causation

As a matter of positive law, it is difficult to identify differences in the causal rules that apply when the conduct is purely omissive. Chapter 11 considered whether, as a normative matter, this should be the case. It argued against special causal proof rules turning on whether the conduct is purely omissive, and argued that omissions can have 'causal potency' in the sense relevant for apportionment of liability. It considered the claim that pure omissions cannot be causes in cases in which the omission does not satisfy the simple but-for test. It showed that this is not the case in relation to cases of 'material contribution', in which a pure omission may alter the positive causal mechanism by which an outcome was produced. It suggested a response to views which hold that there can be no causation in cases of omissive overdetermination.

(iii) Remedial Orders

It was argued that the mandatory nature of a court order—that it orders the performance of a positive act—is alone of no significance when the court is ordering the performance of a duty. It is the fact that certain orders—orders to perform personal services for another being the paradigm case—are particularly invasive, or give rise to invasive forms of enforcement, that justifies less wide-ranging entitlements to such orders.

5. Paths Not Taken

The descriptive and normative views taken in this book contrast with views which hold that tort law is and should only be concerned with negative duties.

In Chapter 1, we encountered Abraham and Kendrick's view that there is no such thing as a positive duty in tort; the apparent positive duties are, on analysis, negative duties in disguise.[11] Although these authors do not characterise their

[10] For a well-known analysis of negligence in terms of a cost-benefit standard, see R Posner, 'A Theory of Negligence' (1972) Journal of Legal Studies 29.

[11] See Chapter 1, p. 28.

position in this way, McBride and Bagshaw also come close to endorsing this kind of view: the situations in which a person is liable for an 'omission', on their view, are typically ones in which a person has done something which, if nothing further is done, will cause harm to another.[12] Thus they insist that an assumption of responsibility should only give rise to liability when one person changes their position on the basis of a promise or representation made to them. In such cases, however, the duty is really a duty to take care to act so as to prevent a person being worse off than if one had not made the promise or representation; it is a duty to prevent *worsening*.

There is an alluring neatness to the position that private individuals only have general enforceable duties not to worsen each other's lives, with P-duties being the domain exclusively of contract, trust, fiduciary law, and public law. This would provide a relatively bright-line division of labour between tort law and other parts of private law, on the one hand, and between tort law and public law, on the other. If these lines were accepted, then private law would, roughly, be concerned with one person's duties not to worsen others' positions, unless they have assumed a contractual, trust, or fiduciary duty, and public law would be the domain of duties to improve the positions of others owed by public authorities.

I have argued against this position, descriptively, on the basis that the P-duties arising by virtue of assumption of responsibility and control cannot be entirely understood as instantiations of negative duties.

Normatively, I have also rejected this position by reference to the fundamental considerations that bear upon the distinction between positive and negative duties.[13] One example of this is the duty of easy rescue, which can be reconciled with each person's status as free and independent of others, while still generating an enforceable entitlement.[14] Another example are duties that part-constitute certain special relationships, such as the P-duties owed by parents to children and that arise when one person agrees to act as another's doctor.[15] In these cases, the needs of the beneficiary of the duty could only be met if there were a P-duty, the duty is chosen by its bearer, and the value served by the duty will not be eroded with legal enforcement.

6. Implications

If the conclusions of this book were accepted, the main implications would be (i) an increased emphasis upon the distinction between worsening and not-worsening, in determining when a special fact must be shown for a positive duty to arise; (ii)

[12] N McBride and R Bagshaw, *Tort Law* (6th edn, Pearson 2018), ch 6.
[13] For these, see Chapter 2.
[14] Chapter 9.
[15] Chapters 4 and 5.

a better appreciation of the basis of the different special facts that generate positive duties, in particular the need to disaggregate the idea of assumption of responsibility into different grounds; (iii) a need to reconsider objections to a duty of easy rescue on the basis of foundational moral considerations; (iv) a greater willingness, in principle, to recognise P-duties on public authorities, albeit not necessarily through judicial development of the law; and (v) a better appreciation of the extent to which omissions should be treated specially in relation to other issues relevant to liability, such as causation.

Index

For the benefit of digital users, indexed terms that span two pages (e.g., 52–53) may, on occasion, appear on only one of those pages.

Tables are indicated by an italic *t* following the page number.

www.ingramcontent.com/pod-product-compliance
Lightning Source LLC
Chambersburg PA
CBHW072323310726
49122CB00003B/159

* 9 7 8 0 1 9 8 8 6 6 5 9 6 *